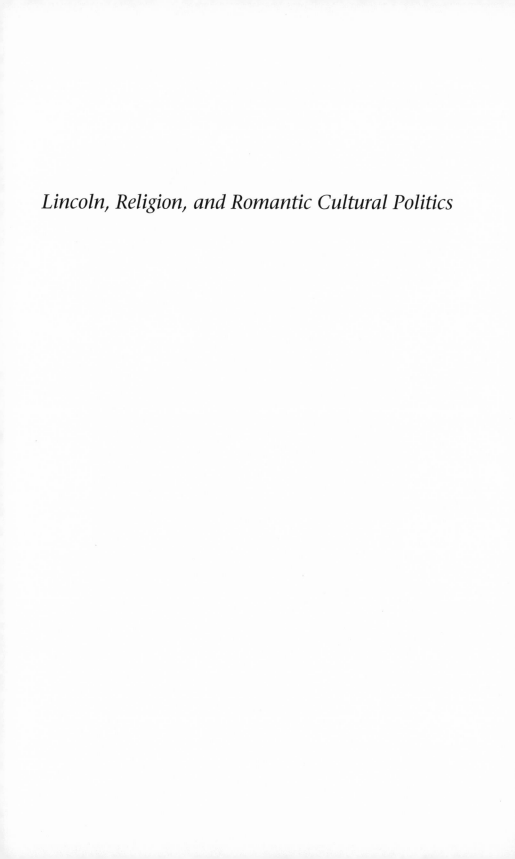

Lincoln, Religion, and Romantic Cultural Politics

LINCOLN, RELIGION, *and* ROMANTIC CULTURAL POLITICS

Stewart Winger

NORTHERN ILLINOIS UNIVERSITY PRESS / DEKALB

© 2003 by Northern Illinois University Press

Published by the Northern Illinois University Press, DeKalb, Illinois 60115

Manufactured in the United States using acid-free paper

All Rights Reserved

Design by Julia Fauci

Library of Congress Cataloging-in-Publication Data

Winger, Stewart Lance.

Lincoln, religion, and romantic cultural politics / Stewart Winger.

p. cm.

Includes bibliographical references (p.) and index.

ISBN 0-87580-300-8 (alk. paper)

1. Lincoln, Abraham, 1809–1865—Views on religion. 2. Lincoln, Abraham,
1809–1865—Political and social views. 3. Lincoln, Abraham, 1809–1865—Oratory.
4. United States—Politics and government—1861–1865. 5. Political culture—United
States—History—19th century. 6. Romanticism—Political aspects—United States—
History—19th century. 7. Religion and politics—-United States—History—19th century.
8. National characteristics, American. I. Title.

E457.2.W77 2002

973.7'092—dc21

200202779

Portions of chapter 4 appeared as "Lincoln's Economics and the American Dream: A
Reappraisal," *Journal of the Abraham Lincoln Association* 22:1 (winter 2001)

CONTENTS

ACKNOWLEDGMENTS

• I wish to thank my many teachers for their patience and support, beginning and ending with my parents, Rev. Daniel and Donna Winger. Being the
son of a schoolteacher and a minister in the church of the Niebuhr brothers,
I grew up discussing history, religion, and politics—whenever there was
nothing better to do at least—and this planted in me both a habit of discussion as well as many of the desires and interests that eventually grew into
this book. Along with the constant loving support of my family, my parents
also helped sustain me financially through a long period of education, and
in the end, both my father and mother were able to help me prepare my
work for publication in this form. Both sympathetic and critical, the manuscript benefited from their well-read layman's point of view.

My work on Lincoln originated with a course I took as an undergraduate
at the University of Chicago with J. David Greenstone, who passed away
soon after I returned to Chicago for graduate work. I was thus an orphan in
the Committee on History of Culture, and I want to thank Karl Weintraub
for his patient academic foster care. He remains an inspiration. I could not
have found better mentors in American Religious, Legal, and Intellectual
History than Martin E. Marty, Jerald Brauer, and William Novak, and I especially want to thank them. Brauer's avuncular presence and devotion to the
Green Bay Packers sustained me at an institution perhaps best described as a
prolonged boot camp for intellectuals. Sadly, like Greenstone, he is no
longer with us.

I want to thank Saul Lerner of Purdue University Calumet for the teaching experience he gave me, as well as for his patient editing of my work. His
dedicated service more than made up for the ludicrously low pay adjuncts
routinely suffer nowadays, at Purdue and elsewhere.

Along with The Committee on History of Culture at the University of
Chicago, I wish to thank my college teachers. During the early 1980's, the
College of the University of Chicago provided a stirring intellectual atmos-
phere. Leon Kass and A. K. Ramanujan were standouts. On typewriters students battered out reactions to then emerging cultural neo-conservatism, to
then vogueish neo-liberal economics, and to a host of other intellectual possibilities. Fighter pilot veterans of the London Blitz fear the ringing of a telephone: the sound of a real typewriter still sets me on edge. Though I later

came to disagree with many of my teachers in the Fundamentals: Issues & Texts program, in particular with their virulent anti-historicism, nevertheless I remain grateful for the intellectual excitement they brought to their teaching. Much of this book can be seen in dialogue with those neo-conservative college teachers; thus while it rejects most of their conclusions, it reflects many of their concerns. The University of Chicago was the only university I ever applied to and I have never regretted the choice.

I want to thank Thomas F. Schwartz and the Abraham Lincoln Association for giving me a platform, and for allowing me to republish material from "Lincoln's Economics and the American Dream: A Reappraisal," which appeared in the *Journal of the Abraham Lincoln Association* (winter 2001). I was especially gratified to receive from the Abraham Lincoln Association and the Lincoln Institute of the Mid Atlantic the Hay-Nicolay Dissertation Prize 2001.

I also want to thank my choral conductors, Bruce Tammen and Randi von Ellefson, and all of my fellow singers in the Motet and at Rockefeller Memorial Chapel Choirs. In the music of religion, they gave me life.

Finally I want to thank Elyse for encouraging me to believe in my work.

Lincoln, Religion, and Romantic Cultural Politics

. . . the ideas of economists and political philosophers, both when they are right and when they are wrong, are more powerful than is commonly understood. Indeed the world is ruled by little else. Practical men, who believe themselves to be quite exempt from any intellectual influences, are usually the slaves of some defunct economist. Madmen in authority, who hear voices in the air, are distilling their frenzy from some academic scribbler of a few years back. I am sure that the power of vested interests is vastly exaggerated compared with the gradual encroachment of ideas. Not, indeed, immediately, but after a certain interval; for in the field of economic and political philosophy there are not many who are influenced by new theories after they are twenty-five or thirty years of age, so that the ideas which civil servants and politicians and even agitators apply to current events are not likely to be the newest. But soon or late, it is ideas, not vested interests, which are dangerous for good or ill.

—John Maynard Keynes,
The General Theory of Employment, Interest, and Money

INTRODUCTION

• Upon the almost endless prairie expanse of Lincolniana, perhaps no single section or mile has seen more intense controversy than Lincoln's religion. His assassination on Good Friday seemed only too appropriate to a grieving Victorian public who raised him to sainthood even before his body reached Illinois for burial. As the funeral toured the country over endless miles of rail, and as everywhere the train was met with black drape and solemn procession, not even an ecstatic pagan like Walt Whitman could resist the somber mood of religious awe. Shocked by his experience as a war nurse, the poet of optimism and celebration found in Lincoln's death a deeper truth: suffering might, after all, be real. Receiving last letters from dying sons was apparently no easier for the public than taking them in dictation had been for Whitman. Only days after the celebration of the North's victory, four years of pent-up grief found cathartic release in Lincoln's funeral. In a somewhat more orthodox theological habit than Whitman's barbaric rags, pulpits across the North also found in Lincoln's death a fit symbol for public grief, which they projected onto a world-historical and even cosmic screen. Lincoln was now seen in familiar prints entering heaven, where George Washington met him with open arms. He now played Christ to Washington's God, a popular image soon reinforced in several biographies of Lincoln. Though there had probably been as much political calculation as personal compassion in his willingness to pardon deserters and the like, Lincoln now became the Christlike redeemer of Washington's creation.[1]

Such adoration soon became too much for William Herndon, who felt compelled to restore his former law partner to humanity by portraying him as an impious scoffer. Herndon knew Lincoln the man, a man who enjoyed bawdy stories and who held himself aloof from any particular religious denomination, suffering some politically for this choice. He had supposedly written a book denying the truth of Scripture, which, as the story goes, was then thrown into the fire by his remarkably farsighted friends to protect his political career. And he had routinely denied the freedom of the will, which for post-Enlightenment thinkers was presumably the basis of all moral accountability. Thus ensued a debate about Lincoln's beliefs that continued through the twentieth century.[2]

For Edmund Wilson, Lincoln's religious language began as a politically motivated sop to the conventions of the time.[3] But to say that a figure of speech is conventional in no way implies that it has no meaning. On the contrary, precisely because Lincoln's religious words were in part conventional formalities, an examination of those conventions sheds light on the nature of mid-nineteenth-century American political culture. Even if Lincoln's religious language were entirely manipulative (which I do not believe), it would remain important to know whether he managed to use the well-worn formulae in creative new ways, or whether he simultaneously created and exploited new rhetorical and cultural possibilities. As one of Lincoln's religious biographers pointed out, "a speech delivered to a religious body can be modified to suit the particular occasion, just as an address delivered at a political meeting can be made to fit a particular situation. Neither statement in spite of some differences need be untruthful or hypocritical."[4] Thus the suggestion that Lincoln may not really have believed what he was saying is only unsubstantiated by the existing record and counter to the general honesty of the man—an honesty that even Stephen Douglas had to acknowledge—but it does not account for Lincoln's originality in his use of religious ideas, it does not do justice to the possibility that there are different ways to "believe," some literal, some more figurative, and it is almost irrelevant to the question of historical significance.[5] The record of Lincoln's words and deeds and the record of their context are what concern the historian, and unfortunately the need for a secular history has often blocked sympathetic investigation into the world of religious expression that surrounded Lincoln and in which his words had meaning.[6]

The twentieth-century debate about Lincoln's religion has presented a false choice between Lincoln as a conventional nineteenth-century evangelical and Lincoln as a skeptic in the tradition of Thomas Paine. That dichotomy excluded an important third possibility, namely, that Lincoln's use of religious language reflected a Romantic and poetic understanding of religion. Romantics typically passed through an Enlightenment stage, skeptical of religious authority, but they found little rest there. More often they were religious seekers who found unorthodox ways to reaffirm surprisingly traditional, Christian descriptions of the human condition. (In some ways the Romantics were more orthodox than were evangelicals, who, ironically enough, generally remained children of the Enlightenment epistemologically as well as ethically.) Romantics often achieved their scandalous orthodoxy by means of poetry. A powerful religious urge drove the Romantics as a group, which helps explain the enormous appeal of poetry both for Lincoln and for his Romantic contemporaries. Romantics were not always literal believers; they did not always affirm the factual truth of Scripture, though they sometimes did. But neither were they Enlightenment skeptics who reveled in a newfound freedom from religious dogma. For Theodore Parker, for example, the poetic and spiritual truths of Christianity assumed far greater importance than the historicity of the biblical account itself, the truth or falsity of this or that miracle.[7] Simply put, Lincoln's religious rhetoric reflected the rise of Romantic poetry and Romantic thought in America.

In 1947, Benjamin Thomas wrote, "The controversy over Lincoln's religion seems now to have been a bandying of words. Neither side defined its terms. Had they done so they might have found they were not too far apart. . . ."[8] Though the interpretation of Lincoln as a skeptic has always been based on Herndon and on Herndon's sources, ironically Herndon himself had not actually denied that Lincoln was a deeply religious man. On the contrary, in order to show Lincoln's true greatness Herndon first sought to make him understandable as a human being who had not been born a saint. Lincoln's elevation to Romantic hero would appear all the more remarkable in light of his earlier skepticism. Romantics showed a particular fondness for the apostle Paul, for conversion narratives, and for the notion of rebirth to a new life. Passing through the spiritual death of Enlightenment skepticism, they rediscovered what for them were the moral truths of Christianity, and through poetry they were reborn to a higher moral, aesthetic, and spiritual life.

Thus Herndon and his collaborators, Ward Hill Lamon, Chauncy F. Black, and Jesse Weik, primarily sought to deny that Lincoln was a conventional evangelical of the mid-nineteenth-century stripe. In the culture wars that followed the Civil War, they wanted to hold on to Lincoln as the champion of Romantic revolt against religious conventionality. "Your knockdown argument," wrote Black, "is . . . to challenge the other side to state which church Mr. L. belonged to, or else [make them] take the ground that a man can be a Christian and repudiate the Church." In contrast to what he said in his book, Black here affirmed that, although Lincoln never made any false pretenses to faith in the Christian creed, he was nevertheless "an *eminently religious man*—as unaffectedly pious as Mahammet, George Washington or Theodore Parker."[9]

While Herndon emphasized Lincoln's early "infidelity," his overall picture of Lincoln, it turns out, was something else altogether: in Herndon's portrayal, Lincoln was never a conventional mid-nineteenth-century evangelical. His scoffing gave way to—or rather made way for—a deeper, truer kind of faith. Lincoln was an "apostle," not indeed of traditional Christianity, but of the American Romantic faith in the meaning of America.

> His name will ever be the watchword of liberty. His work is finished, and sealed forever with the veneration given to the blood of martyrs. Yesterday a man reviled and abused, a target for the shafts of malice and hatred: today an apostle. Yesterday a power: today a prestige, sacred, irresistible. The life and the tragic death of Mr. Lincoln mark an epoch in history from which dates the unqualified annunciation by the American people of the greatest truth in the bible of republicanism—the very keystone of that arch of human rights which is destined to overshadow and remodel every government upon the earth. . . .[10]

In several ways, Herndon did not quite capture Lincoln's religious sensibilities here. Lincoln may never have used the phrase "human rights."[11] No autograph draft Lincoln document contains the phrase, and its absence indicates just how far Lincoln strayed from rights-based Enlightenment thought. In addition, Lincoln did not go quite as far as Herndon in equating America with the Kingdom of God. While he was concerned about America's "just influence in the world," his Whiggish reaction to the Mexican War revealed that he was less sanguine than Herndon about "remodeling" every other government on earth.

In fact Lincoln was still more orthodox than Herndon. But the two men did share a unique literary as well as legal partnership. Both shared post-Enlightenment longings to recover a higher moral and spiritual purpose in life. Though Lincoln's political writings generally used Romantic formulations more circumspectly than Herndon did, the two men discussed intellectual developments with one another for fifteen years, and Lincoln inhabited the role of Romantic hero more than even Herndon imagined.[12] Until recently, most historians have taken up only Herndon's more skeptical-sounding interpretations. For reasons that have to do with North-South reconciliation, racial politics, and a preference for interpretations that were materialistic, pragmatic, and liberal, these historians played up the practical politician in Lincoln at the expense of the Romantic idealist. Thus Herndon's real point has been obscured by the unwillingness of historians to take seriously the impact of Romanticism on American politics.

With the possible exception of Jefferson, Lincoln stands for America more than any other figure, and historians have generally dismissed the obvious religiosity of his speeches and writings, viewing it as politically expedient hokum or as evidence of a kind of battle fatigue that altered a war-torn president's personality, made him more compassionate, and otherwise mattered very little.[13] In this latter strand of analysis, one began with a freethinker who mistrusted religious creeds and rivalries. Lincoln was then seen to have developed a personal obsession with the idea that, through this terrible war, God was working out the redemption of the American people. The strength of this interpretation lay in the way it accounted both for the early, more secular, and even anticlerical Lincoln of the New Salem years and for the writer of the Gettysburg Address and the Second Inaugural Address. But, along the way, little was typically made of the way Lincoln's religious language actually functioned in the antebellum period, when even the elites were more religious than enlightened founders like Jefferson and Madison had been.

In spite of those secular interpretations, a tradition of religious biography also arose that took Lincoln's biblical rhetoric more seriously, challenging the agnostic interpretation. Following the majestic lead of William E. Barton's *The Soul of Abraham Lincoln* of 1920, some half-dozen historians wrote accounts of Lincoln's religious life. They focused not on whether Lincoln believed but on the precise nature of his beliefs. Unfortunately, on the most mundane level there was a problem with sources in this tradition of religious biography.[14] And, beyond the question of sources, these religious biographers joined the skeptics in concentrating almost exclusively on Lincoln's personal beliefs.[15] Rather than placing Lincoln's religious language in its context to find out what it meant historically, they attempted to reconstruct what ideas were in Lincoln's head—a dubious effort, especially when applied to matters of faith. What Lincoln implied one day, he may have questioned the next, and even the hidden yet living God of the Second Inaugural appears in a rhetorical question.[16] David Hein was probably correct to see in Lincoln's words some version of Christian realism that reemphasized human limitations and original sin, but even this reading risks misplacing Lincoln in a mid-twentieth-century context. This book is an attempt to properly contextualize Lincoln's words.[17]

Allen C. Guelzo's *Abraham Lincoln: Redeemer President* addresses many of these concerns, but I hope to delve more deeply into the intellectual and cultural contexts surrounding Lincoln than is possible in a biographical study. Moreover, Guelzo relies on the work of Charles Sellers, Harry Watson, and Daniel Feller, who emphasized the growth of capitalism and, with it, a secular, materialistic worldview. For Guelzo, as in the secularist and skeptical tradition of biography, Lincoln's religious language became an essentially sentimental, Victorian response to the loss of religious belief. Instead I suggest we take the American Romantic more seriously, resisting the temptation, so compelling in a post-Darwinian world, to see secularization as the predestined victor of modern, Western history. Indeed, even Lincoln's economic views were permeated with antimaterialistic, Romantic, and religious notions, few of which survived the later onslaught first of Darwinism and then of religious pluralism in America. In their time, however, the Romantics were without doubt the most powerful thinkers in America. They critically challenged Enlightenment thinking that had long been mired in lazy and conventional intellectual compromises. Lincoln's religious rhetoric reflected and expressed this intellectually serious, albeit mostly doomed, Romantic insurgency.[18]

In part, the relatively slight treatments of Lincoln's religious language reflect a broader tendency in American historical scholarship to downplay the role of religion in American life. Although several recent popular historians have rediscovered the importance of a Romantic Protestant context in the American past, we are not yet fully comfortable with a non-Jeffersonian interpretation of America in the nineteenth century.[19] Seeing just how Lincoln's religious rhetoric fit into the debates of the antebellum period is essential to understanding the very meaning of his thought. Though he remained a lawyer and a politician, Lincoln was a genuinely curious intellectual who responded to the leading lights of his time on everything from politics and the law to history, theology, and technology. Lincoln brought the perspective of these running theoretical disputes to bear on his public life, ultimately defining the central event of American history in religious terms.

Eric Foner was in part correct when he noted that "the view of the Republican party as the political expression of pietistic Protestantism [could] hardly encompass a figure like Lincoln, who was southern-born and whose religious beliefs were akin to the deism of that infidel Thomas Paine." If Lincoln's ethnic and cultural background were the only factor, Foner continued,

"Lincoln should have been a pro-slavery Democrat. At best he was a historical accident, an ecological fallacy."[20] Questions about the pietism of Lincoln's family aside, in his early years Lincoln may well have associated with
the artisan tradition, as Foner suggested, thereby dismissing the environ-
mental determinism of early ethnocultural interpretations.[21] But Lincoln did
not rest with the artisan tradition, and it is difficult to account for Lincoln's
words at Gettysburg in Foner's terms. This was the Romantic period, and
Foner's treatment of Lincoln as a deist in the tradition of Paine and Jefferson
is not unlike treating a Romantic like Brahms as a classicist akin to Mozart.
There are affinities, and one might even stretch the terms "classicist" or
"deist" to fit. But little would be gained, and much, indeed, has been lost. By
making Lincoln "something of a deist" more directly connected "with the
artisan anti-slavery tradition than with evangelical abolition," it was Foner
who created "a historical accident, an ecological fallacy."

The so-called "new political historians" who emerged out of the ethnocultural school broadened their approach to include political as well as ethnic
factors in historical analysis.[22] Alongside ethnic and religious issues like temperance, free schools, and nativism, Michael Holt and William Gienapp established the importance of an underlying political consensus on economic
issues in the breakdown of the second party system. Gienapp in particular
limited the importance of an economic "free-labor" appeal to the years after
1857, when Democrats used similar appeals. Because the Whigs and Democrats no longer disagreed on basic issues of economic development, they no
longer appeared to have any underlying ideological or policy differences.
And because Whigs rejected nativism and did not take a clear antislavery
stand, first the nativist Know-Nothings and then the antislavery Republican
Party replaced them. Instead of Foner's "free-labor ideology," Gienapp
stressed the importance of fears in the North that slavery might expand to
become national. This of course was the heart of Lincoln's 1858 House Divided speech, and the decision in *Dred Scott* reinforced the fear that slavery
might spread nationwide. A series of events including the caning of Charles
Sumner and the outrages of Kansas further lent credence to the threat of
southern encroachment on northern liberties. Thus Gienapp's rich chrono-
logical account allowed him to stress the role of contingent and unpredictable events in the coming of the Civil War.[23]

Unfortunately, Gienapp's interpretation illuminated less of Lincoln's political language than might be expected. While he acknowledged that, for
some, genuine moral outrage against slavery played a role, like Foner he
downplayed that outrage because of the relative absence of sympathy in
northern society for the slaves themselves.[24] But if fear and loathing of the
"slavocracy" and its encroachment on the northern way of life explain the
remarkable rise of the Republican Party (and on this Gienapp is convincing)
the question remains, why not adopt the southern way of life? What was
wrong with becoming a slave-based society? This question becomes all the
more interesting and pressing if, as Foner and Gienapp maintain, Republican

voters did indeed lack concern for blacks. George Fitzhugh did his best to convince northerners to adopt the southern system, but to little effect. Why? Similarly, Stephen Douglas told everyone not to worry about slavery one way or another, as did his archenemy within his party, President James Buchanan. Thus, the question remains, why did significant portions of the northern population dismiss the opportunity to take advantage of slave labor? Blow-by-blow political history does an excellent job of identifying precisely what kinds of appeals to the electorate were successful and when, but it does not explain ultimate motivation. Only an analysis of the ideological or moral underpinnings of political policy can begin to do that.

Gienapp and Holt studiously avoid anything like intellectual history, and thus, apart from relatively abbreviated references to "republicanism" or "the Protestant work ethic," they remain surprisingly silent on major issues of interpretation. The cursory references to "republicanism" or other concepts borrowed from intellectual history constitute at the very least tacit recognition that reference to political discourse remains unavoidable in political analysis. Furthermore, though there is no reason to adopt a sociopsychological or neo-Marxist approach to ideas, in large part language constitutes experience, especially common experience.[25] Along with the onrush of unpredictable events, conscious and unconscious moral assumptions about the direction of events and about just what constituted a worthy life shaped Republican perceptions of the slave power in the South. It takes nothing away from the achievements of Gienapp and Holt to say that the ideas behind the formation of political persuasion are worthy of closer analysis. In fact, the intellectual and narrowly political approaches to history ought to be entirely complementary. The attempt here is to supplement the history of party formation, not to supplant it. If references to Romantic theories of epistemology and to Protestant theories of justification seem far-fetched in a book about Lincoln, it is well to be reminded that the periodic literature of the antebellum period was rife with such discussions. If the *Whig Review* could discuss post-Kantian metaphysics, so, one would think, might a historian of the Whigs.[26]

Joined by Mark Noll and William Brock, Richard Carwardine stressed the role of evangelical activism in the sectional tensions leading up to the Civil War.[27] Carwardine acknowledged that, while the Republican Party was not simply the political wing of evangelicalism, Foner's ideological interpretation "miss[ed] the point that without the moral imperatives of evangelical Protestantism the Republican party would have been less energetic, less visionary, less indignant, less self-righteous—and less successful. Lincoln's candidacy, far from being in tension with the party's Protestant morality, served its purposes well. The party was in no simple sense 'the Christian party in politics,' but in the eyes of northern antislavery evangelicals it both deserved that mantle more than any other political force they had ever known and had in Lincoln an admirable standard-bearer."[28]

Recent intellectual historians have joined the scholars of evangelicalism in taking the evangelical reform impulse of the antebellum period seriously.

A consensus seems to be emerging that acknowledges "a relationship between evangelical reform and modern capitalism without using this connection to disparage reform. . . . Evangelical reform had a logic and appeal of its own in the modern world and was not merely imposed by employers on employees."[29] But I would go further. Though not against market capitalism per se, antebellum reformers, including relatively reluctant reformers like Lincoln, held antimaterialistic attitudes that could be critical of market capitalism when it led to exploitation.[30] Indeed, Lincoln saw slavery as just such an instance of unduly exploitative, market capitalism. The utilitarian doctrine of promoting "the greatest good for the greatest number" could justify slavery as easily as it could justify big capital, especially if slavery could be seen as good for the slaves. In the existing record, Lincoln used the phrase only once, to justify plans for a homestead act. By Lincoln's own arguments, the aggregate economic interest—and therewith, presumably, the "greatest good for the greatest number"—lay on the side of perpetuating, rather than eliminating, the institution of slavery. The point is worth repeating: Lincoln did not justify antislavery on utilitarian grounds, but rather saw utilitarian reasoning as favorable to the interests of slavery. This hints at an underlying antiutilitarian, Romantic impulse behind antebellum reform and behind antislavery. While not typical of the eighteenth-century Enlightenment, the insistence that the dictates of conscience must ultimately be heeded *apart from moral calculus of self-interest and personal happiness* was more commonly held by thinkers in the mid-nineteenth century.[31]

Reference to Romanticism, then, is indispensable both in describing the antebellum political landscape and in understanding Lincoln's religious rhetoric. Given the parallel transformation of both economic and political life, it surely overstates the case to say that "the most revolutionary change in nineteenth century America was the conversion of the nation from a largely de-Christianized land in 1789 to a stronghold of Protestantism by mid-century."[32] Still there is much truth in the assertion that the revivals succeeded in Christianizing American culture by the mid-nineteenth century.[33] Yet scholars of American evangelicalism are mistaken on one point: revivalism and evangelicalism were not the only forces working toward making American culture increasingly Christian. Though powerful, these forces do not explain much about a man like Lincoln who, especially after the mid-1840s, remained carefully aloof from any direct association with revivalism.

The eighteenth century had its revivals, and yet intellectuals like Jefferson hardly noticed them long enough to dismiss them; the world would be Unitarian soon enough. In fact, revivals occurred more or less continually throughout the eighteenth and nineteenth centuries, and from the perspective of the end of the twentieth century they seem to be an almost permanent background condition of American history. The question is, why did they emerge as a potent intellectual, cultural, and political force in middle class and elite circles when they did? The revival hardly touched the Brahmins of Boston, for instance, and yet they too experienced a re-Christianization of sorts. Even among these Unitarian opponents of revivalism, transcendentalists were busy recasting the Reformed Christian inheritance and taking their Scripture quite seriously, if not quite literally. In the general context of Western intellectual history, the mid-nineteenth century saw evangelicalism gain a newfound prestige. Religion was again taken seriously by intellectuals, politicians, and the great mass of people—and by Lincoln.

Lincoln's aloofness from evangelicalism lends itself to the further interpretation that he used religious rhetoric to manipulate a religious public. But a close contextual reading of Lincoln reveals that his religious words were neither calculated concessions to the supposedly naive religion of the time nor the personal testimony of an anguished soul. Radically liberal thinkers like Stephen Douglas cut themselves off from any theological justification for their worldview. In order to give direction to their politics, they made an idol of the nation itself. Lincoln's religious words were part of an antiutilitarian, Romantic movement that challenged Jeffersonian or liberal attempts to define American national purpose in a morally and theologically neutral way. When Whigs such as Lincoln opposed Democrats such as Bancroft and Stephen Douglas, they rejected the proffered liberal consensus itself. Like the Democrats, evangelicals connected American destiny with the coming Kingdom. Lincoln guardedly opposed both of these tendencies. In order to grapple with the moral crisis of slavery, Lincoln eventually returned to an even more orthodox religious vocabulary, denying any connection between American life and the City of God. In the end, it was Lincoln's *rejection* both of liberal and of evangelical forms of postmillennialism (the belief that the Kingdom of God was already at hand) that elevated his Second Inaugural above the efforts made by "the distinguished theologians of Lincoln's generation."[34] Thus, Lincoln differed with evangelicals in a most important way, but he used Romantic religious language to make sense of the complex world that surrounded him and to change that world.

The Romantic in America was a broad intellectual movement not confined to a few disaffected Brahmins, an eccentric Hartford Congregationalist, and a tiny isolated German Reformed seminary in Pennsylvania headed by a German historian and a cranky renegade Presbyterian.[35] Mass-circulation magazines brought the new Romantic sensibility to a very literate society, and, while this Romantic sensibility could be downright hostile to conventional, evangelical morality, it generally encouraged a positive reevaluation of religious thought and life. The most widely read American historian of the antebellum period, George Bancroft, was full of Romantic notions. With the exception of Gary Wills, who saw in the Gettysburg Address something of Bancroft and of Parker's transcendentalism, Lincoln scholars have almost entirely overlooked the impact of Romanticism on American political life that Lincoln's speeches and writings represented.[36]

Nor is the distinction between Enlightenment and Romantic merely the ideal-typical cartoon of latter-day historians. If not always the terms, the distinction was very present to the participants themselves, who everywhere attempted to distinguish between their own positions and mere utilitarianism. Any fair understanding of the period requires a full appreciation of this Romantic revolt against both the Enlightenment and its utilitarian afterglow. Among other things, the Romantic movement helps explain how the man who for Mark Noll and Reinhold Niebuhr most clearly saw the theological significance of the Civil War could be so disconnected from the revival.

With Lincoln a Romantic spirit came to power. The momentary ascendancy of the Protestant reform impulse in 1860, both evangelical and Romantic, has enormously important implications for American political thought. Stephen Douglas was perhaps not entirely correct to suppose that Jefferson treated slavery as an indifferent matter of policy, but Douglas had at least as strong a claim to the liberal legacy of Jefferson as Lincoln did— probably a stronger one. More than the great consensus historians would have us believe, Lincoln was a man of ideas. The "rail-splitter" image has obscured the fact that, for Lincoln, ideas about God and morality mattered greatly. In the hands of Lincoln, to take but one example, Douglas's Kansas-Nebraska Act would become a "prospective principle." And, far beyond its concrete consequences, it was the ethical and moral implications of Douglas's "popular sovereignty" that troubled Lincoln. Not unlike Herman Melville, Lincoln preferred the honest cynic to the self-righteous hypocrite. If the American republic became the means of extending slavery, then America's pretensions to democracy became hypocrisy. As William Brock points out, it was not the material consequences of slavery's extension but its effect on "the nature and purpose of national existence" that aroused passions in the North.[37] While Lincoln clearly loved the political game, what gave politics its savor was not so much the desire for office as the higher principles that, however remotely, lent direction to action. Foremost among leading Republicans, Lincoln took it upon himself to remind the nation that above the political battle hovered a more important war of words and ideas and, behind this, somewhere hidden, lurked the will of God.

PART ONE

Lincoln and Young America

Chapter One

DEBATING THE
MEANING OF AMERICA

• Lincoln's "Second Lecture on Discoveries and Inventions" is an obscure document that presents the twenty-first century reader with a puzzling array of half-lost meanings and half-discernible intentions.[1] Lincoln first delivered some form of the lecture before he was nominated for the U.S. Senate in 1858 and again almost immediately after his loss to Stephen A. Douglas in the famous campaign that followed. Shortly thereafter he traveled to Ohio to confront Douglas yet again and to campaign for local officials in the fall of 1859.[2]

The famous clash between Lincoln and Douglas in 1858 was really part of an ongoing debate between Douglas and the opponents of the Kansas-Nebraska Act, who had formed the Republican Party. The Republicans had only recently outstripped the Know-Nothing, or American, Party in the contest to replace the old Whig party in America's two-party system. Though Lincoln lost the immediate contest for the U.S. Senate, the debates thrust him into the national limelight and set the stage for his election in 1860. At issue was the future of chattel slavery on the North American continent. Douglas contended for a more or less permanent division between slave and free territory running across the continent and based on local control. Lincoln and the Republicans insisted that slavery be "condemned to its *ultimate extinction*," because the nation could no longer endure permanently half-slave and half-free.

Beneath the disagreement about the morality of slavery lay another divide about the status of morality in American politics. For Douglas, local preferences were the irreducible raw material out of which any common political action had to be fashioned. For Lincoln, communal consensus had to be molded to conform to the dictates of morality—historically, biblically, or rationally based. Any common political life necessarily presupposed some basic moral consensus. Whereas Douglas would let local governments decide *for themselves* whether slavery was wrong, Lincoln insisted on a national antislavery policy. For the moment, Douglas had regained his Senate seat, but Lincoln could take solace from the fact that he had won a majority of the popular vote in Illinois; and, though it was not yet fully apparent, he had eclipsed Douglas to become the fastest ascending star in the American political sky.

In this context, then, Lincoln's lecture seems particularly bizarre. An active aspirant to the nation's highest office placed himself in the role of public intellectual and addressed what were, at least on the surface, relatively abstract and—to our eyes—politically irrelevant questions. Discoveries, inventions, science, and progress all belong among the stock topics of the mid-nineteenth-century lyceum circuit.[3] But, as Herndon said, Lincoln's ambition was "a little engine that knew no rest," and it is not at all obvious what "nonpolitical lectures on discoveries and inventions" had to do with preventing the further spread of slavery into the western territories or with gaining the White House.[4]

Adding to the difficulty, the lecture employed an elaborate literary conceit in which Lincoln seemingly, though not altogether clearly, mocked "Young America." This is satire: the punch lines can be recognized even when we miss the jokes. And, though Lincoln was particularly busy with his legal practice and his political activism at this time, the lecture showed much of the literary craftsmanship that made Lincoln's set speeches famous, then as now.[5] But any peroration is absent from the existing draft, and thus, if there was a final pronouncement on the subject of Lincoln's derision, it does not appear in the historical record.

Making matters still worse, it is unclear whether this is anything like the complete body of the lecture as Lincoln delivered it. There exist two large fragments that Roy P. Basler's generally authoritative *Collected Works of Abraham Lincoln* incorrectly treated as two distinct works from two different times, one before and one after the great debates. Basler gave each fragment the name that has come down to us: The First and the Second Lectures on Discoveries and Inventions. But based on a contemporary description there is reason to believe that these two lectures were really the first and second halves of the same speech.[6] *The Daily Pantagraph,* of Bloomington, Illinois, reported both that the lecture commenced by saying that "the whole creation was a mine, and men were miners," which agrees with the First Lecture as Lincoln's *Collected Works* has it, and that it later included the "we have all *heard* of Young America" material, which conforms to Basler's Second Lecture. Although the two sections were written on different paper at different times, clearly the Young America material of the Second Lecture originated at least as early as April 1858, the date Basler gave for the First Lecture.[7]

It seems unlikely, however, that Lincoln would have delivered these two parts as one lecture in exactly the form we have them, because he then would have repeated a reference to steam power with no evidence in the second telling that he alluded to a story already told. In addition, while no mention of music appears in either lecture as found in the *Collected Works,* Henry Clay Whitney reported Lincoln saying "that all other pleasures had a utility, but that music was simply a pleasure and nothing more, and that he fancied that the Creator, after providing all the mechanism for carrying on the world, made music as a simple, unalloyed pleasure, merely as such."[8] Thus Whitney seems to have detected an overt antiutilitarianism in these lectures. Admittedly subject to all the tricks of memory, Whitney's recollection nevertheless resonates with a passage in the extant draft, in which, after noting that Adam spoke immediately to Eve, Lincoln said that "from this it would appear that speech was not an invention of man, but rather the direct gift of his Creator."[9]

Whitney is corroborated by the *Pantagraph*, which reported the following material for which we also have no autograph draft:

> The subject of Laughter was treated of and illustrated by the lecturer in his own inimitable way. Music, like flowers, was a gift of pure benevolence from our good Creator. It is the natural language of the heart, and adapts itself to all emotions, from the triumphal exultation of a Miriam to the plaint of the mourner. To plaintive songs especially he paid a feeling tribute.[10]

In response to an invitation to repeat the lecture in Galesburg, Lincoln said in late March 1859: "I regret to say I can not do so now; I must stick to the courts awhile. I read a sort of lecture to three different audiences during the last month and this; but I did so under circumstances which made it a waste of no time whatever."[11] From this Basler concluded that, after repeating the lecture in Springfield on February 21, 1859, Lincoln turned down further invitations to lecture because he was busy with his legal practice.[12] But John G. Nicolay (soon thereafter Lincoln's secretary) heard Lincoln speak on "Discoveries and Inventions" in Springfield on April 26, 1860. According to Nicolay, Lincoln at that time characterized laughter as "the joyous, beautiful, universal evergreen of life."[13] And Herndon too remembered Lincoln's speaking of laughter. Lincoln's partner recalled his saying in a Springfield lecture "it was a common notion that those who laughed heartily and often never amounted to much—never made great men. If this be the case, farewell to all my glory."[14] With this confusion of sources, then, it is little wonder that these lectures have not been a favorite of historians.

Nevertheless the lectures provide some important clues to understanding Abraham Lincoln. Lincoln used this postelection speaking opportunity to advance the ideas of the still nascent Republican party, to advance his political cause. To understand just how the Second Lecture on Discoveries and Inventions could do so means expanding our sense of the political beyond mere electoral positioning to include something like "cultural politics." Recently historians have shown that, in order properly to understand the antebellum period, it is necessary to speak of something like "political conscience." "Whatever its origin," historian William Brock notes, "a political movement acquired significance when it was seen as the instrument by which moral and material aspirations could be fulfilled. It would be too much to suggest that each party became a transcendental phenomenon, but it is impossible to explain the durability of party loyalty without recognizing that, despite the hypocrisy of individual politicians, the mass of voters saw in 'principles' something more elevated than a horse race or a faction fight."[15]

If only to justify the existence of this new political party, then, Lincoln found it necessary to revisit American history and to rearticulate the meaning and destiny of America in the broadest intellectual context he could imagine.[16] Since America was a country that thought in the language of Reformed Protestantism, Lincoln would perforce find this meaning and destiny in a Reformed or quasi-Reformed world of meaning.

Thus the lectures on discoveries and inventions are perhaps best seen as a species of political theology or, at the very least, theological positioning. Writing on Lincoln and the doctrine of necessity, Allen C. Guelzo noted that Lincoln "burrowed deeper into the mazes of Anglo-American intellectual life in the nineteenth century—through the competing Springfield lyceums, the religious conflicts of predestination and perfection, and the distribution networks of books and the culture of print in the trans-Appalachia before 1860—than his interpreters have given him credit." Indeed, "the next biographer of Lincoln is going to have to pay far closer attention than has been the habit (especially since J. G. Randall) to the bits of cultural substance that lie scattered and unsystemized throughout Lincoln's surviving writings."[17] These particular bits of cultural substance beg explanation.

YOUNG AMERICA

Difficulties begin with the very first sentences of Lincoln's Second Lecture on Discoveries and Inventions: "We have all heard of 'Young America.' He is the most *current* youth of the age. Some think him conceited, and arrogant; but has he not reason to entertain a rather extensive opinion of himself? Is he not the inventor and owner of the *present*, and sole hope of the future."[18] Of course we have not all heard of Young America, or of his nemesis, Old Fogy, but the two terms were commonplace in the 1850s; they had become the slang of the day. Part of a carefully prepared style, the italics in Lincoln's second sentence are his. He underlined heavily in the drafts of his speeches as a guide to pronunciation, and here he set the overall tone of the address by comically overemphasizing a broad pun: Young America was not only a recent coinage and a current slang term, but it was also a style of thought that dismissed the authority of the past and equated virtually all that was good with what was new, or *current*. Old Fogy, by contrast, referred disparagingly to anyone who resisted the rapid changes in traditional ways of life brought about by the tumultuous drive westward and by the simultaneous expansion of a new market economy. But the terms were still fresh, and as time passed different layers of meaning accrued.

By 1859 the two terms had been in use for about 15 years, and Lincoln adroitly played with several shadings of meaning in this lecture. At root, Young America was an attempt to give contemporary events some larger meaning by placing America at the forefront of cosmic history. It was a proposed national self-image, to which Lincoln and others took exception. Young America was also a hazy, Democratically oriented constellation of intellectuals, which on a clear night looked a lot like the Little Giant himself.[19] Lincoln's quarrel with Stephen Douglas gave Lincoln's life direction.[20] The issues between them involved the meaning of God, history, American life, and everything else. One cannot understand their conflicting opinions without first looking at the politics in the 1850s and Lincoln's personal rivalry with Douglas as well as the Enlightenment and the subsequent rise of Romanticism in America. For this reason, an explanation of how Young America figured in Lincoln's short speech offers a good introduction to the political culture that surrounded him in the 1850s.

Compared to manifest destiny, Young America has received relatively little scholarly attention, probably because historians dealing with the 1850s have concentrated on sectional tensions and the ever-impending crisis that led to the Civil War.[21] Manifest destiny, most often treated in connection with the election of Polk in 1844 and the subsequent Mexican War, garners less attention in the study of the 1850s, when the coming of the Civil War becomes the lead story. But, if only to understand Lincoln more fully, and in particular his lectures on discoveries and inventions, his words need to be contrasted with the doctrines of his most vigorous northern opponent. And, while popular sovereignty has received ample scholarly attention because of its obvious connection with Lincoln and the slavery debate, the meaning of Young America remains more obscure.

Young America had three major dimensions: literary nationalism, which pushed for the development of an American literary tradition apart from and even superior to English literature; manifest destiny, the more familiar, expansionist analog to literary nationalism that celebrated American political power and righteousness; and modernist capitalism, a faith in technological progress and the potential prowess of worldwide free markets. These three aspects of Young America shared a radically liberal or socially atomistic political theory, a theory that somewhat ironically resembled British utilitarianism and linked Young America closely with the Democratic Party. Historian David Danbom writes, "Young America stances on domestic issues were the traditionally Democratic ones—born under Jackson or even Jefferson and nurtured by the Loco Focos and the New Jacksonians. Free trade was one measure that had long been advocated by a few Democrats, although the normal Democratic position stated that the tariff should be used for revenue only. Most Young Americans wanted to abolish tariffs altogether and establish free trade." On the issues of banking and the monopoly, Young America likewise conformed to the Jeffersonian-Jacksonian tradition. The emancipation of the individual from the constraints of tradition and of historical community would give American letters a liberating spirit; American expansion would "enlarge the area of freedom" in North America while the American example helped bring free democratic institutions to oppressed nations around the world; and individualism would triumph in a new, world-market economy devoid of "artificial" corporate privilege.[22]

The term "Young American" seems to have been coined by Emerson in an essay of that title published in *The Dial* of April 1844, but Young America had its roots in the literary nationalism of the *Democratic Review*, a magazine founded in 1837; and for a time the Young America literary movement would include the likes of Melville, Hawthorne, and Whitman.[23] Several of the more important elements of the Young America sensibility can be found in Emerson's essay. "It is remarkable," he began, "that our people have their intellectual culture from one country, and their duties from another. This false state of things is newly in a way to be corrected."[24] A cosmic optimist at this point, Emerson equated America with the Garden of Eden under the watchful eye of a "friendly Destiny." "How much better," he said, "when the whole land is a garden, and the people have grown up in the bowers of a paradise." Emerson wanted to construct, or rather build upon, a sense of American identity that contrasted the New World America with the Old World, mired in sin as it was. American letters "should speak for the human race" and "disclose new virtues for ages to come." In Emerson's imagination, America was to become, through her literary productions, some sort of re-deemer nation—but in a very peculiar way. Literary Young Americans would occasionally equate America with Christ, but it was never the suffering Christ of the Cross, the way it would be for the South after the Civil War.[25] Rather, in this loose metaphorical system, America more often corresponded to Adam redivivus, an innocent yet exemplary figure in a new Garden of Eden.[26] American letters would reveal the meaning of America: sin was an il-lusion probably perpetuated by corrupt priests and their Puritan analogs to keep "the people" in line. In America, mankind would overcome what were previously considered to be inescapable human limits.

Beyond literary nationalism, Young America also came to mean a belief in the manifest destiny of America to control at least the entire North Ameri-can continent. This aspect of Young America was the hallmark of Stephen A. Douglas and of his allies at the *Democratic Review*. It had its roots in the 1844 presidential campaign and the movement to annex all of Mexico. Manifest destiny generally evokes a racialist sense of entitlement to expansion based upon the presumed superiority of American life. But it is important to recog-nize that manifest destiny in its pre–Civil War, Young America form was asso-ciated with Democratic politicians like Stephen Douglas and was generally im-migrant friendly. While it was hostile to Mexicans, blacks, and Native Americans, only later did the term assume an Anglo-Saxon, anti-Catholic cast.

Romantic nationalism in America, insofar as it exists as a category, has most often been organized around the term *manifest destiny,* but it is impor-tant to note here that manifest destiny was not the only form of Romantic nationalism in America. By overgeneralizing, Albert K. Weinberg's book *Manifest Destiny* obscured the partisan political nature of this set of doc-trines.[12] Rather than seeing it as a program specific to the Democratic Party, Weinberg mistakenly applied manifest destiny to all Americans of the pe-riod. But as Lincoln's lectures attested, Whigs and antebellum Republicans emphatically did not subscribe.[27]

Douglas and Young America also stood for the new market economy and for "progress." Recently, this third aspect of the Young America persuasion has captured the interest of historians. Whereas older scholarship either treated Young America as a literary movement or as a militantly nationalist and rabidly expansionist foreign policy option, a recent dissertation asserts that, "at the grassroots level, Young America lived as a concept, not as a movement, and that concept emphasized the economic and de-emphasized the interventionist aspects of the Young America rhetoric."[28] While Young Americans saw themselves as the legitimate heirs of Jackson, their un-abashed celebration of progress represented an important development away from the ambivalence of the 1830s when a Janus-faced Jacksonian persua-sion expected that freer markets and less government intervention in the economy would lead back to the simple virtues of the early republic.[29] Now that general incorporation laws had dampened the controversies of the 1830s, Douglas himself championed government subsidies to the railroads; and, in spite of its generally liberal economic theory, Young America stood for exuberant, even impetuous, action—government or otherwise—to push forward the frontier, advance material progress, and bring on all that was new and better. Often the Democrats have been seen as the party of prein-dustrial life while Whigs and Republicans are portrayed as the champions of unbridled market exploitation.[30] But that dichotomy clearly did not hold for Lincoln's northern Democratic opponent in 1860.

It would be a mistake to overlook the enthusiasm for world-market capi-talism so rapturously expressed by the Young America writers (and so sav-agely parodied by Lincoln). Indeed, there was considerable commercial mo-tivation for the sudden burst of expansionism in the 1840s.[31] All these ideas—literary nationalism, expansionism, and liberal market capitalism—were linked and in fact formed a remarkably coherent and recognizable school of thought. Commerce was an "anti-feudal" power, said Emerson, and the growing reliance on trade would bind people and regions together because of their very diversity. Manifest destiny, or expansionism, was a part of the more comprehensive Young America program that included a celebra-tion of the market and of material progress. The world market was celebrated because it could bring diverse regions into relations with one another, and diverse institutions benefited everyone. Slave-grown cotton from the South, for instance, fed the hungry mills at Lowell. Potentially, this commercial em-pire could expand indefinitely, the natural expression of the latent destiny that American letters celebrated. Intellectually, politically, economically, and even spiritually, America was in the vanguard of world history, and world history knew only one direction.

In the wake of the Mexican War, sectional tensions became more and more unbearable. Some sought relief in the national self-image of Young America and used it to justify an expansionist foreign policy. For one histo-rian, "The Mexican War and the acquisition of vast new lands in the south-west had quickened the belief in American Manifest Destiny. The liberal Eu-ropean revolutions of 1848 focused attention on the American experiment and suggested a more vigorous world role for the young nation."[32] But the liberal revolutions of 1848 failed, after all, and their failure could just as easily have strengthened isolationist impulses—as the failure of the First World War to result in worldwide democracy would do.

A note of anxiety that belied the bellicose overconfidence of Young America and that was to resound as a pedal-note beneath all of Young America's words sounded even in Emerson's earlier essay.[33]

> This rage for road building is beneficent for America, where vast distance is so main a consideration in our domestic politics and trade, inasmuch as the great political promise of the invention is to hold the Union staunch, whose days seemed already numbered by the mere inconvenience of transporting representatives, judges, and officers across such tedious distances of land and water. Not only is distance annihilated, but when, as now, the locomotive and the steamboat, like enormous shuttles, shoot every day across the thousand various threads of national descent and employment, and bind them fast in one web, an hourly assimilation goes forward, and there is no danger that local peculiarities and hostilities should be preserved.[34]

For Emerson, economic interconnectedness decreased the chances for civil war. Even more than Emerson, Stephen Douglas hoped that Young America could reduce sectional rivalries. At the New York State Fair in Rochester in 1851 he said "the very diversity of the nation, in products, climate, and soil, should serve as a common bond, imparting strength and stability to its institutions." For many Southerners, the perpetuation of the slave economy depended on American expansion and commercial imperialism. "The label 'Young America' came to identify the movement of ardent, evangelical nationalism that included in its ranks reformers, businessmen, newspaper editors, and political figures," notes Robert Johannsen. "In 1851 and 1852 it had a more specific application to the group within the Democratic party that was determined to restore the party to its former Jacksonian vigor." But if Young America looked backward as it looked to the future, it looked to Jackson the way Jackson had looked to Jefferson. Thus the expansion and trade would prevent the creation of an impoverished urban working class. Young Americans did not feel anxious or ambivalent about the new market economy per se; they embraced it wholeheartedly. Instead, their anxiety focused almost exclusively on America's sectional difficulties, British intrigue, and the question of race.[35]

LINCOLN'S RESPONSE

The most obvious intent of Lincoln's lecture, then, was his criticism of Young America's excesses and, not surprisingly, the excesses of Judge Douglas. After a parody of the way Douglas and Young America uncritically rejoiced in the new market economy (and this alone indicates the degree to which it was the Democrats, rather than the Republicans, who unambiguously championed capitalist development) Lincoln continued his satire:

He owns a large part of the world, by right of possessing it; and all the rest by right of *wanting* it, and *intending* to have it. As Plato had for the immortality of the soul, so Young America has "a pleasing hope—a fond desire—a longing after" territory. He has a great passion—a perfect rage—for the *"new"*; particularly new men for office, and the new earth mentioned in the revelations, in which, being no more sea, there must be about three times as much land as in the present. He is a great friend of humanity; and his desire for land is not selfish, but merely an impulse to extend the area of freedom. He is very anxious to fight for the liberation of enslaved nations and colonies, provided, always, they *have* land, and have *not* any liking for his interference. As to those who have no land, and would be glad of help from any quarter, he considers *they* can afford to wait a few hundred years longer. In knowledge he is particularly rich. He knows all that can possibly be known; inclines to believe in spiritual rappings, and is the unquestioned inventor of *"Manifest Destiny."* His horror is for all that is old, particularly "Old Fogy"; and if there be any thing old which he can endure, it is only old whiskey and old tobacco.[36]

The remark about "those who have no land, and would be glad of help from any quarter," remains somewhat obscure. It may refer to Douglas's opposition to the colonization efforts championed by moderate Republicans like Lincoln. In that case the slaves would be the ones who on Lincoln's view of Douglas's position "could afford to wait a few hundred years longer." But that is doubtful, since Lincoln himself was willing at this point to let slavery die out slowly, perhaps over the course of a hundred years. Most likely it referred to southern Democratic opposition to proposals for a Homestead Act, and thus Lincoln here made an appeal to the interests of free labor.

A look at other details of this passage, especially in the last sentence, reveals that Lincoln was not above sniping at his political opponents in what purported to be an apolitical, academic setting. Douglas was a lover of cigars who on his way from New Orleans to New York at about this time made a brief stop in Cuba to chat with local officials, assess the prospects for American annexation, and order 2,000 Havanas.[37] And, while Lincoln was not prone to self-righteousness or grandstanding on the temperance issue, the close of the passage could be construed as a relatively cheap shot at the hard-drinking Democrats, of which Douglas was certainly only one.[38]

It may seem equally capricious for Lincoln to have connected Young America with "spiritual rappings," but Douglas routinely connected Lincoln with abolitionism and other isms of the radical 1840s. Here, Lincoln turned the tables on Douglas by connecting Young America with the excesses of the age: the Young Americans, not the "Black Republicans," were the wild-eyed innovators. Transcendentalists like George Ripley, William Cullen Bryant, and their friend, the historian George Bancroft, were peculiarly attracted to the Rappite religious sect and attended séances with the Fox sisters.[39] In spite of the dalliances with Romantic excess in the form of superstition, Democrats had a reputation for Painite skepticism that Whigs and

Republicans routinely turned to their own advantage.[40] Thus Lincoln posed as the man of common sense and good Protestant morality standing up to Douglas's recklessly misguided idealism and exaggerated commitment to progress. Less sarcastically put, if Douglas really believed in all that was new, then he would have a lot of bunk to own up to.

It seems Lincoln was letting his guard down somewhat in these lectures. Indeed his Second Lecture on Discoveries and Inventions contains one of the few off-color or bawdy jokes that survived the well-intentioned censorship of his more fastidious contemporaries, jokes for which Lincoln was nevertheless renowned.

> And this reminds me of what I passed unnoticed before, that the very first invention was a joint operation, Eve having shared with Adam in the getting up of the apron. And, indeed, judging from the fact that sewing has come down to our times as "woman's work" it is very probable she took the leading part; he, perhaps, doing no more than to stand by and thread the needle. That proceeding may be reckoned as the mother of all "Sewing societies"; and the first and most perfect "world's fair" all inventions and all inventors then in the world, being on the spot.[41]

As Olivier Fraysse pointed out, threading the needle was a euphemism for sexual intercourse.[42] Lincoln was going for a relatively cheap laugh, and he treated Young America in this same spirit of send-up.

Beyond the light-hearted parody of Douglas, the more important point in these introductory sentences was to satirize Young America in its foreign policy incarnation, manifest destiny. Young America did not appear in what we have come to know as the First Lecture on Discoveries and Inventions, and Lincoln may have added the satire in response to speeches Douglas was making at the time.[43] Lincoln wrote to Senator Lyman Trumbull, "Since you left, Douglas has gone South, making characteristic speeches, and seeking to re-instate himself in that section."[44] Lincoln continued in the same letter to give a remarkably clear presentation of Douglas's difficulties. Douglas had to make his solution to the problem of slavery in the territories—popular sovereignty—appeal to both North and South. As Lincoln predicted in this letter, the South would "push a Slave code upon him, as a test," and Douglas would "bolt" the Democratic National Convention of 1860. (Actually it was the South that eventually seceded from the Charleston Convention, but the issue was the same.)

When Douglas opposed Buchanan and the Lecompton Constitution, many in the antislavery ranks, including many Republicans, hailed him as a "conquering hero," an impression Douglas did nothing to dispel.[45] Lincoln feared that, if Douglas were expelled from the Charleston Convention because of a principled popular sovereignty stand against the "slave power," important Republicans like Horace Greeley, William Seward, and John J. Crittenden might again push for the nomination of Douglas as a Republican, as they had done in the 1858 Senate race just ended. Lincoln took it therefore as his task to prove that, if "the Republican principle can, in no wise live with Douglas; then it is arrant folly now, as it was last Spring, to waste time, and scatter labor already performed, in dallying with him."[46] The electoral logic of Lincoln's position therefore forced him to discredit Douglas's popular sovereignty as a solution to the territorial question.

Lincoln had to respond to Douglas blow for blow, which eventually led him east to Ohio and then on to the Cooper Institute in a dogged effort to prove that Douglas's stand on slavery was inadequate even if local majorities could be counted upon to prohibit slavery in the territories. He had to show that, if slavery were treated in the morally neutral way Douglas proposed, it would lead to the nationalization of the "peculiar institution." This, in turn, entailed arguing, first, that the *Dred Scott* decision, in principle, amounted to the nationalization of slavery; second, that slavery was not a morally neutral thing but in fact wrong; and, third, that the nationalization of this wrong would be inconsistent with the national purpose. Since Lincoln and Douglas agreed on many things as a practical matter, and since Douglas appeared to some to be antislavery enough when circumstances pitted him against the "slave power," Lincoln had to emphasize the theoretical difference between them. Lincoln supplemented the material now known as the First Lecture on Discoveries and Inventions with material that more directly undermined Douglas's position.

While Senator Trumbull was in Washington, Lincoln generally kept him informed of attitudes back in Illinois. In one letter, Lincoln coolly assessed the potential fallout Trumbull might encounter if he were to oppose annexation of Cuba: "I do not perceive that there is any feeling here about Cuba; and so I think, you can safely venture to act upon your own judgment upon any phase of it which may be presented."[47] This captured exactly Lincoln's attitude toward morality and politics. As a politician, Lincoln could not always "safely venture to act upon [his] own judgment." But, though he often labored to create a space for himself in which he could so act, it was this practical side that sometimes led his reform allies to despair of his antislavery convictions. (Douglas had a much different conception of statesmanship.) In this particular case, Lincoln felt fully at liberty to attack Douglas's expansionist rhetoric. A week later, he gave his lectures on discoveries and inventions.

With a grave sectional crisis threatening both the country and his career, Douglas nevertheless continued to preach his expansionist doctrine in an attempt to woo the South.[48] Only two months before Lincoln's lecture, Douglas shared a platform in New Orleans with Pierre Soulé, a radical Young American and a long-time associate:

> If we recognize and observe this principle of states rights and self-government for the people of the territories, there will be peace forever between the North and South, and America will fulfill the glorious destiny which the Almighty has marked out for her. She will remain an example for all nations, expanding as

her people increase and her interests demand more territory. . .[Mr. Douglas was apparently about to bring his remarks to a close at this point, when, in a response to calls of Cuba! Cuba! from the audience, he proceeded thus:]

It is our destiny to have Cuba, and it is folly to debate the question. It naturally belongs to the American Continent and the body of the American Nation. . . . The same is true of Central America and Mexico. It will not do to say we have territory enough. When the Constitution was formed, there was enough, yet, in a few years afterwards, we needed more. . .

If experience shall continue to prove, what the past may be considered to have demonstrated, that those little Central American powers cannot maintain self-government, the interests of Christendom require that some power should preserve order for them. Hence, I maintain that we should adopt and observe a line of policy in unison with our interests and our destiny. I do not wish to force things. We live in a rapid age. Events crowed upon each other with marvelous rapidity. I do not want territory any faster than we can occupy, Americanize and civilize it. I am no filibuster. I am opposed to unlawful expeditions; but on the other hand, I am opposed to this country acting as a miserable constabulary for France and England. I am in favor of expansion as fast as consistent with our interest and the increase and development of our population and resources. But I am not in favor of that policy unless the great principal of non-intervention and the right of the people to decide the question of slavery, and all other domestic questions, for themselves shall be maintained. If that principle prevail, we have a future before us more glorious than that of any other people that ever existed. Our Republic will endure for thousands of years. Progress will be the law of its destiny; it will gain new strength with every state brought into the Confederacy. Then there will be peace and harmony between the free states and the slave states. The more degrees of latitude and longitude embraced beneath our Constitution, the better; for then we shall have the principles of free trade apply to the important staples of the world, making us the greatest manufacturing, the greatest commercial, as well as the greatest agricultural power on the globe.[49]

That sentiment, which in all essentials captures both the mood and substance of the Young America movement, was exactly what Lincoln attacked in his prefatory remarks. Douglas's comments could have appeared in the *Democratic Review* in 1852, before the Kansas-Nebraska Act of 1854 rent an already frayed political fabric and called the Republican Party into being. At all costs Lincoln had to prevent Douglas from successfully equating popular sovereignty with moral right, and he therefore found it galling that Douglas posed as a "great friend of humanity." His introductory remarks on Young America ironically pointed to the hypocrisy of Douglas's manifest destiny aspirations. What kind of popular sovereignty was it that sought to absorb territories without the consent of those who lived there? And Douglas was guilty of the lowest form of demagoguery in promising Cuba to the South, where he knew such a prospect would be popular.

There was a further, subtler comment in Lincoln's remarks. During the campaign for Zachary Taylor in 1848, Lincoln had said "that he honestly believed that all those who wished to keep up the character of the Union; who did not believe in enlarging our field, but in keeping our fences where they [were] and cultivating our present possession, making it a garden, improving the morals and education of the people; devoting the administration to this purpose; all real Whigs, friends of good honest government;—the race was ours."[50] Now, by ironically referring to Mexico and Cuba as "enslaved nations and colonies," Lincoln called to mind the fact that Douglas and Young America had "extended the area of freedom" by bringing more slave territory into the Union, some of which had been free under Mexican law. In his debates with Douglas, Lincoln had sought to show that popular sovereignty was amorality masquerading as a moral maxim. Here he went further. Since manifest destiny would make slave territory of free Mexico, this corollary to popular sovereignty was positively immoral.

Lincoln and Douglas had disagreed on issues relating to American expansion at least since Lincoln's famous "Spot Resolutions" in the House of Representatives in December 1847. Lincoln was skeptical of the reasons President Polk (along with the historian George Bancroft) gave for declaring war on Mexico, and in his "Speech on the War with Mexico" he performed the same savage analytical surgery on Polk's rhetoric that he would later administer to Douglas, revealing the origins of Lincoln's argumentative style. Self-consciously a lawyer, he began by clarifying both the "issue and evidence" in Polk's War Message.[51] The real issue was whether American blood had in fact been shed *on American soil.* Lincoln believed Polk had illegally and unconstitutionally provoked the war on Mexican soil in order to divert attention away from his abandonment of "fifty-four forty or fight" on the Oregon question.[52] After divesting the issue of its ambiguities, he teased out the inconsistencies and evasions in the evidence. Lincoln stayed close to the text of his opponent's brief, noting at one point that he had "sometimes seen a good lawyer, struggling for his client's neck, in a desperate case, employing every artifice to work round, befog, and cover up, with many words, some point arising in the case, which he *dared* not admit, and yet *could* not deny." From "just such necessity," noted Lincoln, came "the President's struggle in this case."[53] Then, in a line that reflected his love of *Macbeth,* young Congressman Lincoln suggested that Polk's guilty conscience explained his bad logic: "How like the half insane mumbling of a fever-dream, is the whole war part of his late message!" After a close reading of Polk's message he impatiently exclaimed that Polk's "mind, tasked beyond it's power, is running hither and thither, like some tortured creature, on a burning surface, finding no position, on which it can settle down, and be at ease."[54]

Stressing the rail-splitter and log-roller side of Lincoln, a long line of scholars has echoed the sentiment that "Lincoln rarely sought rigorous consistency in doctrine; he usually sought the politically possible."[55] While it is true that he rarely if ever sought consistency at the expense of the possible,

Lincoln's treatment of Polk in 1848 and of Douglas throughout his career reveals that he sought both consistency *and* the possible. And it ought to have long since become part of the Lincoln legacy that when it mattered most—in his support for government-sponsored internal improvements, in his resistance to the Mexican War, in his refusal to compromise as states seceded in the winter of 1860–1861, and in his refusal to make peace with Jefferson Davis at the expense of emancipation—Lincoln showed himself to be a man of firmest principle.[56]

When he had to be, Lincoln could be a bit overnice, as when he carefully chose his words when in southern Illinois to mute his relatively friendly stance toward blacks,[57] or when he was more openly antiexpansionist while campaigning for Taylor in New England, where opposition to expansion was popular.[58] In his zeal for William Henry Harrison in 1840, he may even have played upon antiblack sentiment in Illinois because it suited him politically. (Though the report is sparse and the spirit of his remarks is by no means clear, Lincoln made reference to Van Buren's early support for black suffrage in New York.)[59] And it would be safe to say that, most of the time, Lincoln was not a speculative writer. What interested him as a lawyer, a politician, and a student of Euclid was argument and demonstration.

As time went on, however, the debates over slavery in America challenged the fundamental assumptions of American politics. The line of argument forced politicians to answer fundamental questions, and men who sought to avoid the deeper issues, men like Douglas, were simply pushed aside. Especially in his earlier years, Lincoln was not entirely above expressions of contempt for the intellect of his opponents; he even questioned on one occasion whether Stephen Douglas might be "stupid" for assuming that anyone would believe such ridiculous arguments.[60] Behind the malaise of the 1850s and the breakup of the second party system lay voter discontent with political parties that seemed no longer clearly to address issues of concern to the voters. Into this vacuum first rushed the American Party, or Know-Nothings, clearly ministering to anti-immigrant sentiment.[61] But when the Know-Nothings were unable to take a clear stand on the issue of slavery expansion the Republicans rushed in with an unequivocal stance of their own.[62] With the best of them Lincoln could dodge an issue he regarded as secondary, but—in his carefully crafted letters and speeches—clarity and consistency in doctrine remained the hallmarks of his style.

Obfuscation, on the other hand, was the favorite rhetorical tactic of Stephen Douglas. A biographer captures it admirably, quoting one contemporary who said that "when he was unable to turn an argument to his own advantage he would hopelessly befog it for anyone else" while another said that "he can run through the whole diapason of political falsehood with unrivaled skill, from the delicate note of suggested prevarication down to the double-bass of unmitigated lying."[63]

Thus, despite any momentary agreement on policy regarding the sectional disputes, Douglas and the Republicans viewed each other across a deep intellectual divide. The epithet of "demagogue" was typical, and on this point the Republicans were heirs to the Whigs.[64] Whereas the Republicans looked for political courage that would oppose even the will of the people where justice might seem to demand it, Douglas defined statesmanship as ministering to the will of the people, even to their whims. Appealing to the passions was simply part of the business. Even where the logic became strained, a proposal could still be defended as the "will of the people." The notion that the people might be wrong rarely occurred in this way of thinking. Perhaps more than any theoretical difference, it was this somewhat softheaded sentimentality in popular sovereignty that so frustrated the onetime Whig in Lincoln.[65]

Predictably, then, Douglas and the Democrats responded to Lincoln's tightly reasoned assault on Polk by questioning Lincoln's patriotism in not wholeheartedly supporting the popular war effort, and a decade later Lincoln still had to respond to their epithet "Spotty Lincoln." While "no published Whig dissent from Lincoln's views has been found" in Illinois (Lincoln's partner Herndon was apparently a minority of one), the Democratic press called Lincoln the "Benedict Arnold" of Illinois.[66] Opposition to territorial acquisition served Whig political purposes, to both "preserve Whig Party unity and distinguish Whigs from Democrats," but for Lincoln and his fellow Whigs the high ideals articulated by the founders were not a justification for unlimited expansion so much as a call to self-scrutiny.[67] Lincoln had demanded that Polk declare the *spot* where the Mexican War had commenced: "Let him remember he sits where Washington sat, and so remembering, let him answer, as Washington would answer. As a nation *should* not, and the Almighty *will* not, be evaded, so let him attempt no evasion—no equivocation." As Lincoln further suggested, the president's evasions revealed that he was "deeply conscious of being in the wrong," that Polk felt that "the blood of this war, like the blood of Abel, [was] crying to heaven against him." In the debates over the Mexican War, Lincoln already revealed a tendency both to question the inherent justice of American expansion and to hold the nation to a transcendent standard, historically and biblically rooted. Nothing could have been further from the mind of Judge Douglas and Young America.

YOUNG AMERICA AS RELIGIOUS MOVEMENT

On the surface, Douglas and the Young Americans pushed for a radical separation of church and state in the tradition of Jefferson and the Enlightenment. This strand in Douglas's thought showed itself, for instance, when he confronted a clerical petition protesting the Nebraska Bill. The petition gave rise to a remarkable little firefight on the floor of the Senate that spilled over into a letter from Douglas to "Twenty-five Chicago Clergyman" and revealed the extent to which the debate over the status of slavery was also a debate over the relationship of church and state in America.[68]

The petition stated that the clergymen, "in the name of Almighty God, and in his presence, do solemnly protest against the passage of what is known as the Nebraska bill . . . as a great moral wrong, as a breach or faith eminently unjust to the moral principles of the community, and subversive of all confidence in national engagements; as a measure full of danger to the peace and even the existence of our beloved Union, and exposing us to the righteous judgments of the Almighty."[69] The petition itself seemed simple enough, but Douglas saw in it a conspiracy by the "abolition press" to "furnish capital for organizing a great sectional party, and trying to draw the whole religious community into their schemes of political aggrandizement . . . of stimulating excitement for political ends."

Sam Houston, who as a southerner acquitted himself remarkably throughout the debates over the Kansas-Nebraska Act, responded that this was hokum. "I do not believe," he said, "that these ministers have sent this memorial here to manufacture political capital, to have it entered on the records of the Senate, so that it might be taken back, and disseminated through the country. Sir, it comes from the country." But Douglas virtually worshipped at the shrine of popular opinion, and he could hardly consider resistance to the idea of popular sovereignty to be a legitimate expression of popular sentiment. Houston pressed the point: "I told you that there would be agitation; but it was denied upon this floor. Is not this agitation? Three thousand ministers of the living God upon earth—his vicegerents—send a memorial here upon this subject; and yet, you tell me, that there is no excitement in the country! Sir you realize what I anticipated. The country has to bear the infliction."[70]

While Houston and the clergy of New England turned with prophetic tone toward Douglas, other Senate colleagues rallied to his defense. They claimed that the petition assaulted the traditional separation of church and state because the petitioners styled themselves as ministers of the gospel, not as citizens. "The great effort of the American people has been, by every form of defensive measures, to keep that class away from the Government; to deny to them any access to it as a class, or any interference in its proceedings," said James Mason of Virginia, to which Andrew Butler of South Carolina added, "they do not protest as ordinary citizens do; but they mingle in their protest what they would have us believe is the judgment of the Almighty."

In an argument that betrayed its origins in a South where the fear of slave insurrection had long since silenced any prophetic murmur from an active politician, Stephen Adams of Mississippi remarked that "it is so unlike the apostles and the ministers of Christ at an early day, that it loses the potency which they suppose the styling themselves ministers of the Gospel would give to their memorials. The early ministers of Christ attended to their mission, one which was given to them by their master; and under all circumstances, even when the Savior himself was upon earth, and attempts were made to induce him to give opinions with reference to the municipal affairs of the Government, he refused."[71] Here was a two kingdoms doctrine so radical that heaven had become safely irrelevant.

Undaunted, the maverick Texan rejoined in a surprisingly Whiggish manner that, "if ministers of the Gospel are not recognized by the Constitution of the United States, they are recognized by the moral and social constitution of society. They are recognized in the constitution of man's salvation. The great Redeemer of the world enjoined duties upon mankind; and there is the moral constitution from which we have derived all the excellent principles of our political Constitution—the great principles upon which our Government, morally, socially, and religiously, is founded. . . . No man can be a minister without first being a man. . . . He has a right to interpose his voice as one of its citizens against the adoption of any measure which he believes will injure the nation. These individuals have done no more."[72] This actually served to advance the debate, for when the group of twenty-five clergymen presented an almost identical petition they added that they petitioned "as citizens"; everyone in the Senate agreed that the clergy had no special prerogative when petitioning Congress.[73]

But that did not settle the matter for Douglas and his allies, for the grudge ran deeper than the mere status of the petitioners. Senator John Pettit of Indiana began his remarks with a utilitarian catch phrase common to the Democrats; he was "for the greatest liberty to the greatest number."

> But, sir, the Senator from Mississippi [Stephen Adams] says he has a great respect and great reverence for the clergy, for the ministers of the Gospel, as such, while they keep their robes pure and unspotted; but when they descend to the turbid pools of politics, and bedabble their garments all over with the mud, and slime, and filth which he would make you believe is to found there, he loses all respect for them. So should I, if I could be led to believe that the waters of the pool of politics were any more turbid or filthy than the waters which flow through their contradictory streams of theology. I do not believe it, sir. I hold, on the contrary, that the waters of the pools of politics are infinitely more pellucid, and pure, and cheering, and refreshing, than the pool which surrounds their stagnant waters of theology—no two of them agreeing on any proposition which can be presented.[74]

Here was militant secularism worthy of Thomas Paine, and it captures pretty well the Enlightenment-style skepticism to which Young America sometimes pretended. The spirit of Voltaire seems to have breathed in Pettit; he elicited laughter by moving that the petition be referred, not to committee, but to "the officer of the Senate whom we have elected and appointed to expound the divine law and the divine will to us," the chaplain. Pettit had a long-standing reputation for Painite radicalism stemming from his attempts to eliminate military chaplaincies, which dismayed fellow Democrats who knew that an infidel reputation only played into the hands of the Whig and later Republican opposition.[75] More significantly, this kind of talk sounded increasingly heretical, if not vapid, to a nation facing its gravest spiritual crisis. For many both North and South, the times seemed too dire for Pettit's blithe skepticism.

"So far as I am concerned, I am willing that the memorial shall be allowed to lie upon the table," replied an unamused Douglas remembering the petition battles that had earlier disrupted Democratic attempts to suppress antislavery sentiment. He only called attention to the petition, he said, because he had "seen a deliberate attempt to organize the clergy of this country into a great political sectional party for Abolition schemes. That project was put forth clearly in the Abolition manifesto which I had to expose in my opening speech upon the Nebraska bill."[76] Douglas's humorless analysis of the changing political scene was prescient. Only two weeks after his Nebraska Bill passed in the Senate and before it had even been voted on in the House, he perceived the threat of the same sectional party that would rise up in opposition to his bill and eventually destroy him. In classic Jacksonian style, he attributed his opposition, not to a legitimate difference of opinion respecting slavery, but to what Jackson himself referred to as corruptionists who sometimes succeed in "sinister appeals to selfish feelings" and to "personal ambition."[77] In this case the threat was the clergy and the transcendent moral perspective they represented. Like his southern colleagues, Douglas sought to prevent any moral agitation from disturbing the business of America. To do this, he put forward the radically liberal claim that moral concerns were illegitimate in the realm of national politics.

There was, in fact, an abolition scheme of sorts. Men and women like Theodore Dwight Weld and Harriet Beecher Stowe had been working tirelessly for twenty years to convince northern public opinion that slavery was a great evil that demanded a political response. The idea was to educate the public, to make sure that slavery was treated as a wrong, and to push for the denationalization of slavery in Congress. *Uncle Tom's Cabin* grew directly out of this movement, and it was beginning to have a decisive effect on public opinion. Weld's *Slavery as It Is* was essentially a position paper developed by one of the first hired lobbyists of the Congress, and Stowe used it freely as a source for her much-celebrated novel.[78] Now this effort to change public opinion began to bear fruit as a huge tide of protest swept the North in response to Douglas's Nebraska Act.

The antislavery lobby had become a well-oiled machine by 1854, and Douglas reeled in shock at the speed with which they had gotten up the "Appeal of the Independent Democrats in Congress." The petition, he said, was "a response to that Abolition manifesto," "an attempt to give in the adhesion of the religious societies of this country through the clergy to the Abolition and political schemes of that organization," by which he meant that the petition was part of a conscious effort to mobilize public opinion against his bill.[79] Douglas had been an innovator in the development of party organization at a time when "old fogies" challenged the legitimacy of political party conventions and other innovations that seemed to undermine the power of traditional political elites. Faced with the first independent lobby, it was Douglas who now played the old fogy. Ironically, it was the Democrats who now failed to grasp the realities of mass democratic politics—in the face of grassroots efforts, no amount of leadership finesse could make the Nebraska Act acceptable.

Like Senator Pettit, Douglas drew from a well of somewhat anachronistic, anticlerical rhetoric. The protest "in the name of Almighty God" rather than "as citizens," he said, was "an attempt to establish a theocracy to take charge of our politics and our legislation," "to make the legislative power of this country subordinate to the church." Said Douglas, "If we recognize three thousand clergymen as having a higher right to interpret the will of God than we have, we destroy the right of self-action, of self-government, of self-thought, and we are merely to refer each of our political questions to this body of clergymen to inquire of them whether it is in conformity with the law of God and the will of the Almighty or not."[80] To this intemperate outburst, the senator from Texas, Sam Houston, calmly pointed out the unlikelihood of the various denominations combining "to establish theocracy in our country" and added, more importantly, that it was not the petitioners who had created the agitation but the repeal of the Missouri Compromise. Douglas was himself the author his troubles.[81]

All this debate about a petition that had already been tabled may seem trivial, but Douglas was groping for something that went to the heart of his disagreement with the Republicans. The almost identical petition from twenty-five Chicago clergymen, presented to the Senate through him, gave him an opportunity to explain why he found such petitions so offensive. Douglas denied that the clergy spoke "in the name of Almighty God" in these matters. So far there was fairly broad consensus; in a similar situation, Lincoln would take a similar position.[82]

But Douglas went further:

> You "disclaim all desire," also, "to mingle in the conflicts of political parties." This sentiment is admirable. It will meet the cordial approbation of every patriot and Christian. But you immediately follow it with the declaration that "it is our duty to recognize the moral bearing of such questions and conflicts!" You do not desire to engage in war nor to fight the battles of your country, but you do claim that "it is your right, and if you please, your duty, by virtue of your office as ministers, through the agency of this divinely-appointed institution, to declare, in the name of Almighty God, a war, in which your country is engaged with a foreign power, to be immoral and unrighteous, although the representatives of the people and of the States, in pursuance of the Constitution, have declared it to be just and necessary.[83]

For Douglas, the idea of popular sovereignty precluded any appeals to a higher law than the Constitution and the will of the people constitutionally expressed. Nearly everyone but the Garrisonians, the Quakers, and transcendental individualists like Thoreau professed allegiance to the Constitution and the laws of the country. Nevertheless, for men like Lincoln and Seward there was a higher standard than the Constitution and the laws as embodied in American life. For Douglas, the slightest hint of a higher moral standard was in itself theocratic and undemocratic. As George E. Badger of North Carolina put it, the Senate did not recognize "the gift of prophecy."[84]

Seward pointed out that the Senate began each day with an invocation of the blessing of Almighty God in much the same way that the petitioners had voiced their appeal, but that was not really the question.[85] Seward's "Higher Law" speech of four years earlier might have been more to the point. But while it established for Seward an undeserved reputation for anti-slavery radicalism it also made an easy target for Douglas. Douglas treated the slavery issue as a matter of local control and personal choice. Defending the South on these liberal grounds, he sought to remove morality and theology from politics. Douglas ruthlessly followed the logic of his position to its conclusion: *vox populi, vox Dei*. He could acknowledge no higher law and, therefore, no higher standard than American life itself. For similar reasons, the nation had become for him what it was to become for a later generation of liberals, a "normative concept."[86] Generalizing too broadly but speaking truly of Democrats like Douglas, Albert K. Weinberg summed up the theology of Young America: "In his anthropocentric theology, in which God himself served chiefly as a Providence watchful for mankind and human values, the American approached perilously close to changing the traditional dogma, that man exists *ad majorem gloriam Dei*, into the heresy that God exists *ad majorem gloriam hominis*. And Providence had entrusted the fullest achievement of the moral glory of man to the best of human material, the mighty American democracy."[87]

But to Douglas's lasting credit he did attempt to establish an American identity that would avert disunion by appealing both to northern and southern whites. As Lincoln noted, the speech he gave at New Orleans quoted above was indeed characteristic. Douglas wanted to keep oil and water together by maintaining a coalition between free-soilers, the northern working class interested in the economic potential of free soil in the territories, and the South.[88] As early as 1852, he sought to pull the South into his Young America orbit by holding out the prospect of expansion into Cuba and Mexico.

At age thirty-nine Douglas had sought to capitalize on the Young America fever that struck the nation upon the arrival in America of the Hungarian revolutionary Louis Kossuth.[89] After his revolution had been crushed by the combined imperial powers of Europe, Kossuth came to America to elicit support in a liberal crusade against Austria and Russia, and for a time it seemed that Americans might actually take up the slogan "intervention for non-intervention" and send military aid somehow to Hungary. Almost by definition, Young America pushed for American involvement overseas, but the radical Democracy was not alone. Secretary of State Daniel Webster expressed some support, as did such unlikely interventionists as the pacifist Charles Sumner and a whole host of future Republicans like William Seward, Salmon P. Chase, and Abraham Lincoln. Flush with victory over Mexico and sincerely outraged at the plight of Hungary, huge crowds greeted Kossuth almost wherever he went. Seemingly the last republic of any importance in the world, America had a duty to help the Hungarian revolutionaries if she could.

Initially only two sorts of people remained aloof from Kossuth's attempted seduction: such Old Fogy National Whigs as President Millard Fillmore or the dying Henry Clay, and southerners. These men combined a respect for the diplomatic tradition of neutrality that went back to Washington's Farewell Address with a kind of realism (even anti-Romanticism) unlikely to be swayed easily by appeals to moral fervor. In addition, the South generally rejected anything new from the North, especially if it attached itself to the word *intervention*. Douglas was a great improviser. Already bent on a southern strategy in the 1852 presidential campaign, he ended his potentially embarrassing toast to Kossuth, "intervention for non-intervention," by condemning President Fillmore for interfering with a southern attempt to filibuster Cuba. "It was within this context of a slave-state issue that Douglas attacked the principle of neutrality and called for 'a foreign policy in accordance with the spirit of the age.'" Douglas's brilliant gambit, hopelessly doomed in retrospect, was the attempt to make exuberant nationalism a southern cause.[90]

In this he was not without help—if it can be called help. The initial suggestion that Kossuth be rescued in Turkey by the U.S. Navy and transported to safety came from Senators Henry Foote of Mississippi and Pierre Soulé of Louisiana.[91] In spite of the general southern defection, these men supported Kossuth to the end. They were joined by John O'Sullivan, who as editor of the *Democratic Review* back in 1845 had probably coined the term "manifest destiny," and by George Nicholas Sanders, likewise a rabid nationalist and, as of January 1852, himself editor of the same radically Democratic monthly.[92] With Sanders at the helm, the *Democratic Review* was understood to be a Douglas ship, and Sanders pushed hard for Douglas's nomination as the Democratic presidential candidate—a little too hard. As usual, Douglas walked a very narrow line, but Sanders began by identifying Douglas with the interventionists in incendiary terms. And, as if that were not bad enough, he went on in the first issue and in subsequent ones as well, to denounce Douglas's Democratic rivals as old fogies for hedging on intervention.[93] Lewis Cass, Martin Van Buren, and James Buchanan were "senile," "a beaten horse," and "a mere lawyer," respectively, and Young America demanded "young blood," "young ideas," and a "new generation of statesmen" to transform American foreign policy into an international crusade to aid beleaguered republicans everywhere. Despite Douglas's attempts to distance himself from Sanders, the *Democratic Review* articles probably cost him the nomination.[94]

Douglas never dissociated himself completely from Young America, even though it became a source of embarrassment continually thrown in front of him. Not only had Young America alienated Douglas's fellow Democrats with the epithet Old Fogy, but the expansionist designs on Cuba in violation of international law had unsettled the international community as well. The Clayton-Bulwer Treaty, which was intended to harmonize U.S. and British interests in Latin America and to facilitate a canal either at Panama or Nicaragua, included a requirement that both sides refrain from meddling in the internal affairs of neighboring countries. Douglas took it personally: "I feel," he said, "there may be a lurking insinuation in these two clauses, having a little bearing towards an individual of about my proportions. It is the vocation of some partisan presses and personal organs, to denounce and stigmatize a certain class of politicians, by attributing to them unworthy and disreputable purposes, under the cognomen of 'Young America.'. . . I have never either assumed or disclaimed it."[95] Douglas enjoined his Senate colleagues to attend only *his* carefully worded disclaimers, but few could have been fooled. Douglas said in a letter that, "while I am a radical and progressive Democrat, I fear the Review goes too far in that direction—especially in regard to European affairs."[96] But he eventually patched up his working relationship and personal friendship with Sanders, and he remained at the center of the Young America orbit, as his 1858 speech in New Orleans shows.[97] This then was the wound that Lincoln attempted to salt in his remarks on Young America of six years later, when once again Douglas made bold for the presidency.

For a rabid expansionist, Douglas could be surprisingly touchy about American purposes toward Cuba and Latin America. He opposed the Clayton-Bulwer Treaty in part because it seemed to endorse a Mexican view of the late war. He called it a "humiliating and degrading acknowledgment" that the U.S. had been wrong in the cause of the war, a "stain . . . fastened upon the history of our country." Then, remarking that England had stolen Jamaica and Gibraltar from Spain, Douglas erupted, "The whole system of European colonization rests upon seizure, violence, and fraud," adding that we "have never invaded the rights of other nations. We do not hold in our hand the results of rapine, violence, war, and fraud, for centuries. . . ."[98] Douglas chose not to listen to Lincoln's speech on the Spot Resolutions, to say nothing of taking even passing notice of the "heathen" American Indian the way, for instance, Sam Houston did.[99] How could he? To join in Lincoln's frank willingness to acknowledge national sin would have destroyed his entire conception of American history and destiny.

In fairness to Douglas one has to add that, though he promised to do more when the Civil War was over, Lincoln avoided taking any political risks on behalf of Native Americans.[100] But Whigs opposed Indian removal and westward expansion, and Lincoln does seem to have understood the enormity of U.S. Indian policy, a possibility that for Douglas literally did not exist. The British might have sins to atone for, but Britain was everything America was not. That the novus ordo seclorum of America included nothing resembling sin, original or otherwise, was the secret heart of American exceptionalism in its Young America, manifest destiny form. With the notable exception of Hitler's Third Reich, perhaps, any attempt at empire must apologize for itself, but this *anti*apology made Young America—and perhaps America—unique.[101]

Rather than acknowledging the deliberate near-genocide of the Native Americans and then appealing to some higher good that might justify the act as a necessary evil, rather than acknowledging the unalloyed exploitation that defined chattel slavery and at the same time working to end it, Young America echoed Jefferson's remarkable assertion of American innocence in his original draft of the Declaration of Independence. For Young America there was no reason to apologize at all.

To make that claim, Young America gave added impulse to racial views otherwise pervasive in 1850s America and especially common in the Democratic Party. Always implicitly and usually explicitly, these views were thus built into manifest destiny. In order to justify ignoring the claims of Native Americans, black slaves, or, in this case, the Mexicans, and yet to maintain its high-flown humanitarian rhetoric, Young America routinely defined those groups either as less than fully human or as being in a kind of training stage of civilization. Mexico, the *Review* said, "started with every chance in her favor except one: *her people were not white men; they were not Caucasians.*" "*Such men did not know how to be free.* They have not learned the lesson to this day, nor will they learn it till they are taken into the district school of American democracy, where the master will govern them till they learn how to govern themselves."[102] Douglas went further in the direction of scientific racism. "No one," he said, "can vindicate the character, motive and conduct of the signers of the Declaration of Independence, except upon the hypothesis that they referred to the white race alone, and not to the African, when they declared men to have been created free and equal." Blacks were decidedly inferior, and any "amalgamation between superior and inferior races" would only bring the higher "down to the lower level of the inferior, but never [elevate] them to the high level of the superior race."[103] In this important sense Young America had always been ready for the *Dred Scott* decision: white men alone had rights that it was bound to respect.

Notoriously subtle and controversial, Lincoln's attitude on race differed.[104] In the lecture he asked rhetorically, "but for the difference in *habit* of observation, why did Yankees, almost instantly, discover gold in California, which had been trodden upon, and over-looked by Indians and Mexican greasers, for centuries?" Lincoln certainly embraced the prevalent notion that Christian civilization was superior to any of the available options. And, though he did not talk of Anglo-Saxon or Caucasian superiority, Mexicans were decidedly on a lower rung of the ladder.

Coupled with a curious remark about the Lutheran Reformation, Lincoln's comments imply a mild form of nativism, or at least a nod in the direction of Know-Nothingism, at a time when Republicans desperately sought to bring as many American Party voters into Republican ranks as possible.[105] But that might also be reading too much into Lincoln's remarks, especially since the point he was making was that the "habit of observation" was not natural but cultural. Forward-thinking, modernist, former Whigs like Lincoln and Seward embraced immigration for its positive economic effects.[106]

In the debates just ended, Lincoln had unequivocally rejected Know-Nothingism as counter to the principles of the Declaration of Independence, a document that on his reading included "the whole family of man."[107] To embrace xenophobia or even anti-Catholicism immediately after the election would have unraveled his entire challenge to Douglas.

The solution to this puzzle is clear. A little later in the lecture Lincoln said that the utility of phonetic writing "may be conceived, by the reflection that, to *it* we owe everything which distinguishes us from savages. Take it from us, and the Bible, all history, all science, all government, all commerce, and nearly all social intercourse go with it." Lincoln was a culturalist who looked to history for his moral bearings. Thus, unlike Douglas, he shared none of the scientific racism that would come to dominate Republican discourse after the war. Unlike most Know-Nothings, Catholicism was not for him inconsistent with American institutions. But on the other hand he did assume the *cultural* superiority of American life. Lincoln helped to formulate a substantive moral vision of self-sufficient farmers and entrepreneurs, and this egalitarian Republican vision welcomed immigrants and even blacks and, with the Dawes Act, "savages," but always with the assumption that they would become in some sense "Yankees."

Here, as in a great many things, the differences between Lincoln and Douglas, between the Republicans generally and Young America, seem very small. Lincoln's remark on "greasers" could easily imply the patronizing stance Young America took toward Mexican civilization. But the great difference lay in the general outlook that surrounded these words. Douglas wanted to mute sectional tensions both by minimizing the humanity of blacks and by diverting attention from the "slavery agitation" to an expanding frontier where, Indians and Mexicans notwithstanding, there would be ample opportunity both for slaveholders and free labor. In common with the antebellum reform movements, Lincoln and the Republicans adopted a critical stance toward their own culture, even while they shared in—or merely acquiesced to—-its prejudices. The real meaning of America was not for them the status quo or even the dream of a vast continental empire; the real meaning was an ideal that, as they saw it, had been articulated by the founders, one that stood apart from the reality and that could always be used to judge and criticize the real, existing America.

While they may seem prejudiced by twenty-first-century standards, the justice of the Republicans' cause did not presuppose racial inferiority, and thus they could remain open to learning, even curiosity, in regard to race.[108] Even after advocating colonization and "separation of the races," Lincoln could accurately distinguish the two positions: "The Republicans inculcate, with whatever of ability they can, that the Negro is a man; that his bondage is cruelly wrong, and that the field of his oppression ought not to be enlarged. The Democrats deny his manhood; deny, or dwarf to insignificance, the wrong of his bondage; so far as possible, crush all sympathy for him, and cultivate and excite hatred and disgust against him; compliment themselves as Union-savers for doing so; and call the indefinite outspreading of his bondage 'a sacred right of self-government.'"[109]

Though subtle, the difference between Lincoln and Young America on this point was important. Free from any need to regard the aspirations of blacks and Indians, Young America was able to invest manifest destiny with a real religious zeal. "Unfold the whole scroll of history," said the *Democratic Review*, "and show us the nation which, from its cradle to its manhood, has bristled so ceaselessly at every step with the movements of the electric machinery of Divine Providence. Our history was borrowed from none of the stereotyped forms of national life in the elder world. It had no antetype in the past. It began alone—it exists alone."

Having characteristically defined the United States as a nation without a history—and thus without sin—the *Democratic Review* went on to equate America with Christ, stating that Mexico is "dead" but that the "American republic is strong enough to do anything that requires strength. It is vital enough to inject life even into the dead. That she can do it to Mexico we believe, we know it. It was done to Florida and to California. . . . We, of all nations, can show a history and example of progress, order, and power, without monarchy or hierarchy," continued the article. It concluded:

> Our republic was conceived only in the holy embrace of liberty. It was born amidst the jeers of monarchy. Only a few wise men from the East followed the star as it traveled toward the West, till it halted over the manger where the newborn lay. But those wise men paid homage, and the new political dispensation has not disappointed their predictions. Our nation has grown till it can measure its strength with the mightiest powers of the earth; and the question now comes up: *Shall we not begin as a republic to emancipate nations, as monarchies have long been crushing republics?*"[110]

So much, one might say, for the separation of church and state. Douglas himself was not this openly blasphemous. But in a theologically minded, even theology-obsessed Romantic Age a doctrine of radical separation that recognized no higher law than the state could only result in making an idol of the nation. So far was anything like national self-criticism from Young America that, astonishingly—yet typically—enough, there was no hint of irony whatsoever in the use of the word "emancipate," which alone speaks volumes about the difference between Lincoln and Douglas.

As Douglas had in his speech, the article asserted that "we have acquired by legitimate purchase or friendly negotiation every foot of ground over which our flag waves today" and then said that, as a "disgrace to North America, an opprobrium to the whole system of republicanism, and consequently a disgrace to the United States . . . we should absorb Mexico for her own sake." "She should be dragged up from her degradation and raised into the constellation of free states," and it was "the business of statesmanship to determine the manner of its accomplishment." About as explicitly as possible, this defined statesmanship as the devising of means to meet given ends. Since southern senators would block any attempt to organize Nebraska under the free-soil provisions of the Missouri Compromise, Douglas faced a procedural stumbling block, or so he thought. He moved therefore to remove the obstacle and revoke that compromise. Rather than preclude the possibility of slavery north of the compromise line, why not leave it to the people themselves to decide? This would remove the moral question from Congress, something Douglas typically sought when morality seemed to intrude into the political process. (In 1860 his solution to the sectional controversy would be a sedition law banning all declarations that slavery was wrong.)[111] Let both North and South accept a local decision. Thus Douglas saw popular sovereignty as a way to prevent the moralistic agitation over slavery from interrupting what to him seemed a natural course of events.

In denying the legitimacy of religiously and morally motivated antislavery agitation and dismissing its "allied army of isms," however, Douglas forgot that he himself actively pursued Young America's moral program.[112] The call to "emancipate" Mexico was a kind of messianism after all. And, perhaps better than anything else, this religious zeal of Young America explains why he brought up the Kansas-Nebraska Act in the first place.

"The Indian barrier must be removed," Douglas argued. "The tide of emigration and civilization must be permitted to roll onward until it rushes through the passes of the mountains, and spreads over the plains, and mingles with the waters of the Pacific. . . . No man can keep up with the spirit of the age who travels on anything slower than the locomotive, and fails to receive intelligence by lightning. We must therefore have Rail Roads and Telegraphs from the Atlantic to the Pacific, through our own territory."[113] Of course Douglas wanted a Pacific railroad. And he may have been thinking in terms of a bisectional Know-Nothing opposition, rather than an explicitly sectional Republican Party that would defeat him in 1860 but which as yet did not exist. But, more than any other man, the senator who steered the compromise measures through a bitterly divided Congress in 1850 should have known how delicate the sectional balance was.

On the one hand, ideas mattered very little to Douglas. To Douglas, it did not matter, or so he thought, that the Compromise of 1850 rested on no real consensus for compromise. It did not matter to him whether slavery were voted up or voted down. That was Douglas the consummate tactician and phenomenally adept legislator. Given a particular project, the man was virtually tireless in its execution and remarkably creative in solving the practical political problems he faced. The Kansas-Nebraska Act, perhaps even more than the Compromise of 1850 or the Illinois Central Railroad, testified to Douglas's legislative skills. As Douglas put it, "I passed the Kansas-Nebraska Act myself."[114] On the other hand, at each stage of Douglas's maneuverings he seems to have believed what he said. Popular sovereignty pretended to be concerned only with process, not with results, but that was the illusion of a man who took his ends for granted. In fact, popular sovereignty was the tactical wing of a substantive Romantic vision, manifest destiny. Douglas had a dream; he even had a religion. He had Young America.

EMANCIPATION OF THE MIND

On some level, Lincoln's audience would have had much of this in mind when he lectured on discoveries and inventions. And they probably laughed at the jokes, especially the line about the land being "sadly divided out since [Adam] had dominion over all the earth." "Never fret," said Lincoln, "Young America will *re-annex* it." They would have recognized this for what it was: an old Whig mocking a Democrat who had fallen out with the leadership of his party over just how to adjust the sectional rivalry over the territories, and who was paying bitterly for it. But satire was a device Lincoln put to serious purpose. He blended his comments on Young America with the substance of what his editors have called the First Lecture on Discoveries and Inventions. "If the said Young America really is, as he claims to be, the owner of all present, it must be admitted that he has considerable advantage of Old Fogy." Lincoln then said that Adam, as the first of the old fogies, was no worse than Young America for the chance he was given. Indeed Young America carried a heavy burden of debt to the past, because "the great difference between Young America and Old Fogy, is the result of *Discoveries, Inventions, and Improvements*" that accrued over time and through history.[115]

As Thomas Arnold, English historian and favorite of the *Whig Review* put it, "Two things we ought to learn from history; one, that we are not in ourselves superior to our fathers; another, that we are shamefully and monstrously inferior to them, if we do not advance beyond them."[116] Arnold was active in English church reform and advocated as the mission of the established church the Christianizing of British culture, and there were deep affinities between Arnold's project and the goals of the American Whigs.[117] True to his own American Whig Party background, Lincoln lightly imputed a kind of impiety to Young America by recalling that writing was invented "as early as the time of Moses; from which we may safely infer that it's inventors were very old fogies."[118] But, again, that was not his *main* point, and it would be a mistake to think that Lincoln wanted to defend old fogyism or that he wanted to establish a greater reverence for tradition per se.

The consensus historians of this century correctly minimized the importance of European or Burkean conservatism in the political culture of the North, and Lincoln's lecture was not about cherishing inherited customs and traditional forms of life.[119] Though Lincoln and the Republican Party showed a greater interest in historical precedent than Young America, they were hardly traditionalists. Lincoln noted the "fact that a new country is most favorable—most necessary—to the immancipation of thought, and the consequent advancement of civilization and the arts. . . . In anciently inhabited countries, the dust of ages—a real downright old-fogyism—seems to settle upon, and smother the intellects and energies of man. It is in this view that I have mentioned the discovery of America as an event greatly favoring and facilitating useful discoveries and inventions."[120] Douglas and Young America would have had very little difficulty with this idea. Working hard for Lincoln's nomination at the Republican National Convention of 1860, for instance, David Davis telegrammed to Lincoln, "Nothing will beat us but old fogy politicians."[121]

No less than their Democratic counterparts, Lincoln and the Republicans believed that America stood in the vanguard of world history. The Republicans promoted settlement of the West with practically Young American zeal. Lincoln himself was the very model of the self-made man and, therefore, an almost unreflective believer in social mobility. As Gabor Boritt has amply shown, Lincoln's "Whig Party stood not for the past but the future of America."[122] It was not by accident that future Republicans, both Conscience Whigs and Independent Democrats, showed almost as much enthusiasm for Kossuth as Douglas did.

"To be fruitful in invention, it is indispensable to have a *habit* of observation and reflection; and this *habit* our steam friend [James Watt, the inventor of the steam engine] acquired, no doubt, from those who, to him, were old fogies." From this starting point, Lincoln listed the discoveries and inventions that facilitated other inventions: "the inclination to exchange thoughts with one another"; and "the Divine gift, or invention of speech" had led to writing, which, Lincoln said, was "the great invention of the world." Next came printing, "the true termination of that period called 'the dark ages;'" the discovery of America; and finally, the introduction of patent laws. Obviously Lincoln shared Young America's enthusiasm for technological innovation and fully believed in progress—at least in the sense of material and technological advancement. The acceptance of permanent ongoing technological revolution separated Old Fogy from both Young America and younger future Republicans.

While Lincoln was not skeptical of innovation per se, however, Gabor Boritt rightly concluded that for Lincoln "the material road was merely the means leading toward intellectual and moral elevation."[123] Even with his treatment of patent laws, Lincoln chose to make the moral point that the patent system "added the fuel of *interest* to the *fire* of genius"—a classic Lincolnian concern. Lincoln looked to harness the principles of self-interest and ambition and to make them compatible with the common good. At the 1859 Wisconsin State Fair Lincoln again elaborated his point about patent laws:

> And not only to bring together, and to impart all which has been *accidentally* discovered or invented upon ordinary motive; but, by exciting emulation, for premiums and for the pride and honor of success—of triumph, in some sort—to stimulate that discovery and invention into extraordinary activity. In this, these Fairs are kindred to the patent clause in the Constitution of the United States; and to the department, and practical system, based upon that clause.[124]

For Lincoln, intellectual discoveries and inventions did not constitute progress merely because they facilitated other discoveries. He was at least as concerned here with the moral effect of patent laws and the like.

Similarly, in the Second Lecture on Discoveries and Inventions, Lincoln noted:

> It is very probable—almost certain—that the great mass of men, at that time, were utterly unconscious, that their *conditions*, or their *minds* were capable of improvement. They not only looked upon the educated few as superior beings; but they supposed themselves to be naturally incapable of rising to equality. To immancipate the mind from this false and under estimate of itself, is the great task which printing came into the world to perform. It is difficult for us, *now* and *here*, to conceive how strong this slavery of the mind was; and how long it did, of necessity, take, to break it's shackles, and to get a habit of freedom of thought, established.

Lincoln here described the historical consciousness about as well as anyone. The very way people thought had a history. In his lecture, the "goldmine" that interested Lincoln was—note the odd word choice—the "immancipation of thought and the consequent advancement of civilization and the arts."[125]

As an aside Lincoln added two additional things to his list of discoveries and inventions that facilitated progress: "Though not apposite to my present purpose, it is but justice to the fruitfulness of that period, to mention two other important events—the Lutheran Reformation in 1517, and, still earlier, the invention of Negroes, or, of the present mode of using them, in 1434."[126] Lincoln's reference to the Reformation coincided with the Republican appeal to former Know-Nothings on the grounds of anti-Catholicism and might therefore have hinted at a nativist appeal.[127] But with the ironic little aside about the "invention of Negroes" Lincoln meant either to imply that slavery ran counter to the most important currents of history or that the currents of history were not so swift and sure after all. Thinkers of Lincoln's generation from George Bancroft to Alexis de Tocqueville saw in the Reformation, as much as in the advent of printing, the emancipation of the mind from "the dark ages." And men like Theodore Parker claimed that slavery went against progress and denied the spirit of the age.[128] For Lincoln, however, even the Reformation had not ushered in the age of goodness and light.

Lincoln's point in challenging Young America was not that progress was illusory or dangerous. Along with nearly everyone in 1850s America, Lincoln did not as yet question the view that history continuously culminated in an ongoing, ever-upward present. He even conceded to Young America the commonplace that civilization worked its way "principally Westward."[129] "Westward the star of empire takes its way" was the motto George Bancroft chose for his history, and this telling misquote of Bishop Berkeley became a standard Young America slogan.[130] Lincoln emphasized that, because the present owed so much to the past, Young America had no right to be so "self-complaisant," and thus his main point was to shift the emphasis to the moral and intellectual side of things.[131] The really important progress was not merely a matter of ever-greater prosperity and material splendor but the progress of ideas and, more specifically, the progress of *moral* ideas. "Gold-mines are not the only mines overlooked in the same way," he said. "There are more mines above the Earth's surface than below it. All nature—the whole world, material, moral, and intellectual,—is a mine."[132] In the face of Douglas's unabashed and therefore honest celebration of material progress, Lincoln and the Republicans continued the Whig tradition of emphasizing moral and spiritual concerns.[133]

The opening remarks of the Second Lecture, then, should now make more sense. In the first paragraph, Lincoln painted a colorful portrait of bounty that the world-market economy laid upon Young America's table.

> Men, and things, everywhere, are ministering unto him. Look at his apparel, and you shall see cotton fabrics from Manchester and Lowell; flax-linen from Ireland; will-cloth from Spain; silk from France; furs from the Arctic regions, with a buffalo-robe from the Rocky Mountains, as a general out-sider. At his table, besides plain bread and meat made at home, are sugar from Louisiana; coffee and fruits from the tropics; salt from Turk's Island; fish from New-foundland; tea from China, and spices from the Indies. The whale of the Pacific furnishes his candle-light; he has a diamond-ring from Brazil; a gold-watch from California, and a spanish cigar from Havanna. He not only has a present supply of all these, and much more; but thousands of hands are engaged in producing fresh supplies, and other thousands, in bringing them to him. The iron horse is panting, and impatient, to carry him everywhere, in no time; and tidings in a trifle less than no time. He owns a large part of the world, by right of possessing it; and all the rest by right of *wanting* it, and *intending* to have it. As Plato had for the immortality of the soul, so Young America has "a pleasing hope—a fond desire—a longing after" territory.[134]

The warmth of Lincoln's descriptions here, along with his known enthusiasm for technological innovation during the Civil War, should not lead us to read these lines as celebratory of Young America, rather than as critique or parody.[135] Make no mistake; as a representative of the supposedly market-oriented Republican Party, Lincoln chastised the Democrats for their excessive faith in market capitalism. Coupled with the remark about Plato and the immortality of the soul, it is clear that Lincoln playfully criticized the excessive and impious materialism of Young America. In their unbridled enthusiasm for an expanding world-market economy and an expanding nation, Young America neglected matters that should have been more important.

Lincoln did not wish to halt progress or technological innovation, but he did want to remind his listeners of what was really important. Later in the lecture he suggested that speech might not be "an invention of man, but rather the direct gift of his Creator."[136] In the parts of the lecture of which we have no autograph draft, Lincoln reportedly said, "music, like flowers, was a gift of pure benevolence from our good Creator. It is the natural language of the heart, and adapts itself to all emotions, from the triumphal exultation of a Miriam to the plaint of the mourner."[137] Not only were there more important things than the bounties of the market, but the greatest gifts were not necessarily the result of human effort at all. In these lectures, Lincoln replaced Young America's arrogance and complaisance with an attitude of humility, even gratitude. To counter the Romantic vision of manifest destiny, he introduced his own equally Romantic vision of America's place in history.

Lincoln last delivered his lectures on discoveries and inventions on April 26, 1860.[138] On September 30 of the previous year he delivered an address at the Wisconsin State Fair and, since that address touched on many of the same themes, its concluding paragraph may well include all or part of the missing conclusion to the lecture.

> It is said an Eastern monarch once charged his wise men to invent him a sentence, to be ever in view, and which should be true and appropriate in all times and situations. They presented him the words: "And this, too, shall pass away." How much it expresses! How chastening in the hour of pride!—how consoling in the depths of affliction! "And this, too, shall pass away." And yet let us hope it is not quite true. Let us hope, rather, that by the best cultivation of the physical world, beneath and around us; and the intellectual and moral world within us, we shall secure an individual, social, and political prosperity and happiness, whose course shall be onward and upward, and which, while the earth endures, shall not pass away.[139]

Here at the Wisconsin State Fair, and in the lectures on discoveries and inventions as well, the task Lincoln urged his listeners to take up was the intense cultivation of the land and of the mind "in a world less inclined to wars, and more devoted to the arts of peace, than heretofore."[140] By 1863 the notion that the reign of peace was come would stick in the throat a little more; and by 1865 the Civil War would temper Lincoln's optimism still further. At Gettysburg, "the great task remaining before us" was the completion of a war, the rebirth of the nation in freedom, and the preservation of self-government, but the Gettysburg Address would end with an almost identical phrase: "shall not perish from the earth."

Lincoln stated his hope that America would not be subject to what had been seen as the inevitable fall and decay of nations and empires—a notion near and dear to Young America. Lincoln clearly shared some of what is a characteristic brand of American optimism. Thus, in the lecture on discoveries and inventions, in the Wisconsin State Fair speech, and even in the Gettysburg Address, Lincoln more than flirted with a species of postmillennialism, the belief that through progress American life was ushering in the fulfillment of sacred history.[141]

Still, it is also important to recognize that already in 1859 Lincoln considered the possibility that American civilization might "pass away." In this he revealed not only the somewhat pathetic tendency (common in the Romantic Period) of dwelling on the transience of all earthly endeavor, but, more important, he applied this principle of transience to the *American* endeavor. In order to head off the possibility that America too might pass away, he exhorted his listeners to "renewed exertion."[142] Indeed, in all of his occasional addresses from the Lyceum Address of 1838 through Gettysburg, Lincoln made similar exhortations to communal moral striving. And in each of these instances he used two seemingly contradictory though in fact complementary rhetorical strategies. On the one hand, he held out an almost postmillennial promise that bordered on the impious equation of America with the coming Kingdom. On the other hand, he nearly always included an element of criticism that raised the possibility that, without self-conscious moral striving, all might soon be lost.

In Lincoln's occasional speeches there was always an element of Romantic culturalism, for lack of a better term. Though he was not a nativist, we should not miss his rejection of the liberal internationalism that Young America celebrated. Where Young America saw in tradition and historical community only an artificial set of constraints, for Lincoln historical community was a source of inspiration and meaning. In general, Young America set its expansionist sights on Mexico and the Gulf. "A few idealists believed that America's destiny lay in bringing the entire world into one union," noted historian David Danbom, and "the colorful Senator Robert J. Walker of Mississippi wrote that American expansionism would bring the same result that English liberals hoped free trade would bring—world unification free from international conflict." Prophetically, as it turns out, Walker predicted a world order in which "a vast majority will speak the English language; the general convenience will in the end make it universal."[143]

Lincoln, on the other hand, was one of those who "did not have the Young America faith in the feasibility of expansion into racially and culturally alien areas."[144] Thus Young America had more in common with late-twentieth-century economic liberalism and internationalism than Lincoln did. Lincoln was faithful to America in the cultural sense of seeking to perfect America on its own terms. Young America accepted cultural difference, including Roman Catholic voters, and sought to expand American institutions on that liberal basis. But it could afford to do so only because, from the perspective of economic liberalism, such cultural differences were at best irrelevant and more often a nuisance. Racial solidarity was apparently enough.

Cultural concerns were not irrelevant for Lincoln, and his rejection of radical liberalism was complete; he was simply too concerned with moral community and with substantive morality to accept Young America's internationalist vision. It is almost fair to say that, for Young America, historical community and culture did not matter at all. This was not quite true: Young America actually saw its liberalism as the culmination of all history. But for

Whigs a concern with the traditions of learning and religion was more typi-cal, and the heartland of Whiggery was New England. Thus, despite his pro-fessed admiration for Henry Clay, especially as regarded the slavery issue, Lincoln directed his economic and cultural allegiance almost completely to-ward the Northeast. In his life choices as well as in his legal and public ca-reers, Lincoln rejected the subsistence agrarianism of his youth in favor of industrialization, projects like railroads and the Illinois and Michigan Canal, and close economic and cultural ties with the Northeast, which goes a long way toward explaining why Lincoln was a Whig and not a Democrat.[145]

Along with a belief in the power of what we might call emergent capital-ism, Lincoln also absorbed much of New England's spirit of humanitarian re-form. David Danbom summed up the difference between Young America and humanitarian reformers: "While the humanitarian reformer was at-tempting to achieve moral perfection in America, the Young American was attempting to achieve political perfection throughout the world by Ameri-canizing it."[146]

Thus Lincoln's preoccupation with ethics and with the mind linked him (along with his fellow northern Whigs) to the humanitarian, Protestant tra-dition within antebellum American culture, a tradition opposed to the self-interest-oriented liberalism of Douglas and one that, according to Gilbert Barnes, gave rise to the "antislavery impulse."[147] The hero of that book was Theodore Dwight Weld, with whom Lincoln would have disagreed on many points, but with whom he also shared certain important underlying con-cerns. In *Slavery as It Is,* Weld did not cite examples of mistreatment of slaves because, "however numerous or well authenticated, they would be either scouted as incredible or met with the cry 'exception.' . . .treatment, however bad, is but an appendage of slavery." Instead, as Barnes noted, Weld empha-sized "the inflictions of slavery on *mind*—its prostration of conscience . . . its destruction of personality—its death-stab into the soul of the slave."[148]

. . .

Beginning with his praise of "all-conquering mind" in the 1838 Lyceum Address and continuing through the Wisconsin State Fair speech of 1859 and beyond, Lincoln consistently expressed the same arch-Victorian anxiety for the control of passions like self-interest and ambition by the mind. What linked him with political antislavery men like Seward, Chase, and Sumner as well as with reformers like Theodore Dwight Weld and Harriet Beecher Stowe was the belief that this control must be asserted in the political as well as the personal realm.

The lectures of 1858–1860 reveal something of Lincoln the Romantic in-tellectual, and it is this Lincoln that shows the piety of his great war speeches as something more than the musings of a momentarily tortured conscience. Lincoln belonged with neither Young America nor the old fogies. Neither was he an unambiguous herald of progress like the Democrats, whose chief spokesman in this regard was George Bancroft, nor was he the partisan of a revered past, which for the old fogies provided the only model for future action. While he revered parts of the past, and while he had high hopes for the future, both the past and the future remained morally ambiguous.

In his classic of 1955, *The American Adam*, R. W. B. Lewis mentioned but never fully explored a middle term between what he called the parties of memory and of hope. To this category he ascribed such "off-beat traditionalists" as Herman Melville, Nathaniel Hawthorne, and the elder Henry James, and he called it the "party of irony."[149] Similarly, Christopher Lasch recently made essentially the same distinctions and argued for the importance of the ironic point of view and the sense of human limitations in writers like the later Emerson, Carlyle, and William James.[150] What is remarkable, however, is just how explicitly ideas about progress were argued in antebellum America, and just how political they were. Beyond the immediate jabs at Douglas, Lincoln used the lecture on discoveries and inventions to position himself in that ongoing debate. There was another, related debate that Lincoln took up when he challenged Young America, a theological debate about the meaning of America. It is in the context of this debate that the meaning of Lincoln's religious rhetoric can be discovered. Douglas quite literally spoke for George Bancroft, who made America the telos of history and thereby precluded any prophetic or morally critical stance. Drawing on his Whig heritage, Lincoln countered that argument with an ironic Protestant perspective.

Chapter Two

OF PRIESTS AND PROPHETS

• In January 1821 Thomas Jefferson congratulated John Adams for his role at the recent Massachusetts constitutional convention. Adams had proposed an amendment to the commonwealth's bill of rights abolishing state recognition of religious sects, and Jefferson hailed this as proof of "the advance of liberalism." Yet Jefferson worried about the slavery question:

> This country, which has given to the world the example of physical liberty, owes to it that of moral emancipation also. For, as yet, it is but nominal with us. The inquisition of public opinion overwhelms in practice the freedom asserted by the laws in theory.
>
> Our anxieties on this quarter are all concentrated in the question What does the Holy alliance, in and out of Congress, mean to do with us on the Missouri question? . . . The real question, as seen in the states afflicted with this unfortunate population, is Are our slaves to be presented with freedom and a dagger? For if Congress has a power to regulate the conditions of the inhabitants of the states, within the states, it will be but another exercise of that power to declare that all shall be free. Are we then to see again Athenian and Lacedemonian confederacies? To wage another Peloponnesian war to settle the ascendancy between them?[1]

Here Jefferson clearly touched on the conflict that eventually resulted in the Civil War. But, more important, he characterized opposition to Missouri statehood as a "Holy alliance" or "inquisition," and he equated "moral emancipation" with a relatively apologetic stance toward slavery. The author of the Declaration of Independence reacted here not only to a widening chasm between North and South but to an intellectual and historical divide as well, one that separates the eighteenth century from the nineteenth. From the 1820s through the 1850s, northern antislavery rode in on a wave of religious feeling alien to the skeptical rationalism of the founders, and Jefferson marked well the new mood. Eventually, revivalism and transcendentalism would ignite to threaten both the Union and Jefferson's liberalism.

Not missing the point, Adams replied:

> Slavery in this Country I have seen hanging over it like a black cloud for half a Century. If I were as drunk with enthusiasm as Swedenborg or Wesley, I might probably say I had seen Armies of Negroes marching and countermarching in

the air, shining in Armour. I have been so terrified with this Phenomenon that I constantly said in former times to the Southern Gentlemen, I cannot comprehend this object; I must leave it to you. I will vote for forcing no measure against your judgments. What we are to see, *God* knows, and I leave it to him, and his agents in posterity.[2]

Both Adams and Jefferson equated religious enthusiasm with irrationality and superstition. For Jefferson, "angry," "unwise and unworthy Passions" had caused the Missouri agitation and threatened men's ability to reason dispassionately.[3] This "enthusiasm" menaced the delicate sectional balance and, to the elder statesmen, represented the religious enslavement of the European past that America had explicitly rejected with disestablishment.

To many of the younger generation, however, it seemed absurd to equate moral emancipation with acquiescence in slavery's expansion the way Jefferson did. The fight to disestablish religion was all but over, and these men and women longed for some absolute commitment. For some of them, this longing transformed Jefferson's enlightened acknowledgment that slavery was wrong into a positive moral duty to work for its abolition. For others, the new Romantic sensibility in no way led to an antislavery commitment. Young America, for example, was a form of Romantic nationalism that expressed a desire to serve on the side of history but that was *not* antislavery. The South of course developed its own brand of Romantic identity. It was increasingly difficult to acknowledge a wrong, however, and then leave it in the hands of God to correct. After ages of darkness, the world seemed perfectible to many, entailing a duty to work toward that perfection. "Posterity" had arrived, and God was not lacking volunteer "agents."

William Brock captured the shift admirably: "In Europe a tradition of respectable antiquity had maintained that governments served a moral purpose and that rulers were ordained by God as instruments in the divine plan. In the United States the Revolution had replaced this sanction for authority by the assertion that governments derived their just powers from the consent of the governed, that their primary purpose was the protection of rights that could not be abridged, and that utility and expediency were the sole tests that should be applied. Now the idea that government had a moral character, and should have a moral purpose, was reentering American life."[4] Even one of the great consensus historians, Merle Curti, had to admit that "by the early thirties the Northeast was becoming so rapidly industrialized that, to many, America seemed to stand for canals and railways, wharves and factories. From this industrialization sensitive souls drew back in horror and dismay, for it seemed to them that the mechanical trend in American civilization, the preoccupation with 'curious mechanical contrivances and adaptations of matter, which it discovered by means of its telescopes, microscopes, dissections and other mechanical aids,' was destroying human and spiritual values. And was not all this mechanism in our industrial organization, in morals, and in politics the inevitable and direct result of a sensationalist philosophy which denied the primary intuitions of the soul? Was not the solution for misfortunes to be found, in part at least, in a repudiation of Locke and the empiricists and in drinking deeply of the spiritual nourishment of the Cambridge Platonists, Coleridge, and the German idealists?"[5]

Despite the obvious importance of this Romantic revolt against the Enlightenment, it is often assumed that American politics have been untheoretical, practical, and un-Romantic.[6] More than any other figure in antebellum America, George Bancroft articulated that conception. According to his interpretation, American life represented a radical break with the past, especially with its theology. In America, "the terrors of religion, as interpreted by a priesthood" and "the bayonets of a standing army" had finally been overthrown, leaving a natural society of individuals contracting to govern themselves in freedom.[7] All the essential theoretical questions had been answered, leaving only matters of practical application yet to be solved. History, culture, and theology had been overcome, with natural, political, and economic sciences replacing inherited sources of understanding, wisdom, or authority. Bancroft's great ten-volume *History of the United States, from the Discovery of the American Continent* provided the competent and credible historical narrative Americans needed to solidify this Jeffersonian conception of American identity. And this liberal consensus has had remarkable staying power. It was, in a sense, a frontier thesis as well; confronted with the tabula rasa of an uncharted wilderness, the colonists cast off the burdens of their past way of life and formed themselves anew on the principles of nature, natural science, and common sense. Unlike in the Old World, in America mankind had the opportunity to found a society on the principles of nature, thus putting the principles of the Enlightenment into practice. As Bancroft told the story, Americans shed more and more of the past until they arrived at the culmination of all world history, the American Revolution and the U.S. Constitution.

Ironically, an examination of Bancroft's miscellaneous speeches and writings, as well as of his *History*, reveals that his antitheoretical conception of American identity was itself a historical, cultural, and theological achievement. Like Marx, Bancroft studied under Hegel, and though his writings lacked much of the urgency of Marx's, like Marx he invested history with a goal, or telos, and subordinated individual events to that guiding purpose. An excessive concentration on "the founding fathers" has misled generations of Americans. America is not merely the land of the Enlightenment; for America, too, had a Romantic period. Bancroft's great ten-volume history helped solidify the myth that Americans were the one people who had no myths. One of the ironies that resulted has been that those most inclined toward a "scientific," value-free, or liberal explanation of the American community have been, for that reason, the most inclined to accept the Romantic myth. More cleverly even than Marx, who wanted his history to be science, Bancroft obscured the mythological character of his history when he made American life a step out of history into the Enlightenment world of static scientific nature.[8] This paradox is particularly maddening because the central player on the American cultural stage at the time not only saw this, but saw through it. With increasing clarity over time, Abraham Lincoln fought a mostly losing battle against this vision, and subsequent generations have honored his name while ignoring his message.

That is not to say that Lincoln himself was less invested in theory than Bancroft; on the contrary, Lincoln shared the deepest tendencies and longings of the Romantic. The Romantic endeavor was an attempt to recapture and revitalize religious modes of thought and feeling that were thought to have been lost during the rationalistic and mechanistic period now known as the Enlightenment; and from Keats's odes to Rachmaninov's Vespers, from Thomas Carlyle's *Signs of the Times* to the Virgin at Chartres of Henry Adams, the full colors of virtually any intellectual in the Romantic period appear only in the light of a fundamentally religious effusion.[9] Often the attempts to recapture religious commitment took on a scientific—or, rather, a scientistic—garb, as when Karl Marx attempted to give scientific legitimacy to his historical theories. But, in retrospect, Marx's historical theory was clearly an urgent millennialist vision of world history, difficult to comprehend without the moral outrage that informed it. And beneath the surface of even the most scientific and skeptical sounding antebellum writing lay similar transcendental longings.

AMERICA'S ROMANTIC MYTH AND LINCOLN AS LECTURER

Such are the grand cultural stages on which local political controversies play out, often with comic effects. According to the *Illinois State Journal,* Lincoln's lecture at Illinois College in Jacksonville "was received with repeated and hearty *burate* of applause," and one week later it was announced that Lincoln would repeat the lecture, this time at the Concert Hall in Springfield for twenty-five cents admission. A little further a similar notice appeared with the added exhortation, "Let us, one and all, compliment [Mr. Lincoln] with a full attendance. His lecture, we are assured, will be an 'intellectual feast.'"[10] Lincoln's lecture was part of the energetic politicking that pervaded the intellectual life of America even as the possibility of secession and war dampened the spirits of more prescient politicos. And immediately beneath this invitation to banquet on Lincoln's intellectual feast there appeared a notice for a new periodical, the *Democratic Age,* which attempted to replace the faltering *Democratic Review.* According to the notice, this new monthly was "evidently of the 'Young America' order of Democracy and its style has all the slap-dash freshness pertaining to that particular order." Young America was also an association of young men who met at places like fire stations and who, like their counterparts, the Republican "Wide-Awakes," generated enthusiasm and voter turnout with torchlight parades or serenaded favorite politicians at victory celebrations. Perhaps in response to Lincoln's lecture, an entry the next day read: "Attention Young America. You are notified to meet at your Hose House at two-o'clock in full uniform, for parade."

Despite the narrow politics of the matter, despite his lifetime personal rivalry with Stephen Douglas, Lincoln had much higher aspirations that took him to the rostrum of the lyceum circuit. His literary ambition led him to experiment with his own stories and poems and eventually found expression at Gettysburg and in the Second Inaugural Address.[11] He said of his favorite poem that he would give all he was worth, and go in debt, to be able to write so fine a piece as he thought that was.[12] Following Mr. Lincoln, the Springfield Concert Hall booked a "Lecture on Astronomy" by "Rev. Mr. Springer, from Maine, who brings high testimonials from scientific gentlemen of the East, of his qualifications," and whose "splendid apparatus," they again felt "assured," would "furnish a delightful treat to his audience."[13] The lecture circuit was an important avenue of intellectual ambition in mid-nineteenth-century America, and virtually all of the important cultural spokesman of the day embarked upon it at one time or another: Melville, Emerson, Twain, Parker, Sumner, and a host of less well remembered but nevertheless important figures who explained the implications of rapidly advancing scientific discovery and often sought, consciously or unconsciously, to reconcile these advances with inherited wisdom and religious belief.

More than in the Second Lecture on Discoveries and Inventions already discussed, the elements of what appears in the *Collected Works* as the First Lecture was of this type.[14] And if Lincoln intended the material of the Second Lecture to undermine Douglas and Young America, the questions remains: what was the so-called First Lecture about? In it, Lincoln discussed the origins of various discoveries and inventions; among other odd-seeming tidbits, he dated the creation at six thousand years ago, more or less.[15] His principle sources for the lecture were the Bible and the *Encyclopaedia Americana*, edited by Francis Lieber.[16] Lieber was one of the chief critics of social contract thinking (and ipso facto a leading exponent of organic and historical theories of state), and he eventually helped Lincoln formulate the North's theory of the laws of war.[17] His was by far the most important popular encyclopedia of its day. Lieber translated and adapted it from the German *Conversations-Lexikon*, soliciting articles from the likes of Joseph Story and Edward Everett.[18] Thus, along with the magazine press, publications like the *Encyclopaedia Americana* did much to popularize Romantic thought. Lincoln not only owned it, he used it.

"All creation is a mine," Lincoln began, "and every man, a miner."

> The whole earth, and all *within* it, *upon* it, and *round about* it, including *himself,* in his physical, moral, and intellectual nature, and his susceptibilities, are the infinitely various "leads" from which, man, from the first, was to dig out his destiny.
>
> In the beginning, the mine was unopened, and the miner stood *naked,* and *knowledgeless,* upon it.
>
> Fishes, birds, beasts, and creeping things, are not miners, but *feeders* and *lodgers,* merely. Beavers build houses; but they build them in nowise differently, or better now, than they did, five thousand years ago. Ants, and honey-bees,

provide food for winter; but just in the *same way* they did, when Solomon referred the sluggard to them as patterns of prudence.

Man is not the only animal who labors; but he is the only one who *improves* his workmanship. This improvement, he effects by *Discoveries,* and *Inventions.* His first important discovery was the fact that he was naked; and his first invention was the fig-leaf-apron. . . .[19]

Even less has been said about Lincoln's First Lecture on Discoveries and Inventions than the Second; it certainly lacks the racy jokes and the sarcastic punch. He first delivered the lecture immediately before the Illinois Republican Party nominated him for the Senate in 1858, and he did not revisit his lecture circuit ambitions until after losing to Douglas. Because Douglas himself encouraged public support for internal improvements, and because the dispute over slavery in the territories overshadowed all else, the traditional Whig theme of "improvements" was not important in 1858–1859.[20] Along with the biblically based, pre-Darwinian time line, the use of the Bible to determine the origins of spinning and weaving, of wheels and boats, of plows and flour mills, seems very quaint. But even this is not surprising coming from a known student of Scripture in the years just before *The Origin of Species and the Descent of Man.* What Lincoln found interesting about the natural world, and by implication what he did not, is significant. Not attracted to grizzly bear claws and exotic new plants, what interested Lincoln most in retelling the Creation story was its *moral* import.

While the elements of the Second Lecture that attacked Young America added rhetorical teeth to the otherwise conventional Whig reminder that government-sponsored internal improvements were a moral duty, the material now known as the First Lecture led up to the story about steam power.

The advantageous use of *Steam power* is, unquestionably, a modern discovery.

And yet, as much as two thousand years ago the power of steam was not only observed, but an ingenius toy was actually made and put in motion by it, at Alexandria in Egypt.

What appears strange is, that neither the inventor of the toy, nor any one else, for so long a time afterwards, should perceive that steam would move *useful* machinery as well as a toy.[21]

Though elements of this story appeared in what we call the Second Lecture, Lincoln made his point more clearly here. Former Whigs who became Republicans favored such improvements as public institutions of higher learning, and here Lincoln emphasized the active participation of the mind in the making of discoveries. Technological progress was *not* inevitable. Rather it depended upon a contingent *"habit* of observation and reflection," which, if not properly cultivated, would wither.[22] Adam's first important discovery was not the "fig-leaf-apron" but "the fact that he was naked." Each example Lincoln cited made the same point: "even the plow, could not have been conceived of, until a precedent conception had been caught, and put into practice—I mean the conception, or idea, of substituting other forces in nature, for man's own muscular power."[23] As in the Second Lecture, Lincoln articulated what we would call a Romantic or idealist epistemology.

Olivier Fraÿssé, one of the few historians to deal with the First Lecture, found evidence of Lincoln's abiding hostility to farm work and agriculture. He wrote that, in Lincoln's view, "the farmer is not far removed from the beast. In the lecture on inventions, agriculture is the last industry mentioned (after spinning and weaving, metallurgy, and transportation)," because, "in consequence of the first transgression, *labor* was imposed on the race, as a *penalty*—a *curse*."[24] These observations were part of Fraÿssé's convincing case that, for his entire adult life, Lincoln ran from the farm labor of his youth. In this context, however, the interesting points to be gained are, first, that for Lincoln discoveries and inventions were a way of overcoming original sin. Lincoln saw in technology an escape from Adam's curse, and thus his thought about progress in this period had postmillennial tendencies, typical of most Americans then as now, but inconsistent with Lincoln's own later words. Second, the only improvement in agriculture Lincoln mentioned was "the conception or idea, of substituting other forces in nature, for man's own muscular power."[25] As a Romantic, Lincoln was preoccupied with the power of mind over matter.

The Romantic strain in Lincoln's thought appears more clearly in his two-paragraph meditation on Niagara Falls from ten years earlier. "Niagara Falls!" he began, "By what mysterious power is it that millions and millions, are drawn from all parts of the world, to gaze upon Niagara Falls?"

> There is no mystery about the thing itself. Every effect is just such as any intelligent man knowing the causes, would anticipate, without it. In the water moving onward in a great river, reaches a point where there is a perpendicular jog, of a hundred feet in descent, in the bottom of the river,—it is plain the water will have a violent and continuous plunge at that point. The mere physical of Niagara Falls is only this. Yet this is really a very small part of that world's wonder. It's power to excite reflection, and emotion, is it's great charm.[26]

Already Lincoln's use of "mystery" and "emotion" reveal the stirrings of a Romantic sensibility, but Lincoln then rehearsed, with all of his love of geometry and physics, what a geologist and a philosopher would say about the great cataract. "The geologist," he mused, "will demonstrate that the plunge, or fall, was once at Lake Ontario, and has worn it's way back to it's present position; he will ascertain how *fast* it is wearing now, and so get a basis for determining how *long* it has been wearing back from Lake Ontario, and finally demonstrate by it that this world is at least fourteen thousand years old." (Interestingly enough, this did not coincide with the biblical time line that Lincoln seemed to endorse ten years later in the lecture on discoveries and inventions.) The philosopher, according to Lincoln, would discuss the amount of water pouring over the falls and point out that all that water had to be lifted up by the sun over a vast area of the earth's surface. Finally, said philosopher would be "overwhelmed in the contemplation of the vast power the sun is constantly exerting in quiet, noise-less operation of lifting water *up* to be rained *down* again."[27]

Though it ended with this expression of awe in the face of the natural world, the philosopher's dry, prosaic perspective on nature only provided an artful foil for a second paragraph in which Lincoln confessed what amounted to a Romantic credo: "But still there is more," he wrote. Niagara Falls

> calls up the indefinite past. When Columbus first sought this continent—when Christ suffered on the cross—when Moses led Israel through the Red-Sea—nay, even, when Adam first came from the hand of his maker—then as now, Niagara was roaring here. The eyes of that species of extinct giants, whose bones fill the mounds of America, have gazed on Niagara, as ours do now. Cotemporary with the whole race of men, and older than the first man, Niagara is strong, and fresh to-day as ten thousand years ago. The Mammoth and Mastadon—now so long dead, that fragments of their monstrous bones, alone testify, that they ever lived, have gazed on Niagara. In that long—long time, never still for a single moment. Never dried, never froze, never slept, never rested,

We can only guess what might have followed the last comma, and one wonders how Lincoln would have reconciled the geologic age of the earth with the biblical story of Creation—this, surely, was a great topic for the lyceum. Like many of his generation to visit Niagara Falls, Lincoln was puzzled by the chronology that the recession of the falls suggested. "The most important breakthrough in solving the chronology problem, widely accepted in Anglo-American geological circles by 1820, was to read the Mosaic accounts not literally but figuratively; the six days of creation were now understood merely as literary terms to convey to unsophisticated people the events of what actually had been six ages of geological activity by means of which God effected the creation of the earth."[28]

Lincoln found in the falls an image of God. In spite of the troubling chronology, Lincoln here saw an image for divine watchfulness or superintendence, a consistent theme of his religious words. As with Theodore Parker, Walt Whitman, and a host of lesser literary lights, it was the ongoing miracle, rather than the particular timing of the Creation, that seemed most important. (Unlike some of his cohort, Lincoln did not find in Niagara Falls any impetus toward literary nationalism or any occasion for exaggerated patriotic fervor.)[29] Most important for us, finally, Lincoln here revealed his conversion from any Enlightenment skepticism (or its Common Sense school extension) to a Romantic and poetic relationship with nature, which eventually allowed him to reconnect with his biblical and Augustinian past. The ultimate meaning of nature transcended utilitarian and materialist considerations.

Lincoln's predestinarianism came at a crucial moment in intellectual history when the providential worldview had been giving way before more mechanistic theories for more than a century. No question could have had deeper intellectual ramifications than whether reasonable people could still find ultimate meaning in historical development, which was why Lincoln later found it necessary to address the issue of discoveries and inventions. In the 1840s, for instance, Robert Chambers's *Vestiges of the Natural History of Creation* momentarily stemmed the tide of scientific determinism, allowing a respite from the onslaught of mechanism by providing a credible teleological account of the history of the universe.[30] It was a theory of evolution that accounted for things like mastadon bones and the like but that did not rely on the mechanism of natural selection. Instead Chambers postulated a divine purpose: God was at work in evolution. Some thirty years later the growing acceptance of Darwin and social Darwinism would bury even this formidable Victorian bulwark under a crushing wave of amoral science, consigning the book to relative oblivion. While evangelicals and the *Whig Review* both hated *Vestiges*, everybody read it, including Lincoln.[31] But, as this meditation as well as the Lincoln's lectures attested, he preferred a more concrete, biblical God to the abstract teleology of Chambers. Lincoln justified his position not by turning to natural science to prove the literal facticity of the biblical narrative—the way conservative, Common Sense clergymen did—but by turning to poetry and to a powerful poetic reappropriation of biblical language and imagery.[32]

Dismissing the fragment altogether, one Lincoln biographer speculated that here Lincoln's "pen stopped as he recognized that he was not good at this sort of thing. Later, when Herndon asked him what reflections he had when he saw the falls, he remarked solemnly that he wondered where all that water came from."[33] But Lincoln was teasing Herndon, whom he knew to be a very Romantic young man indeed. This use of irony would find a parallel in Lincoln's famous letter to Horace Greeley in which he appeared to make union (rather than antislavery) the reason for the war, when unbeknownst to Greeley and to almost everyone else the Emancipation Proclamation was written and ready in the desk drawer. Herndon had no idea Lincoln was indeed impressed with Niagara Falls and thus failed to see Lincoln's dismissive remark as a joke. He took it as proof that Lincoln "had no eye for the magnificence and grandeur of the scene."[34] Herndon was a better historian than has often been thought, but here Lincoln's irony successfully obscured his self-conscious Romanticism, both from Herndon and from some later historians.[35]

But even if Lincoln did stop writing his meditation on Niagara because he did not like his work—a thesis for which there is no evidence one way or another—he clearly *was* "good at this sort of thing." The fragment shows the same pacing and antithesis that marked Lincoln's great meditations later in his career. Consensus historians also used a passage from Lincoln's eulogy of Henry Clay to suggest that Lincoln's own productions owed their eloquence, not to "types and figures—of antithesis, and elegant arrangement of words and sentences," but to "great sincerity and a thorough conviction in the speaker of the justice and importance of his cause."[36] Lincoln certainly spoke with sincerity and conviction on occasion, but his sheer mastery of the meditation form at Gettysburg could not have come without practice, and this "Fragment on Niagara" shows the self-conscious stylist at work.[37] He may not have achieved literary greatness or even gone beyond the conventional in this meditation, but Lincoln did situate himself in his intellectual world. While natural history interested him some in itself, he found moral questions more important; and while, as when lecturing on discoveries and inventions, he could draw ethical conclusions from history, what interested Lincoln most was not ethics but a kind of *piety*. By dwelling for a moment in awe and wonder at the beauty and the power of nature, Lincoln sought to set himself in the proper relationship to his "maker." Lincoln's use of language here was a Romantic, "symbolic-imaginative response to nature."[38] In Niagara he found a figure for the watchfulness of some mysterious power, and this attitude of awe and wonder was what the Romantic was all about. On all sides of the slavery controversy, the desire to set oneself right with God, the Romantic quest for righteousness, would inform, shape, distort, and even drive the debate.

In Lincoln's "Speech on the Subtreasury," a speech in which he called Douglas "stupid," he said of the upcoming 1840 presidential campaign:

> I know that the great volcano at Washington, aroused and directed by the evil spirit that reigns there, is belching forth the lava of political corruption, in a current broad and deep, which is sweeping with frightful velocity over the whole length and breadth of the land, bidding fair to leave unscathed no green spot or living thing, while on its bosom are riding like demons on the waves of Hell, the imps of that evil spirit, and fiendishly taunting all those who dare resist its destroying course, with the hopelessness of their effort; and knowing this, I cannot deny that all may be swept away. Broken by it, I, too, may be; bow to it I never will. The *probability* that we may fall in the struggle *ought not* to deter us from the support of a cause we believe to be just; it *shall not* deter me. If ever I feel the soul within me elevate and expand to those dimensions not wholly unworthy of its Almighty Architect, it is when I contemplate the cause of my country, deserted by all the world beside, and I standing up boldly and alone and hurling defiance at her victorious oppressors. Here, without contemplating consequences, before High Heaven, and in the face of the world, I swear eternal fidelity to the just cause, as I deem it, of the land of my life, my liberty and my love. And who, that thinks with me, will not fearlessly adopt the oath that I take. Let none faulter, who thinks he is right, and we may succeed. But, if after all, we shall fail, be it so. We still shall have the proud consolation of saying to our consciences, and to the departed shade of our country's freedom, that the cause approved of our judgment, and adored of our hearts, in disaster, in chains, in torture, in death, we NEVER faultered in defending.[39]

This fiscal policy speech by an Illinois Whig assemblyman in 1839 sounds as if it might have come from the "Lost-Cause" religion of the postwar South.[40] And that is precisely the point: along with a market economy, North and

South shared a common Romantic culture, as they had shared an Enlighten-ment of culture one or two generations before. In case anyone wondered, John Brown's raid would soon attest that, deluded or not, heroic Christian martyrdom remained in the cultural repertoire. Though it may well repre-sent the writing of Seward or Hay, Lincoln himself would compliment work-ingmen in Manchester for their "sublime Christian Heroism" in supporting the Union war effort to the detriment of their livelihoods, and the redemp-tive power of vicarious suffering permeates the Gettysburg Address as well.[41]

While the bombast of his speech on the subtreasury was unusual for Lin-coln, throughout his life he would continue to express a willingness and even desire to fight and die in a just cause, a desire that in the end, of course, was gratified. As president-elect he said the Declaration of Independence "gave promise that in due time the weights should be lifted from the shoulders of all men, and that *all* should have an equal chance. . . . But if this country can-not be saved without giving up that principle—I was about to say I would rather be assassinated on this spot than to surrender it."[42] And again in June 1862 he expressed his grim determination to press forward in a just cause even on his own: "I expect to maintain this contest until successful, or till I die, or am conquered, or my term expires, or Congress or the country forsakes me; and I would publicly appeal to the country for this new force, were it not that I fear a general panic and stampede would follow—so hard is it to have a thing understood as it really is."[43] The slavery debate was replete with explicit religious language and feeling unlike anything in the debates surrounding the Constitution in 1787, and much of it acknowledged a responsibility to the Creator beyond the mere pursuit of happiness in the garden of creation.[44]

The phrase "without contemplating consequences" is particularly star-tling because it flirts explicitly with anticonsequentialist ethical theory, and such theories were typical of post-Kantian, Romantic thought. Yet "duties are ours, events are God's" was the dictum of a kind of antislavery activism that Lincoln wholeheartedly rejected.[45] As much as Jefferson or even Ben-tham, Lincoln contemplated consequences. Nevertheless, it was most un-Jeffersonian for Lincoln to accept the Civil War rather than to have compro-mised his principles by allowing slavery to expand into the territories. One could say that Lincoln feared compromise would destroy his Republican Party, but what made that party so important to Lincoln was the cause of condemning slavery to its ultimate extinction. For Lincoln, as for a signifi-cant portion of the northern population, the antislavery meaning of Amer-ica had become more important even than life itself.[46]

As Lincoln and political antislavery activists like Salmon P. Chase saw it, the principles of Jefferson's Declaration—that all men were created equal, that government rested on consent—were a transcendent ideal, an a priori moral principle, never attained but always striven after. This was a major reinterpretation of Jefferson. Jefferson would have liked to claim that his epistemology admitted of no a priori principles, moral or otherwise. To Jef-ferson, the equality of blacks appeared less and less "self-evident" as the data came in. Radically liberal, and therefore almost amoral, Jefferson was un-compromising only in his defense of individual freedom from governmental control.[47] The world was "a matter of calculation," the art of life "the art of avoiding pain." With these words he broke off a potentially disturbing love affair and returned to the serenity of his "intellectual pleasures"; similar sentiments surrounded his decision not to push for the end of slavery. "Justice is in one scale, and self-preservation in the other," he wrote, and in the end the Epicurean of Monticello preferred not to have his teacups rattled, for neither love nor justice. Lincoln, on the other hand, though he kept his longings for righteousness carefully reined in, continued to express them, and he continued to insist that they were the reason he stayed in politics.[48]

In the following fragment from the time of the debates, for instance, Lincoln apologized for his ambition.

> I have never professed an indifference to the honors of official station; and were I to do so now, I should only make myself ridiculous. Yet I have never failed—do not now fail—to remember that in the republican cause there is a higher aim than that of mere office. I have not allowed myself to forget that the abolition of the Slave-trade by Great Britain, was agitated a hundred years before it was a final success; that the measure had it's open fire-eating opponents it's stealthy "dont care" opponents; it's dollar and cent opponents; it's inferior race opponents; its negro equality opponents; and its religion and good order opponents; that all these opponents got offices, and their adversaries got none. But I have also remembered that though they blazed, like tallow-candles for a century, at last they flickered in the socket, died out, stank in the dark for a brief season and were remembered no more, even by the smell. School-boys know that Wilbe[r]force, and Granville Sharpe, helped that cause forward; but who can now name a single man who labored to retard it? Remembering these things I can not but regard it as possible that the higher object of this contest may not be completely attained within the term of my natural life.[49]

Much has been made of Lincoln's adroit political skills. If a man's lifework can be said to have a theme, however, Lincoln's was the effort to reconcile the demands of morality with the demands of self-interest or political calculus. Indeed, this tension provided a theme for the entire era Lincoln came to represent. It was, after all, the tension between utilitarianism and Romanticism. Lincoln devoted considerable energy in every phase of his career to schooling his audiences and colleagues in the art of maintaining that balance. Take the above passage: Lincoln never used this fragment publicly, perhaps fearing it would have linked him to more radical elements in the antislavery movement. William Wilberforce and Sharp were the heroes of the revival-based evangelical wing of the antislavery movement and the models for political antislavery activists who had come to oppose the fugitive slave law that Lincoln supported.[50] Support for the fugitive slave law made Lincoln seem less avidly antislavery, and the Republicans nominated Lincoln in

1860 in part because he *seemed* less radical than Seward and because he would therefore have greater appeal in the lower North.[51] (One should add that there might also have been other factors at play.)[52] To himself, however, he acknowledged these leaders of the antislavery movement, along with pragmatic statesmen like Clay, and he made them his model. He justified his ambition by giving it a "higher aim than that of mere office." At this point in his career, he longed to put himself on the side of history, which, since it was the nineteenth century, was the side of God.

One of the earliest remarks regarding religion that we have in Lincoln's own hand came from 1832, when Lincoln published his candidacy for the Illinois General Assembly in the *Sangamo Journal*. In his "Communication to the People of Sangamo County," otherwise devoted to issues surrounding improving navigation on the Sangamo River, Lincoln endorsed some form of public support of education.

> That every man may receive at least, a moderate education, and thereby be enabled to read the histories of his own and other countries, by which he may duly appreciate the value of our free institutions, appears to be an object of vital importance, even on this account alone, to say nothing of the advantages and satisfaction to be derived from all being able to read the scriptures and other works, both of a religious and moral nature, for themselves. For my part, I desire to see the time when education, and by its means, morality, sobriety, enterprise and industry, shall become much more general than at present, and should be gratified to have it in my power to contribute something to the advancement of any measure which might have a tendency to accelerate the happy period.[53]

Of interest here is the emphasis Lincoln placed on what is known in the twentieth century as the liberal arts—and nothing could have been less Jeffersonian. Of course Jefferson himself enjoyed an ample liberal education, but he did not wish it upon others. True to the Enlightenment, he prescribed a course of applied natural science, practical and useful, that avoided both the theology of the past and the "intuition" of the new Romantic sensibility.[54]

Lincoln's campaign document dealt primarily in very practical matters, but the aims of education for the young Lincoln were not of the vocational, Jeffersonian sort. The first aim was moral: to inculcate appreciation for free institutions by teaching history. Next Lincoln included the benefit of reading Scripture and other moral works. Only toward the end of the passage did he come to anything very practical. He obviously identified completely with the Whig Party, the forward-thinking party of "morality, sobriety, enterprise and industry." The "Communication" ended with an oft-quoted passage: "Every man is said to have his peculiar ambition. Whether it be true or not, I can say for one that I have no other so great as that of being truly esteemed of my fellow men, by rendering myself worthy of their esteem. How far I shall succeed in gratifying this ambition, is yet to be developed. . . ." Here Lincoln already hit on the formula with which he would reconcile his burning ambition with his reverence for American institutions. Whether completely genuine or not, he would adopt the pose of the humble petitioner striving to be of true service. Lincoln provided a thorough, even overwrought treatment of the moral issues involved in running for public office. His passionate involvement in the slavery question may have been aroused as late as 1854, but his concern with political morality and political theology began much earlier.

In their own way, the Democrats were as Romantic as the Republicans. The really important controversies of the period centered on the question of who, if anyone, was entitled to the mantle of righteousness, and Lincoln's chief difficulties with the way Young America viewed history were theological. He objected to what was then becoming the primary American version of the nation's place in world history, the dominant American self-understanding. He objected because it encouraged a "self-complaisant" and exaggerated self-estimate.[55] Since the Young Americans saw America as the telos of world history and narrowly equated American civilization with the will of God, they were therefore blind to the faults in American life, blind to its own transgressions, incapable of reform, and athwart the path of true progress. In the lecture on discoveries and inventions, Lincoln took time from his law practice and political campaigning to challenge this dominant version of history. This was no trivial undertaking, for behind Douglas and Young America stood a colossal figure, a man who formulated the entire historical theology that in some ways still dominates the American imagination.[56] According to one eyewitness, Lincoln decided to write the lecture after examining George Bancroft's *Literary and Historical Miscellanies* of 1855.[57] Directly and indirectly, Lincoln challenged George Bancroft.

GEORGE BANCROFT'S ROMANTIC HISTORICAL THEODICY

Perhaps a good date for the advent of the Romantic in America would be July 4, 1826.[58] On this day, exactly half a century after they both signed the Declaration that Jefferson had written for the Continental Congress and that Adams had defended before that now venerated assembly, both Adams and Jefferson died. The last words of Adams were reportedly, "Thomas Jefferson still survives," which, poignantly enough, was no longer true.[59] Symbolically, we might say that the Enlightenment, for which Jefferson in particular has come to stand, also died that day. As if to fill the void in American thought left by Jefferson's departure, George Bancroft that day gave his first major public address, a Fourth of July oration in Boston. Like his friend Edward Everett, most noted now for his warm-up speech at Gettysburg, Bancroft had studied in Germany, and unlike the older William Ellery Channing, whose exposure to German transcendental philosophy had come too late in life to have deep effects, Bancroft returned to America ready to apply these ideas to American life, thought, and history.[60]

In his address, Bancroft attempted to put the fiftieth anniversary of American independence in a meaningful historical context, and what is remarkable in retrospect is how explicitly theological his views were. He began, in most un-Jeffersonian fashion, by saying that "our act of celebration begins with God. To the eternal Providence, on which states depend, and by whose infinite mercy they are prospered, the nation brings its homage and the tribute of its gratitude."[61] In addition to becoming a prominent American historian, George Bancroft became a leading Democratic politician who Van Buren appointed collector of the port of Boston. Bancroft in turn handed out positions to Nathaniel Hawthorne and Orestes Brownson. Later he would serve under Polk as secretary of the navy, acting secretary of war, and minister to London. He was an advisor to Democratic presidents as well as to Stephen A. Douglas, and he eventually delivered both Lincoln's official eulogy and wrote Andrew Johnson's "First Annual Message to Congress," which earned him an ambassadorship to Prussia. He was also called upon to deliver Johnson's official eulogy. In these political capacities as well as in his role as historian, he was one of the chief intellectual spokesmen for a Democratic Party that insistently claimed title to the true Jeffersonian tradition. And Jefferson, of course, authored the "wall of separation" between church and state. It seems somewhat paradoxical, then, that while we might have expected him to begin a semicentennial of Jefferson's Declaration with popular sovereignty and "the people" he in fact began by invoking God's blessing.

Nor was this merely a required formality. Bancroft's invocation of God signaled a shift in the entire American epistemology. "In the name of humanity," Bancroft welcomed his listeners to the festival, which commemorated "an improvement in the social condition; in the name of religion [he welcomed them] to a profession of the principles of public justice, which emanate directly from God."[62] While Jefferson may have given passing mention to "Nature's God," for him nothing emanated from God except through the created order. Similarly, the most characteristic religion of the Enlightenment, Unitarianism, had no place for the divinity of Christ revealed through Scripture—or for a Holy Ghost of any kind. When they mentioned God at all, thinkers like Jefferson generally spoke in terms of the First Person of the Trinity, the creator of heaven and, more often still, of earth. Christ was a great moral teacher, perhaps, but hardly "the Savior," or the Son of God *natum ante omnia saecula*. As for the Holy Spirit, Jefferson's disparaging remarks about "enthusiasm" summed up his attitudes well.

More skeptical about human nature, the Federalists were nevertheless as eudaemonistic as Jefferson, that is, they too made human happiness the focus of their ethical theory. According to Sacvan Bercovitch, they "had set forth the most pragmatic, anti-enthusiast program on record for realizing the dreams of mankind."[63] The Enlightenment was itself a reaction to the religious wars of the seventeenth century, and if there was one element of Christianity that troubled contractarian liberals from Hobbes and Locke to Madison and Jefferson it was the kind of religious enthusiasm that might disturb the delicate status quo, either with an appeal through Scripture to the words of Christ or, worse still, a direct appeal to God in the third person.[64]

Like Thomas Carlyle, however, Bancroft explicitly rejected the materialism of the Enlightenment and its "afterbirth," positivism. German idealism attracted him chiefly because it helped him to undermine positivism, which he described as "A system which professes to re-construct society on the simple observation of the laws of the visible universe, and which is presented with arrogant pretension under the name of the 'Positive Philosophy,' scoffs at all questions of metaphysics and religious faith as insoluble and unworthy of human attention; and affects to raise the banner of an affirming belief in the very moment that it describes its main characteristic as a refusal to recognize the infinite." He concluded, "How those who own no source of knowledge but the senses can escape its humiliating yoke, I leave them to discover."[65]

There was a source of knowledge beyond the five senses, and it allowed for a more personal relationship with God than the observation of regularities in the natural or moral order; it made room, once more, for a poetic relationship with nature. Unlike the literalists of the Enlightenment, who at best found only bare shelves when they looked into the religious thought of the past, a poetically minded Romantic could find a rich storehouse. The book of theology was now reopened and out of it tumbled ideas about Providence and predestination, mystery and imagination, rapturous joy, wonder and enthusiasm, sin and redemption—in short, a whole menagerie of bêtes noires from Jefferson's worst nightmares.

Among the first American Romantics, Bancroft put the new epistemology to his own peculiar uses. Unlike the Enlightenment founders, who reserved a place in a democratic polity for a disinterested elite that arbitrated disputes arising from conflicting interests, Bancroft used the German philosophy to postulate a kind of General Will.[66] There was a faculty beyond the five senses that every human being shared, an intuition or "reason," higher than the "understanding," "which deduces inferences from the experience of the senses."[67] Bancroft's "reason" went beyond the faculties recognized in the empiricism of an Adams or a Jefferson and eliminated the need for elite leadership of the type the founders took for granted. This, for Bancroft, was the very meaning of democracy, and it is what attracted him to the party of Jackson: "Thus then the people governs, and solely; it does not divide its power with a hierarchy, a nobility, or a king. The popular voice is all powerful with us; this is our oracle; this, we acknowledge, is the voice of God."[68] Bancroft used the new German idealism to justify the claims of a more militant kind of democracy, one in which there was little place for positive government action in the economy (and no room at all if it resulted in elite institutions like the "monster bank," the Bank of the United States). These ideas, expressed in his massive histories, provided an intellectual foundation for young Romantic democrats like Stephen Douglas: "the people" were always right, and America, by a kind of historical definition, was always on the side of God.

Nourished from childhood on theological debate between his father and his father's friends, Bancroft knew well enough to anticipate a challenge on this point.[69] In spite of the agnosticism of the founders, Americans had conflated

their country with the Kingdom of God almost since the first discovery, tiptoe-
ing around the heresy in a variety of theologically intriguing ways.[70] But laying the heresy this bare still required a defense. Bancroft hastened to add that
some people (like the Whigs) might prefer the judgment of the enlightened
few, "but true political science [did] indeed venerate the masses." "It main-
tains, not as has been perversely asserted, that 'the people can make right,' but
that the people can DISCERN right. Individuals are but shadows, too often en-
grossed by the pursuit of shadows; the race is immortal: individuals are of limited sagacity; the common mind is infinite in its experience." Indeed, "individuals claim the divine sanction of truth for the deceitful conceptions of their
own fancies; the spirit of God breathes through the combined intelligence of
the people."[71] As a matter of practice it made little difference whether the people *made* right, or only *discerned* it; in either case, Bancroft had to accept the
voice of the electorate uncritically. Bancroft's reasoning here was entirely di-
vorced from practice, and in spite of his loudest protestations he was a pedant
and theory-monger of precisely the sort Jefferson had so detested.

More striking still, not only did he say outright that "democracy was practical Christianity," Bancroft anticipated a theological challenge on this very
point from his Whig friends, and he moved to head it off.[72] Again and again in
the antebellum period one sees this kind of self-conscious theological positioning in the public debate. To say that the people could *make* right would obviously usurp the divine prerogative, and Bancroft could not quite bring himself
to make public opinion his God. Nevertheless, that was the obvious tendency
of his thought, and at a time in American history when people knew their theology he was a remarkably thorough religious thinker who left little for the
reader to infer. Original sin, that relic of past barbarism, had been overcome;
"the race had been redeemed." With these optimistic words, the transcendence
of the divine and, with it, any prophetic or critical voice was all but drowned
out in a genial worship of the democratic order and of America itself.

This of course could lead to some absurdities, especially if "the people"
decided to abandon the Democratic Party. The election of the Whig Harrison
in 1840 called forth some elaborate apologetics. To Democrats, the election
of Jackson in 1828 had signified the final triumph of the people, and, again,
history knew only one direction. They were baffled, then, by the result of
1840, in which the people had chosen the "party of aristocracy" in a free
and fair election; and it is amusing in retrospect to observe their bewilder-
ment. The Democrats could never admit, as the Whigs charged, that Jackson's war against the national bank had something to do with the economic
calamity of 1837. For the Democrats, these were not matters of experimental
public policy but questions of political faith, and they clung tenaciously to
the belief that government intrusion in the natural economic order was not
only bad policy but immoral and un-American as well. America, remember,
meant a break with the past, and elite institutions, such as the Bank of the
United States, betrayed an old-fashioned mistrust of the people's ability to
know their own best interest and to order the economy for themselves.

The subtreasury plan of 1839 was the Democratic attempt to finesse their difficulty and stabilize the currency by depositing federal money, not in any bank, but with a government agency. Of course all the Democratic objections to the elite institution of a national bank applied even more strongly to a government agency, and Lincoln lunged after this exposed jugular in the same subtreasury speech in which he called Douglas "stupid" and in which he expressed a desire to fight on the side of God, alone if necessary.[73] Lincoln also pointed out that, as a practical matter, money deposited at the subtreasury would bear no interest and would remain, quite literally, useless. The subtreasury scheme failed to convince the voters, who turned Van Buren out of office in 1840. Since "the principles of public justice emanating directly from God" had failed to flow directly into the electorate, Democrats struggled. They needed to believe both that the national bank was an unnatural and undemocratic intrusion in the economy *and* that the people were always right. In a characteristically deft piece of theology, Van Buren amended the theory only slightly; the Whigs might have duped the people momentarily by nominating a military hero and by accusing Van Buren of being the aristocrat, but "the sober second thought of the people" would again discover the true principles of public economy.[74]

In a democracy it is probably never good politics to claim that the people are to blame for anything, or that they might have made a misstep, even inadvertently. And it would be easy to see in the phrase "the sober second thought of the people" a rather pathetic attempt at demagoguery. In fact, it became a heartfelt mantra for the Democrats, because it allowed them to escape having to choose between the two pillars of their creed: to continue believing both that there was no source for political truth other than the electoral process and that an unregulated economy was normative, natural, and godly. As one of his biographers wrote, Bancroft "rationalized Harrison's triumph into a component of the divine plan, designed to foster vigilance and exertion. One setback did not curtail the reign of the general laws that swayed the moral world."[75] After the election of Polk four years later, Democrats emerged with their faith both in Jacksonian economics and in undiluted popular government fully restored.

Already in 1826, Bancroft revealed many of the intellectual and religious tendencies reflected in the ideas of Stephen Douglas and Young America. "Our moral condition," according to Bancroft, was "indeed superior to that of the old world in the present, or in any former age."[76] America stood "in the eye of Heaven and the world in all the comeliness and strength of youth, yet swayed by a spirit of mature wisdom, exemplifying in her public capacity the virtues and generous affections of human nature, a light to the world, an example to those who would be free, already the benefactress of humanity, the tutelary angel of liberty."[77] Like Young America in the 1850s, Bancroft in 1826 saw America, not just as a "redeemer nation," but also as Christ himself: "As on the morning of the nativity the astonished wizards hastened with sweet odors on the Eastern road, our government had hardly come into being and the star of liberty shed over us its benignant light, before the nations began to follow its guidance and do homage to its beauty."[78]

Bancroft might argue before the inquisitor that the word "as" made the whole figure a simile and thereby save himself from a charge of blasphemy or idolatry, but such language showed the tendency of his entire historical theology, which was not an idiosyncratic or minority view. It was a view shared by an entire political party, articulated and defended by one of America's most prominent public intellectuals, and one that remains, implicitly, an important part of the American self-understanding. America was the light unto the nations, the end and purpose of all history. Nor was the overt theology in Bancroft merely the careless use of religious rhetoric. National freedom and independence "were not the offspring of deliberate forethought; they were not planted or watered by the hand of man; they grew like the lilies, which neither toil nor spin."[79]

Even while he defended a view far more optimistic about the possibility for human goodness and perfection than such orthodox professions at first glance might lead one to suspect, Bancroft took great pains to articulate and to claim it as his own, an orthodox Augustinian position. Because Lincoln addressed precisely these same themes (and in an arguably more genuinely Augustinian way) Bancroft's discussion of perfectability ought to be of added interest to us.

> Yet while the common mind of New England was inspired by the great thought of the sole sovereignty of God, it did not lose personality and human freedom in pantheistic fatalism. Like Augustin, who made war both on Manicheans and Pelagians, like the Stoics, whose morals it most nearly adopted, it asserted by just dialectics, or, as some would say, by a sublime inconsistency, the power of the individual will. In every action it beheld the union of motive and volition. The action, it saw, was according to the strongest motive, and it knew that what proves the strongest motive depends on the character of the will. Hence the education of that faculty was, of all concerns, the most momentous. . . . The Calvinist of new England, who longed to be "morally good and excellent," had no other object of moral effort than to make "the will truly lovely and right."
>
> Action, therefore, as flowing from an energetic, right, and lovely will, was the ideal of New England. It rejected the asceticism of entire spiritualists, and fostered the whole man, seeking to perfect his intelligence and improve his outward condition. It did not extirpate, but only subjected the inferior principles. It placed no merit in vows of poverty or celibacy, and spurned the thought of non-resistance. In a good cause its people were ready to take up arms and fight, cheered by the conviction that God was working in them both to will and to do.[80]

Bancroft fully identified with his Puritan forebears, and he used them here to define an orthodox position regarding the freedom of the will and the ultimate sovereignty of God; and this was perhaps as good an explanation of the orthodox Protestant position as any. (Bancroft's quotation marks refer to his favorite theologian, Jonathan Edwards.) In the face of God's sovereignty, Lincoln's "Malice toward none and Charity for all" would constitute essentially the same theological move toward a "truly lovely and right" will. And, if there was any immediate contemporary relevance in the passage, it might be found in the references to "pantheistic fatalism" and "non-resistance." On the grounds of orthodoxy, Bancroft challenged any transcendentalist inclined toward pacifism.

But Bancroft could be as slippery theologically as he was politically. He praised William Ellery Channing, for instance, because Channing "knew that man was made in the image of God; that the gift of reason opened to him the path to the knowledge of creation, and to mastery over its powers. Having the highest reverence for genius, Channing yet acknowledged the image of the divine in every human being."[81] The juxtaposition of Channing's "mastery over the powers of creation" with Edwards's absolute sovereignty of God is troubling. But the contradiction resolves itself in part, at least, with the observation that Bancroft constantly apologized for Jacksonian democracy. He therefore sought to minimize any possible inconsistencies between modern American life, as it was emerging at the time, and the beliefs of the great ancestors, whether that meant the founders of 1776 and 1787 or the Puritans of the Massachusetts orthodoxy. American history could know no real conflict; all had to be of one piece. Whereas in the eighteenth century apologetic descendants of the Puritans recast their ancestors as lovers of liberty, Bancroft made democracy the essence both of the Puritan idea and of William Ellery Channing's.[82] Thus Bancroft's professions of orthodoxy need to be taken with a grain of salt. In his actions, as well as in many of his words, he was as entirely optimistic about the human condition as any transcendentalist, and he was probably farther than most of them from any truly prophetic stance. Bancroft stood at the beginning of a long line of historians who saw it as their chief duty to apologize for American life.[83]

The son of a Unitarian minister, Bancroft attempted to reclaim Trinitarian dialectics. "From the time that this truth of the triune God was clearly announced, he was no longer dimly conceived as a remote and shadowy causality, but appeared as all that is good and beautiful and true; as goodness itself, incarnate and interceding, redeeming and inspiring; the union of liberty, love, and light; the infinite cause, the infinite mediator, the infinite in and with the universe, as the paraclete and comforter. The doctrine once communicated to man, was not to be eradicated. It spread as widely, as swiftly, and as silently as light, and the idea of God with us dwelt and dwells in every system of thought that can pretend to vitality; in every oppressed people, whose struggles to be free have the promise of success; in every soul that sighs for redemption."[84] To Adams and Jefferson, the Trinity was an absurdity on its face. From the perspective of Jefferson's natural theology, Trinitarian doctrine only gave credence to the arguments of atheists, while Adams dismissed the Trinity because human understanding was a revelation from its maker, "nature and nature's God"; and all know that "one is not three; nor can three be one."[85] But if the new German philosophy caught on in large measure because it facilitated the reappropriation of religious modes of thought and feeling, this included a return to the neglected Second and Third Persons of the Trinity. Perhaps more important is the question of whether, by making the voice of the people the voice of God, Bancroft had not himself compromised the divinity of Christ and made Christianity the ally of a new kind of empire. But at least he knew what was at stake, and in terms of Protestant theology at least he knew what he was about. In an overtly theological and even pedantically orthodox way, Bancroft built on an already long line of New England thinkers who sought to give America a place in sacred history or who tried to make American history sacred.[86]

In fact, the chief attraction for Bancroft, both in his reading of Jonathan Edwards and in his writing of history, was the endeavor to find a place for America in sacred history. As the first American historian trained in the German critical method, Bancroft took great pride in the scientific pretensions of his work, and he knew the sources he had painstakingly gathered very well. But for Bancroft, what lent history coherence was the attempt to discover "the principles that govern human affairs" and thereby to demonstrate "the superintending providence of God." The German word *Weltgeschichte* generally refers less to the history of the world per se as to the history of salvation, and Bancroft's translation of the German as "universal history" was similar.[87] Bancroft quoted Edwards, "Universal history does but seek to relate 'the sum of all God's works of providence,'" concluding, "Nothing appears more self-determined than the volitions of each individual; and nothing is more certain than that the providence of God will overrule them for good. The finite will of man, free in its individuality, is, in the aggregate, subordinate to general laws."[88]

Bancroft ran fairly roughshod over Edwards here, who would not have agreed with the majoritarian and Jacksonian implications that Bancroft drew for the general popular will. God's general laws prevailed, to be sure, but Edwards would never have implied that "in the aggregate" sin had been overcome. Bancroft's treatment of Edwards here coincided with his entire historical interpretation of the Reformation and of Puritanism as—at heart—democratic movements. Nevertheless, like some of his German colleagues, Bancroft sought to reclaim a pre-Enlightenment vision of history, a vision not merely of "one damn thing after another" but one in which events had some discernible cosmic meaning. Like Edwards, Bancroft found that meaning in "the gradual regeneration of humanity." For Bancroft, the U.S. Constitution accomplished the "grand event of the thousand years of modern history."[89] Like Edwards, Bancroft gave America the lead part in the grand drama of sacred history.[90]

In his effort to give America a place in sacred history, Bancroft did not simply equate America with the Israel of old; in fact he seldom compared his nation with that undeserving, backsliding rabble. Unlike Israel, the importance of America in history made sense. God's choice was comprehensible in human terms, and the task of history was to show how. History for Bancroft was thus a kind of theodicy.[91] Bancroft's propensity to put the best possible face on matters eventually allowed him to fold even the Civil War into his seamless Democratic worldview. This remarkable trait carried over also into his personal experience. Unlike Melville and Whitman, who were profoundly impacted and even shattered by the war, Bancroft would ride it out seemingly untouched. When the trauma began to recede, he remained blithely poised to interpret the meaning of the events and to reassert, remarkably enough, the consensus vision of America as a land without real conflict.

Throughout the antebellum period and on all sides of the cultural debate, America was spoken of in reference to "Christian Civilization," and Bancroft was not alone when he synthesized the relatively secular Enlightenment American identity he inherited with a new Romantic Christian image. Nearly everyone agreed that true Christianity and true democracy were identical, though there were ways other than Bancroft's to affect this synthesis. Lincoln mentioned the Reformation in his lecture on discoveries and inventions as well, but he immediately followed that remark with a mention of the "invention of Negroes." True to his more orthodox upbringing, Lincoln denied any equation of American life with the church triumphant. For Bancroft, Augustine's great divide between the City of Man and the City of God, between the church militant and the church triumphant, had been overcome. That was the meaning of American democracy: America was the church triumphant.

Technically speaking, then, Bancroft was a postmillennialist. (On a less Romantic epistemological basis, many if not most evangelicals of the period likewise articulated postmillennial positions.) The millennium had arrived; and now that original sin had been overcome mankind could achieve perfection in this world. "Submission," wrote Bancroft, "is due to the popular will, in the confidence that the people, when in error, will amend their doings; that in a popular government injustice is neither to be established by force, nor to be resisted by force; in a word, that the Union, which was constituted by consent, must be preserved by love."[92] This was hopelessly naive of course. There were some people, Whigs like Lincoln for example, who, even though they believed in progress of a sort, did not share this rosy, chiliastic view of human nature and society. One can imagine, for instance, the grimace on the face of a clear-sighted slaveholder like John Calhoun at the notion that society did not rely on force but strictly on the law of love. In the North, skeptical Whig intellectuals remembered the long march Jackson had inflicted on the Cherokee and the daily use of force necessary to preserve the slave system, which led to a more realistic appraisal of their own political reality. There were also those who preserved the pessimism of old-fashioned premillennial Calvinism. These latter two streams would meet in Abraham Lincoln. If the law of love preserved the Union, then it was tough love indeed—tough enough at least to make Georgia howl. After the Civil War, Bancroft's optimistic brand of liberalism would become the whipping boy for the cynical generation that had served and survived. "What like a bullet can undeceive?"

Melville would ask, referring in no small measure to himself.[93] Whereas Bancroft was sure the bayonets of a standing army were no longer necessary, Oliver Wendell Holmes, Jr., knew well that in any society conscripts were marched to the front, "bayonets to the back if necessary."[94] Caught without intellectual immunities against the transcendental giddiness of the 1840s, however, Bancroft not only embraced that optimism, he lent it intellectual respectability with his intricate historical and theological apologetics.

Naturally, this put America in the van of world (read always, of course, European) history, and Young America would later seize upon this point. It had become a majority view that all of history had been preparation for the advent of America. While a genteel Whig like Daniel Webster could proclaim that the American Revolution brought with it a millennial promise, this powerful historical interpretation informed virtually every aspect of Democratic politics, beginning with Jackson and increasingly thereafter.[95] "If there be patriotism," said General Jackson himself, "in the effort to increase the wealth and happiness of all classes in our society—to diffuse the blessings of equal laws, and a just government—if there be love in the spirit which finds in this free land of ours the means to spread the light of the Gospel, and to teach fallen man throughout the world how he may recover his right to civil and religious liberty—it seems to me that all this patriotism—all this philanthropy—all this religion—appeals to us in favor of the addition of Texas to our Union."[96] The annexation of Texas and the Mexican War were in Bancroft's future, but Jackson's words here make clear the relationship between Old Hickory, Young America, and Bancroft's pedantic Fourth of July oration of 1826. In the essentials and, to a remarkable extent, in the details, all three shared the same theological understanding of America's place in history.

CONSCIENCE MONEY AND THE PROPHETIC VOICE

As perhaps the chief intellectual spokesman for young and radical northern Democrats after the death of William Leggett, Bancroft perceived no difference between the policies of Jefferson and Jackson. It was this static theory of a timeless American consensus that lay behind the Janus-faced character of the Jacksonian persuasion.[97] In an 1844 campaign speech Bancroft expressed the radical side of this Democratic persuasion, saying, "The present contest involves the highest considerations—the purity of the Constitution, civil liberty, free suffrage, justice to adopted citizens, the boundary of an extent of our country." Indeed, "It involves in an especial manner, whether American industry shall be allowed to prosper under the action of general laws, or whether it shall be kept in conflict with those laws and subjected to all the hazards and uncertainties of an artificial system. (Renewed cheering.) The great restrictive system which overhung the world for centuries, was shaken by American independence."[98]

In the battle against the protective tariff and against the bank, Bancroft saw a continuation and a fulfillment of the antimercantilist American Revolution.

Democrats saw the conflict as one between a natural system of politics and economy and the relics of an oppressive past. Any interpretation of the Democratic Party as anticapitalist in this period, though, must be rethought. For the Democrats, government involvement in the economy was "artificial," opposed to the natural operation of economic laws. At the same time that Bancroft made this radically liberal, potentially laissez-faire or libertarian argument however, he maintained that "the idea of a discriminating revenue tariff, and no more, as sufficient for American labor, [came] sanctioned by all the weight of the fathers of the revolution—by the fears of England; by the early judgment of America."[99] Thus the Democrats could pose simultaneously as radical Jeffersonian liberals and as the defenders of a historical orthodoxy that belied Jefferson's assertion that the earth belongs to the living.[100]

The Democrats certainly considered themselves radical, and on several issues they were. Bancroft pushed for "the opportunity for instruction and intellectual culture," which was a traditional Whig theme; and, in flagrant contradiction to his libertarian professions, he and the Democrats supported a ten-hour rule to limit the workday. Bancroft's unflagging public support for Polk from the convention on earned him an appointment as secretary of the navy in spite of his known antislavery leanings.[101] As navy secretary, he not only presented Congress with the new Naval Academy in Annapolis as a fait accompli but, in a move that symbolized Democratic solidarity with the common working man and resonated with the work of literary Young Americans like Herman Melville and Richard Henry Dana, he limited the practice of flogging in the navy.[102] Democrats could take the lead on reform measures that demanded positive government action if they could conceive of the problem either as a relic of past barbarism or as a foreign, usually British, intrusion in the American natural order. Their libertarianism thus remained subordinate to their historical vision.

Beyond the rhetorical bows to "the fathers," however, this Democratic persuasion was ultimately conservative and demagogical, because it rested on a scheme of sacred history designed to flatter the electorate at every turn. The habitual view of the Democrats as the progressives and the Whigs as the procapitalist conservatives is misleading. Unlike Leggett, Bancroft lacked the courage of his convictions in the antislavery matter, which was true of most opponents of slavery who survived within the party. Bancroft's rise in Democratic politics was contingent on his ability to downplay the antislavery implications of his thought, and he did this in classic Jeffersonian and Democratic fashion: he blamed slavery on the British.[103] And Bancroft's conservatism went beyond merely prevaricating on the slavery question. He urged the "reannexation of Texas," a Democratic position that Lincoln still sneered at in the Second Lecture on Discoveries and Inventions. By this convenient constitutional theory, the territory west of the Sabine originally included in Jefferson's Louisiana Purchase but thereafter ceded to Spain in the treaty of 1819 remained American territory, because, as General Jackson wrote in a letter in 1844, a question arose "whether this government can dismember its territory, and disfranchise its citizens without their consent."[104] Consent in fact had very little to do with it, and the "re-annexation" theory was designed to give America a clear moral field to attack Mexico. "The people" remained free of sin, and Bancroft was not shy about inciting the "young democracy of New York" to cast stones: "for the vindication of our territory in its full extent, the merchants, and manufacturers, and agriculturists are equally interested. The harbors of Oregon are for American ships; it's markets for American labor; its soil for the American ploughs; its wide domain for American institutions and American independence. (Terrific cheering, and shouts of 'Oregon is ours, and must be ours,'—'Yes, and Texas too,' and so on.)"[105]

Bancroft's support for annexation of Texas, and with it a probable war with Mexico, came at an important juncture in Democratic politics and in Bancroft's political career. Van Buren resisted immediate annexation of Texas, but this stand was rapidly becoming unpopular with the young Democracy. In addition, the old Democratic Party slogans had begun to wear thin; Democrats themselves had begun to push for government development projects like railroad land grants. Bancroft's Massachusetts Democrats in particular were in trouble, and the loss of the White House in 1844 might have been disastrous for a minority state party dependent on federal patronage. At the Democratic Convention in 1844, Bancroft abandoned his longstanding commitment to Van Buren and lent crucial support to the candidacy of James K. Polk. Bancroft now sided unequivocally with Young America. As Lilian Handlin noted, "territorial expansion would replace the anachronistic problems of aristocracy, monopoly, and corporations in the party's vocabulary. Bancroft had been willing to abandon those terms for some time, and had criticized the 'fanatical exaggeration of abstract principles' that fostered 'collisions with established interests.' Never at ease with his own early class-warfare visions, Bancroft had long hedged his pronouncements and sounded more like an enlightened Whig than a radical Democrat."[106] Of course, for Bancroft, the people in the aggregate remained the nearest approximation to the voice of God on earth. Thus what resulted was a corporate kind of Democracy unlike the individualism one associates with Thoreau or Emerson, to say nothing of Jefferson. This big, bellicose, corporate Democracy had immediate designs on Mexico.

Bancroft lobbied hard to parlay his early support of Polk into an attractive appointment. Polk eventually rewarded him by making him secretary of the navy. Bancroft was made acting secretary of war just in time for the war with Mexico, and he was the man who sent Zachary Taylor to the Rio Grande and John Fremont on a "scouting" expedition to California. Bancroft issued instructions for a fleet to proceed to California in the event of war. "The policy was President Polk's," noted one historian, "for he wished to obtain California by negotiation or by force; and inside the cabinet, Bancroft opposed Polk's desire to declare war before the skirmish at the Rio Grande offered a handy pretext. Still when the time came, Bancroft helped Polk draft his message to Congress."[107] Thus the first time Abraham Lincoln sparred with

George Bancroft was in his reply to Polk's War Message already discussed. In that reply, Lincoln deprecated the intellect of the War Message's author for his bad logic, and, more important, he decried the depravity of the crimes Bancroft meant to conceal with his professions of American innocence.

Bancroft's assertion of American innocence in the Mexican War parallels Stephen Douglas's defensiveness on precisely this point discussed in chapter 1. Like Douglas, Bancroft was cautiously in favor of absorbing as much of Mexico as possible. He was cavalier about this "little war," and he joked about a "second conquest of Mexico with his friend and fellow historian, William Prescott, author of *The Conquest of Mexico*." He believed that Mexico would be regenerated and that the war proved the vigor of American civilization to the rest of the world.[108] All of this was standard Young America fare, and like Young America Bancroft recognized the long-standing tradition that America acquired her territory by purchase rather than conquest. With his keen sense for theological apologetics and a life's work dedicated to the idea that America was one nation not mired in sin, Bancroft grasped the significance of exchanging money immediately. Even though Mexico lay prostrate at the conquering army's feet, even though the treaty had been negotiated under dubious circumstances, and even though the purchase terms conformed to U.S. demands made *before* the conquest of Mexico, terms which now appeared overgenerous to more rabid All-Mexico men, he heartily approved the "purchase" of California that concluded the war.

The historian Frederick Merk chastised the leaders of the movement to annex all of Mexico, noting that Young Americans like Stephen Douglas were something less than "intellectual giants" and exonerating the Whigs of complicity in the All-Mexico movement. While critical of the All-Mexico movement and its Young America leadership, however, Merk nevertheless accepted Bancroft's position as "a correct view of the payment to Mexico," because it preserved the idea that no American territory had been acquired by conquest. For Merk, "This tenacity on the part of Americans in adhering to an old ideal [was] evidence of the failure of expansionists to convert much of the American public to the concept of conquest and absorption of All Mexico." But the Whigs saw through Bancroft's deceptive theologizing and evasive claims of innocence, even if Bancroft and Young America did not. The Whigs could admit that California had been acquired by conquest because they had maintained the ability to be critical of their country when necessary. Though Democrats called it a libel on the president, the Whigs called the payment for California exactly what it was, "'conscience money'—atonement for a wrong done Mexico."[109]

Lincoln remained relatively indifferent to territorial expansion, a point probably underappreciated in the popular view.[110] As a loyal Whig, this was in part a matter of party expediency and in part a matter of principle.[111] While "Lincoln's ideas about expansion were not trammeled by any Federalist or Eastern residue of fear of expansion *per se*," as a Whig he pushed for a greater cultivation, moral and physical, of the territory already under the

American flag, and he opposed or ignored the possible extension of American sovereignty depending on its relationship to slavery.[112] Thus, in the 1830s, he "ignored Texas, Alamo and all, except for labeling it, once, a foreign land 'where a villain may hope to find refuge from justice.' In the following decade, while expansionism mounted to a frenzy in Illinois, he explained that he was 'never much interested' in the Texas question."[113] Since slavery was already in Texas, annexation would have little effect. Nevertheless, in 1844 he opposed annexation as inexpedient. "In 1846 he refused to support a forceful stand on Oregon. In 1848 he took an advanced position against the Mexican War and, realizing that some land acquisition was unavoidable, he labored to minimize it; he then tied expansion to the aggravation of the slavery dispute. When Democrats accused him of wanting to return to Mexico the bounty of the Treaty of Guadalupe Hidalgo, he made no denials. In 1858, when pressed by Douglas, Lincoln declared he was not against 'honest acquisition of territory' in principle. This was as close as he ever came to appearing to endorse in plain words expansion."[114]

In 1859, Lincoln attacked the notion of manifest destiny and ridiculed Jackson's expansionist views.[115] For Young America, the mere existence of democratic American institutions entailed such a degree of moral superiority and perfection that expansion of American territory became a positive duty. Instead of building empires, President Lincoln was, to one congressman, "a hindrance and a calamity" to those hopes. According to one historian, Lincoln lacked "any belief in the superiority of northern civilization, or its right to rule this continent."[116] This probably goes too far. Lincoln does seem to have had a sense of American superiority not only regarding political institutions of republican government but regarding learning and invention as well. Nevertheless Lincoln's nationalism was qualified by a critical stance toward America, as revealed in his opposition to a war of aggression and his hostility to the institution of slavery.

This points to a profound and potentially troubling tension in the writings of Abraham Lincoln. Lincoln belonged to the party that insisted that there was a higher law than the national will. He held the nation to transcendent standards that could not be equated with the rule of institutions as earthly as the electoral college. America had no God-given right to conquer the continent. On the other hand, Lincoln invested the Union (and later the "Nation") with, at the very least, quasi-religious significance. In his own day, his patriotism was questioned because of his opposition to territorial expansion, but he would also be accused of reverencing the Union with "religious mysticism." Generally only the latter impression has been carried down to our own time. Lincoln is seen negatively as a Bismarck or Lenin for his commitment to unifying the country, allegedly at all costs, or more positively as the greatest exemplar of the political type who "acted to enhance and extend, not subvert, the social and political authority of postmillennialist Protestants."[117] These impressions were not without justification. Lincoln's use of biblical language came near on more than one occasion to connecting God's purposes with the purposes of America as interpreted by the Republican Party. But Lincoln also attempted to head off precisely that interpretation. In the First Lecture on Discoveries and Inventions, Lincoln challenged a pattern of thought that in different forms prevailed both in evangelical circles and in the Democratic Party. He attempted to articulate a centrist (and ironic) vision of America's place in history, one that admitted the unique role America had as the only large and successful democratic republic in the world at the time and yet sought to curtail the hubris that both Young America and some post-millennialist Protestants in the Republican Party coalition exhibited.

Reading Lincoln's speeches without some awareness of Bancroft, Douglas, and Young America is analogous to listening in on only one side of a telephone conversation. Given the insights into Lincoln's literary method and the theories of George Bancroft as background, his lecture on discoveries and inventions should not seem so odd after all. His theme was his generation's place in history, and with it he sought, in part, to pursue politics by literary means. In his 1892 reminiscences, *Life on the Circuit with Lincoln,* Henry Clay Whitney claimed that Lincoln determined to write his lecture on progress as a response to Bancroft's *Literary and Historical Miscellanies* of 1855.[118] It does not appear that Lincoln took up Bancroft's work as a direct object of parody the way he took up the speeches of Stephen Douglas and James Polk. Bancroft's oration shared little with Lincoln's lecture beyond the attempt to put the accomplishments of America into some larger historical framework. Nevertheless, placing Bancroft's work side by side with Lincoln's lectures clarifies some of Lincoln's remarks and hints at the differences between Whig and Democratic worldviews, differences that expose the significance of Lincoln's religious vocabulary.

At first glance, Lincoln and Bancroft seemed very close in their views of history and human progress. Lincoln too believed in progress, and he too sought to give old fogies like Adam and Abraham their due. More than this, both thinkers saw history providentially. Behind the chaotic-seeming events of history there was the will of God, and Bancroft—to say nothing of Georg Friedrich Hegel—might have endorsed Lincoln's teleological interpretation that "to immancipate the mind from this false and under estimate of itself, is the great task which printing came into the world to perform."[119] But that was an unusual overreaching for Lincoln and was probably no more than a figure of speech. For Lincoln the great task remained always before us—hence, perhaps, his use of the present tense, *"is* the great task," for an invention more than four hundred years old. At this time Lincoln was busy making the case that in fact there had been a great "degeneracy" in the moral sense of the American people regarding slavery.[120] Supported by Bancroft, Douglas openly espoused the belief that freedom might include the freedom to hold slaves. Since Lincoln interpreted the Constitution and the Declaration of Independence as antislavery documents, he saw Bancroft and Douglas to be falling away from those statements of high moral principle. And, again, Lincoln's sneering aside about the "present mode of using Negroes" was calculated to cast doubt on the Bancroftian belief in the inevitability of moral progress.

Thus the chief disagreement between Lincoln and Bancroft about the nature of progress might be said to have been on the issue of contingency versus determinacy. Bancroft's entire narrative was teleological: progress was inevitable and irresistible; every change was always for the better; accident was an illusion of an incomplete understanding; every historical event had a purpose that could be discerned. From this, he confidently predicted the course of history and expounded upon the purposes of Providence. For Lincoln, on the other hand, the toy that exploited steam power had been in existence ages before it chanced to occur to someone that the principle upon which it operated might be generalized and used in more practical applications. Lincoln's radical Calvinist background led him to downplay the capacity of human beings to discern the will of the God of history. Thus from a human perspective Lincoln's world was a morally messier place than Bancroft's.

This profound difference in the way Lincoln and Bancroft looked at history had immediate moral and political implications. In "The Progress of Mankind" Bancroft insisted on the inevitability of progress in large measure because he feared that the self-conscious reform zeal of the abolitionists would lead to civil war. "The good time is coming," he wrote, "when humanity will recognize all members of its family as alike entitled to its care. . . . But this result must flow from internal activity, developed by universal culture; it cannot be created by the force of exterior philanthropy; and still less by the reckless violence of men whose desperate audacity would employ terror as a means to ride on the whirlwind of civil war." If progress were irresistible, it could be neither checked nor accelerated; again, it would not be overstating the case to say that Bancroft's entire historical project was intended to preach complacency. "Since the progress of the race appears to be the great purpose of Providence, it becomes us all to venerate the future. We must be ready to sacrifice ourselves for our successors, as they in their turn must live for their posterity."[121] But this line about sacrifice for posterity was at best empty cant, for in fact Bancroft was willing to sacrifice little, if anything, on the altar of freedom. Worse still, the sacrifice he had in mind here seems to have been the patient acceptance of gross inequity—cold comfort indeed. The belief in progress was Bancroft's chief theodicy, and he used it here to preach a rather easy contentment. Though Bancroft seemed to be preaching a reliance on God, on another level he was saying that mankind had already been redeemed and that the sins of the world would take care of themselves. Since the dictates of Providence could be deduced from the history of an evolving public opinion, reliance on God was little more than a formality. God spoke through public opinion, and in public opinion Bancroft put his trust.[122] Working through the instrument of a slowly ripening public voice, God would right the wrongs of the world in His own good time.

Bancroft and Lincoln both saw a "last hope" in American democracy, but for Lincoln there was a real possibility that we might meanly lose it.[125] Paradoxically, Lincoln's exhortations to overt moral action proceeded from a more pessimistic sense of human nature than Bancroft's. In keeping with both Whig theory and his Calvinist heritage, Lincoln emphasized the need for self-consciously moral self-government as well as the self-conscious education of public opinion by "statesmen" (or, in our terms, "opinion shapers"). Lincoln rejected both the belief in the inevitability of moral progress and the idea that original sin had somehow been overcome.[124] Already in 1842 Lincoln had derided precisely the kind of intergenerational responsibility to which Bancroft pretended.

> Few can be induced to labor exclusively for posterity; and none will do it enthusiastically. Posterity has done nothing for us; and theorize on it as we may, practically we shall do very little for it, unless we are made to think, we are, at the same time, doing something for ourselves. What an ignorance of human nature does it exhibit, to ask or expect a whole community to rise up and labor for the *temporal* happiness of *others* after *themselves* shall be consigned to the dust, a majority of which community take no pains whatever to secure their own eternal welfare, at a no greater distant day? Great distance, in either time or space, has wonderful power to lull and render quiescent the human mind. Pleasures to be enjoyed, or pains to be endured, *after* we shall be dead and gone, are but little regarded, even in our *own* cases, and much less in the cases of others.[125]

Unlike Bancroft, Lincoln did not assume that American democracy necessarily brought with it the spiritual regeneration of humanity. Again, there were elements of Bancroft's vision in Lincoln. Lincoln did not question progress in the sense that man's mastery of nature was on the increase or even that human freedom was now more completely realized than ever before. But he did deny that progress was inevitable, that America was inevitably progressive, and, most important, that human depravity was a thing of the past. He also questioned the value of any material advancement that neglected or evaded the moral and spiritual problems that had always confronted humanity and that therefore still confronted America. Thus, even while he took pride in America's legitimate achievements, Lincoln attempted to temper the more outrageous theological claims made for American democracy. If democracy equaled "practical Christianity" in any way, it was not the simple equation that Bancroft suggested. America was not quite the Kingdom of God on Earth.

PART TWO

The Romantic Whig Response

Chapter Three

ROMANTIC PROTESTANTISM
AND WHIG RHETORIC

• A political party may originate as collections of interest groups pushing for specific pieces of legislation, as did the American Whigs. In the initial stages, the Whigs were a somewhat diverse group, perhaps best thought of negatively as the opposition to Jackson and the Democrats rather than positively as the adherents of a single, coherent set of ideas or ideology.[1] But a list of specific proposals is not enough to get elected. If only to articulate arguments for or against specific proposals, politicians necessarily grope for themes that they hope will strike a chord with the electorate and lend coherence to their programs. If not always a complete philosophy of government, some recognizable cultural vision, some overarching set of metaphors, themes, and images seems necessary for long-term political success.

The American Whigs were no exception to this rule, but the intellectual and religious turn of the Whig mind made them a puzzle to twentieth-century historians. From the point of view of the popular imagination, they have been banished to the dark realm of the completely forgotten. Where once schoolboys memorized his speeches, Daniel Webster is now remembered, generally speaking, only in connection with the nationalism of his "Reply to Hayne." The significance of Henry Clay's American System, a program for positive moral government in the life both of the nation and of the states, is now only vaguely understood. Whether or not they did justice to any lingering republicanism in Jacksonian rhetoric, Whigs saw the explicitly liberal "Loco-Focos" as their chief ideological adversaries. Whig "modernizing" or procapitalist impulses are generally well delineated, but the fact that they developed in opposition to an explicitly liberal Jacksonian ideology goes unnoticed. Ironically enough, the party most associated with "the market revolution" in America was strangely at odds with the liberal political values and utilitarianism one usually associates with the industrial transformation of the nineteenth century.

A full appreciation of Lincoln's originality in his war speeches cannot come without understanding the degree to which he shared his general outlook with an entire political tradition. And yet most nonhistorians remain completely unaware of Lincoln's first political party, a party he believed in as passionately as he later did the Republicans. While students of Lincoln are generally aware of the positive government ideals of his Whig early manhood, most do not grasp the thoroughgoing rejection of utilitarianism that his moral vision entailed. This is unfortunate. The obscurity of the Whigs has meant, for instance, that opposition to Indian removal has vanished from American memory, as has opposition to manifest destiny, utilitarianism, and the Mexican War. Finally, neglecting the Whigs has meant the disappearance of the tradition of positive moral government in America. In the twentieth century, this philosophy of government appeared to be an orphan child abandoned on the American doorstep, perhaps helpful for sweeping any nasty byproducts from the stables of mass capitalism, but deeply suspect, philosophically speaking, on the grounds of Jeffersonian individualism. In fact, however, positive moral government was not an intruder upon the life of the American family. Rather, the United States, like other Western nations, has a long history of positive moral government, and the Whig Party was perhaps the clearest expression of that tradition.

According to the traditional interpretation, "the most salient characteristic of American Whig political thought was that it remained within the tradition of the 'commonwealthmen,' that remarkable group of English and Scottish writers whose importance to eighteenth-century American political culture has been emphasized by recent historians. It was their compound of common law, Protestant piety, moral philosophy, and classical learning that constituted the American Whigs' political frame of reference."[2] This interpretation stressed classical republican elements in Whig thought such as mixed constitutions, the separation of powers, the secret ballot, and acceptance of the leadership of propertied gentry as well as the Florentine Renaissance inheritance and Machiavelli.

The emphasis on classical republican ideas has been somewhat unfortunate, however, and the four elements of Whig belief—common law, Protestant piety, Scottish moral philosophy, and classical republican thought—are best kept distinct. In formulating their response to the tightly reasoned and comparatively more homogeneous Democratic persuasion, Whigs were drawn to each of the four traditions, and different traditions became central for different thinkers. In addition, younger Whigs were often heavily influenced by the new Romantic sensibility. Especially for northern Whigs, so much of whose thinking was later taken up into Lincoln's Republican Party, Reformed Protestant thought accompanied by Scottish moral philosophy or Romantic thought predominated while classical republican themes faded to at most an occasional reference by the 1850s and 1860s.[3] In important ways, young Whigs in fact *rejected* classical republican models. In 1840, "Harrison's candidacy . . . reinforced the image of the Whigs as the party of moral rectitude and Christian influence in politics, an image which helped give to the 'discordant combination of the odds and ends of all parties,' some cementing coherence."[4]

Michael Holt's recent blow-by-blow electoral analysis of the Whig Party largely endorsed the traditional interpretation. Nevertheless, Holt also laid especial stress on the Whig Party's opposition to Jacksonian despotism. Jackson appeared to have perfected the art of demagoguery and to have usurped the parliamentary prerogative when, for instance, he put the veto power to new uses.[5] Throughout his interpretation, Holt relied on supposedly "republican" fears of tyrannical Jacksonian despotism to explain the principled nature of Whig opposition to the Democrats. Whigs wanted to "save public liberty." "Thus, at the end of 1832, the National Republicans developed the credo upon which the Whig party would be founded and which would remain its central principle." But Holt also acknowledged other principles for which the Whigs were willing to fight, and along the way he echoed the traditional treatment of the Whigs as a blend of secular republican ideology, evangelical religion, and Common Sense moral philosophy.[6]

In addition, there was in Holt's book a strand of analysis that needs to be reinforced: Whigs sought to justify a positive moral state. "In 1837, for the first time, the two parties articulated clear, coherent, and conflicting philosophies about the proper role of *both* state and national governments in the economy and framed concrete legislative programs reflecting those philosophies."[7] This program for "internal improvements" and the philosophy of positive moral government Whigs articulated to defend their program is central to Whig thought. As Holt pointed out, for Van Buren and the Democrats, "any positive government action created privilege" while "Whigs, in diametric contrast, believed government must promote prosperity." This was Henry Clay's American System of using high tariff revenue to finance government civil engineering and educational projects as well as using a national bank to ensure a sound currency. Believing also that it would appeal to the electorate, Whigs launched "a full-fledged defense of positive government." As Holt showed, Whigs carried the economic nationalism of the old National Republicans into the Harrison campaign of 1840. Whigs "voted against every Van Buren recommendation that entailed a retreat by government from its role as partner to, and abettor of, private economic interests." To do this, "Whig politicians, editors, and pamphleteers articulated a coherent and sophisticated philosophy of the positive state that underlay the position they took in battles over specific policies in Congress and state legislatures."[8] Voters in 1840 knew that Harrison stood for subsidization of internal improvements and had for a long time. And they were disappointed when the states' rights proponent (though classically republican) John Tyler failed to follow through on Whig positive government ideas.

As they attempted to articulate a national self-conception decisively at odds with George Bancroft and Young America, Whigs took part in a decreasingly secular republican, and increasingly theological, discussion. In fact the origins of an important strand of Whiggery can be traced to the Antimasonic rejection of Painite radicalism. The Republican party of the 1850s can be seen as extending this same impulse. In absorbing Antimasonry, Whigs were able to craft a synthesis of commerce and virtue quite unlike the classical republican ideology of the founding period.[9] Historians generally agree that neither the Whig party nor the early Republican Party were straightforwardly "the political expression of pietistic Protestantism." Naturally the Whig and Republican parties remained coalitions of what could be called interest groups. Nevertheless, "a form of postmillennial political evangelicalism, with its roots in Antimasonry and sabbatarianism, nourished the Whig, Free Soil, temperance and Know Nothing parties, and reached its apotheosis in the Republicans."[10] Whigs loathed the amoral and antigovernment tendencies both of utilitarianism and of radically liberal thought because they feared liberal thought hindered the workings of a positive moral state, affecting everything from foreign policy and relations with Native Americans to questions about economic policy, education, and even personal morality. These concerns for positive government, rather than classical republicanism, constituted the ideological cement that held an otherwise disparate coalition together and gave it coherence.

While in his own Romantic idiom Lincoln flirted with postmillennial themes of progress and the coming Kingdom, he was not an evangelical. Yet he nevertheless moved along a genuinely religious trajectory. "The antebellum political landscape is strewn with striking examples of political figures who were scarcely Evangelicals, but whose political course, language, and moral posture derived from their Protestant—and often more narrowly evangelical—roots."[11] Though properly speaking not evangelicals, on their own terms and in their own way Romantic Protestants like Lincoln accepted much of the evangelical worldview—especially as it related to political morality. Even as they pushed for public works to aid economic development, even as they remained forward thinking and entrepreneurial, and even as they rejected the trappings of premodern rural life, Whigs, especially northern Whigs, questioned a belief that now seems almost synonymous with the American way of life: that in material progress *alone* lies the way of salvation.

WHIGS AND THE DECLINE OF CLASSICAL REPUBLICANISM

The American Review: A Whig Journal Devoted to Politics, Literature, Art and Science was a fascinating monthly that ran from the end of 1844 through January 1852. In this official organ of the Whig Party could be found the entire spectrum of Whig thought. It printed pieces by Edgar Allan Poe, James Russell Lowell, John Quincy Adams, Daniel Webster, Edward Everett, John C. Calhoun, and Horace Greeley, and among the leading sponsors of the magazine were Webster, Rufus Choate, and Lincoln's congressional friend and future Confederate vice president Alexander H. Stephens.[12] Like the *Democratic Review,* the *Whig Review* was a political magazine as well as a forum for fiction and poetry, book reviews, and cultural commentary of the highest level. It was a weapon of cultural politics, and its mission was to promote alternatives to the kind of Democratic vision expressed by George Bancroft. It displays the striking diversity of Whig theory as well as the party's unifying anti-Jacksonian belief in positive moral government.

One strategy Lincoln and the *Whig Review* shared with political abolitionists like Theodore Weld, John Quincy Adams, and the "Conscience" wing of the Whig Party was to treat the "Union" or "America" as a moral person. Steeped as he was in both Christian and classical thought, Adams did this self-consciously, as when he complained that the nation as a person was to live hand to mouth. To Stephen Decatur's famous toast, "Our country! In her intercourse with foreign nations, may she always be in the right; but our country, right or wrong," Adams responded, "I cannot ask of heaven success, even for my country, in a cause where she should be in the wrong. *Fiat justitia, pereat coelum.* My toast would be, may our country be always successful, but whether successful or otherwise always right. I disclaim as unsound all patriotism incompatible with the principles of eternal justice."[13]

The *Whig Review* would later refer to "that most abominable maxim—*Our Country, right or wrong.*"[14] With this, Adams and the Whigs rejected Machiavelli and classical republicanism, accepting instead a Protestant view that had roots in the Reformation and the Middle Ages. Machiavelli sought to insulate the "prince" from the ethical critique of a prophetic Christianity; he therefore rejected the concept of the state as a moral person that dominated medieval Christian political philosophy. Machiavelli's prince was to put the interests of the fatherland before all else, even before his own salvation. Lincoln by contrast made the same rhetorical move Adams did. For Lincoln, the nation, like the individual, was accountable to God. He would rather leave his country or die, he said, than surrender the principles of right on which the nation was founded and that alone justified its existence.[15] Unlike Machiavelli, Lincoln could not have supported the country if it abandoned its moral commitments. This impulse was part of the Protestant legacy, and nothing could have been less Machiavellian.

There did appear in the *Whig Review* Old Fogy articles that promoted classical republican themes. One such article, entitled "The Progress and Disorganization," appeared in the second issue and attacked the Democrats for demagogically subverting the Constitution and for replacing the spirit of disinterested virtue with the "wild and disorganizing enthusiasms" of political party. The article began with a direct challenge to the Bancroftian faith in the "spirit of the age." "What is the spirit of the age, among spiritless men."[16] The phrase was associated with Romanticism and "German transcendentalist" ideas generally, and with Stephen Douglas's toast to Louis Kossuth.[17] With sarcasm reminiscent of Lincoln's later remarks on Young America, the *Whig Review* defined the spirit of the age as "Opinion—an enlightened and wide-acting Intellectual Presence, . . . a mighty movement made up of the Bible, Gunpowder, the Printing Press, the Steam Engine, Popular Education, Equality at large, Written Constitutions, the Magnetic Telegraph, and for this country, the great Anglo-Saxon propensity of Land-stealing." Furthermore, "this new and all-accomplishing social force, Opinion, at once the mover of all modern good, and the check upon any excess to which it might run, dates not beyond the invention of Printing," which first gave "a diffusive energy to Thought; made Religion independent of priests, Government of rulers; and set in action those wide forces that lent a fresh power to all old improvements and produced, or is to produce, all the new."[18]

Like Lincoln in his lectures on discoveries and inventions, the author here expressed skepticism about the exaggerated belief in progress. The reference to "Land-stealing" (later echoed by Lincoln) was a snipe at the Polk administration's aggressive policy toward Mexico, a policy that would lead to war less than a year later. But the parallels with Lincoln's lectures do not end there. The second part of the quote functioned as demurrer. In other words, the author chose not to dispute the idea that the advent of printing and the possibility of universal education had led to astounding progress in recent centuries. Lincoln would demur on similar points and in precisely the same manner. The basic belief in progress of some kind was simply beyond challenge in mid-nineteenth-century America.

But even if printing did make public opinion a more powerful force than it had ever been before, as the title "The Progress and Disorganization" indicated, the article raised some Lincolnesque questions about the nature of that progress. Having granted the importance of the invention of printing, the article pointed out that many other, earlier inventions had made the more recent inventions possible. What was printing without alphabetic writing, steam engines without steel, telescopes without glass? It then posed essentially the same question Lincoln did in his lectures on the same topic: "In all these and many other ancient arts, Mind was as admirably exerted as in the modern improvements which have slowly arisen out of them: why claim, then, this intellectual preëminence for the secondary applications?" Much more than Lincoln's lectures, this article was of the Old Fogy philosophy that dared to question the permanence of American progress. "May there not," it asked, "be one great difference as to the social effects of the old and the recent arts, which these magnifiers of the moment have never suspected—that there are arts without the help of which social institutions could never have arrived at any excellence, and other arts that may possibly contribute only to their decline?"

This of course threw a gauntlet at the feet of Bancroft's style of postmillennial optimism, and the author of the article, perhaps Daniel D. Barnard, went on in very republican fashion to claim that civilizations, including this one, were subject to decay, even going so far as to cite failed or failing civilizations like Rome, the Greeks, Persia, China, Carthage, and Tyre.[19] He explicitly attacked "the Benthamites, the Owenites, the Radicals, the Jacobins, and all who make the vanguard of what calls itself 'the Progress;'" and he defended the more orthodox Augustinian view that "the Bible will accomplish God's work in God's own way and time."[20] He denied human perfectibility, and he made an explicit case against the various secularized forms of millennial optimism, including the transcendental synthesis of Christianity and radical liberalism of George Bancroft.

The general effect of progress on war, said the author, "has been to furnish to the civilized man that merciless superiority with which he has trampled over the ruder nations of this continent and of the East: its particular effect, not to make the mass of combatants braver, but to render war mechanical, to banish heroism in its most admirable form."[21] This was an important part of the argument because advocates of pacifism claimed that the new power of public opinion made war obsolete.[22] In part because they wanted to believe that "Christian Civilization" had overcome the need to rely on force, lingering mob violence in American life troubled thinkers like John Quincy Adams and Abraham Lincoln. Even well into the war Lincoln was still unsure. In complete seriousness he suggested to a group of American Indian leaders brought to Washington that, in addition to cultivation of the soil, white people prospered because, "although we are now engaged in a great war between one another, we are not, as a race, so much disposed to fight and kill one another as our red brethren."[23] Correctly, as it turned out, the author of "The Progress and Disorganization" maintained that no such reign of peace and love was at hand, not even in America.

Along with virtually all Whigs, Lincoln would have agreed that the way Democrats typically invested the people with infallibility amounted both to impiety and to an abdication of political leadership: this was a Whig rallying point. Statesmanship had to be more than ministering to the public whim.[24] But the precise nature of moral authority remained a much thornier issue, one on which Whigs from various traditions could never agree. At this point, the author of "The Progress and Disorganization" revealed his antidemocratic, classical republican colors. As opposed both to Bancroft and the Democrats, as well as to future Republicans, he held that the best policy "consults the order of Nature the most, and, depressing none by arbitrary and conventional establishments, leaves the stolid to grovel, and him of strong soul (Nature's nobleman and favorite) to mount, each according to his proper powers." For this "is the republican system: the other is the democratic, the radical, the Jacobin— for all these are only different but inevitable stages of the same thing."[25]

At first glance, some of this might appear Lincolnesque. Lincoln sometimes talked of a meritocratic "race of life." But Lincoln's race of life was part of an egalitarian vision; he did not revel in natural inequality or laud the virtues of "natural superiority." By contrast, this author said that "they who are fit to be free will be free; and so as surely of those who are the contrary. Make the bad, the foolish, the slavish free, and what will such freedom be but a license of everything flagitious, stupid and insolent?"[26] There was little of Lincoln's emancipationist impulse in this kind of classical republican talk. For future Republicans with a capital *R*, condemning slavery was more important than preserving the Union. For this author the converse was true: preserving the Union and the "Constitution as it was" was more important than condemning slavery.[27]

A similar article, "Our Country," conjured "the spirit of the past—the chivalric and thoughtful spirit, that prompted to wise counsels and valorous deeds—when worth was not gauged by the standards of wealth or fashion, and a nation's greatness was not computed by the arithmetic of numbers, nor her glory measured by the geometry of space."[28] This should bring Lincoln's lectures to mind. On the other hand, Lincoln explicitly rejected the spirit of the past and Old Fogy in his Lyceum Address as well as in the discoveries lectures. This put him not in the classical republican but in the progressive Protestant camp more typical of northern, antislavery Whigs. While Whigs agreed on the need for an alternative to Bancroft and the Democrats, and even agreed on the broad outlines of that alternative, northern Whigs like Lincoln did not generally join the South's retreat into the fantastic chivalry of Sir Walter Scott, a retreat that would arouse the endless ire of, among others, Mark Twain, and that helps explain why Twain preferred Connecticut. If they looked backward at all, young Whigs looked toward a Protestant past. But they were generally forward looking.

Lincoln praised entrepreneurial capitalism for its power to develop human potential, making it part of the American mission. But "The Progress and Disorganization" saw in the commercial spirit a threat to the perpetuation of American civilization, first, because—as Malthus argued—greater prosperity only stimulated population growth and, second, because the commercial spirit posed a threat to the civic virtues of patriotism and valor on which any republic necessarily depended. Here was classical republican thought in almost pure form. "Amid incessant buying and selling, immediate personal interest, soon comes to be, with all men, supreme. The social sentiments and feelings, are all lost in the individual passions and habits; all public facts become a selfish calculation, that discreetly values everything by what it will bring in money." More important, in an overly commercial society "liberty itself turns venal, a commodity in common with everything else: the rich man buys, and the poor will sell it."[29] To combat this spirit the author looked to disinterested leadership, to men who could "banish selfish ends, forget uncivic passions, and apply themselves to earnest and wise consultation for the public good alone, as if to some solemn office of Religion."[30] Machiavelli could not have said it better.

The author apparently realized just how anachronistic the republican vision had become. Nothing could illustrate so well as this article the way in which classical republican ideas were hopelessly at odds with the entrepreneurial capitalism that Lincoln extolled and that characterized the economic life of the period.[31]

> Old manners decay, old customs are broken up, local usages disappear, and a great part of whatever in sports or exercises or observances should give a charm to rural life, and beguile toil with innocent pleasures, or confer a manly strength and address vanishes until the mere rustic is haunted all the while by cares as incessant and as eating as attend him who has a hundred rich commercial ventures at sea, or sleeps only among troubled dreams of the fancy stocks in which he deals. The same gnawing solicitudes, turned only to inferior objects, beset all conditions of life.[32]

This was precisely the species of traditionalism that scholars have associated with the backward-looking Jacksonian Democrats rather than with the supposedly forward-thinking Whigs, yet here it was a Whig who spoke for a premodern past.[33] This Old Fogy anticapitalism offers a glimpse, rare in America, of that species of traditionalism Max Weber contrasted with the Protestant ethic and the spirit of capitalism. An older, sleepier, more comfortable way of life had been pushed aside by a new inner-worldly asceticism to which Old Fogy took exception.

Thus "The Progress and Disorganization" explicitly rejected the restless, aspiring spirit that Abraham Lincoln shared with Young America, a spirit that was clearly Protestant in its affinities and origins. And it was precisely this Old Fogy reaction that Lincoln sought to avoid in his lectures, even while he attacked Young America. While most Whigs would have agreed that an excessive concern with commercial values resulted in a lower moral horizon, like Lincoln they favored entrepreneurial capitalism in spite of its materialistic and utilitarian tendencies, not because of them. And moral leadership that embraced progress and capitalism was not to be found in the traditionalism of a classical republican theory that rooted itself in inherited patterns of deference and authority.

AN INTELLECTUALLY VIABLE PIETY

By now it should be clear that Abraham Lincoln was not some intuitive genius from the frontier but in fact the self-conscious interpreter of a rich intellectual inheritance. Less clear is the question of just how much of his outlook was part of the general Whig point of view and how much was original to Lincoln. Many of the themes that arose in Lincoln's occasional writings and that appear odd and even idiosyncratic to us—discoveries and inventions, the threat of Caesar or a Napoleon, a democracy's need of moral leadership and transcendent moral values—actually would have seemed conventional and even hackneyed to someone familiar with Whig thought and language. Lincoln's call for a "political religion" in his Lyceum Address, for example, was entirely in accord with conventional Whig thinking. While Democrats sought to downplay sectional tensions by appealing to the economic interdependence of the sections and therefore to the economic *interest* each region had in maintaining the Union, Whigs sought to maintain unity by generating a common *national feeling*. They attempted to make the Union a more genuinely spiritual community by articulating a set of beliefs that all sections could agree on.

This by itself marked the Whig enterprise as Romantic and antiutilitarian. No longer could some elite hide what in fact had been a class-based agenda behind the seemingly neutral disinterestedness of Madison's classical republicanism. Overt moral categories were back in the debate. Somewhat paradoxically, behind the utilitarian appeals of the Democrats lay a Romantic conception of American identity that received its fullest articulation by the Young America cohort and the *Democratic Review*. No less than the Democrats, the Whigs took part in a general Romantic movement that occurred on both sides of the Atlantic and that included Americans north and south. No less Romantic, the *Whig Review* struggled to articulate a national self-conception clearly opposed to utilitarianism and the Enlightenment.

Perry Miller captured the paradox of this movement most cogently when he noted that the "astonishing fact" about westward expansion is how few Americans at the time would have explained or justified expansion "in any language that could remotely be called that of utility. The most Utilitarian conquest known to history had somehow to be viewed not as inspired by a calculus of rising land values and investments but (despite the orgies of speculation) as an immense exertion of the spirit. Those who made articulate the meaning of this drama found their frames of reference not in political economy but in Scott and Byron, in visions of 'sublimity.'"[34] In the interest of fairness, Miller might have accused the British and French empire builders of a similar self-delusion; but the point should be well taken. (Lincoln, by the way, was particularly fond of Byron.)[35] The *Whig Review* was certainly no exception to Miller's rule that antebellum Americans shunned overt utilitarianism. Born in opposition to James Polk, to Young America, and to the Mexican War, the pages of the *Whig Review* contained a remarkably consistent attempt to define and defend a Romantic position. Since, as Miller noted, "this aversion to the pleasure-pain philosophy became most pronounced in those countries or circles in which a vigorous Christian spirit was alive," the *Whig Review* often attempted to define and defend what looked like a Reformed Christian position as well.[36]

The first number of the *Whig Review* was dated January 1845 but actually appeared in advance of the 1844 presidential election. In the "Introductory," probably written either by the chief political writer, Daniel D. Barnard, or by the editor, George Hooker Colton, the *Review* laid out the Whig position.[37] The Whig party, it said, "is in all things essentially conservative, and at the same time is the real party of progress and improvement." Whigs sought to strengthen "the confederacy and knit together the various sections with common interest and affection."[38] To do this the *Review* proposed a ten-point program: protection to labor, producer, merchant, and manufacturer (this reflected the Whig belief that the classes shared important common interests and denied the class-based rhetoric of the Democrats); fiscal integrity; sound currency; enforcement of law (a reference to Dorr's Rebellion and antiabolition mobs as well as to the fugitive slave provisions of the Constitution); a vigilant defense; a national bank; internal improvements (harbors, roads, and canals); judicial independence (maintenance of an independent elite to interpret the legal tradition); limited executive power (which referred to Jackson's high-handedness in regard to the court, to his vetoes of the Whig legislative agenda and the bank, and, later on, to Polk's solo performance in prosecuting the Mexican War); and the promotion of education (the following article touted national universities, national observatories, and the national bank as "glorious schemes of general improvement").[39]

Much of the Whig program had been thwarted by the libertarianism of the Democrats, who, "professing an exclusively democratic creed" and a desire to advance the "greatest good of the greatest number" (what else needed to be said?), brought a "profligate waste of the national treasures."[40] To the positive program, the editors added a litany of Democratic abuses: the economic depression; inadequate currency; lack of internal improvements; depreciation of property; dishonesty with public debt; blind party obedience against conscience, patriotism, and justice; corruption of the elective franchise; defiance of the civil power; countenance and support of revolutionaries (Dorr's Rebellion again); "perfidy toward an unoffending nation" (Mexico again); selection of a presidential candidate who would carry that perfidy out (Polk); leveling down, not up; and an elective judiciary.

After listing the Democratic abuses, the *Review* summed up its indictment of the Democrats, who "have been disposed to make the stability of legislation dependent on the dominancy of a party, and to consider the idea of law as having no majesty, no authority, no divine force inherent in itself—as not a great Idea enthroned among men, coeval with Eternal Justice, which feeling alone can keep it from being trampled under foot of the multitude—but as derived from, and existing by, the uncertain sanctions of the popular will." What is more, "in all this they are not merely loosening the foundations of order and good government: they are paving the way—first, indeed, to anarchy, but next to despotism."[41] Americans "possess the same passions, weaknesses, and vices, as have the men of all ages and nations; and with us as with them, the demon of popular frenzy crouches ever in the dark cavern of the future, one day, it may be, to spring forth upon us. Seen in this light, "The standard, by which to judge of a nation's greatness, is a standard of the mind and heart; a standard which the materialist cannot apply; whose uses the demagogue cannot understand."[42]

Their list of proposals and complaints pretty well makes clear just what stank so in the nostrils of the Whigs. Certainly the Whigs believed in (and were supported by) educated elites. And there were Old Fogy, "silk-stocking" Whigs around, who—like the author of "The Progress and Disorganization"—bemoaned the loss of inherited elite power. But Whig electoral support did not necessarily correlate very well with wealth; and, if taken at their word, what bothered Whigs most about Democratic thought was its lawlessness. Democrats saw no necessary check on the will of the electorate and, in utilitarian fashion, denied there *was* a higher law transcendentally defined. The utilitarian "greatest good for the greatest number" was in fact a higher law of sorts, but it lacked any transcendent component. There was little in it that could be used to generate a prophetic critique. Democrats such as Bancroft actually blended utilitarianism and Romanticism into a remarkable synthesis that equated higher law with the outcome of utilitarian and liberal processes. But the Whig objection still held: practically speaking, there was no place for a truly transcendent higher law in the Democratic scheme. In Theodore Parker's telling phrase, it was still "practical atheism."[43]

The memory of the French Revolution haunted Whig political thought in the mid-nineteenth century. "Napoleon" became a one-word cautionary tale. Whigs have been portrayed as conservatives distrustful of democracy, but in most cases it was not true.[44] They feared in an unfettered democracy what they would have feared in any unfettered government—the denial that there was a higher law than the claims of that government. This is what Robespierre and Napoleon meant for them. They saw in demagogic appeals for support of Polk's conquest of Mexico—"Our country, right or wrong"—a possible reenactment of Napoleon's own demagogically inspired career of foreign conquest.[45] In order to head off that threat, they sought to find a place for higher law and a voice for learned authority. This was immensely difficult in a nation with no established church, a positive antipathy toward inherited elites, and—outside of New England at any rate—little history of deference to a learned elite as well. There was a strong tradition of deference to the common law, and it is remarkable in retrospect just how well Whigs did in preserving an independent and somewhat nondemocratic court system.[46] The rest of their program, especially the attempt to establish a place for self-conscious moral leadership and an "Eternal Justice" potentially at odds with the will of the people, did not fare as well.

One clearly recognizes something of Lincoln in almost all of these points. Lincoln was to cast the entire Civil War as the enforcement of the Constitution and existing law against rebellious, locally elected authority. While Lincoln's executive style left large areas of policy to Congress (apart from his capacity as commander in chief), the Morrill Land Grant Act of 1862 could find justification in the Whig Party's program, as did the National Bank Act of 1863. Lincoln shared Whig economic views that downplayed class antagonism. When lecturing on discoveries and inventions he questioned the inevitability of progress and doubted whether the new was always better than the old. And in his unceasing quarrel with Douglas he routinely cast the expansion of slavery as irresponsibility toward future generations and a violation of public trust.

Whig Romanticism affected their vision of the law, imparting to it an authority and even majesty far beyond Jefferson's somewhat glib assertions that the country could use a little revolution now and then. Thus the *Whig Review* attached its practical program, which could appear a bit mundane, to a Romantic sense of communal purpose. John Quincy Adams saw in harbors, roads, bridges, universities, and observatories a program of national self-improvement. For him, only the obligation to leave the country a better place for future generations could justify such expenditures. And the Whig program was not that mundane after all. Whigs opposed Cherokee removal and the Mexican War. Though fear of a sectional battle over acquired territory may have played a role, Whigs almost universally opposed the conquest of Mexico on principle. According to the Whig vision, the nation should remain content with its existing borders, encourage "the efforts of the then dawning Republics in South America," and strive for a further perfection of the republican experiment.[47] In addition, there was in the writings the *Whig Review*, as well as in Adams and Lincoln, a still higher appeal: there was "Eternal Justice." To establish a bisectional party and to counteract a potentially amoral utilitarianism, Whigs attempted to foster agreement on the higher ideals for which the nation stood.

While the country was moving away from Enlightenment-style liberalism toward an organic and Romantic view of nationality, and while classical republican ideas faded as a vital intellectual force, the idea of a Christian nation was becoming part of the new Whig sensibility, in both the North and the South. Whigs in particular found a natural albeit troubled alliance with evangelicals on the importance of a transcendent perspective. "Whigs made a bid for the support of evangelicals who, while committed to the classic

Protestant virtues of self-control and self-discipline, also welcomed an interventionist government that would regulate social behavior and maintain moral standards in public life. They commonly portrayed their opponents as atheists and religious perverts, the allies of Mormons, freethinkers, and Roman Catholics." The Whigs touted themselves as "the Christian party."[48] As the *Whig Review* put it in the introductory article its second volume, "When this journal fails to support, with whatever power it may possess, the foundations, and pillars and outposts, of that greatest of all elements at once of conservatism and progress—Christianity—it will be time for it to be abandoned of all men as an instrument of danger to the country."[49] This helps explain why some Whigs would dally with nativism and the American Party. They were striving for an element of cultural unity on a range of issues from temperance to slavery—and to some, Catholicism appeared to block their progress. Many if not most Whigs, including Lincoln, forthrightly rejected nativism.[50] Nevertheless, Lincoln's wartime proclamations of fast days, thanksgiving days, and Sabbath observance eventually reflected his absorption of these ideas. The ideal of the "*Christian Statesman* who recognizes the finger of God in the affairs of men" was one Lincoln would, with careful qualification, come to embody.[51]

Since it was a deliberate response to the *Democratic Review*, the specific tenets of the *Whig Review* were of course part of an ongoing argument with Stephen Douglas, George Bancroft, and Young America, as when the *Whig Review* complained, "They speak of the various lines of communication, which intersect our land in every direction, as so many links in a chain of indissoluble union." Instead, argued the Whig organ, "it must be some deeper and more potential cause than this that shall maintain good feeling among the citizens of our widely extended land. A confederacy of free and popular governments is not to be held together by gross, material bonds— they must be cemented by a spiritual concord."[52] Thus the "political religion" of Lincoln's Lyceum Address was fully in line with conventional Whig thinking about the need for a more spiritual cohesion for the Union. Just as Lincoln's call for a "political religion" had been accompanied by the warning of a demagogic Caesar or Napoleon, the "spiritual concord" desired in this passage was meant to "secure that holy tie against the sword of some daring Alexander," some demagogue preying on a people become "lawless and dissolute," "depraved and reckless." While passages like this from the *Whig Review* make it clear just how much of Lincoln's early thought, which may now seem peculiar, was in fact standard Whig fair, they also show just how deep Lincoln's antagonism to Douglas ran. The call for a political religion in the Lyceum Address was a challenge and an alternative to a Democratic vision that relied on economic interdependence and "interest" as well as demagogic expansionism and millennial patriotism to preserve the Union. For Whigs, false patriotism and financial interests were not enough.

An especially wonderful piece ran in this first issue of the *Whig Review* that laid out an option more congenial to northern Whigs. "Influence of the Trading Spirit upon the Social and Moral Life of America" by Henry W. Bellows took matters up from the Protestant angle, and as the title suggested it too harbored an antiutilitarian animus.[53] Though he was not mentioned, the article agreed with Alexis de Tocqueville: "There are no bounds among us to the restless desire to be better off; and this is the ambition of all classes of society. . . . In other lands, if children can maintain the station and enjoy the means, however moderate, of their father, they are happy. Not so with us. This is not the spirit of our institutions. Nor will it long be otherwise in other countries. That equality, that breaking down of artificial barriers which has produced this universal ambition and restless activity in America is destined to prevail throughout the earth."[54]

This was not Abraham Lincoln talking; in its view of commercial activity "The Influence of the Trading Spirit" was closer to "The Progress and Disorganization" and Old Fogy. One can quote almost at random: "If ever the curse of labor was upon the race, it is upon us; nor is it simply now 'by the sweat of thy brow thou shalt earn thy bread.' Labor for a livelihood is dignified. But we labor for bread, and labor for pride, and *labor* for pleasure."[55] If the Democrats found Tocqueville offensive (though they could not ignore him), the *Whig Review* embraced the Frenchman wholeheartedly—or perhaps one should say that Tocqueville wholeheartedly embraced his Whig informants. Either way, Tocqueville and the Whigs both jabbed at a bellicose Young America that could brook no such criticism. While "Influence of the Trading Spirit" honored the Puritan forefathers, it also claimed that the necessity for such disciplined struggle was past: "What they bore as evil we seek as good." The pithy critique of American life included such insightful remarks as, for instance, one about Victorian architecture: "The best part of the house is for the occasional use of strangers and not to be occupied by those who might, day by day, enjoy it, which is but one proof among many that we love to appear comfortable rather than to be so."[57]

In spite of the anticommercial slant and, even more, in spite of the attack on precisely the kind of restless activity and self-improvement that for many scholars has defined Abraham Lincoln, there were elements in "The Influence" that would echo in Lincoln's writings. While Democrats celebrated public opinion as the voice of God, Whigs talked incessantly of a "corrupt public opinion." American political thought has often been supposed to be untheoretical and practical, but the *Whig Review* was preoccupied, if not obsessed, with epistemology, which self-consciously reflected the embattled rise of Romanticism. The article opened with an epistemological discussion:

> Those influences which affect the characters of a whole people are less observed, although more important, than such as are peculiar to classes or individuals. The exertions which one may make to protect himself from error or demeaning influences are sometimes rendered ineffectual from his ignorance of the tremendous biases which he receives from a corrupt public opinion; as the most careful observations of the mariner are sometimes vitiated by an unknown current which insensibly drifts him from his supposed position. What everybody does in our own community we are apt to suppose to be universal with men; and uni-

versal custom is, by general consent, not to be disputed. We are not disposed to suspect public opinion or to question common custom. Nay, we do not even, for the most part, distinguish between a prevailing sentiment and an innate idea, between a universal or national habit and a law of nature.[58]

This may seem obvious enough to us, but it was still startling and new to Americans in the 1840s. At a stroke, ideas like this rendered an Enlightenment, Common Sense view obsolete. For Jefferson, the senses could be trusted to give a direct impression of the world; everyone would agree if they would but open their eyes. From this followed his interest in the natural sciences to the exclusion of such dark matters as history and theology. To be understood, the world had merely to be examined closely. If forgotten, the misconceptions generated by centuries of priestcraft and monarchy would fall like scales from the eyes as a new order of the ages commenced. But by 1845 Marx was developing notions like "ideology" in Europe. The revolutions of 1848 were only three years away, and on this side of the Atlantic New England transcendentalism was in full flower. Jefferson's comparatively naive empiricism no longer satisfied thoughtful men and women. The *Whig Review* here made explicit the transition from the innate ideas of the moral sense philosophy of the Scottish school, known as the Common Sense school, to a more Romantic historical understanding of the human condition, to what later came to be called cultural relativism.

As John M. Murrin noted, the eighteenth-century Common Sense school "endowed every human with a moral sense, an ingrained and instantaneous response to external stimuli. Until corrupted by their cultures or by habit, people react positively to benevolent actions (for example, a mother nursing her infant) and negatively to malevolence (for instance, teenagers clubbing a dog). Common Sense philosophy provided an antidote to the skepticism of David Hume, first, by establishing what people could take for granted and, then, by building larger philosophical systems upon this foundation. At first, many Calvinists regarded moral sense philosophy as a challenge to the doctrine of original sin, but by the end of the century Scottish learning had triumphed almost completely in American academic life."[59]

"Influence of the Trading Spirit" might be seen conservatively as essentially in accord with the eighteenth-century Scottish theory. Nevertheless, here a more Augustinian and even Pauline conception of the human situation was made possible by emphasizing the ideal side of epistemology. An important part of perception occurred before we even opened our eyes; self-examination and the fear of God were the beginning of wisdom after all.[60] Natural man was fallen, which meant that, without prior knowledge of God, natural perception of the world was unreliable. Throughout the debates with Douglas and especially at the Cooper Institute, Lincoln made precisely the same move that the *Whig Review* did, going into great historical detail to prove that public sentiment toward the slaves had degenerated since the founding. His entire case depended not only on the idea that public opinion had in fact been corrupted but also on the idea that public opinion was all-powerful, that it shaped the very perception of reality. In one striking figure, southerners looked at reality as through a coin: "The plainest print cannot be read through a gold eagle and it will be ever hard to find many men who will send a slave to Liberia, and pay his passage while they can send him to a new country, Kansas for instance, and sell him for fifteen hundred dollars, and the rise."[61] This was not simply the Madisonian point that individuals and groups tended to pursue their material advantage. Rather, the "moral sense," the very *perception* of southerners, had been altered. In this important way, Lincoln's Republicanism continued what had been one of the favorite arguments of the *Whig Review*. For Lincoln and the Whigs, moral ideas shaped perception in a way that for Adams and Jefferson could only have been considered superstitious.

If public opinion could be "moulded," the immediate question was how to mold it, or to what pattern—hence the necessity for a transcendent moral perspective for Lincoln. Democrats made it easy on themselves: *vox populi, vox dei*. Whigs questioned this equation and therefore found themselves drawn to history and religion. Thus the *Whig Review* criticized the American way of life on *theological* grounds in a manner antithetical to George Bancroft and the Young America movement. "If we are doomed to be tradesmen, and nothing but tradesmen," it proclaimed, "if money and its influences and authority are to reign for a season over our whole land, let us not mistake it for the Kingdom of Heaven, and build triumphal arches over our avenues of trade, as though the Prince of Peace and Son of God were now and thus to enter in."[62]

Americans, continued the *Review*, were particularly strict in their morals, but this was "artificial, conventional." "The fear of evil consequences," insisted the *Review*, "is more influential than the love of goodness. There is nothing hearty, gushing, eloquent in the national virtue. You do not see goodness leaking out from the full vessel at every motion it feels." "We fear that the ruling passion of our community, the habits of business which it has established, the anxious and self-concentrated mind which ensues, the morals which it engenders are very hostile to anything like perfected humanity."[63]

Telling also were the words "artificial" and "conventional." These were the bugbears of a Romantic language, in which "Nature" in its many connotations was always good. Romantics tended to see Nature, rather than society, as the source of good, while society came to be viewed as a source of corruption. Thus, on the surface, at least, Romantics seemed to reject the Christian scheme of salvation that began with original sin and the notion that society must both restrain natural impulses and train people to do good. But the words "artificial" and "conventional" as used here were also the sign of what a Reformed theologian and even Luther would have called an unregenerate heart. One might say that these words operated in two theological word-systems at the same time, one Protestant and the other Romantic. For all the loud protestations that the doctrine of original sin belonged to a barbaric past, and for all the talk of man being born good, Romantics postulated a subsequent fall into civilization and artificiality. Thus, they sought redemption from a fallen and corrupt status just as their orthodox forebears had. The complete outline of the Christian drama became evident in the way redemption from an oppressively self-centered conventionality was to be found, as of old, in spontaneity, love, joy, and a rebirth of the "heart." In a sense Romantics attempted to rekindle the older Augustinian piety in a post-Enlightenment context. (From this angle, Rousseau had not so much rejected the Calvinism of his beloved Geneva as reconstructed it.) In fact the link between an Augustinian theological inheritance and a Romantic rejection of the Enlightenment was so smooth that *Whig Review* could make the connection in an almost casual manner.

Finally, the author of "Influence of the Trading Spirit" ventured to question the Pelagian tendencies of American religion in the age of Methodism. In other words, while the characteristic evangelical religion at this time was optimistic about the capacity of human beings both to choose salvation and to do good, the author insisted that the heart, rather than any outward ethical behavior, was at the center of religious life. The chief metaphor was not God's governance and law, as it likely would have been fifty years earlier.[64] Unlike William Paley or John Quincy Adams, the writer did not promote the belief in an afterlife in order to ensure good manners in this world.[65] "How few are aware that Christianity is a call to freedom, a call to happiness," he opined. "Would we but listen, it would break these very chains whose galling wounds we have been opening; it would allay these feverish anxieties; it would restore to us contentment; it would legitimate our pleasures; it would reestablish or, for the first time, build our homes; it would give our children parents, and us parents children; it would teach us that happiness resides ever in the simple and impartial bounties of God: in domestic love, in social intercourse, in generous sympathy, in a mind pleased with little things, in the gratification of our various innocent tastes, in the love of nature, in thought, in doing good."[66]

Some of this was similar to "The Progress and Disorganization." There too the rise of the "self-made man" and the "race of life" (Lincoln's telling phrase) had made life itself an unpleasant task. But "Influence of the Trading Spirit" did not have the bitter tone. It did not cast the conflict as one between a past ideal and a modern machine age or defend a class or slave system. Finally it did not appeal to classical republican and therefore extremely Pelagian ethical ideas. (In classical republicanism, human free will was valued highly and set against the vagaries of fortune.) Rather it was an attempt to bring a fairly straightforward gospel message about love and spontaneity to what it saw as a cramped and artificial American way of life and religion.

The link between Romanticism and a more orthodox Christianity can hardly be emphasized enough. It was as if, before settling down again to call itself "the West," what had heretofore called itself "Christendom" stood back for a moment to examine the empiricism, the positivism, and the utilitarianism it had created. A few gasped in horror at what they saw, and nearly everyone was at least troubled. Like Romantic Democrats, Romantic Whigs expressed a desire for urgency and moral purpose in life, a purpose beyond what was offered either in the conventional moralism of Common Sense philosophy or in conventional evangelicalism. Americans were by no means alone. Parallels can be and have been drawn endlessly between Lutheran or Calvinist hymnody and the Romantic poetry of Germany or the English-speaking world, respectively—between Edwards and Emerson, Calvin and Rousseau, Bach and Brahms, Reformed Orthodoxy and Lincoln, and so on.[67] What is remarkable in retrospect is how self-consciously Romantics made a link with the religious past.

A NEW BIRTH

A particularly revealing article in this regard appeared in the May issue of 1845 entitled "Thoughts on Reading," and behind the conceit of this simple title lay a systematic course in Romanticism. The point of a good book was not to entertain, or even to inform, but to sow the seeds of thinking in the mind of the reader. That may seem a simple enough idea, but it assumed an idealist rather than empiricist epistemology. What the article had in mind was that mere "talent" dealt with the visible world and with evidence that came through the senses while "genius" imparted to the reader the very rubrics of understanding. Just as Kant had postulated a priori categories, the Common Sense school sought to avoid the radical skepticism of Hume by postulating certain "innate ideas." But, as with "public opinion" in the article on the "Influence of the Trading Spirit," the "innate ideas" of the Common Sense school were no longer innate. Instead they had become variable and historical, including things such as "the spirit of trade." In this article, full-blown Romantic "Genius" was a creative process that made new and original ways of understanding possible: "It is in this sense, too, that genius is truly said not only to be creative, but to give forth creative ideas; for its ideas are perfect germs, containing in miniature all the elements of the mind from which they sprung; and, if they fall in a genial soil, will vegetate, and grow into the beauty and fruitfulness of the parent mind." In an easier metaphor: "All true books are but spectacles to read nature with; and all true readers employ these, to look *through,* not to look *at.*"[68]

But why this passion for epistemology? Why did seemingly every article or story in the *Whig Review* begin with a lesson on the power of the mind to organize experience? Again, why did Lincoln interrupt his political and legal business to dwell on the ideal preconceptions necessary to facilitate the most important kinds of discovery and invention? Or why, a little later, would a painter like Monet dedicate walls of canvas to revealing and indeed reveling in the subjective element of perception? Why did Poe develop the mystery genre in which active powers of the mind beyond any merely passive empirical experience were always necessary to solve the crime? (And why would the *Whig Review* immediately recognize this idealism to be the core of Poe's work?)[69] Why was the fiction, not only Poe's *Tales,* but even the pulp fiction, prefaced with the author's assurance that the events about to be narrated would bear witness to the mysterious possibilities of mind? Why celebrate what to old fogies of the Common Sense school amounted to an epistemological quagmire?

The answer may be discerned by reviewing the traits that "Thoughts on Reading" ascribed to "genius" and "talent."[70]

Talent	*Genius*
The logical concatenations of Locke's *Essay on the Understanding.*	The living breathing pages of Milton's "Paradise Lost."
The speculative subtlety of Locke and Reid.	The untutored Bunyan and Burns.
Ben Johnson.	Shakespeare.
Gives information of the objects and agencies around us.	Gives life and reality to the slumbering possibilities of our being.
Tells us wherein life, and thought, and feeling and action consist.	Causes us to live, and feel, and think and act.
Tells us how, or why or what to sing and feel.	Puts a song in our mouths, and a feeling into our hearts.
Does our thinking and feeling for us.	Sets us thinking and feeling for ourselves.
Imparts his knowledge but not his power.	Transforms us into what he is himself.
Proves inductively by marshaling external evidence.	Authenticates intuitively by creating the tribunal to which it appeals.z
Appeals to the head or the heart but not both.	Head and heart act together in concert.
Mechanically and lifelessly combines the elements of experience to a given end.	Organically creates according to vital animating principles.
Brings thoughts and images together in verse.	Images and numbers *grow up* into poetry.
Combining power.	Natural growth.
Ends and means separate.	Ends and means inseparable.
Logic, calculation.	Imagination, inspiration.
Macauley's inimitable art makes one wonder at the well-ordered bouquet of arrangement and skill that has ordered his examples thus.	Carlyle's flowers, scattered naturally, lead one to wonder at the divinely mysterious agency that wrought them.

Clearly these lists display an anti-Enlightenment animus. "Thoughts on Reading" preferred poets to philosophers (with the predictable exception of Plato), and it preferred idealist epistemologies to empiricism. The reason that the Romantic preferred idealism so militantly can be found in its antiutilitarianism: "To class the logical concatenations [of Locke's *Essay on Understanding*] with the living, breathing pages of [Milton's "Paradise Lost"] were nearly or quite as unphilosophical as to refer the actions of a man and a brute to the same constitution of nature."[71] To a Romantic, the prolonged Enlightenment attack on religion threatened to sap human life of all that was higher and to reduce human beings to mere animals.

Scorning "artifice," "calculation," and "lifeless mechanism," "Thoughts on Reading" expressed a longing for a more immediate kind of life, one in which music and poetry were valued more highly than steamboats, in which "head and heart acted in concert," in which ends and means were inseparable, and in which ethical behavior consequently sprang naturally from the spontaneous feeling of the heart. "Human life, too, was once a serious piece of work, and people could afford time for no reading but such as would tend to make them wiser and better; and hence authors crowded as much matter into as little space as possible. But now, since human life has become but an idle jest or farce, and people read only to have their brains tickled and time killed, or because they cannot sleep, authors of course spread as little matter over as much space as possible."[72] To this Thoreau famously added, "as if you could kill time without injuring eternity." In short, Romantics loved the new epistemology because it allowed them once again to feel and live in relation to a higher "agency" and therefore to replicate the piety that had characterized a religious life before Bentham, Mill, and even Newton. For transcendentalists this meant that "Nature" with a capital *N* took on the attributes of divinity. For many writers in the *Whig Review*, however, writers who were more conservative (and, as they argued, more metaphysically and theologically thoughtful as well), the new epistemology meant that they were once again able to replicate some of the specifically Christian piety of their forebears, once again able to live in constant relation to the living God of Abraham, Isaac, Jacob, and Milton.[73]

Some people, admitted the author of "Thoughts on Reading," would not accept this distinction between talent and genius. "The truth is, there are some people, whose faith is only in things that are seen, and to whom a clear and complete explanation is the only rational ground of belief." In reality, the author argued, the things right-thinking people see "force upon us a belief in something unseen; and we are so credulous as to admit the reality of many things which we cannot explain."[74] This was not a simple denial of the scientific evidence. Rather it was an attack on the very notions of evidence on which the scientific materialist relied. "Thoughts on Reading" here argued for the special agency of genius to shape our perceptions. It was not the Romantic believer but the materialist who was epistemologically naive. One did not simply open one's eyes and receive the world more or less as it was. Perception depended on many things, including especially what one had been taught, and what one therefore expected to see. One who read Milton rather than Gibbon might learn to see literally a whole host of different things. The faculty of "imagination," or "Reason," could see in the falls of Niagara a sublime figure for the watchfulness of God. The world of poetry remained, and with it was the possibility of an entirely different relationship with the natural world.[75] Thus against the doubting Thomases of the Enlightenment the Romantic *Whig Review* could restate the ancient faith—*visibilium omnium et invisibilium,* "of all things seen and unseen."

Here again the writers of the *Whig Review* made the link between Romanticism and Reformed Christianity themselves: "Genius is to truth and beauty, what true piety is to religion. . . . With the truly pious man, religion is both the means and the end of his service; his object is, not the reward of religion, but simply the life of religion itself." And so, "With genius, in like manner, truth and beauty are at once the means and the end of its action; at once the light that reveals and the object revealed. . . . Genius does not *pursue* truth and beauty, as external objects to be reached by intermediate means, but lives, and moves, and has its being in them; and its productions are but the expression, the very pulse and breath of that life."[76]

Genius, in other words, was the Romantic equivalent of a regenerate soul working in art. Genius did not pursue a reward. Rather, its works were spontaneous and joyous acts of adoration. This is recognizably Reformed or Augustinian as opposed to, say, Thomistic piety, because works here were in no way the means of gaining God's grace; they were not the effects of calculation but rather grew naturally out of a previous inspiration of grace. Faith was not the crowning achievement of contemplating the natural world; rather grace or "genius" was the precondition of seeing the world truly in the first place.

Again grasping to explain the difference between talent and genius, "Thoughts on Reading" argued that genius "is the possession of a mysterious something, which others have not, and cannot obtain," a "mysterious something" that is "not to be had for study, nor for price; a man may be familiar with all science, as with household words, and yet not have this unacquirable and incommunicable knowledge; he may sport with all languages, as with his mother-tongue, and yet know nothing of the universal language."[77] One should not miss the echoes of 1 Corinthians 13 in this passage. As with the Gettysburg Address, the very cadences made a connection to the religious past, and here they served to cement the relationship between Romantic genius and Christian love. Redemption, the change of state from a soul under the sign of sin to a soul under the sign of grace, happened before the production of great work. A broad generalization holds for the Romantic period: while *inspiration* or *inspired* remained cognate to both languages, the ability to appreciate and feel the effects of *genius*—this "vision and faculty divine"—can be treated as a rough translation into the Romantic of the Calvinist "regenerate" or even "elect."

Not surprisingly, then, the idea of "conversion" can be found in the narratives of the *Whig Review*. In the Romantic conversion narrative, the idealistic epistemology and the possibilities it opened up for a higher and richer life came with the conversion of our hero to that higher life itself.[78] Both William H. Seward and Henry Clay expressed an anxiety for their redeemed status, which led them to adopt not a Reformed denomination but the more liturgical Protestant Episcopal Church that did not expect or demand a particular conversion experience as a prerequisite for membership.[79] But elsewhere the conversion story was revived. From "The Rime of the Ancient Mariner" to *Moby Dick* one finds elements of this familiar narrative line all over the Romantic corpus, not out of fidelity to a past theological paradigm that had to be adhered to—indeed Romantics leaned rather toward iconoclasm—but because conversion had long been part of the self-understanding, something one expected to have happen in life. In fact the habitual iconoclasm of the Romantic pose has probably obscured just how orthodox most Romantics really were. As Perry Miller put it, "in a thousand ways the forms of society were still those determined by the ancient orthodoxy, piously observed by persons who no longer believed in the creed. We do not need to posit some magical transmission of Puritanism from the seventeenth to the nineteenth century in order to account for the fact that these children of Unitarians felt emotionally starved and spiritually undernourished."[80]

The differences between Romantic conversion and the original, more properly Calvinist one were as important as the similarities. Though the Whigs were more favorably disposed to the doctrine of original sin and fallen man than the transcendentalists, George Bancroft, or the *Democratic Review,* they did not seek salvation from a state of sin and depravity, a sense of their own unfitness for the Grace of God—though they made a nod to this requirement of the form. What haunted them, and what they sought to escape, was the old empirical and utilitarian view of a world devoid of meaning and higher purpose. As with Lincoln, a worldview predicated on the selfishness of the individual troubled Romantic Whigs. What bothered Romantics so much about the utilitarian worldview was the pettiness, the futility, and the lack of possibilities either for evil or for moral greatness. The new epistemology literally redeemed them from this sense of futility. Life, for Lincoln, was not a melee but a "race" in the direction of greater moral, intellectual, and economic self-development. And the "new birth of freedom" at Gettysburg would be an installment in the same Romantic genre. The nation would be redeemed and rededicated to a higher democratic, and in some sense Christian, purpose.

Stories and articles in the *Whig Review* often portrayed Christianity as something other than the sentimentality of moral reform evangelicals like Harriet Beecher Stowe. In constructing an intellectually viable piety, it was not enough to establish a credible metaphysical foundation; the degeneration of religious sentiment into Victorian sentimentality had also to be confronted and reversed as well, which must be borne in mind when considering, for instance, Lincoln's use of off-color humor. Even while the Whig

Party courted evangelicals, the *Whig Review* was the adoptive home of those who questioned the Democratic politics as well as those who questioned Democratic views of history and the human situation. The *Whig Review* claimed the Ishmaels of the world who questioned the benevolence of human nature or the innate godliness of the American endeavor as described by George Bancroft, the somewhat cynical people who could still make sense of the drama of sin and salvation, and the people who saw the typical American, not as Adam before the fall, but as already bearing the mark of Cain.

The division of the major Protestant denominations into northern and southern churches was still very fresh. Presbyterians divided in 1837 on theological grounds, and Methodists and Baptists split sectionally the year before the *Whig Review* began, in 1844. Thus, like the Democrats, the Whigs attempted to maintain a neutral stance on slavery in order to make national electoral success possible. At least one author, in his "Study of Plato," was willing to suggest that slavery might not be an "evil in itself."[81] But each of the isms of 1840s America had its metaphysical justification, and the Whigs felt they needed to respond in kind if they were to maintain a national party. "Whence, in short, the energy and success of the destructives, in all ages, in breaking down the old foundations of good institutions, except that the conservatives have either been too negligent to examine whether their foundations were of God, or too remiss to repair the breaches, or too lazy to build when they found and felt the rock."[82] (In the Lyceum Address Lincoln made use of the same rather hackneyed biblical image to explain his devotion to the law.) For this author, the "rock" was apparently some sort of Platonic (and therefore Romantic) Christianity.

Reflecting the philosophy of Common Sense, Jefferson could dismiss the entire tradition of metaphysics in favor of seemingly obvious ethical truth with a flourish at once both more radical and more conventional than Descartes: "What all agree in is probably right; what no two agree in is probably wrong." How, for instance, Jefferson's empty platitudes applied to an issue like slavery was of course never clarified. But Whigs insisted that agreement on the theoretical principles of philosophy and government alone could secure the Union from the manifold error that threatened to divide it; "so long as the convictions of men are based on a sound philosophy, so long will they uphold these institutions."[83] Left unsaid of course was the converse of the proposition, that if no general agreement could be had on the moral and philosophical principles of government (and therewith agreement on the issue of slavery as well) these institutions would fly apart. In the end, there developed, in opposition to what Lincoln called the "pro-slavery theology," an antislavery theology.[84] The Whigs were unable to solidify their identity, and when their specific economic issues lost relevance, the slavery conflict began to divide them, and they found no identity or principles to rely on for their continued existence.

History has been especially unkind to the Whigs. Not only was their vision of an economy of entrepreneurs swallowed up in economies of scale and a vast centralized factory system. After the Civil War, the cult of science returned with a vengeance, almost erasing the Romantic from the American memory. For the most part the idea of America as a moral community would lie dormant until Hitler and the Second World War shocked some "pragmatists" into moral self-awareness and a self-conscious affirmation of faith.[85] Certainly, elements of Whiggery survived, but veterans of the Civil War tended to see only cant in any kind of moral pronouncement—liberal or religious. Men like Philip Sheridan and William Sherman, Oliver Wendell Holmes, Jr., and Charles Francis Adams, Jr., believed in elite leadership, but this would-be oligarchy of experts was no longer an overtly moral let alone *spiritual* leadership. To the higher criticism, which only a few intellectuals had encountered before the Civil War, came Darwin's theory of evolution and, more important, his theory of natural selection. Progress was no longer moral or indeed divine; it was *natural.*

Whigs had been able to articulate a kind of Protestantism that was respectable and intellectually viable, but which no longer seemed possible in the brutal postwar cosmology. The Romantic was not entirely finished, of course, for there was something of a revival of religious fervor in the Progressive era. Standing as he did at Armageddon, and battling for the Lord, Theodore Roosevelt in particular can fairly be called a Romantic Protestant. Jane Addams, William Jennings Bryan, and even Woodrow Wilson owed something to the Whig part of the Republican Party's heritage. Roosevelt reveled in the prophetic voice perhaps even more than Lincoln did—though perhaps not with equal cause. But for a time the religious options dwindled to a choice between a decidedly this-worldly social gospel and an anti-intellectual fundamentalism. Lincoln's religious language becomes intelligible only against the background of that earlier Romantic world in which intellectual life was still dominated by Protestant discourse. According to the *Whig Review*, "when the personal rivalries and partisan asperities of the day shall have been forgotten, and the mellowing hand of Time shall have consigned to the Future only the virtues of the Present, the positions and aims of the Whig party will stand out like watch-towers and beacon-lights on the mountain side, and be referred to and quoted as monuments to inspire, as precedents to guide, another race of statesmen and patriots; etc. etc."[86] Instead the Whigs have been almost entirely forgotten and, when remembered at all, most often misunderstood.

Chapter Four

LAW AND ECONOMICS IN A ROMANTIC AND RELIGIOUS AGE

• The *Whig Review* printed articles representing a range of Whig opinion, and there was nothing anomalous about its Romanticism or its religious focus. The Romantic impatience with the perceived banality of Enlightenment thought found expression across the political spectrum. While Democrats continued to honor the secularism of their Jeffersonian heritage, after the mid-1840s the Romanticism of Young America increasingly dominated their vision as well. A more overt form of Romantic Protestantism came to dominate Whig and later Republican Party thinking, displacing classical republicanism and precluding the kind of liberalism that gained influence after the Civil War. For Daniel Walker Howe, "the American Whigs were poised uneasily between two contrasting views of history. The legacy of classical political thought, stretching across continents and centuries, had made use of history (in words attributed to Thucydides) as 'philosophy teaching by examples.' History was a great storehouse of lessons, for the most part cautionary tales with grim endings. Such had been the use the authors of *The Federalist* had made of history. By the nineteenth century, however, the idea of long-range improvement in the human condition, of history as progress, was also appealing." Eventually, continued Howe, "evangelical religion tipped the scales in favor of belief in progress." "During the nineteenth century a sense of evolution and a reliance on genetic explanations rode the wave of the intellectual future. The state was discussed more and more as an organism; contractualism and natural rights were ideas that were losing ground until, by the end of the century, they seemed positively antique."[1]

Yet the full implications of this increasing reliance on a Romantic view of history have often gone unrecognized, and the history of American law especially has remained under the sway of a liberal interpretation. Whether viewed positively as a "release of energy" or negatively as the favoring of vested interests and big capital, our histories of antebellum law have had little to do with a Romantic sense of historic community.[2] It is of course true that the law did much to facilitate the Industrial Revolution in America, which makes it plausible that the impersonal liberal capitalist state of the twentieth century originated in the nineteenth. But one must avoid reading history backward, projecting later developments onto an earlier period. At issue is what the actors thought they were doing, the way they articulated their social vision as they facilitated the building of railroads, canals, and bridges. Generally they were quite open and honest about it, taking pride in helping to build and expand civilization, which, increasingly, they thought of in terms of "Christian Civilization."

"HAS THE STATE A RELIGION?"

When Lincoln visited Chicago for the River and Harbor Convention in 1847, the burgeoning metropolis boasted just 16,000 inhabitants.[3] He lived in an overwhelmingly rural world in which local self-government was not some lost ideal but still a lived reality, and he had little conception that his generation was replacing that world of self-government with the liberal state as it came to be in the twentieth century. Legal theorists of the period did not even pretend to be "liberal"; that is, they did not postulate a morally and theologically neutral state that governed society from the outside, that adjudicated disputes between citizens, and that otherwise remained aloof from community standards, aspirations, and cultural politics.[4] (They did use the term "liberal," but almost in the precise opposite sense of the "liberal arts.") Even while the classical republican notions of static nature, cyclical history, disinterested virtue, and "paranoid-style" or conspiracy-based reasoning were fading before more impersonal, progressive, and providential notions of historical causation, self-government remained a part of the new Romantic credo. The rise of the industrial economy coincided with the continuing dominance neither of enlightenment and utilitarian reasoning nor of classical republican thought but rather with the rise of various Romantic religious understandings. And, as elsewhere, these understandings would inevitably be felt in the law.

Thus, an examination of jurisprudence in the Romantic period leads back to the queen of the sciences, theology. In that context, one can better appreciate the significance of some of Lincoln's most famous words and writings. As part of the Romantic revival of religious thought and feeling, one of the major themes (if not *the* major theme) of antebellum political literature was the relationship of human to divine law. Even those who disagreed on its content and application seemed eager to acknowledge a higher law. Even Douglas had popular sovereignty to give some direction to constitutional interpretation; it was, as Arthur Bestor noted, his higher law.[5] On all sides of the debate over slavery, another debate about the role of higher and even divine law ensued, and thus any appraisal of Abraham Lincoln must place him in the world of antebellum law and theology.

In the Romantic period, the idea that law was merely the will of the lawgiver, or legal positivism, was the one position to be avoided at all costs. The law was much more, the immanent embodiment of higher law, transcendent and divine. In this respect, legal positivism was akin to and in fact allied with utilitarianism. Even where the lawgiver was "the people," legal positivism smacked too much of utilitarianism, worldly mindedness, materialism, and "Mammon" to interest most antebellum intellectuals—hence, once again, George Bancroft's facile but necessary equation of the will of the people and the will of God. Though Lincoln in his First Inaugural Address said "the intention of the lawgiver is the law," he was not a legal positivist. He said these words in connection with the fugitive slave clause of the Constitution, which he constructed as a statute; and, perhaps reflecting his collaboration with William Seward, in the next paragraph he endorsed certain limitations to the enforcement of the fugitive slave clause based both on "the safeguards of liberty known in civilized and humane jurisprudence" and on the privileges and immunities clause of the Constitution.[6] The will of the lawgiver was only one part of legal interpretation, and in the interpretation of the common law that dominated antebellum American jurisprudence it played almost no role.

In the world of legal theory there was an overtly Christian intellectual tradition available to Lincoln. Daniel Walker Howe noted that the failed liberal revolutions of 1848 reinforced Whig doubts about liberal theory, and the shots of 1848 echoed through all of Lincoln's subsequent writings, including the Gettysburg Address. But scholars have missed how the European struggles gave impulse not only to Whig conservatism but to a progressive Christian theory of the state as well. A now obscure work from Lincoln's bookshelf reveals this dynamic. In 1854, the year of the Kansas-Nebraska act, Charles Bowyer published his *Commentaries on Universal Public Law*, which took the revolutionaries of 1848 to task for misunderstanding the nature of republican institutions. A radical member of Parliament and an Anglo-Catholic with Irish sympathies, Bowyer believed the continental revolutionaries acted as demagogues when they sought to follow public opinion rather than to guide it. For Bowyer, public opinion was plastic and could be manipulated: "In Italy especially, public opinion was deified," and since "no statesman had the power to direct public opinion," the Continental revolutionaries misused emergency powers, thus extinguishing liberty. However important consent might be, the republican statesman needed a moral standard separate from the public whim.

Writing in the grand style of the nineteenth-century legal treatise, Bowyer derived all public law, neither from Scottish moral philosophy nor from classical thought, but from the law of the Gospel: love God and thy neighbor as thyself. Legitimate republican government functioned through consent of the governed, but it fell to the republican statesman to inculcate public morality and to work toward this transcendent Christian ideal. Bowyer pointed out the "maimed and imperfect view of the nature of man" among those who relegate "all that man ought to regard in the observance of Natural Law to his temporary life only" and who "deem themselves more philosophical, in proportion as they separate religion from Natural Law."[7]

Elite legal culture of the mid-nineteenth-century Atlantic world was more favorably inclined toward this theological inheritance than were the founders eighty years previously. In order to avoid the worship of public opinion, both Lincoln and Bowyer rejected contract-based reasoning and instead applied overtly religious categories of thought to public life. There is much of Lincoln in Bowyer's commentary. "By the people, for the people" appears in a quote from Savigny; and by way of rejecting contract theory Bowyer in 1854 gleaned from Joseph Story precisely Lincoln's view of the nature of the American Union: "In the case of federal constitutions, such as that of the United States of America, there is indeed a fundamental law, the origin of which partakes of the nature of that of a treaty or contract; but this is not an original contract in the sense in which the term is used by Locke and Rousseau, nor a compact. It is a constitution of government,—a modification of civil or political society previously existing, by the union of several bodies politic in a form of constitution." For Lincoln, too, the Union was older than the Constitution.[8]

The importance of an overtly Christian theory of statecraft became apparent with the controversy surrounding the Mexican War. William Brock pointed out that "it was the moral aspect of the war rather than its connection with slavery that first assailed the American conscience and shook the assumption that though Americans might differ on material questions, they stood together on the firm ground of 'republican virtue.'"[9] In both the Mexican War and the extension of slavery, northern Whigs especially saw an impious denial that the nation was subject to a higher power. As it did for Bowyer, statesmanship for Lincoln meant guiding public opinion according to transcendent principles. While conservative former Whigs would favor compromise in 1861, Lincoln parted ways with conservative Whigs like Rufus Choate and Daniel Webster when he denied that the traditional order was a legitimate end in itself. Thus a romantic Christian legal theory that grew in reaction to the failed revolutions of 1848 and to the earlier war with Mexico helps explain how, rather than allowing consent or compromise to determine the fate of slavery in the territories, Lincoln mustered the resolve to impose freedom on the nation by war.

Lincoln did not necessarily get any of his ideas from Bowyer; he left no marginalia and may not even have read *Commentaries on Universal Public Law*.[10] He did use the phrase "universal law" in the First Inaugural Address: "I hold," said Lincoln, "that in contemplation of universal law, and of the Constitution, the Union of these States is perpetual."[11] That suggests the president-elect made a study of the field in preparing his address but does not necessarily reflect a reading of Bowyer's volume in particular. The Bowyer volume remained in the Lincoln-Herndon library while Lincoln and Seward collaborated on the First Inaugural in Washington.

In fact the differences between Bowyer and Lincoln are as important as any similarities. Bowyer's Catholicism led him to Thomas Aquinas and the natural law tradition rather than to the more historically minded Romantic Protestantism that dominated the world of Lincoln. In opposition to manifest destiny, Republicans like Francis Lieber, Seward, and Lincoln developed their own visions, rooting the existence of the nation in history, historical necessity, and progressive historical development. Harry Jaffa has probably gone the furthest in reading Lincoln as a natural law theorist.[12] Jaffa essentially discovered what Bowyer and Lincoln had in common: a belief in the necessity for a transcendent perspective in democratic politics. But the dissimilarities between a Romantic Anglo-Catholic and Abraham Lincoln are equally important. In America the overwhelmingly Reformed theological inheritance made any return to Aquinas highly unlikely. And the most prominent Aristotelian in America was an apologist for slavery.[13] Justly or unjustly, the centrality of the debate over slavery reinforced native Protestant tendencies and made Aristotle an unlikely hero. For a man with a strongly Augustinian upbringing, knowledge of the will of God was much too hard to come by to be rendered systematically or to be applied with absolute certainty. Post-Enlightenment uncertainty seems to have reinforced the native American tendency toward Augustinian as opposed to Thomistic piety. When Lincoln claimed not to have controlled events but to have been controlled by them, it was not some "noble lie," as Jaffa had it; rather, it was a classic Augustinian reaffirmation of the absolute sovereignty of God in history.[14]

When, in reaction to Polk's war of aggression, the *Whig Review* asked, "Has the State a Religion?" contrary to the Jeffersonian orthodoxy the answer was a qualified but emphatic "yes." The article came to the defense of Thomas Arnold's "Inaugural Lecture on History," which had been assailed in the *Democratic Review,* and the *Whig Review* used the occasion to express outrage at the Mexican War. After assuring its readers that it intended no return to monarchy and aristocracy, the *Review* began: "Is the State a moral as well as a physical agent? . . . In a word—is it to be guided in determining the duties and relations of men, solely by considerations of their physical well-being, or must it also, in connection with this, have some reference to those truths and those obligations, that concern the spiritual and moral health?"[15]

Against "that shallow doctrine of the Monticello School, which some regard as the ne plus ultra, the last and greatest attainment of political wisdom," against those who denied the state had anything to do with moral considerations and claimed that the law had no right to meddle with anything "that picks no man's pocket or breaks no man's leg," the *Whig Review* asserted that the state invariably legislated morality—and on purely moral grounds. Crimes were punished not simply because they affected persons or property but "because *they are wicked* and abominable." Since the *Whig Review* assumed that "a true morality, and a true justice which is anything more than the barest consulting of convenience, are inseparably connected with considerations drawn from religion and from the invisible world," the state indeed did have a Religion. "Our Democratic notions deceive us on this point," the article continued. Even democratic states had an absolute power located somewhere, and such an absolute power could not be left "destitute of a sense of right and wrong." Men like George Bancroft might claim "that the world has advanced; man has risen in the scale of being; religious sanctions may have been necessary to the security of governments in past ages;

but now "the moral sentiments have been fully developed; in short, man is now prepared for absolute self-government." But, for the *Whig Review*, "the very light within us remains but darkness."[16]

The author postulated a hypothetical case akin to that of Puritan New England in which "a company of religious persons, professing the Christian faith, are cast upon a certain locality, on which is to arise a true State." Even assuming merely material motives, the community would be within its rights if it were to banish those who taught that there was no God. In words that reflected the "well-regulated society" ideal of the common law, the *Whig Review* had this imaginary community say, "We refuse to listen to you ourselves, and we forbid your speaking to our children. We say this as heads of single families, and as the civil guardians of associated families. You are a worse offender, even against the physical good of society, than the man we have punished for selling unwholesome provisions. . . ."[17] The author conceded that, if taken to its logical conclusion, this theory might result in a species of intolerance at odds with the reality of religious pluralism in American life; nevertheless, he stuck to his guns.

Much as it did for Lincoln, nationality for the *Whig Review* presupposed fundamental moral agreement. "We have not the homogeneity of the Puritans, either in Church or State: and yet we still have that without which no nation can long exist, any more than a body without a soul—namely, a national religion," such that, "whatever may be our other differences, we meet on the broad ground of a common professed Christianity; not in the narrow sense of being *established* by law, but as forming the basis on which the law itself is *established*."[18] In a footnote, the author cited Webster's speech on the Girard Will case before the Supreme Court as well as Chancellor James Kent in *People* v. *Ruggles*. Surprising though it may be to those raised on classically liberal interpretations of the American past, the *Whig Review* here articulated a mainstream, mid-nineteenth-century conception of American nationality and its connection to morality and even theology. It was an embattled conception to be sure, but a mainstream and even dominant one.

The twenty-first century should not be too hasty to reject this Whig theory on the grounds of separation of church and state. As a matter of descriptive fact, the Whig theory may be stronger than the liberal description of American legal life. Try as one might to contrive liberal arguments for prohibiting polygamy or the arranged marriage of minors, such laws clearly reflect a latent Christian bias in the law, and it was that bias that Whig theory acknowledged. Said Kent, "Christianity in its enlarged sense, as a religion revealed and taught in the Bible, is part and parcel of the law of the land." In modern parlance one might say that Christianity was central to American culture and that that culture was expressed in the law. "We may very truly say," said the *Whig Review*, "that very few of our institutions would have been what they now are, if our ancestors, who have transmitted them to us, had not been Christians."[19] Thus, despite religious toleration and even disestablishment, Americans remained a "Christian people." Certainly there were differences between the sects on "rights and forms and modes of worship." But Christians agreed—or should have agreed—on the "religious doctrines of national accountability, national retribution, and individual obligation." The point was that, as a moral being accountable to God, the state had no business attacking Mexico. "But alas! when the doctrine of religious national accountability and of a national conscience is dropt out of our political creed, we become far more animalized in our public than in our private relations."[20] Moral man, immoral society.

Lincoln has served as a model of vigorous executive leadership because he did not let every possible formal or legal objection prevent him from prosecuting the war with vigor. Yet at the Cooper Institute he also enjoined the North to "have faith that right makes might."[21] In the end it was Lincoln's appeal to a Christian state *under* God that lent power to his most memorable political oratory. What gave Lincoln's religious language its impact was the fact that it was no mere sentimental gesture but rather part of a hardheaded legal theory, one that was shared by an entire school of writers and thinkers, and one that helped Lincoln to make his case, first for opposition to slavery's expansion, then for the Union, and finally for emancipation.

A HIGHER LAW

In 1850, William Seward—Lincoln's future rival for the 1860 Republican nomination, his secretary of state, and perhaps his only real friend in the cabinet—refused to support Henry Clay's proposed compromise on the slavery question because, among other things, it included a stronger fugitive slave provision. He defended his opposition to the Compromise of 1850 on the grounds that there was a "higher law than the Constitution." Seward articulated this higher-law position to justify opposition to the fugitive slave provisions of the compromise, and there was more than a little political motivation in his stand. Whigs had always professed loyalty to the Constitution. "The Constitution as it is" was the motto of their monthly, and, in opposition to the Liberty and Free-Soil parties, they sought to unite the northern and southern wings of their party. However individual Whigs might have felt about the peculiar institution, they agreed that the federal government had no power to abolish it where it already existed. But by this same logic, or so it seemed, the North owed obedience to the fugitive slave provision equally explicit in the Constitution, a provision unpopular and even openly resisted in antislavery areas of the North. Stung as much by the moral reproach aimed at their way of life as by actual economic damages, but also fearing the loss of economic opportunity entailed in any possible Wilmot Proviso, the South demanded strengthening the fugitive slave clause with a federal Fugitive Slave Act.[22]

Antislavery Whigs were in a difficult position. After being dragged into what they saw as a perfidious war of conquest on behalf of southern interests, many antislavery Whigs saw in the stronger fugitive slave provisions further acquiescence to the slave power. As in the battle over the gag rule and the right of petition, here too the slave power seemed to threaten the very principles of local self-government. The new Fugitive Slave Act eliminated jury trial for the fugitives, denied them the right to testify in their own behalf, and put enforcement of the fugitive slave clause in the hands of federal officers who could issue warrants, gather posses, and require citizens to aid in the return of fugitives under penalty of law. The new provisions were intended to prevent local officials and juries in the North from interfering in the recapture of fugitives. This was less of a problem in relatively proslavery Illinois, where the fugitive slave provisions were more popular. Indeed, throughout the 1850s Lincoln could simply insist that, unpleasant as it was, under the Constitution the North owed the South the faithful return of fugitive slaves. Wendell Phillips might rave and call him "that slave hound of Illinois," but Lincoln remained insulated by geography from such radical antislavery demands.[23]

If anything, Phillips spoke more truly than he knew. In 1841 Lincoln represented a would-be slaveowner, Bailey, who had apparently been cheated in the purchase of "black or negro girl or woman, named Nance," without receiving the necessary papers of indenture. In the course of claiming that Bailey did not owe the Cromwell estate the purchase price for Nance, Lincoln argued that the Northwest Ordinance and the Illinois Constitution forbade slavery in Illinois, that therefore Nance had been free upon entering the state, and that thus the purchase was invalid. Thus *Bailey* v. *Cromwell* has sometimes been seen as consistent with Lincoln's antislavery sentiments. But presumably Bailey would have been happier owning Nance than winning the lawsuit, and Lincoln pressed what was in fact a convenient argument on behalf of a client.[24]

In the Matson slave case of 1847, congressman-elect Lincoln argued on behalf of a slaveowner named Matson in a habeas corpus proceeding—seemingly in the teeth of precedent he helped set in *Bailey*.[25] Some biographers have attempted to excuse Lincoln's action in taking this case, but it seems he took it because, as an ambitious lawyer, he wanted in on an important case. Nor did he "throw the case." Despite the fact that it was a seemingly hopeless cause contrary both to his own earlier arguments before the Illinois Supreme Court and his professed antislavery sentiments, Lincoln gave his client the best case he could, and he availed himself of the only argument open to him: that Matson had intended to keep the slaves in Illinois only temporarily and that he was entitled to keep them *in transitu*. "This," wrote Stephen Oates, "was cold and brutal logic, demonstrating how attorney Lincoln could set aside his personal convictions—for he claimed to hate slavery—and go all out to win for a client, even if that meant sending a family back into bondage."[26] In *Bailey* v. *Cromwell* the court had held that "the presumption of the law in Illinois is that every person is free without regard to color" and that "the sale of a free person is illegal."[27] But no one in the Matson case mentioned the *Bailey* decision, least of all Matson's attorney. Lincoln lost, and the court freed Matson's slaves without citing *Bailey*.[28]

It may be somewhat high-flown to chalk the Matson affair up to Lincoln's devotion to Whig law and order—unless by that one means merely that, as a lawyer, he generally accepted cases regardless of his own personal moral opinions. The prevailing legal ethics of the day held that morality was compatible with taking any and every case.[29] Nor was Lincoln here making a show of Whig willingness to uphold the fugitive slave clause of the Constitution; Lincoln made no effort to publicize his efforts in this case, and Matson's slaves were not persons "held to Service or Labour in one State, under the Laws thereof, escaping into another," and thus they did not come under the provision of that clause. According to David Donald, "neither the Matson case nor the Cromwell case should be taken as an indication of Lincoln's views on slavery; his business was law, not morality."[30] But not to decide is to decide after all. Questions concerning the relationship of morality and law were hotly disputed at the time, and Lincoln was to take a prominent part in those disputes. As a Republican it was Lincoln who would most cogently reject the possibility of moral neutrality in public life. Lincoln did not embrace the enthusiastic position that one's personal moral convictions were to be held above the laws and the Constitution; rather, the law embodied the morals of the community. The lawyer's duty was to communal as opposed to individual moral commitment.

After incorrectly maintaining that Lincoln "had shown no zeal in such a cause and lost his case," Benjamin Thomas added that "the slavery issue had not yet seared itself into his conscience to the point of inducing him to place the plight of a few hapless Negroes above the abstract legal aspects of the question."[31] While his second point is partially correct—Lincoln did become more unambiguously antislavery over time—Thomas's formulation also carried with it the assumption that Lincoln eventually came to a more compassionate view, and thus he sentimentalized the later Lincoln. As president, Lincoln certainly never went soft. To keep his Union coalition together during the early phases of the Civil War, he proceeded cautiously with emancipation with an eye both to legality and to prevailing moral opinion.

Whigs founded law and society on fundamental moral agreement, and it was becoming something of a Whig tenet that a morally neutral liberal order was neither possible nor desirable. But the question was the application of higher law, first, in the case of fugitive slaves and, second, in the case of slavery extension. As with Seward, Lincoln's careful reasoning served his political needs as well. For Lincoln, advocating slavery's extension (but not the Fugitive Slave Act) constituted moral turpitude because it went beyond merely acquiescing in an institution that already existed and prolonged the existence of slavery itself. Thus Lincoln's antislavery conviction became clear only after the Kansas-Nebraska Act of 1854. He was not a leader in these developments. Only in 1856 would he finally come out to join the revival-style Republican Party.[32] In the meantime, he enjoyed the grace of geography on the fugitive slave question and was never made to pay politically for his actions in the Matson case.

Elsewhere, however, the Fugitive Slave Act of 1850 already created more difficulties for northern Whigs. By defending the more stringent provisions for the recovery of fugitive slaves, Daniel Webster remained faithful to the national aspirations of the Whig Party, but in antislavery circles he became the fallen angel and Ichabod of the Bay State.[33] And for Seward, whose base of support remained the Antimason (and later evangelical and antislavery) areas of New York largely settled by New Englanders, the Fugitive Slave Act was potentially even more embarrassing. With his higher-law position, Seward attempted to finesse the dilemma squarely faced by Webster. This is not to say that Seward was insincere. Not unlike Lincoln four years later, Seward had to reconcile Whig constitutionalism with antislavery absolutism. As much for himself as for his constituents, he offered up a remarkable theory, one that William Brock called "the most profound of the controversy" and "one of the most sensitive discussions on the character of the United States presented during the nineteenth century."[34] As Jefferson and Adams had feared, Romantic religious enthusiasm breathed a new spirit into the councils of the nation. With one foot still planted in the Enlightenment, Webster too regretted the new Romantic and religious mood: "When a question of this kind takes hold of the religious sentiments of mankind, and comes to be discussed in religious assemblies of the clergy and laity, there is always to be expected, or always to be feared a great degree of excitement."[35] Whatever Seward's personal motivations, the *terms* of his particular position revealed a Protestant political culture grappling with the issues of slavery in a burst of constitutional and theological creativity.

The first thing to note about Seward's "higher-law" speech is what Seward was *not* saying.[36] Seward did not argue that the Constitution could be disregarded when and where its provisions clashed with some higher law transcendentally defined. That, in fact, was the view of the Liberty Party that had given the Whigs such fits in 1844, particularly in Seward's New York. "We hereby give it to be distinctly understood," said the Liberty Party platform, "by this nation and the world, that, as abolitionists, . . . we owe it to the Sovereign Ruler of the Universe, as a proof of our allegiance to Him, in all our civil relations and offices, whether as private citizens, or as public functionaries sworn to support the Constitution of the United States, to regard and to treat the [fugitive slave clause] of that instrument . . . as utterly null and void, and consequently as forming no part of the Constitution of the United States, whenever we are called upon, or sworn, to support it."[37] This was clearly a higher-law argument.

But if the Liberty Party's position was clear, from a Whig point of view it was also dangerously anarchistic, and it was emphatically *not* the position Seward adopted. Rather, on the relationship between higher morality and the Constitution, Seward took precisely the position that Lincoln would assume four years later. "Slavery must give way," Seward said. The gradual "ripening influences of humanity" made emancipation inevitable and near. The question was whether emancipation would be gradual and peaceful or violent and sudden. "All measures which fortify slavery or extend it tend to the consummation of violence—all that check its extension and abate its strength tend to its peaceful extirpation. But I will adopt none but lawful, constitutional, and peaceful means to secure even that end; and nonesuch can I or will I forgo."[38] Where, then, was the higher law? For Lincoln and the Republicans in 1860 it would be in the resistance to the extension of slavery to new territories, and for Seward in 1850 it was in opposition to the Fugitive Slave Act. Seward's writing was not as clear as Lincoln's, perhaps, but Lincoln and the Republican Party would carry the same kind of mainstream, constitutional antislavery into the election of 1860.

Behind this rather innocuous-seeming gradualism, Seward articulated a complex and rather innovative view of the Constitution. Rejecting the notion that the Constitution rested on the agreement of the states, or even on the consent of the individuals composing the Union, Seward grounded law in something like the social state or society, including the moral aspirations of that society. "The Union," he said, "was not founded in voluntary choice, nor does it exist by voluntary consent. . . . The Union—the creature of necessities, physical, moral, social, and political—endures by these same necessities." Emancipation could not be effected "by merely sounding the trumpet violently and proclaiming emancipation, while the institution [was] interwoven with all [the South's] social and political interests, constitutions, and customs." No power, except the people of the slave states, could abolish it. Nor, for instance, could the South secede. In a "rural republic . . . a democracy of property and persons, with a fair approximation toward universal education and operating by means of universal suffrage," the people had so come to accept their government that they could not be brought to accept revolution. "The Union, then, is," he said, "not because merely men choose that it shall be but because some government must exist here, and no other government than this can. If it could be dashed to atoms by the whirlwind, the lightning, or the earthquake, today, it would rise again in all its just and magnificent proportions tomorrow."[39]

Seward put forward an organic conception of the Union and the Constitution, one rooted in the beliefs, economic practices, and traditions of the American people. He opposed the Fugitive Slave Act (in careful contradistinction to the Constitution's fugitive slave clause) because it ran against the spirit of American legal tradition of locally administered justice. (It was the South that insisted on greater federal authority.) As with Bancroft, Choate, and the pages of the *Whig Review,* Seward traced American origins to "the Pilgrim Fathers." Unlike Bancroft, but like Choate and other Whigs, Seward defined American nationality, not in terms of the triumphant cosmopolitanism of Young America, but in terms of culture. "The question now arises," he said, "Shall this one great people, having a common origin, a common language, a common religion, common sentiments, interests, sympathies, and hopes, remain one political State, one nation, one Republic, or shall it be broken into two conflicting, and probably hostile, nations or Republics." Seward reiterated the general Whig strategy of consolidating the Union by articulating a set of commonly held beliefs as well as a shared past. Even though antislavery Whigs like Seward and Lincoln resisted nativism, and even though they sought to bring blacks into the political community so defined, this culturalist rhetoric was not without exclusionary or nativist potential.

In pressing this noncontractarian view of the state, Seward used elements of the classical republican theory of statecraft: "no man better understood this principle than Machiavelli, who has told us, in regard to factions, that 'no safe reliance can be placed in the force of nature and the bravery of words, except it be corroborate by custom.'" Seward also cited *The Federalist* and thinkers like Burke, Montesquieu, Vattel, and Bacon, and terms like "faction" were scattered thinly about. But the heart of the speech had nothing to do with Machiavellian republicanism or Burkean conservatism. Rather the new theories of progressive development that were voiced by Bancroft and even by Lincoln dominated Seward's conception of the historical process.[41] "The Atlantic States, through their commercial, social, and political affinities and sympathies," Seward wrote, "are steadily renovating the Governments and the social constitutions of Europe and of Africa; the Pacific States must necessarily perform the same sublime and beneficent functions in Asia," and then "a new and more perfect civilization will arise to bless the earth." For Seward, the discussion about the evils of slavery was "part of the eternal conflict between truth and error—between mind and physical force—the conflict of man against the obstacles which oppose his way to an ultimate and glorious destiny."[42]

William Brock noted that, "behind this conviction, shared by so many throughout the North, lay the Puritan heritage and the great tide of intellectual and Romantic revolt which had already caused much stirring in Europe."[43] Everywhere the crisis over slavery was viewed in religious terms, as either a reaction to sin and sinners or to evil. Even southerners who saw slavery as a positive good tended to see it also as part of a difficult journey in a dark, imperfect, and imperfectible world. Thus in northern triumphalism they saw apostasy from their own version of Augustinian orthodoxy, and ruminations on the doctrine of the two kingdoms abounded in this period, especially when the place of slavery in American life was at issue (hence Harriet Beecher Stowe's great character, Augustine St. Claire).[44] Seward's speech as well as Lincoln's carefully ambiguous treatment of this teaching in the Lyceum Address were each part of the same Augustinian conversation.

Seward was forward looking, and, not entirely unlike Stephen Douglas, George Bancroft, and Abraham Lincoln, he looked westward to an expanding American civilization. Slavery was an aberration, an "accidental, and incongruous institution" that would be overcome and eliminated. "Sir, there is no Christian nation, thus free to choose as we are, which would establish slavery. I speak on due consideration, because Britain, France, and Mexico have abolished slavery, and all other European states are preparing to abolish it as speedily as they can."[45] The reference to "Christian nation" should not be dismissed as accidental or unimportant. Christianity was seen as entirely compatible with the new economic order that Whigs and Democrats alike were ushering onto the historical stage. Indeed, that new order was the practical application of Christian teaching. The much-celebrated free-labor ideology, the "freedom of industry," as Seward termed it, was suffused with the doctrine of "calling." Natural rights and even the advance of learning and technology—so much in conflict with evangelicalism in the century after Darwin—were also part of the triumphal march of Christian civilization and were not necessarily seen as a threat. Evangelicals were in the van of important reform movements, and Christianity was intimately connected with the spirit of progress.

Seward invoked at least two traditional Christian theological notions when he claimed there was a "higher law than the Constitution": stewardship and the Trinity. He held that "there is a higher law than the Constitution which regulates our authority over the domain and devotes it to the same noble purposes. The territory is a part—no inconsiderable part—of the common heritage of mankind, bestowed upon them by the Creator of the universe. We are His stewards and must so discharge our trust as to secure, in the highest attainable degree, their happiness. . . ."⁴⁶ Stewardship was a principle that transcended the reliance on a strict legalist order and helped govern the community by love, and Seward's use of the term was entirely orthodox.⁴⁷ While strict adherence to the Constitution was necessary, national salvation did not come through such adherence. It came through the fulfillment of a higher · standard, the law of love or stewardship. Thus Seward did not attempt to establish a neutral liberal political sphere that operated in spite of persistent religious belief and persistent theological contention. For antislavery Whigs, the battle was not about individual rights. Rather, constitutional government was attempting, as far as possible, to embody certain religious ideals. Though Seward might have invented some other, perhaps more philosophical and more secular, language, the words he chose were neither classically liberal nor classically republican but Romantic and overtly Christian—the dominant language of the period. By the time of Lincoln's great war speeches, at least two decades of overt public theology had prepared the public to hear and understand Lincoln's biblical rhetoric.

Of course more radical antislavery activists also used this kind of language. *Uncle Tom's Cabin* would reek of the revival and evangelicalism, and even a self-conscious outsider like Thoreau would find it necessary to go back to the Bible to make his case for refusing to pay taxes to support the Mexican War:

> Christ answered the Herodians according to their condition. "Show me the tribute money," said he; and one took a penny out of his pocket. If you use money which has the image of Caesar on it and which he has made current and valuable, that is, *if you are men of the state* and gladly enjoy the advantages of Caesar's government, then pay him back some of his own when he demands it; "Render therefore to Caesar that which is Caesar's, and to God those things which are God's"—leaving them no wiser than before as to which was which; for they did not wish to know.⁴⁸

Thoreau everywhere assumed a readership that was not only biblically literate but biblically minded as well. Thus, a less biblically minded age, one
without a Calvinist theological inheritance, faces in his writings a nettle-
some obstacle course indeed. Without at least some familiarity with nineteenth-century religion, the better part of Thoreau's irony and meaning remains entirely obscure. The same is true for writers like Herman Melville,
William Seward, and Abraham Lincoln.

Here Thoreau revisited the Gospel and reinterpreted a passage that in
Mark, Matthew, and Luke revealed a sagacious Christ avoiding a clever verbal
trap and turning it on his enemies. If Jesus had said that the tax should be
paid, then he would have lost status with the people as an outsider and chal-
lenger of Herod and the Pharisees. If, on the other hand, he told them not to
pay the tax, then the Roman authorities could have arrested him. Traditionally the passage was interpreted as foundational for Augustine's two kingdoms
teaching; the state and the Kingdom of God were distinct realms that did not
conflict, each having its legitimate place and role, and each therefore deserving proper obedience.[49] During the Mexican War, Thoreau objected to precisely that sort of divided loyalty among his nominally antislavery neighbors.
(Lincoln's action in the Matson case would have horrified him.) Much like
Melville's use of Father Mapple's sermon on Jonah in *Moby Dick,* in this passage Thoreau found a more subtle and subversive reading of a biblical text.
For Thoreau, Christ also meant to imply that his interrogators were about the
business of Caesar rather than the business of God, as they should have been.
After all, they carried with them Caesar's craven image contrary to scriptural
command. Thoreau then radicalized the point by demanding separation from
a wicked state and suggesting that service to God and service to Caesar were
incompatible. This typically Romantic bit of intellectual naughtiness took the
vox mei, vox Dei of the *Whig Review* toward anarchism. Having reinterpreted
this crucial passage on the issue of taxation, Thoreau could preach obedience
to God to the exclusion of obedience to Caesar, reversing the traditional interpretation. He could tell the abolitionists of Massachusetts that the Constitution was irrelevant; it was enough if they had God on their side: "any man
more right than his neighbors constitute[d] a majority of one already."[50]

Like the *Whig Review,* Seward responded to the radicalized Christianity of
abolitionism and transcendentalism, not by rejecting as inappropriate the
theological terms of the debate—as indeed he could have, and as a good son
of Paine and the Enlightenment like Senator John Pettit in fact did—but by
articulating a defense of gradualism on even more orthodox grounds. In addition to the notion of stewardship, Seward appealed to the Trinity. Unlike
George Bancroft, however, Seward gave the Trinity an activist spin by emphasizing the Second and Third Persons. Seward did not believe, as Thoreau appeared to, that one could abolish slavery "merely by sounding the trumpet
violently and proclaiming emancipation, while the institution [was] interwoven
with all [the South's] social and political interests, constitutions, and customs."
The existing state of society was of God, after all, and could not simply be disregarded. This would seem to result both in a conservative validation of the created

order and, in Trinitarian parlance, in replacement of the transcendentalist emphasis on the Holy Spirit with a Unitarian emphasis on the First Person and the created order reminiscent of the Enlightenment. Yet Seward ridiculed "our statesmen" who said that God permitted slavery and alone can end it. "As if the Supreme Creator, after giving us the instructions of His Providence and revelation for the illumination of our minds and consciences, did not leave us, in all human transactions, with due invocations of His Holy Spirit, to seek out His will and execute it for ourselves."[51]

Seward here voiced the kind of self-conscious theological positioning that characterized American cultural debate in the antebellum period. Like the Unitarian "Cotton" Whigs, who resisted antislavery appeals, Seward recognized the presumptive rationality of the existing order and the difficulties that must accompany any attempt at change. But, like the transcendentalists, he also accepted the revealed illumination of "conscience," which here he associated with the scriptural revelation of the Second Person. Rounding out the Trinity he added "due invocations of His Holy Spirit" as well. Seward's orthodox presentation of the Trinity was meant to defend a position that accepted the Constitutional protection of property in slaves where it already existed but that also insisted on the eventual end of slavery by constitutional means. He could synthesize Webster's conservatism with the enthusiasm of a Thoreau or even a John Brown by reconstructing a gradualist and prudential Trinitarian whole. While remaining loyal to the Constitution, he could nevertheless join his evangelical allies and Thoreau in opposing both the Fugitive Slave Act and the expansion of slave territory on the grounds of revealed truth and even on the grounds of a charismatic (potentially anarchic) invocation of the Holy Spirit. With the ideas of stewardship and the Holy Trinity, Seward gave overt moral and theological direction to the Constitution.

Though others, such as Thoreau, reached other conclusions, in the context of Romantic Protestant nationalism, Seward's "higher-law" speech was a brilliant effort. Viewed as a matter of political calculation on the other hand, the speech was a disaster. It was read as an endorsement of a Liberty Party–style position and helped give Seward an undeserved reputation for radicalism, a reputation that would not serve him well in the Republican nomination fight of 1860.[52] Though politically helpful to him in the short run, Seward's subtle position cannot be dismissed as mere political calculation. Rather, the episode reveals the striking theological thoughtfulness of the period as well as the degree to which the controversy over slavery forced a reevaluation of fundamental principles.

The master of political calculation in this matter was not Seward but Abraham Lincoln. In 1852 Lincoln took a very careful position in relation to Seward: "His supposed proclamation of a 'higher law' is the only specific charge I have seen for a long time. I never read the speech in which that proclamation is said to have been made; so that I cannot by its connection, judge of its import and purpose; and I therefore have only to say of it now, that in so far as it may attempt to foment a disobedience to the constitution, or to the constitutional laws of the country, it has my unqualified condemnation."[53]

Whether or not it was true that the successful lawyer had not read Seward's speech (and there is no reason to assume that it was not *technically* true), Lincoln said these words in the context of a general defense of Seward, and he was surely aware that Seward's speech did not countenance disobedience to the Constitution. Lincoln knew that his own position was almost identical to Seward's. And he went on to add that there were plenty of higher-law men in the Democratic Party as well. Of course in 1852 he could not have foreseen the Republican Convention of 1860, but, in the context of northwestern and, more specifically, Illinois politics, he had positioned himself most adroitly. As it turned out, Lincoln's careful positioning would make him more attractive than Seward to the lower North in 1860.

While Lincoln was more willing to comply in the return of fugitive slaves, when the political squeeze finally reached Illinois in 1854 he too began to see the issue of expanding slave territory as one between right and wrong for which, consequently, there could be no honorable compromises. Seward was more interested in compromise or diversion from the main moral issue in the winter of 1860–1861, but that only revealed that Lincoln was not only the better writer but the more consistent and cool-headed thinker as well. The differences between Seward and Lincoln were both subtle and short-lived. They shared a common vision that sustained a political and personal friendship until Lincoln's death. It takes nothing away from Lincoln to acknowledge that, on the most important points, Seward was out in front of him. Thus William Brock was right to restore Seward's "higher-law" speech to the place of honor it deserves, for it was not only a political position that the two men shared.[54] They agreed on the entire theologico-constitutional rationale for that position as well. Lincoln allowed Seward to help pen the great Fast Day and Thanksgiving Proclamations, a remarkably generous act from a man as conscious of the written word (and as gifted) as Lincoln.[55] And this was not because Lincoln was above such things as religious observances. Both Seward and Lincoln thought of America as a community of moral purpose. Theirs was what William Brock called a "moral nationalism," a Romantic Protestant nationalism that resisted unprincipled expansion and the Mexican War as contrary to that communal moral purpose.[56] Lincoln and Seward collaborated on the peroration of the First Inaugural, sentences that are today more often memorized than read carefully. The "mystic chords of memory" were not rhetorical icing on the more substantive cake of constitutional argument; rather, these words represented an appeal to historic community by two Romantic nationalists. As such, it was the last Whig attempt to avert civil war by appealing to a shared moral vision and a shared past.

MATERIALISM AND MORAL AUTONOMY

According to Gabor S. Boritt, the leading historian of Lincoln's economic thought, "Lincoln was possessed by the optimism of Western Civilization, reborn in the Renaissance, grown to maturity in the Enlightenment, and triumphant in nineteenth century America, which saw man as the master of his own destiny."[57] Leaving aside, for the moment, the fact that both Lincoln and the leading American historian during Lincoln's lifetime, George Bancroft, repeatedly claimed, in one way or another, that man was *not* the sole master of his destiny, it is hardly unusual that historians now see in the sweep of Western history a unidirectional progression toward the materialistic opportunity society of modern America. Most twentieth-century American historians shared this vision.[58] But at least two of the most important figures in mid-nineteenth-century American life, George Bancroft and Abraham Lincoln, did not write history in quite this way; neither would have claimed that "endless material progress" was "the heritage of Western Civilization."[59] And both would have mentioned nonmaterial aspirations they considered more important. Many of their contemporaries used the term "Christian Civilization" either to describe a reality or to characterize an ideal, and with that they sought not just to "cleanse" materialism and utilitarianism but also to redeem it. After the war, a Mark Twain or an Oliver Wendell Holmes, Jr., would see mostly hypocrisy in this prewar Romanticism, but, however deserving of derision, it pays to remember just what the pretensions were that the postwar cynics skewered in their now-familiar works.

Whether or not they were deluding themselves, Americans before the Civil War almost universally sought to make material advancement a means to something still higher. "This religious impulse fused in the minds of many Whigs with their desire for economic development to create a vision of national progress that would be both moral and material." For their part, Young Americans "expressed grave reservations about industrialization. They believed that the industrial revolution threatening to engulf the United States posed a grave danger to what they most valued in their country: widespread ownership of property; agrarianism and a dispersed population; and geographical and social mobility. To ward off the anticipated consequences of rapid modernization and to recreate an idealized Jeffersonian past, they sought to acquire new lands, to encourage agriculture, and to promote foreign trade."[60] For Bancroft, materialism belonged to the Enlightenment (and an emasculated Europe), and though doubtless a necessary stage in the progress of mankind this Enlightenment materialism was to be overcome as part of the providential scheme. In Bancroft's words, "the senseless strife between rationalism and supernaturalism will come to an end; an age of skepticism will not again be called an age of reason; and reason and religion will be found in accord."[61]

Bancroft projected his own democratic idealism onto the Enlightenment world of Jefferson and even onto the Puritans, just as later historians projected their democratic materialism onto the world of Bancroft and Lincoln. Thus, ironically, our teleological histories turn George Bancroft precisely on his head. We have simply replaced his Romantic idealist assumptions about the past with modernist materialistic assumptions of our own. For, however strongly Lincoln promoted material advancement, as a Romantic intellectual there were matters for him of greater importance.

In *Lincoln and the Economics of the American Dream,* Gabor Boritt reconstructed Lincoln's Whig economic vision, pointing out that economic opportunity was one of the unifying themes of Lincoln's public career from his first campaigns for a place in the Illinois legislature until his death. For Lincoln, government had a moral obligation to provide economic opportunity for the people, especially the poor. Accordingly, he stood for positive government intervention in the economy in the form of a national bank and various public works projects. In articulating this thesis, Boritt used "the American dream" or, simply, "the dream" as shorthand for a cluster of primarily economic values that recurred in the sayings and doings of Abraham Lincoln. Lincoln himself never used such terms, but that in itself is no critique. Boritt's economic dream was a powerful heuristic device. While Boritt pushed the interpretive limits of his thesis, he openly acknowledged the points where it seemed unable to account fully for Lincoln's words and actions. Even as Boritt pressed forward with his portrait of a very economics-minded Lincoln, he acknowledged that, in Lincoln's speeches, economics always remained subordinate to a moral vision. "Lincoln," he said, "found pure raw materialism unpalatable—however much he relied on it in his attempts to lead men. Life had to have deeper meaning." If Lincoln did not organize his own thoughts around the American dream, it may be of some interest to know what language he *did* use to put his economic as well as his political and moral thought into a larger perspective.[62]

Boritt's American dream essentially corresponded to what Richard Hofstadter more derisively called "the Self-Made Myth."[63] Whether one celebrates or derides it, both terms point to the way Lincoln consistently stood for the same relatively stable set of beliefs throughout his public life, including the belief in rising standards of living, endless material progress, social mobility, and each individual's opportunity to rise.[64] Lincoln also shared the labor theory of value common in the period, which, like the Marxists in Europe but unlike most American economic thinkers, led him to emphasize the rights of labor and to favor the use of strikes to protect the interests of workers.[65] While phrases like "rising standards of living" savor perhaps too much of the twentieth century—and, again, Lincoln did not use them—Boritt nevertheless found a consistent pattern of concern in Lincoln's early stand on the national bank, the tariff, internal improvements, public land policy, and, oddly enough, his antiexpansionism. Lincoln was also consistent in later presidential activities, such as military strategy, peacemaking efforts, and his plans for reconstruction. In each of these areas, Lincoln either sought to use public power to advance the opportunities of individuals, especially the poor, to have a fair chance in the "race of life" or made appeals to the economic interests of those whom he sought to persuade.[66] Boritt convincingly showed that for Lincoln social mobility, equal opportunity, and entrepreneurial market capitalism were normative ideals. "The key to this persuasion," said Boritt, "was an intense and continually developing commitment to the ideal that all men should receive a full, good, and ever-increasing reward for their labors so that they might have the opportunity to rise in life."[67]

But viewing Lincoln's thought through the lenses of a twentieth-century American dream is difficult to square with Lincoln's moralism. For example, the Democrats saw in the acquisition of Mexican territory a possible economic expansion. Lincoln, however, remained impervious to their economic arguments, and in the lectures on discoveries and inventions and elsewhere he chided them for their greed and materialism.[68] Even a casual reader of Lincoln has to be struck by the consistency with which every argument, however technical or legal or economic, took on a moral dimension as well.

Boritt managed this problem in two ways. First he noted that, for Lincoln, economics itself was a moral science or, rather, that Lincoln's economic arguments always included a self-consciously moral appeal. "Lincoln's assignment of a fundamental role to the labor theory makes crystal clear that the moralist in him 'never abdicated before the economist.'"[69] "In economic terms '*useless* labour' was the same as '*idleness,*' Lincoln explained. Thus, as always in his thinking, economics and ethics merged. . . ." Lincoln and Marx, Boritt suggested, were both attracted to the labor theory of value because it enabled them to give their economics a moral tone. Second, Boritt acknowledged that, at certain points in Lincoln's career, economic appeals seemed entirely to disappear in favor of an ethical appeal, as in the case of his opposition to Polk's war with Mexico, when Lincoln "subordinate[d] economic matters to his antiwar stand."[70]

To a certain extent, this latter way of viewing the matter undermined Boritt's effort to unify Lincoln's career on economic principles. The problem can perhaps best be seen in Boritt's attempt to bring Lincoln's antislavery convictions under the umbrella of the American dream. Here Boritt employed both of his strategies for reconciling Lincoln's moralism with the economic dream. First he pointed to the economic arguments Lincoln sometimes employed in making his antislavery appeal and argued that the antislavery appeal flowed naturally from an ethical economics.[71] For instance, Lincoln thought blacks ought to have the same right to rise in life and the same right to the fruits of their labor as anyone. To Lincoln, the slaveowners were "idlers," and the same labor-theory/work-ethic moral that permeated Lincoln's economic arguments could be and were applied especially to his criticisms of slavery. Slavery was indeed antithetical to the way of life that Lincoln and the Republicans endorsed.

The problem, however, is that there were others who shared Lincoln's belief in material progress, economic opportunity, and all the rest, but who were *not* antislavery. This applied especially to Stephen Douglas. Historians have missed this point in part because they have generally contrasted the Whigs and Republicans with the supposedly backward-looking and economically unsophisticated Jacksonians rather than with the forward-looking Young America of George Bancroft and Stephen Douglas: "Lincoln sensed, to borrow the words of Marvin Meyers, that the Whigs tended to speak to the 'explicit hopes of Americans' and the Jacksonians to their 'diffuse fears and resentments.'"[72] Thus, as long as it appeared that Lincoln's Democratic opponents were old fogies who opposed the new commercial economy and tried to preserve a quiet, premodern way of life, historians could treat forward-thinking entrepreneurial capitalism as inherently antislavery, reinforcing the notions of postwar southern apologists who wanted to see in the South and slavery a critique of modern industrial capitalism.

On the one hand, there were Whigs like the author of "The Progress and Disorganization," who sought to preserve a premodern way of life. By the 1850s, on the other hand, Young America had replaced the Jacksonians as Lincoln's chief ideological opponent.[73] Young America was unambiguously bullish on almost precisely the same economic vision that Lincoln consistently maintained, and yet Yound America was not antislavery. The internal improvements debate had died down by 1859 not just because the slavery issue overshadowed all else but also because Lincoln and Douglas agreed on the need for railroads and the like. Douglas introduced the Kansas-Nebraska Act in part to facilitate western development and the transcontinental railroad, the very same Nebraska bill that aroused Lincoln's indignation and fired the soul of the Republican Party.[75] Douglas was as much a self-made man as Lincoln, but from Lincoln's point of view it was Douglas, not Lincoln, who wanted Americans to put economic development (and political compromise) above morality.

In Lincoln's First Inaugural Address, he and Seward reiterated Seward's argument that for economic reasons North and South could not separate.[76] Nevertheless Lincoln's most important and consistent argument for Union was political, not economic: acquiescing to the demands of a minority that had no legitimate constitutional grievance would have destroyed the principle of majority rule on which popular government necessarily depended. And throughout the 1850s, it was Douglas who pressed the economic argument for Union in his southern strategy and in his Young America speeches.[77] Douglas there argued that civil war could be averted if slavery were treated as just another regional segment of a diverse American economy, an economy made strong by that diversity. For Douglas, the North and South formed an economic unit. Northern economic interest lay with tolerance for the institution of slavery. Lincoln conceded the point, and it was in the teeth of such economic arguments that Lincoln and the Republican Party made their appeal.[78] According to Lincoln, it was Douglas who said that "the question of negro slavery is simply a question of dollars and cents." Republicans by contrast treated slavery as "a moral, political and social wrong."[79] Lincoln's opponents used the economic arguments for Union to defend, not the Republican Party, but popular sovereignty and the Kansas-Nebraska Act.

The attempt of some historians to unify Lincoln's thought on the economic issues of the American dream stumbled over the fact that, even more than Lincoln, Douglas trumpeted the promises of an expanding economy and the American dream. It also took the apologists for slavery at face value and implicitly assumed that the institution of slavery was something other than market capitalism pushed to an absurd extreme. Supposedly, emancipation was "inherent" to the American dream.[80] Yet, for many upwardly mobile southerners, the American dream consisted of owning slaves and a plantation; for Douglas, one man's economic dream was as good as another's. It ought to be difficult for us to accept uncritically the idea that the South was a premarket society when it dedicated its economy to producing cotton for a world market and when certain human beings had become just another commodity on the block.[81] Far from sharing in any of George Fitzhugh's Romanticism about a paternalistic southern way of life, both Lincoln and Douglas saw it for what it was: market-driven exploitation.[82] They simply did not see the South as antimodern in an economic sense. Lincoln well knew that the institution of chattel slavery was of modern origins.[83] If Lincoln identified "the right to rise as the central idea of the United States," it is not immediately clear how that excluded the right to rise to the status of slaveowner.[84] Lincoln integrated both his economic convictions and his antislavery into a unified vision he maintained consistently throughout his career. But there was nothing anticapitalist about slavery, George Fitzhugh notwithstanding, and thus the sources of Lincoln's antislavery arguments are not to be found in his economic vision. Rather, his antislavery convictions and his economic thinking shared a more fundamental common source.

As Boritt pointed out, Lincoln even downplayed the appeal to northern economic interest in the free-soil cause because "he recognized that emphasizing materialistic self-interest weakened his high moral tone." "Lincoln's opposition to slavery was expressed in moral terms, and he raised the moral ingredient of politics perhaps to its highest level in the dominant stream of American politics. Under the all-important moral superstructure, however, he often buttressed his thought with economics—not surprising for one who had placed the good science at the heart of his efforts for more than two decades." Lincoln clearly addressed economic, legal, or political issues as they arose. Since many if not most of the issues that confronted him as a frontier legislator centered on economic development, economics necessarily occupied much of his time. "Of course improvements, for [Lincoln] and many others, were ultimately part of broad advancement that was 'material, moral, intellectual'—to quote his words from 1859. The material road was merely the means leading toward intellectual and moral elevation." Because he was "a politician in a state where economic battles were also the main political battles," economics was the central theme in much of Lincoln's early political life. "Antislavery was also there but was pushed far in the background with its triumph placed at a very distant day. After 1854 antislavery became Lincoln's immediate goal, and the economic policies that he continued to esteem highly and work for when possible were relegated to the background and to a future triumph."[85]

Phrases like "rising standards of living" or "endless material progress" have their roots and their meaning in the context of a twentieth-century economy in which large numbers of people worked their entire lives as employees. In 1861, Lincoln could still deny that a system of permanent wage labor even existed.[86] He explicitly rejected the Jeffersonian ideal of the independent yeoman farmer.[87] At the Wisconsin State Fair in 1859 he refused, as he said, "to employ the time assigned me in the mere flattery of the farmers, as a class. My opinion of them is that, in proportion to numbers, they are neither better nor worse than other people."[88] Lincoln's doubts that farmers were morally better than other people merely because they worked on the land should not overshadow the premodern ethical elements of Lincoln's economic thought. Though it had little to do with Jefferson, that each man should have a kind of "independence" was important for Lincoln and the Republicans; and this moral independence or autonomy, rather than the more modern-sounding American dream, is a better choice for naming and organizing Lincoln's economic views.

Lincoln's economic thought represented a middle term between the static world of Jefferson's imagination and what can be called "modern" economic relationships. For Lincoln, the opportunity to rise meant that "many independent men everywhere in these States, a few years back in their lives, were hired laborers."

> The prudent, penniless beginner in the world, labors for wages awhile, saves a surplus with which to buy tools or land for himself; then labors on his own account another while, and at length hires another new beginner to help him. This is the just, and generous, and prosperous system, which opens the way to all—gives hope to all, and consequent energy, and progress, and improvement of condition to all. No men living are more worthy to be trusted than those who toil up from poverty—none less inclined to take, or touch, aught which they have not honestly earned. Let them beware of surrendering a political power which they already possess, and which, if surrendered, will surely be used to close the door of advancement against such as they, and to fix new disabilities and burdens upon them, till all of liberty shall be lost.[89]

No less than Young Americans, who looked to expansion and slavery to prevent the rise of urban factory labor, Lincoln still thought in terms of economic independence. A rising standard of living in modern society usually refers to rising wages in real terms, yet Lincoln and the Republicans envisioned an economy in which every individual could become self-employed if he or even she so strove. Rising wages and, with that, more material wealth was not for them the goal of political economy. "The Common Sense philosophy was still the ruling one," wrote Joseph Dorfman. "Jeremy Bentham had his devotees in the United States, but his apparently exclusive emphasis on the pleasure-pain calculus, and the greatest happiness for the greatest number without reference to a theological sanction, unlike Paley, made him appear dangerous to college teachers."[90] As Daniel Walker Howe put it, "the Whigs justified not only the new technology but the system of industrial capitalism on the grounds of moral benefit to society. They never employed the argument later apologists for American business would sometimes use, that profitability itself is an indicator of social utility."[91] Thus, in the relentlessly systematic hands of an old fogy like Francis Wayland, political economy was still a branch of moral philosophy, which itself was ultimately subordinate to theology.[92] For young Romantics like Lincoln, Thoreau, and Emerson, the goal of political economy was something roughly analogous to moral autonomy, or what they called "independence." Though Lincoln was not sentimental about farming the way Jefferson was, he saw the self-made man not as a permanent wage earner but as a moral paragon by no means unrelated to Emerson's "Self-Reliance."[93]

Nevertheless, the shift from the Jeffersonian ideal to the independent self-made man of Lincoln's imagination was of historic importance. As Boritt noted, Lincoln's arguments in favor of a high protective tariff "took part of the tendency of protectionist thinking to move away from the politically oriented tariff policy of Hamilton and the generation that followed him, which had an air of apologia, a call to sacrifice, about it."[94] This phenomenon has been described as the decline of republican thinking and the rise of modern liberal social theory, a cultural shift that corresponded with an ongoing economic transformation from the mercantile and apprentice systems to a capitalist society and the wage-labor system. If James Madison, for example, could balance passion against passion and thereby reserve a place of power and authority for a "disinterested" elite, it was certainly no longer possible in the world of Jackson and Clay.[95] Even more than Henry Clay, Lincoln based his arguments on the welfare of individuals; he rarely if ever used the classical republican language of public virtue. For him, the concept of disinterestedness so crucial to republican thinking amounted to a theological absurdity.[96] (Lincoln extended a notion of original sin or natural depravity to everyone, including both "the people" and any pampered elite.) Thus Boritt was correct to point out that the vocabulary of classical republicanism and disinterested virtue were absent in Lincoln's writings.

In describing Lincoln's economic appeals, which sound forthright to our ears, Boritt stumbled over Lincoln's moralism and found himself forced to add that Lincoln's economic arguments "never overshadow[ed] his moral perception."[97] It did not follow that because Lincoln rejected republican language he could only have been the forthright Epicurean liberal (albeit one with a quirky moral streak) of Boritt's American dream—and this is of tremendous significance. Before the cult of scientific expertise rose in the late nineteenth century to replace it, Protestant categories again dominated the American imagination. This was true not just for evangelicals but for young Romantic intellectuals like Lincoln as well. While the Old Fogy rhetoric of inherited wealth and classical virtue seemed wooden and even petrified in a wide-open economy, Protestantism remained alive and well.[98] Not only did the Romantic, anti-Enlightenment tendencies of the time lend renewed intellectual respectability to religious thought—witness educated

Brahmins like Emerson and Bancroft—but the evangelical movement "manifested a resurgence of middle-class Protestant culture."[99] Protestantism had always remained a potent intellectual force outside of the elite cosmopolitan circles, even in Jefferson's day. Thus the election of Jackson that ended elite domination of the political debate contributed to the rise of a more overtly religious political discussion. As a self-educated intellectual from the bottom of border-state and then Illinois society, Lincoln was perfectly positioned to take part in these tendencies.

Whigs accepted the new social mobility. Nevertheless, they attempted to temper the spirit of unbridled acquisitiveness with appeals to what they imagined were the higher ends of man. Increasingly, they based that appeal on religious grounds. Lincoln's religious utterances reflected the Whig orientation. While "silk-stocking" elite leadership and the classical republican rhetoric of disinterested virtue were rapidly waning, a Protestant vision began to replace those more secular ideals in the three decades before the Civil War.[100] Lincoln received the overwhelming support of Protestant religious groups in 1860 and 1864. He was elected by skilled workers and professionals who felt they had the most to gain from the economic prosperity of market capitalism, by native-born farmers, and by voters of New England descent.[101] His rhetoric reflected his constituency perfectly: he combined the forward-thinking, prodevelopment, and positive-government Whiggery of Clay's American System with the moral concerns of New England and of the evangelical movement.

In the Wisconsin State Fair speech, Lincoln painted a vivid picture of what he meant by free labor. In it, he associated permanent wage labor with the "mud-sill" theory put forth by slavery apologists like George Fitzhugh. By the 1850s southerners had begun to defend slavery with a claim that the slave was better off than a factory worker because they were cared for in old age and because a slaveholder had an interest in caring for his property that the factory owner could not have.[102] Implicitly accepting the premise of the argument, Lincoln conceded that a permanent wage-labor system would be unacceptably oppressive. He therefore had to deny that such a system existed in the North at all. Lincoln's understanding of the northern economy reflected his own experience as a successful man who rose almost from the bottom of the social ladder; he believed in the right to rise. Lincoln professed great admiration for Clay, owing not only to the politically moderate antislavery views shared by both men and to the positive government impulse of Clay's American system but also to the ideals captured admirably in that star-fated coinage of Clay's, "the self-made man."[103]

But free labor for Lincoln was not permanent wage labor; it was neither the necessary drudgery of lower orders, as it was in classical republican thought, nor the somewhat unpleasant means to material acquisition, as it is in modern economic thought. Labor for Lincoln was a divine "charge" with its own ends. At the State Fair he encouraged farmers to adopt modern agricultural techniques of "thorough cultivation":

The effect of thorough cultivation upon the farmer's own mind, and in reaction through his mind, back upon his business, is perhaps quite equal to any other of its effects. Every man is proud of what he does *well;* and no man is proud of what he does *not* do well. With the former, his heart is in his work; and he will do twice as much of it with less fatigue. The latter performs a little imperfectly, looks at it in disgust, turns from it, and imagines himself exceedingly tired. The little he has done, comes to nothing, for want of finishing.[104]

Or again:

By the *"mud-sill"* theory it is assumed that labor and education are incompatible; and any practical combination of them impossible. According to that theory, a blind horse upon a tread-mill, is a perfect illustration of what a laborer should be—all the better for being blind, that he could not tread out of place, or kick understandingly. According to that theory, the education of laborers, is not only useless, but pernicious, and dangerous. In fact, it is, in some sort, deemed a misfortune that laborers should have heads at all. Those same heads are regarded as explosive materials, only to be safely kept in damp places, as far as possible from that peculiar sort of fire which ignites them. A Yankee who could invent a strong *handed* man without a head would receive the everlasting gratitude of the "mud-sill" advocates.

But Free Labor says "no!" Free Labor argues that, as the Author of man makes every individual with one head and one pair of hands, it was probably intended that heads and hands should cooperate as friends; and that that particular head, should direct and control that particular pair of hands. As each man has one mouth to be fed, and one pair of hands to furnish food, it was probably intended that that particular pair of hands should feed that particular mouth—that each head is the natural guardian, director, and protector of the hands and mouth inseparably connected with it; and that being so, every head should be cultivated, and improved, by whatever will add to its capacity for performing its charge. In one word Free Labor insists on universal education.[105]

Here Lincoln couched even his economic views in a larger theocentric moral argument about the meaning of human life and about our duties to God. His characteristic humor should not mask his seriousness of purpose. If, as some historians have suggested, the antislavery movement was in some way a moral smoke screen for the injustices of wage-labor capitalism, the same cannot be said for the antislavery convictions of Lincoln.[106] Lincoln thought the whole person should be engaged in the work; not just the hands and back but the whole person, mind, body, and "heart." Indeed, Lincoln extended the critique of slavery to the wage-labor system as well. In one of the only references we have that he made to the emerging northern factory system, Lincoln treated it as a perversion of God's design for humankind.

This is not to say that Lincoln was the captive of some dogmatic religious rule or that he blindly accepted some article or other of faith. In almost all areas Lincoln was a remarkably independent thinker who, even when he used the ideas of others, insisted on sharpening their formulations, passing them through his own filters. He had a sense of human experience and psychology that was simply too rich and subtle for the self-interest calculus of a Bentham or, for that matter, Bentham's neoclassical, "Chicago School" imitators. He was too much of a Romantic to accept material acquisition as a legitimate purpose in life. "The leading rule for the lawyer, as for the man, of every calling, is *diligence*," he said.[107] The term "calling" still implied service to God, and by invoking it Lincoln placed himself in a tradition of providential thought about the human condition. He tended to overwork himself not out of a desire for gain, or even to "get ahead," but rather out of a constant and pressing sense that his life had to have a higher meaning and that that meaning was to be found chiefly in what a less theological age would call his "career." He was well aware of his superior talents, and his ambition was to find a worthy outlet for them. Lincoln was subject to depression when he felt his career was faltering, and he knew whereof he spoke when he talked about doing the work well only when the heart was in it. Like Francis Wayland, Lincoln too quoted Genesis: "in the sweat of thy face, shalt thou eat thy bread." Unlike Wayland, he turned this argument against the slaveholders.[108] Permanent wage labor with a rising material standard of living was explicitly *not* a part of Lincoln's economic thought. Instead Lincoln stressed the right—indeed the divinely appointed duty—to labor in one's calling and to rise therewith to moral autonomy and economic independence.

Though there is some justice in the speculation that, had he survived, Lincoln would have sided with labor in the upheavals of the late nineteenth century, he did not see permanent wage labor as a reality, and he did not see those upheavals coming. Henry Carey was perhaps the chief economic theorist for the Whigs, and he therefore had great influence on Lincoln's economic thinking. Daniel Walker Howe has suggested that, had he lived, Lincoln may well have shared Henry Carey's deep disquiet over the economic developments of the postwar period. "The triumph of the northern bourgeoisie ushered in an era very different from anything Lincoln could have expected or wanted," Howe argued. "His objective, in the broadest sense, was to defend and extend the kind of free society he had known in Springfield. This was a society of small entrepreneurs, market-oriented farmers, young men working for others until they could save enough to set up for themselves, and striving professionals like himself."[109]

Just as Carey was "horrified when he saw the new economy," "Lincoln, too, would have been grieved by its oppression and its sordid materialism."[110] In Old Fogy fashion, Carey was more reluctant than Lincoln to join in the purely antislavery Republican Party, but eventually he came around. Lincoln and Carey shared similar economic ideals, and since a Romantic outlook generally led to heightened moral sensitivity, Howe is probably correct: we should be careful not to make Lincoln the champion of modern economic relationships.

On the other hand, Phillip S. Paludan has warned us that we should know Lincoln "as a man of his age, not as a man too good for it."[111] When southern apologists, most notably George Fitzhugh, attacked the northern free-labor system by citing abuses like child labor and long factory hours that led to a life of harsh subsistence, Lincoln reacted as defensively to these attacks as Douglas had to aspersions cast on the ethics of American expansion.[112] "Republican politicians and abolitionists were stung by this critique, and as Lincoln's partner William Herndon recalled, 'Sociology for the South aroused the ire of Mr. Lincoln more than most pro-slavery books.'"[113] Even while Lincoln actively worked to increase opportunities for men like himself to rise, he was also led, somewhat inconsistently, to mistake his free-labor ideals for the realities of antebellum life. In this limited way, slavery may have blinded Lincoln to the emerging problems of industrialization that, as Paludan pointed out, others of Lincoln's time saw more clearly. Dickens, Hawthorne, Melville, Thoreau, and Emerson all had reservations about the direction economic development was taking. Lincoln, in the act of mustering northern self-confidence for the antislavery battle, took little note of such nay-sayings. And Lincoln's belief in the reality of social mobility was not without its harsh side. Perhaps he was at his worst in his dealings with his own family, people who from Lincoln's point of view failed to pursue greater personal economic success and who he may therefore have felt justified in leaving behind.[114] It seems that hubris, Lincoln's pride in having come up from the bottom on his own, at least partially blinded him to the fact of his extreme good fortune.

Still, Lincoln worked to make economic opportunity a reality for the straggling and struggling. Lincoln and the Whigs advocated positive government action to make the free labor system equitable and thus cannot be considered heralds of unregulated capitalist exploitation. Because the slavery issue necessarily distracted his entire generation from economic issues that otherwise might have absorbed more of their attention, it does not follow that antislavery was a smoke screen for northern industrial development. "As industrialization entered a stage with which Lincoln had little first-hand familiarity, as factories and increasingly mechanized farms came to dominate the land, new opportunities opened up," Gabor Boritt noted. "Lincoln's understanding of this coming change was very restricted, but it permitted him to maintain his support of economic development unwaveringly."[115]

Lincoln was able to support economic development unwaveringly because his experience and understanding were very restricted, and this lapse in his discernment seemed so glaring in the Progressive era that a spurious Lincoln quotation appeared to fill the gap: "As a result of the war, corporations have become enthroned, and an era of corruption in high places will follow. The money power of the country will endeavor to prolong its rule. . . ."[116] Boritt pointed out that, as Lincoln worked to bring the giant railroad corporations into being, he seemed to have had a "totally innocent lack of foreboding" regarding large-scale capitalist enterprise.[117] The large corporations would soon transform his world of small independent entrepreneurs into a Gilded Age of big labor and big capital. Though the Civil War separates the Romantic antebellum period from the harsh scientism, social Darwinism, and literary realism of the Gilded Age, Lincoln prosecuted the war to preserve that older world of moral and economic independence. As Eric Foner put it, "The foundations of the industrial capitalist state of the late nineteenth century, so similar in individualist rhetoric yet so different in social reality from Lincoln's America, were to a large extent laid during the Civil War. Here, indeed, is the tragic irony of that conflict. Each side fought to defend a distinct vision of the good society, but each vision was destroyed by the very struggle to preserve it."[118]

Because Lincoln and his generation did not have modern American life in mind when they unwittingly set its big industrial wheels in motion, it is inappropriate to read them as cheerleaders of the American way of life as it came to be. But it is especially disturbing in view of Lincoln's Second Inaugural Address. Lincoln in particular almost always maintained a critical, even prophetic, stance toward the society he knew. In 1859, when he necessarily had to make the strongest case he could for the northern way of life and its free-labor economy, Lincoln came the closest he ever would to claiming God's particular favor for American institutions.[119] Even then he was able to discriminate between the free labor he celebrated and the existing New England factory system. Like English Romantics such as Thomas Carlyle and William Blake, Lincoln could echo the prophetic question: "was Jerusalem builded here, amid these dark satanic mills?" By the time Lincoln wrote his Second Inaugural, he denied outright that God's purposes could be equated with our own. It is fair to say that Americans have lost much in the way of theological discernment and sophistication in the last century and a half. However foolishly, Bancroft could dream that "the husbandman or mechanic of a Christian congregation solves questions respecting God and man and man's destiny, which perplexed the most gifted philosophers of ancient Greece."[120] Rather than the repository of his deepest gut-level ruminations, Lincoln's religious vocabulary might sound to modern ears as the sign of a soft head.

For a brief period, the Romantic held sway in American public discourse. Along with Whig economic thinkers like Henry C. Carey, Lincoln rejected the constraints of an old apprenticeship economy that doomed individuals to the trades and callings of their parents and that favored deference to hereditary elites. But Lincoln also rejected an economics that made money and material the measure of all things. This was the forward-thinking Whig message, and abolitionists and temperance advocates joined the Whigs in their admiration of entrepreneurship.[121] Romantics tended to look to the religious thought of the past for inspiration, and since for many the American past was, roughly speaking, Calvinist and even Puritan, American Romantics returned to Reformed understandings of the human condition, reactivated and revitalized them and, inevitably, adapted them to their own purposes.

The religious feeling of the period lends the Civil War its particular flavor. As much as any other factor, this pathos probably helps explain the war's enduring appeal to readers of history.[122] Thus, to recover the full colors even of Lincoln's economic thinking means explaining the religious dimension of Whig and Republican thought as well. Though their overall economic outlook differed greatly from that of their Puritan forbears, Lincoln and his generation reactivated the idea of a "calling" and adapted it to the socially mobile economy that existed just before the rise of mass industrialization. In the twentieth century, even the left generally accepted the materialism generally associated with capitalism. Thus, somewhat ironically, Lincoln and the Whigs submitted their economic system to an ethical critique rather more stringent than has been applied since. They made moral independence the goal of political economy, and moral independence must therefore replace the idea of the American dream in our understanding of the period. In this narrow window of American history, it was possible to justify market capitalism on the grounds of higher human aspirations.

Chapter Five

THE TRAGEDY OF THE
WHIG RESPONSE

• The Whig response to Jacksonian libertarianism was threefold. First, Whigs denied that self-interest was equivalent to moral right transcendentally defined, which led to an aversion to utilitarianism and to an emphasis on genteel, noneconomic endeavors like poetry, religion, and music. In younger and more Romantic Whigs this tendency was especially pronounced. They apologized for capitalist development by conceiving of it as a means to higher ends. Second, Whigs insisted that the people might not always be the best arbiters of self-interest or morality; the electorate could be and therefore had to be educated. The statesman was to educate the electorate by making the best case for what was right, even at the risk of failing to be elected. Third, since (as the rise of the slave power attested) real progress was not automatic, positive moral legislation remained necessary to promote that progress—even in America. The doctrines of laissez-faire and free trade amounted to little more than an abdication of moral responsibility. Each of these three responses permeated Whig thought and not surprisingly, therefore, Lincoln's response to Stephen Douglas as well.

More specifically, northern Whiggery provided Lincoln with a thoroughly articulated Protestant nationalism. Northern Whigs tended to reject classically republican notions, such as disinterested virtue and the authority of a propertied elite, in favor of individual opportunity, a capitalist economy, democratic government, and scientific progress. They were eclectic, but based on a Reformed tradition of language and symbolism they rejected the apotheosis of individual desire. Instead they insisted on making substantive moral claims about what a "civilized" and "Christian" nation should look like. They conceived of the economy, not as a morally neutral marketplace and an opportunity for individuals to get wealthy, but as a mechanism that needed to be fine-tuned so that individual self-striving became consonant with the common good. Finally, they perceived of the individual, not as a producer and consumer merely, but as an eternal soul.[1] Individuals therefore had both a right and a duty to develop their faculties in service to themselves, to others, and to God. When he came out against Douglas's radically liberal apology for the Kansas-Nebraska Act, Lincoln spoke with the Yankee accents of northern Whiggery in spite of his Kentucky drawl.

Whigs sought to eke out a place for leadership in a democracy by appealing to higher laws, standards, or values that they hoped a majority in a democracy might share. Obviously their effort would fail on the question of slavery. In the meantime, however, it was only natural in an overwhelmingly Protestant nation that some Whigs would turn to that particular religious heritage as a source of spiritual cohesion. Before the Mexican War exacerbated America's sectional troubles, the Whig appeal to a shared vision might have seemed possible, but with the triumph of Young America and the Mexican cession came a dispute between North and South over the spoils of conquest that laid bare a fundamental difference over the extension of—and ultimately the right or wrong of—slavery. Ironically, the prophetic strain within Protestantism, rather than fortifying the forces of cohesion as planned, exacerbated centrifugal tendencies and helped tear the country apart.

It is worth repeating the fact that the major Protestant denominations split before the political parties did, and only then did the nation divide. Perhaps even more quixotic than Douglas's attempt to make expansionism a bisectional cause was the Whig attempt to foster agreement North and South about "Eternal Justice." In retrospect it seems inevitable that neither the Whig Party nor the *Whig Review* would survive. No agreement on the principles of earthly, let alone eternal, justice was possible between those who came to convince themselves that slavery was the antidote to an excessively materialistic northern factory system and those who saw the plantation system itself as an especially brutal cotton factory. In an era when "utilitarian" was a term of derision, North and South would each accuse the other of lacking any higher spiritual calling. As a former Whig, Lincoln was prepared for the task of shaping public opinion, an act that embodied the Whig definition of statesmanship. With the death of Henry Clay and his generation came an end to the openly antislavery southern politician. When it became obvious that the Whig Party could not be revived, Northern former Whigs could move toward a more openly antislavery position and Lincoln could help shape northern public opinion to his own antislavery beliefs.

A WHIG LINCOLN CONFRONTS DOUGLAS

In a now famous speech at Peoria in 1854, Lincoln returned to active political life after a four-year hiatus with words that directly challenged Douglas's Kansas-Nebraska Act. In what appears to have been a period of self-searching after a disappointing term in Congress, Lincoln had written his "Fragment on Niagara Falls," and for four years he had concentrated on his legal career (and Euclid) when Douglas's Nebraska Bill unexpectedly provided an outlet for his Romantic and heroic ambition. If American intellectuals were to read but one Lincoln speech, this should probably be the one.

At Peoria, Lincoln articulated his objections to Douglas's doctrine of popular sovereignty, and in the essentials his position remained unchanged for the rest of his life. The speech not only defined him politically, it came to be the expression of a northern majority opinion and the law of the land. Lincoln articulated his objections to the Nebraska Act and the doctrine of popular sovereignty that Douglas used to justify it, but he also argued that slavery itself was the heart of the difficulty. In one of those carefully crafted little nuggets that invite close attention, Lincoln summed up his case.

> This *declared* indifference, but as I must think, covert *real zeal* for the spread of slavery, I can not but hate. I hate it because of the monstrous injustice of slavery itself. I hate it because it deprives our republican example of its just influence in the world—enables the enemies of free institutions, with plausibility, to taunt us as hypocrites—causes the real friends of freedom to doubt our sincerity, and especially because it forces so many really good men amongst ourselves into an open war with the very fundamental principles of civil liberty—criticizing the Declaration of Independence, and insisting that there is no right principle of action but *self-interest*.[2]

Behind this passage lay twenty years of debate, not only between Lincoln and Douglas personally but between Whigs and Democrats more generally. Thus the language was distilled and concise. If construed as a reference to Douglas's personal intentions, the accusation of real zeal for the spread of slavery was probably excessive. Nevertheless, Lincoln knew his man. Douglas claimed that whether one held slaves was a matter of personal preference and state's rights, a matter of local interest only. Lincoln perceived that Douglas's "don't care" doctrine of popular sovereignty represented the collapse of American liberalism into amorality.[3] Lincoln also knew his own Whig lines. The broad perspective was typically Whig; the Democrats were defensively patriotic and openly contemptuous of world opinion, especially British opinion. Whiggish too was the willingness to engage in national self-criticism. While Douglas identified with the self-government strand in Jefferson and restricted the scope of the phrase "all men are created equal" to white men only, Lincoln would have none of it: "Near eighty years ago we began by declaring that all men are created equal; but now from that beginning we have run down to the other declaration, that for SOME men to enslave OTHERS is a 'sacred right of self-government.'"[4] Paradoxically, then, Lincoln identified with the Declaration of Independence as a statement of moral principle and equality but *not* as the radically liberal, eudaemonistic, and potentially libertarian document it in fact was.

Most striking, however, was the last reason Lincoln gave for his hatred of slavery: the peculiar institution taught that there was "no right principle of action but *self-interest*." It was not even the practical matter of human suffering that troubled him most. The sentimentalized—indeed Christlike—portraits of Lincoln should not blunt the hard edges of his words and deeds. What bothered him most was a theoretical point, a "prospective principle," and in this he was quite unlike Jefferson, for whom ideas played no such central role. Lincoln was most troubled by the idea that the fundamental principles of civil liberty might be reduced to self-interest, which led him to make a startling connection. He suggested that slavery (rather than, for instance, northern industrialism) had helped to foster a radically liberal and utilitarian political theory. Slavery was the logical extension of what could be called the eudaemonism of the Enlightenment, the belief that human happiness is the measure of all things. In Lincoln's language, it amounted to the worship of "mammon." A liberal theory that denied any higher moral law beyond individual desire and self-interest was powerless in the face of slavery. In a universe bleached of any moral possibility one could hardly object to a slaveholder maximizing his own utility, his own happiness. But, said Lincoln, doing so involved a rejection of the moral principle of equality: "In our greedy chase to make profit of the negro, let us beware, lest we 'cancel and tear to pieces' even the white man's charter of freedom."[5] For Democrats to be consistent, Lincoln was saying, they would have to join Senator John Pettit in claiming that the phrase "all men are created equal" was a self-evident lie, thus canceling the Declaration of Independence.

In the Peoria Speech, Lincoln revealed himself to be a cultural historian of considerable insight, for there was, in fact, an intimate connection between the institution of slavery and the self-interest-based theories of limited government that characterized the Democratic Party. Herbert J. Storing described a tendency within Jefferson's thought itself that connected the defense of the institution of slavery with liberal political theory, which allowed "for justice to be reduced to self-preservation, for self-preservation to be defined as self-interest, and for self-interest to be defined as what is convenient and achievable." In this way, "the slave owner may resolve that it is necessary to keep his slaves in bondage for the compelling reason that if they were free they would kill him," and so slavery, "in this ironic and terrible sense, can be seen as a radicalization of the principle of individual liberty on which the American polity was founded."[6] Storing essentially echoed Lincoln when he noted a connection between Jefferson's belief in limited government and slavery. The desire to reassure the South and defend slaveholders led many, especially in the Democratic Party, to adopt an antigovernment, laissez-faire position. Thus, slavery contributed to the exceptionalist tendencies that have characterized American political theory ever since.[7]

The Jeffersonian legacy was itself ambiguous. At times Jefferson pushed the idea that less government was necessarily better; at other times he supported such improvements as the Cumberland road.[8] At the expense of its plausible positive government and egalitarian animus, southern apologists for slavery and their northern Democratic allies drew upon and reinforced the libertarian potential of Jefferson's thought. Another historian noted that the internal improvements proposals of President John Quincy Adams found a harsh reception from some leading southerners, because "some states' rights radicals like Nathaniel Macon and John Randolph had been warning that power to build roads suggested power to free slaves, as if the purpose of internal improvement was tyranny followed by emancipation."[9] And Michael F. Holt has suggested that, in Andrew Jackson's first term, southerners were attracted to strict construction and limitations on the powers of the national government because they were determined to protect the institution of slavery. Jackson's own strict-constructionist line against internal improvements was at least in part an effort to shore up southern support.[10]

Moving still closer to Lincoln and Douglas, the founding issue of the *Democratic Review* (1837) also made the connection between its own libertarianism and the Democratic Party's southern wing, when it equated those "desirous of the emancipation of the Negro race" and those "desirous of the emancipation of credit" and concluded that "the duty of the General Government, of non-intervention, dictated by the States-Rights principle, is equally clear and imperative in both cases."[11] In their constant efforts to prevent a southern defection to the Calhounites, Democrats like Jackson, Martin Van Buren, and later Stephen Douglas were each led to adopt radically antigovernment positions on a whole range of issues from internal improvements and the national bank to federal power in the territories. And to do this they were willing to rely on ever more tortured constitutional interpretations that denied federal power even when those interpretations ran afoul of fairly clear language, precedent, practice, and intent. This rendered the liberal, postbellum apologies for the Confederacy feckless; from the very beginning, libertarian political thought was little more than a moral smoke screen for slaveholding.

Lincoln had spent a good part of his life frustrated by Douglas's penchant for clothing what were essentially arguments of convenience in the robes of high moral principle. Like most Whigs, Lincoln had spent a good part of his life frustrated with a government unable to address the needs of citizens because it hobbled itself with what he regarded as spurious libertarian doctrines. Thus Lincoln's antislavery convictions were in part a continuation of his Whig belief in moral government. Though at this point in time he had no intention of pushing for emancipation, he joined in the antislavery crusade not only because he saw in popular sovereignty the threat that slavery would become national but also because he feared that this liberal doctrine would eliminate the possibility for Whig positive moral government. Beyond Lincoln's specific economic views, what connected the Whig Lincoln with the Republican Lincoln and with Lincoln the Emancipator was his fear that, in American democracy, self-interest would displace any more substantive moral vision.[12]

Lincoln devoted most of this speech to fears of slavery's expansion and to a historical disquisition on the antislavery meaning of American history. In "Fragments on Government," Lincoln took up and rejected the tradition that emphasized libertarian possibilities in Jefferson. For unknown reasons, John Nicolay and John Hay dated these fragments just before the speech at Peoria, but they may not have come from precisely that time. The motto of the *Democratic Review* was from Jefferson: "that government governs best, which governs least." Democrats routinely construed this to mean that less government was better simply because it was less, which accorded with their view of liberty as the absence of constraint. On this view, government could not conceivably be construed as a positive source of liberty, but only as a negative restriction on private freedom. What the sage of Monticello had in mind was that in a well-governed country—like America of course—less government was necessary. Because there was little arbitrary rule or oppression, authority was respected; and vigilence patrols for unruly slaves notwithstanding, there was little need for the constant policing that characterized French society under Louis XVI. Thus, Jefferson had not necessarily intended to say that less government was *always* better, though his remarks were open to that interpretation. For their part, Whigs claimed that they were the true heirs of Jefferson. However one evaluates Jefferson's flirtations with libertarian radicalism, the Whigs claimed Jefferson even while they believed in positive moral government. They had to defend Clay's American System of public works against a quasi-libertarian Democratic opposition; and to do this they first had to establish a place for positive government in the American mind.

It was all but inevitable, then, that Lincoln would see popular sovereignty as yet another libertarian argument, this time for the perpetuation of slavery. In response, he not only argued that it was perverse to defend arbitrary rule over slaves on the grounds of limited government, but in the "Fragments on Government" he attempted to amend (or replace) the Jeffersonian epigram with one of his own devising, one that would be free of libertarian implications.

> The legitimate object of government, is to do for a community of people, whatever they need to have done, but can not do, *at all*, or can not, *so well do*, for themselves—in their separate, and individual capacities.
>
> In all that the people can individually do as well for themselves government ought not to interfere.
>
> The desirable things which the individuals of a people can not do, or can not well do, for themselves, fall into two classes: those which have relation to *wrongs*, and those which have not. Each of these branch off into an infinite variety of subdivisions.
>
> The first—that in relation to wrongs—embraces all crimes, misdemeanors, and not-performance of contracts. The other embraces all which, in its nature, and without wrong, requires combined action, as public roads and highways, pubic schools, charities, pauperism, orphanage, estates of the deceased, and the machinery of government itself.
>
> From this it appears that if all men were just, there still would be *some*, though not *so much* need of government.

In another draft Lincoln added that "the best framed and best administered governments are necessarily expensive" and that many of the legitimate objects of government existed "independently of the injustice in the world." Even if all men *were* angels, Lincoln suggested, government would still be necessary.[13]

Lincoln knew only too well that the libertarian defense of slavery had debilitated the government: a libertarian critique of slavery would surely come back to haunt him. Thus the Peoria speech shows Lincoln the Whig becoming Lincoln the Republican. Lincoln was anything but a one-issue thinker; he looked beyond the slavery question to things like homesteads, land-grant colleges, and uniform currency. He wanted to use government to create opportunities for hardscrabble people like himself. He therefore sought to clarify, if only for himself, just where he thought legitimate government resided, rejecting the Democratic Party's version of Jefferson and injecting his own Whig version into the new Republican persuasion. This gave Lincoln's antislavery appeal a tone entirely different from the way it might have sounded if had he been a former Democrat. It opened up a world of moral and religious rhetoric that made his appeal much more powerful.[14]

But there was a catch. "In reworking the founding synthesis, Lincoln had to engage his moral absolutism in dialogue with the founders' inherently more relativistic concept of union."[15] Lincoln reconciled his transcendent morality with liberal politics in two ways. First, he insisted that morality be a legitimate interest among the other contending interests in the political game, thus politicizing the sacred. Moral principles could be legislated as legitimately as any other "interest," Lincoln argued:

> Have we no interest in the free Territories of the United States—that they should be kept open for the homes of free white people? As our Northern States are growing more and more in wealth and population we are continually in want of an outlet, through which it may pass out to enrich our country. In this we have an interest—a deep and abiding interest. There is another thing, and that is the mature knowledge we have—the greatest interest of all. It is the doctrine, that the people are to be driven from the maxims of our free Government, that despises the spirit which for eighty years has celebrated the anniversary of our national independence.[16]

The appeal to northern interest in free territory was part of what Foner called the "free-soil" ideology, and Lincoln certainly made no effort to disguise the appeal here.[17] But to the free-soil appeal he added that preserving "the maxims of our free Government" constituted an even greater political "interest." Elsewhere Lincoln was careful not to reduce morality to self-interest: "Will springs from the two elements of moral sense and self-interest."[18] Because of his lifelong battle with Douglas and the Democrats, Lincoln was conscious of the theoretical difference between them. Douglas claimed that his doctrine of popular sovereignty would lead to the same free-soil result as Lincoln's more overt free-soil position, but Lincoln reiterated and reemphasized that it was the *wrong* of slavery and not just northern self-interest on which he based his case.[19] Lincoln self-consciously sought to make room for moral reasoning in democratic politics. He claimed that the extension of slavery into the territories was not strictly the business of the Nebraskans. Slavery violated the fundamental principles of free government in which everyone had an interest. Moral concerns were as legitimate in politics as self-interest, Lincoln contended—even more legitimate. Moral sentiments were politically relevant.

Second, Lincoln enshrined the Constitution and more especially the Declaration of Independence as religious creed, thus exalting politics and (from Douglas's point of view) blurring the distinction between church and state. He was not a theocrat; he did not even consider a Cromwell-style protectorate, and he would have ample opportunities to behave more like Oliver Cromwell. During the Civil War, Lincoln resisted pleas from Illinois governor Richard Yates to use federal troops to pressure the Democratically controlled Illinois legislature.[20] Instead, Lincoln stood for reelection in the midst of the Civil War at a time when all his hopes for American democracy and even for mankind depended upon the outcome. He willingly acquiesced to democratic process, but he never held that the people or the process were infallible. On the contrary, it was not the process but the *maxims* of free government that had a sacred character. This resembled the free-church world of his early life, in which the confession of faith provided the basis of institutional loyalty. "His solution was to elevate the Union itself to a higher moral plane."[21] For Lincoln, the Union was valuable only insofar as it promoted higher moral principle.

> Our republican robe is soiled, and trailed in the dust. Let us repurify it. Let us turn and wash it white, in the spirit, if not the blood, of the Revolution. Let us turn slavery from its claims of "moral right," back upon its existing legal rights, and its arguments of "necessity." Let us return it to the position our fathers gave it; and there let it rest in peace. Let us re-adopt the Declaration of Independence, and with it, the practices, and policy, which harmonize with it. Let north and south—let all Americans—let all lovers of liberty everywhere—join in the great and good work. If we do this, we shall not only have saved the Union; but we shall have so saved it, as to make, and to keep it, forever worthy of the saving. We shall have so saved it, that the succeeding millions of free happy people, the world over, shall rise up, and call us blessed, to the latest generations.[22]

In this familiar quote from the same 1854 speech in Peoria, Lincoln cloaked American republicanism in sacred vestments and read American history as part of sacred history, as nearly everyone did in the antebellum period. For Lincoln—and for the political antislavery movement generally—the Constitution was an *antislavery* document: it protected slavery where it already existed, but it also left it doomed to its "ultimate extinction." Slavery was contrary to the principles of the Declaration and was admitted into the Constitution only where it already existed and only as a necessity. The "ultimate extinction" doctrine that Lincoln shared with the political antislavery movement allowed him to reconcile his reverence for a founding that included slavery with his abhorrence of slavery itself. Thus, in two distinct but tightly interwoven ways, by politicizing religious concerns and by sacralizing American politics, Lincoln, along with others of his generation, brought theology back into the political debate.

Implicit in Lincoln's "ultimate extinction" was a Romantic conception of history and of progress. Scholars have generally credited Lincoln with a reinterpretation of Jefferson's Declaration that transformed the phrase "all men are created equal" from a description of natural fact into a statement of moral purpose.[23] Because he saw equality as a matter of *rights*, Lincoln could avoid arguing that equality was a natural *fact*. He therefore did not have to trouble himself with a scientific racism that treated as an empirical question what the Declaration of Independence seemed to proclaim as an almost a priori truth. Of the black woman he said, "in some respects she is not my equal; but in her natural right to eat the bread she earns with her own hands without asking leave of anyone else, she is my equal, and the equal of all others."[24] Lincoln thus Romanticized Jefferson by construing the "self-evident truth" of equality, not as empirically obvious natural fact of the Common Sense philosophy, but as a moral maxim.

In addition, the power and importance he gave to ideas ran counter to the tenor of Jefferson's writings and belies much of what has been taught about the practical, nonideological character of American thought and life.

> Our government rests in public opinion. Whoever can change public opinion, can change the government, practically just so much. Public opinion, on any subject, always has a *"central idea,"* from which all its minor thoughts radiate. That "central idea" in our political public opinion, at the beginning was, and until recently has continued to be, "the equality of men." And although it was always submitted patiently to whatever of inequality there seemed to be as matter of actual necessity, its constant working has been a steady progress towards the practical equality of all men. The late Presidential election was a struggle, by one party, to discard that central idea, and to substitute for it the opposite idea that slavery is right, in the abstract, the workings of which, as a central idea, may be the perpetuity of human slavery, and its extension to all countries and colors.[25]

The notion that public opinion was derivative of some "central idea" was intellectualist in the extreme. As it had for the Whigs, American political life for Lincoln revolved around a credo. But, after reading the Declaration of Independence as a statement of moral purpose, it remained for Lincoln to reconcile abstract right with a messy historical reality. He did this by moving the Declaration from the beginning to the end of American history, making it the goal of the American endeavor. While the Enlightenment was characterized by a static view of human nature, Lincoln relied on the dynamic Romantic view of progress; over time, progress would reconcile right with reality, a view of history shared by Romantic Democrats. Like George Bancroft, Lincoln relied on a belief in progress, if not quite for a theodicy, then at least for a way to justify his patient (and, to immediate abolitionists, complaisant) attitude toward the evil of slavery.

Unlike Bancroft, who made America itself the telos, or goal, of all history, Lincoln made the now transcendental principles of the Declaration his moral lodestar. Unlike Bancroft, Lincoln questioned the inevitability of progress. Lincoln feared that, after Douglas had taught the public not to care, slavery would spread nationwide. At this point he decided to draw his line. If northerners accepted the southern definition of slaves as personal property like any other, then by the rules of comity that property would remain property in the free states and would enjoy the legal protection of property. This was the other half of Lincoln's "House Divided" position. If northern public opinion came to share Douglas's indifference to the institution of slavery, then the house would become "all slave" rather than "all free." The mere "formality" of another *Dred Scott* decision, said Lincoln, would make slavery lawful in all the states.[26] He was not merely protecting a northern, free-soil way of life—though he was doing that also. Much more, it was the meaning of America that was at stake. The trigger for Lincoln's uncompromising attitude, the point at which he could no longer agree to compromise, was not, as it was for Douglas, a physical line across the continent dividing slave from free soil.

Lincoln drew his line, not in the sand, but in the realm of ideas.

> I am not a Know-Nothing. That is certain. How could I be? How can any one who abhors the oppression of negroes, be in favor of degrading classes of white people? Our progress in degeneracy appears to me to be pretty rapid. As a nation, we began by declaring that *"all men are created equal."* We now practically read it "all men are created equal, *except negroes.*" When the Know-Nothings get control, it will read "all men are created equal, except negroes, *and foreigners, and catholics.*" When it comes to this I should prefer emigrating to some country where they make no pretence of loving liberty—to Russia, for instance, where despotism can be taken pure, and without the base alloy of hypocracy.[27]

In his own form of Romantic nationalism, Lincoln bound the idea of America to a higher purpose, equality of rights—and even equality of conditions—for "all men everywhere." If America became the instrument of the extension and perpetuation of slavery, then Lincoln was no longer interested in being American.

In the winter of 1860–1861, as southern states began to secede from the Union, Lincoln was no longer willing, as he had been as late as Peoria in 1854, to compromise on the issue of slavery's expansion.[28] "There is, in my judgment," he said, "but one compromise which would really settle the slavery question, and that would be a prohibition against acquiring any more territory."[29] This helps explain why Lincoln took the trouble to assail Douglas's belief in manifest destiny in his lectures on discoveries and inventions. Douglas wanted the nation to expand southward to make room both for free-soilers from the North and for plantation owners from the South, and had Lincoln's sole concern been the free-soil interests of northerners he would have been more willing to engage Douglas's manifest destiny solution to the problem of slavery on the continent. But Lincoln thought that any compromise on slavery's extension, "either the Missouri line extended, or Douglas' and Eli Thayer's Pop. Sov. would lose us every thing we gained by the election; that filibustering for all South of us, and making slave states of it, would follow in spite of us, under either plan."[30] As it had in the wake of the Mexican War, slavery would again follow the flag, thus defiling it. Again, it was Douglas who appealed chiefly, if not exclusively, to northern self-interest. Between the debates and his inauguration Lincoln repeatedly expressed anxiety that the nation might expand southward, making formerly free territory a home for slavery, subverting the very meaning of America in his imagination.

Lincoln's "House Divided" position also revealed his deep hostility to Douglas's self-interest-based liberal theory. If public sentiment were "debauched" to the point where it would acquiesce in the perpetuation of a wrong like slavery, then there was no hope for a moral outcome in an otherwise amoral political process, and the "spirit of the age" could not be a reliable guide to transcendent right, or the will of God.[31] Similarly, if individuals could learn, it could not be said that they were always the best arbiters of their own interests. What would they have to learn? It was perfectly obvious to Lincoln that people *did* learn. Men like Douglas had been teaching the public mind not to care about slavery and that it was an indifferent thing; public sentiment regarding slavery had degenerated with the potentially disastrous effect of perpetuating and extending slavery. Consistent with the general Whig didactic program of Victorian respectability, Whigs like Lincoln sought to educate the electorate and to counter the inroads of Democratic Party amorality by keeping moral concerns before the public. At this point the frontier "rail-splitter" image of Lincoln becomes positively misleading, for if there was something of Huck Finn in Lincoln, there was good bit of Aunt Polly as well.[32] Whigs had counseled temperance, the rule of law, literacy, and respect for learning and for traditional Protestant doctrine and piety. All of this ran counter to "the Democracy," with its celebration of "intuition" and the "common man." An untutored mob could not be trusted, because fallen man could not be trusted. Since this was so, there could be no Bancroftian faith in a transcendent general will of the people.

Thus while Lincoln struggled to keep the moral lights burning—risking war in the process—Douglas took refuge in ever more obscure appeals to process. He wanted to avoid letting moral claims illuminate, or inflame, the debate. Popular sovereignty was only one in a series of such moves. During the course of the debates, Douglas appealed both to individual choice and to the decisions of the Supreme Court as final arbiters beyond which supposedly there could be no legitimate appeal. Before 1854 it was the Compromise of 1850 that, as the result of constitutional process, supposedly had a sacred quality for Douglas. Seen in this light, Douglas's celebrated "Freeport Doctrine" was an especially tortured attempt to avoid a moral stand by relying on the *absence* of positive legislation to shape a positive moral outcome. Douglas saw appeals to religion as antidemocratic and, indeed, theocratic.

The Democratic appeal to the decisions of the Supreme Court was particularly hypocritical because, as Lincoln reminded his audience with his snidely repetitive use of the honorific "Judge Douglas," the Little Giant had once been made judge as part of a court-packing scheme. Now suddenly the Court had become a holy tribunal for Douglas. Lincoln put no stock in the intellectual integrity of Stephen Douglas.[33] He knew that, for Douglas, ideas were but arguments to be used at his convenience and that, when it suited him, Douglas was capable of abandoning his principles entirely. (In his disdain for the power and meaning of ideas, Douglas was probably the truer Jeffersonian.)[34] Adding to the hypocrisy of the Democratic position was the fact that Chief Justice Roger Taney had helped Jackson with his denial of Court authority in the name of popular government. Now Douglas appealed to Taney's decision as final, and he claimed that Lincoln's position was subversive of the Court's authority. Lincoln's memory was too good for this: "Again and again have I heard Judge Douglas denounce that bank decision, and applaud Gen. Jackson for disregarding it. It would be interesting for him to look over his recent speech, and see how exactly his fierce philippics against us for resisting Supreme Court decisions, fall upon his own head." Lincoln went further. Douglas was willing to abandon his principle of popular sovereignty in the case of Utah, where the question was not slavery but polygamy. Here Douglas joined Lincoln in the view that the territory should be "coerced to obedience" (Lincoln's telling phrase). Thus Douglas's attachment to the doctrine of popular sovereignty disappeared when it became inconvenient. For Lincoln, this was "only additional proof of what was very plain from the beginning, that that doctrine was a mere deceitful pretense for the benefit of slavery."[35]

It is fair to say that, for many, the entire point of liberal contract theory had been to prevent moral and especially theological reasoning from disrupting the smooth and peaceful functioning of a supposedly secular order. The theory had been the eighteenth century's reaction to the religious wars of the seventeenth. For Lincoln, however, independent moral thought and moral leadership remained necessary because institutions and processes could not be relied upon to produce a moral outcome transcendentally defined. The principle of right could not rest upon a mechanism, such as popular sovereignty, the decision of the Supreme Court, or even upon a realm of law that was somehow separate from political and moral reasoning. Inevitably, all those mechanisms were shaped positively by education or swayed negatively by flattery, demagoguery, and self-interest. Lincoln conceded to Bancroft and the Democrats the point that in a democracy public opinion was everything. But, rather than surrender to popular whim, he insisted on educating public opinion. "In this and like communities," he said, "public sentiment is everything. With public sentiment, nothing can fail; without it nothing can succeed. Consequently, he who moulds public sentiment goes deeper than he who enacts statutes or pronounces decisions."[36]

Lincoln's "House Divided" position implied that the liberal solution to the problem of morality in a democracy was impossible. On a moral issue like slavery there could be no middle ground; either one supported the expansion and perpetuation of slavery or one resisted it. Even as habitually slippery a character as Stephen Douglas could not avoid taking a moral stand. In effect, his attempted evasions only served to perpetuate slavery.

Thus Lincoln's theological language was neither a reaction to personal trauma nor a sop to the religious convictions of weaker souls. Lincoln's chief objection to Douglas was gut revulsion to the cynical, glib, and hollow libertarian worldview that made self-interest the only principle of right action. He had been arguing with Douglas along these lines for twenty years, and he was eager to meet the Little Giant in the arena of public debate. In the wake of the Kansas-Nebraska Act, Lincoln's reply to Douglas at Peoria in October 1854 defined him politically and, in retrospect, made his career. Since morality was not derived from natural reason or "common sense" (as the Enlightenment everywhere assumed) but was learned in the context of a specific historical community (as the conflict over slavery and Romantic theory alike made glaringly obvious), argument based on the theological tradition and history of the community was likewise inescapably necessary. Thus Lincoln rejected Douglas's libertarianism on grounds that reflected the rise of Romantic Protestantism and Whig political theory.

In response to the belief that "the Will of the majority" or "the people" determined justice, the *Whig Review* had said "the true republican, who understands his own rights and those of others, will have no *Will* to govern him, but Justice only—the Will of God. Only when the voice of 'the People' is for justice, will he admit that their voice is the voice of Deity. And no less so is his own, when he *alone*, for justice, cries against a nation,—the word is then, *vox mei, vox Dei*, and not, *vox populi, vox Dei*."[37] Here was Lincoln's keen and Romantic insight, the insight of his entire generation. Even in a republic there could be no escaping public theology.

BANCROFT STEALS LINCOLN'S TRIUMPH

Lincoln seemed destined to cross paths with George Bancroft. He had challenged Bancroft for the first time when he picked apart Polk's War Message of 1848. At that time he may have been unaware that the historian had helped Polk prepare his message. Then when preparing the lectures on discoveries and inventions, he once again challenged Bancroft's complaisant version of history. Lincoln responded to Young America with a historical vision that emphasized the continuing need for moral and intellectual struggle. But the Lincoln-Bancroft debates did not end there. In the late 1850s, a working relationship developed between Stephen Douglas and George Bancroft. Bancroft was the leading Douglas supporter in New York during Douglas's battle against the Buchanan administration over the proslavery Lecompton Constitution for Kansas, and during the Lincoln-Douglas Debates of 1858 Bancroft provided the historical background that Douglas eventually used in his famous *Harper's Magazine* article.[38] Without necessarily knowing it, Lincoln had also been up against Bancroft during his debates with Douglas.

Lincoln again attacked this Bancroft/Douglas version of American history in a speech at the Cooper Institute in 1859 that helped launch Lincoln's presidential aspirations by making him known and respected in the Northeast. After some two decades of disappointing struggle, Lincoln finally triumphed over Bancroft and the Democrats in the presidential election of 1860. In the end however, the wily Bancroft exacted a quiet revenge. He delivered the official eulogy of Lincoln, and his depiction of Lincoln as a man of the people has figured large in our understanding of Lincoln ever since. As Richard Current noted, "Bancroft had a conception of history that, in itself, was perhaps more a hindrance than a help to a true understanding of Lincoln."[39] In the end, Bancroft triumphed over Lincoln by obscuring the memory of his Whig vision and casting him in the mold of a Romantic Democrat. This is unfortunate because Lincoln's quarrel with Douglas had been a quarrel with Bancroft's transcendental democracy all along.

Douglas's Young America vision and the great historical syntheses of George Bancroft were almost interchangeable. It is not surprising, then, that as the Civil War approached the two men would work together. Bancroft approved of the Nebraska Act and popular sovereignty as a solution to the problem of slavery in the territories both because it relied on the same "will of the people" that he had transcendentalized and made the sole font of political legitimacy, and because it accorded precisely with his view that the Constitution vested all authority over local concerns in state and territorial legislatures. As Lilian Handlin put it, "Douglas's bill would free the nation for more important tasks than dealing with such insoluble problems as bondage. Having already assumed that the West would unify the country and fulfill manifest destiny, Bancroft regarded Douglas as the new Jackson who would save the party and the nation. Douglas, like Bancroft, would gladly have buried the slavery controversy. Neither man had any special sympathy for the blacks, and both acquiesced in the existence of bondage for the foreseeable future. Pacific railroads and the prosperity of America's heartland were the shared components of a nationalistic vision."[40]

The intraparty struggle over the Lecompton Constitution, however, finally brought the like-minded Douglas and Bancroft together. While Douglas's popular sovereignty required that the people decide for themselves what kind of constitution they should have, Buchanan decided to accept Kansas's proslavery Lecompton Constitution though it lacked a legitimate popular mandate. As in the case of the Fugitive Slave Act, the South once again abandoned the pretext of concern for local rights and liberties and demanded from the federal government protection for slavery. Douglas was in turn forced to abandon the largely southern leadership of his party. Rather than make a complete hypocrite of himself and lose all free-soil credibility in Illinois at a time when he was approaching a reelection fight against the new anti-Nebraska Republican Party and Abraham Lincoln, he led the fight against the administration. Upon hearing that Douglas intended to stand by his Nebraska bill "in its plain signification," Bancroft offered his aid to Douglas in early December 1857. Both Bancroft and Douglas saw the rival Topeka constitution as "probably the voice of the people," and they were willing to accept it as the bona fide antislavery verdict of Kansas. Bancroft's letter to Douglas included several colonial precedents for this popular sovereignty idea and concluded with an offer of extended help: "if you should think with me on this subject as I confidently trust you do, pray let me hear from you. It can do no harm, and I may be able to render you aid."[41] Later the same month Bancroft sent Douglas more detailed historical notes and colonial precedents.[42]

In addition to supplying Douglas with colonial precedents for the doctrine of popular sovereignty, precedents that lent the authority of the founders to what were in fact radically democratic ideas, Bancroft presided over a mass meeting of what was left of the radical wing of the Democratic Party in New York to encourage resistance to Buchanan's high-handed cracking of the patronage whip in support of Lecompton. This was an open and active show of support for Douglas. Douglas responded by keeping Bancroft abreast of developments in Washington.[43] Bancroft had been comparatively inactive politically since his return from the Court of Saint James in 1849.[44] Living in New York, he wrote volumes 4 through 8 of his *History* in the decade before the Civil War, thus completing an original plan that culminated in the Declaration of Independence.[45] Bancroft was willing to interrupt his work to help Douglas because Douglas stood for precisely the principles Bancroft wrote into his *History.*

No wonder Bancroft's "The Necessity, the Reality, and the Promise of the Progress of the Human Race" sparked a response from Lincoln. As Bancroft saw it, both southern fire-eaters and northern abolitionists threatened the Union because they failed to rely on the forces of history and public opinion to effect change gradually and naturally. It was the belief in some higher law apart from the will of the people that had led to anarchy in Kansas and had threatened the Union.[46] The God of history would emancipate the slaves in good time. Since the will of God was made manifest through the will of the people and since this, in turn, was expressed through a dialectical historical process, the only proper response was to allow the will of the people to express itself over time. Bancroft and Douglas therefore shared similar ideas both about the proper approach to the current situation and about what it meant to be a statesman in a democracy. The statesman was to embody and *follow* the will of the people, not lead and educate it. In addition, Bancroft and Douglas shared the Young America belief that expansion in the West would somehow resolve the question between North and South. Finally, though they expressed it differently, both Bancroft and Douglas believed that the time for theological reasoning and moral struggle was past; history had ended in a placid liberal democratic order, which made theology (in the hands of anyone other than Bancroft himself) a positive nuisance.

Though one had to look carefully to see any disagreements, Douglas and Bancroft did not agree on every issue. Unlike Douglas, Bancroft disagreed with Chief Justice Taney's opinion in the *Dred Scott* case.[47] Bancroft believed that blacks were fully human and that, in the State of New York at least, there had been black citizens at the time of the ratification of the U.S. Constitution. At the very bottom of his thought Bancroft was antislavery in a way Douglas was not. But Bancroft was willing to subordinate his beliefs about race and any disagreements with Douglas on black citizenship because, like Douglas, his transcendental view of democracy was more important than any other moral consideration. The will of the people really was the will of God. In the long run public opinion would come to itself and abolish slavery without activism or self-conscious effort on the part of public figures and politicians. Because Douglas saw it as his role to embody public opinion, Bancroft hoped that the senator would be able to calm the sectional tensions. In his speech on Douglas's behalf, Bancroft hoped to put the anti-Lecompton movement "on grounds that we may stand upon in Charleston or New Orleans as well as Chicago or New York." Of course Bancroft could not believe that the people of the South would abandon Douglas and popular sovereignty, and he found a convenient scapegoat for southern actions in southern politicians, who sought to use the Kansas issue to push for a southern presidential candidate in 1860.[48] In spite of differences on some of the relatively minor points in Douglas's complex political positioning, Bancroft was willing to help Douglas both with historical precedents and with active campaigning for both popular sovereignty and the Little Giant.

With this in mind, Bancroft's changing reactions to the presidency of Lincoln take on a special significance. The first influential professional historian to evaluate Lincoln was a cultural and political player—and a partisan Douglas supporter at that.[49] He initially had little good to say about the new Lincoln administration. In September 1861, he wrote to his wife: "We suffer for want of an organising mind at the head of the government. We have a president without brains; and a cabinet whose personal views outweigh patriotism." A few days later he wrote again: "the only trouble of mind I have springs from my want of confidence in our present administration." But a month earlier his remarks already showed that he had begun to assimilate into his providential scheme Lincoln's victory, southern secession, and the Civil War. Conveniently enough, his latent antislavery now became overt. Secession did "not spring from any element of a free government" but was "an anomaly in a democratic country." Indeed the war bore "witness to the capacity of a nation of the free to govern themselves wisely." "The doctrine of liberty [was] proved true by the fact that it [would] not be reconciled with slavery." Seemingly nothing, not even the Civil War, could dent Bancroft's belief in the redeemed status of democratic mankind.[50]

Here again Bancroft manifested his extraordinary ability to fold any and every occurrence into his master narrative. Now, remarkably, he derided the same manifest destiny aspirations that only two years earlier figured so prominently in the common appeal of Douglas and Bancroft, finding that "the masters, see, or fancy that they see, that freedom will come to the black man at any rate, unless a way should be found for the continual expanse of slavery over new territory. . . . A slave empire, surrounding the Gulf of Mexico, and the Caribbean Sea, was the dream of the most excited; but the calmest men held fast to the idea that the continuous extension of slavery was essential to its durability."[51] While Bancroft abandoned manifest destiny entirely, Douglas transformed it into a proposal for a zollverein or tariff union that would allow the course of commercial empire to take its way uninterrupted, and allow the seceded South to enjoy complete control of its peculiar local institution.[52] Bancroft rejected Douglas's idea for a zollverein as unworkable, and given their differing pasts and the political pressures on the senator it was not surprising that Douglas initially clung to the local diversity and internationalist capitalism in manifest destiny rather than to the "spirit of the people" and the corporate democracy of Bancroft. Not unlike Lincoln in his First Inaugural, Bancroft saw in secession "the doctrine of individualism pushed to its extremist limit: it would have dissolved the country, society itself, into atoms as lifeless and unconnected as the particles of sound." In the end, Douglas came to agree with Bancroft's view that the South might legitimately be "coerced to obedience."[53]

Thus, despite his abandonment of manifest destiny and his earlier private reticence on the slavery question, Bancroft continued to celebrate his transcendental democracy. After the firing on Fort Sumter, he said, "I witnessed the sublimest spectacle I ever knew; the uprising of the irresistible spirit of the people in behalf of law and order and liberty." "In no one southern state," he continued, "was there an opportunity given for a free expression of popular opinion; the revolution was effected in every state except South Carolina by a minority; and is now maintained by a free use of passion and terror." In keeping with Bancroft's long-held convictions, the people themselves could not have erred. Bancroft's postmillennial faith also remained unshaken, and already in 1861 he had found a framework for understanding the war.

> Have no fears that after victory, we may use the victory unmercifully. We are more in danger of being too eager to kill the fatted calf for the returning prodigal; but the four millions of semi-barbarous labourers will remain; and here as everywhere else, the palingenesis from an intolerable wrong cannot be hoped for without suffering; so that I cannot vouch for our ability to build up at once the walls of a perfect Jerusalem. Slavery will remain but will no longer be king; and the element of freedom will gradually but surely develop itself in its light and purity.[54]

Bancroft's view bears remarkable similarities to Lincoln's Second Inaugural of four years later. In a letter to Lincoln himself in 1861: "Civil War is the instrument of Divine Providence to root out social slavery; posterity will not be satisfied with the result, unless the consequences of the war shall effect an increase of free states. This is the universal expectation and hope of men of all parties."[55] Characteristically, Lincoln would avoid the abstract theological terminology in favor of grand biblical cadences. Still, the idea of the war as blood atonement for collective sin was clearly not just the possession of fire-and-brimstone evangelicals. Here, a rather effete product of Harvard and Boston unitarianism, one of America's most prominent intellectuals and a Democrat, also saw the Civil War as Christian sacrifice. The difference, then, between Lincoln and Bancroft, between Republicans and Democrats, was not that the one played to a religious audience while the other preferred Thomas Paine. The important differences were to be found in the precise details of their theological musings. Unlike Lincoln, Bancroft showed no signs of tempering his basic optimism about the human condition. Unshaken by the war, he simply folded it into his scheme of cosmic optimism.

Bancroft became a staunch Union Democrat who not only supported the Emancipation Proclamation but fully understood Lincoln's reasoning that, as a war measure under the necessary and proper clause, emancipation could legitimately apply only to the areas then in rebellion.[56] Afterwards he also supported the Thirteenth Amendment.[57] Bancroft met Lincoln on several occasions, and ironically enough, in view of his recent good offices for Douglas, he found himself supplying *Lincoln* with historical precedents when the president applied for help in justifying the suspension of the habeas corpus writ.[58]

Lincoln played rather well on Bancroft's vanity, a vanity that seems to have temporarily disabled the historian's ordinarily keen sense of irony: "He took me by one of his hands," Bancroft reported after attending a reception at the White House, "and trying to recall my name, he waved the other a foot and a half above his head, and cried out, greatly to the amusement of the bystanders: 'Hold on—I know you; you are—History, History of the United States—Mr.—Mr. Bancroft, Mr. George Bancroft,' and seemed disposed to give me a hearty welcome—expressing a wish to see me some day apart from the crowd."[59] Lincoln had a politician's gift for remembering names and almost certainly knew who Bancroft was; thus the joke was probably at the famous historian's expense. Without perceiving any slight or irony from the somewhat dim Illinois lawyer with the "defective education" and hence the ability to speak with clarity "but not with eloquence," Bancroft used Lincoln's apparent good will to make a request.[60] For a facsimile book entitled *Autograph Leaves of Our Country's Authors,* he received from Lincoln a copy of the Gettysburg Address along with a laconic note: "Herewith is the copy of the manuscript which you did me the honor to request." It seems Lincoln got the better of Bancroft in this particular encounter since, in addition to the opportunity to revise and republish his most cogent and ringing defense of the war effort, Lincoln solidified Bancroft's goodwill and received his implied endorsement in arguably the most crucial election year of American history.[61]

Even though Bancroft's chameleon-like political capabilities would also lead President Grant to keep him on as ambassador to Prussia after Andrew Johnson's term expired, it would be a mistake to assume that he had gone over to the Republicans. "The imperative call of duty cheers us on to the struggle more than ever; for unless we succeed, the power of the people which pervades all history as a prophecy, is beaten down, and there is no other Western hemisphere where the struggle can be renewed," Bancroft declared in April 1863. "We have no choice; we must persevere. If we would build up the home of humanity—if we would safely transmit the regenerating principles that give life its value—we must persevere."[62] Again it would be easy to see in this passage an abstract of Lincoln's views. But the postmillennialism here was more overt and unapologetic than it was with Lincoln. Where Lincoln sometimes speculated on the purposes of Providence, Bancroft was sure he knew them. More important for the moment, there was a different conception of the nature of political life hidden in Bancroft's phrase "the power of the people." In this Union League speech, given just six months before the Gettysburg Address, Bancroft went on to imply that Lincoln had endorsed a popular sovereignty settlement of the territorial question and that the South had rejected it. A motion, he said, "made and countenanced, by intimate friends of the incoming President" would have brought into the Union an enlarged state of New Mexico without reference to slavery. Slowly Bancroft began to cast Lincoln in the image of the now-deceased Stephen Douglas. By the time Bancroft was called upon to speak at funeral service for Lincoln in New York, the transformation was complete. Even before his death, Lincoln's Whiggery was being erased from public memory.

Bancroft accomplished this Democratization of Lincoln in spite of the fact that he now accepted some of Lincoln's view, articulated at the Cooper Institute, that, "when the Federal Constitution was framed, general emancipation was thought to be near" and that "since that time the attempt has been made in what are called Slave States, to render the condition of slavery perpetual." "Events have proved with the clearness of demonstration," he continued, "that a constitution which seeks to continue a caste of hereditary bondmen through endless generations is inconsistent with the existence of republican institutions."[63] Moving in Lincoln's direction, he now saw slavery as incompatible with the American purpose.

"Events," Bancroft said, had proven it. In fundamental ways, then, he remained as far from Lincoln as ever. Had events like secession not occurred, Bancroft was saying, it would have been presumptive evidence that slavery was *not* counter to republican institutions and the spirit of history. Obviously enough, Lincoln was antislavery *before* secession. As he had with all his heroes, Bancroft obscured Lincoln's moral leadership by emphasizing an all-powerful popular will. Bancroft was ready to ratify any status quo, and since Lincoln now spoke for the current state of things Bancroft dutifully, if reluctantly, ratified Lincoln. Bancroft may not have realized, however, how his historical theory eliminated the very prophetic voice that had characterized the dearly departed Lincoln. Just as "the people" arose in 1776 to support the Declaration of Independence, in 1861 "the people with one united voice" had determined to resist secession. (One wonders just who it was who did the seceding, to say nothing of "people" like Douglas who considered letting the South go in 1860–1861.) Now at the death of Lincoln, arguably the most contentious time in all of American history, Bancroft claimed, "in serene majesty the country rises in the beauty and strength and hope of youth, and proves to the world the quiet energy and the durability of institutions growing out of the reason and affections of the people."[64]

In his official eulogy of Lincoln before a joint session of Congress, Bancroft revisited his popular sovereignty position of the 1850s. Had the nation "let freedom and slavery compete for the territories on equal terms, in a fair field, under an impartial administration; and on this theory, if on any, the contest might have been left to the decision of time."[65] Bancroft's audacity was remarkable. "As the Presidential election [of 1860] drew on," he continued, "one of the great traditional parties did not make its appearance [the Whigs]; the other reeled as it sought to preserve its old position, and the candidate who most nearly represented its best opinion [Douglas], driven by patriotic zeal, roamed the country from end to end to speak for union, eager, at least, to confront its enemies, yet not having hope that it would find deliverance through him." This was a strange way to eulogize Lincoln, who made his career fighting precisely this man and precisely these doctrines. With slavery out of the way, Bancroft wanted to reestablish the old Democratic Party resistance to active moral government. Douglas had been the true martyr, the true prophet of the great American democratic God. Lincoln came in at the last minute with his Emancipation Proclamation to steal the Giant's place in "universal history," that is, the history of salvation.

But Bancroft was using the superiority of Douglas and popular sovereignty to set up the Romantic place in history he was creating for Lincoln. Douglas now played John the Baptist to Lincoln's Lamb of God. Bancroft had written in the *Atlantic Monthly* that Lincoln's "temper was soft and gentle and yielding; reluctant to refuse anything that presented itself to him as an act of kindness; loving to please and willing to confide; not trained to confine acts of good-will within the stern limits of duty." Bancroft's Lincoln "was of the temperament called melancholic, scarcely concealed by and exterior of lightness of humor,—having a deep and fixed seriousness, jesting lips, and wanness of heart."[66] Wanness of heart, indeed. Recycling much the same material he had used in his eulogy of Andrew Jackson in 1845 (or for that matter any number of heroic American figures in the pages of his histories), Bancroft made Lincoln the child of the frontier whose scanty education and illiterate parents made him the perfect channel and passive medium for the voice of the democratic God.[67] Unlike Jackson, however, Lincoln had no heroic force of will—and indeed no will of his own. Lincoln "lived the life of the American people, walked in its light, reasoned with its reason, thought with its power of thought, felt the beatings of its mighty heart, and so was in every way a child of nature, a child of the West, a child of America."[68]

For Bancroft, the sixteenth president had not been a great leader, or really any kind of leader at all. The people were in control, and Lincoln "was led along by the greatness of their self-sacrificing example; and as a child, in a dark night on a rugged way, catches hold of the hand of its father for guidance and support, he clung fast to the hand of the people, and moved calmly through the gloom." This was a striking description of Lincoln's administration, and one wonders what Bancroft made of the New York draft riots. But for his fixity of purpose, the people might have pulled Lincoln in all directions at once. According to Bancroft, however, rather than providing any overt moral leadership, Lincoln had trusted "the intuitions of the people and read those intuitions with rare sagacity."[69]

Moral leadership was clearly a problem for Bancroft. Though it really had no place in his scheme of transcendental democracy, and though he distrusted would-be moral leadership to say the least, in retrospect he always admired successful leaders. This compromise in fact helped make his histories interesting. Bancroft loved to portray great individuals in their moments on the grand historical stage. As his listeners had every right to expect, he treated them to what in many ways was an insightful portrait of Lincoln.

> The habits of his mind were those of meditation and inward thought, rather than action. He delighted to express his opinions by an apothegm, illustrate them by a parable, or drive them home by a story. He was skillful in analysis; discerned with precision the central idea on which a question turned, and knew how to disengage it and present it by itself in a few homely, strong old English words that would be intelligible to all. He excelled in logical statement, more than in executive ability. He reasoned clearly, his reflective judgment was good, and his purposes were fixed; but, like the Hamlet of his only poet, his will was tardy in action; and for this reason, and not from tenderness of feeling, he sometimes deplored the duty which devolved on him had not fallen to the lot of another.[70]

For all his grandeur, Hamlet was not the kind of Christian statesman one wanted to emulate. Bancroft still smarted over Lincoln's delay in proclaiming emancipation, and here he attributed to indecision what was in part clear, cold, realpolitik. Still, some of this description of Lincoln's intellectual character was apt. Remarkably, Bancroft was even aware of the difference between his own Latinate prosody and Lincoln's more muscular style.

As chief eulogist, Bancroft was uniquely situated to affect the way people remembered Lincoln; and no one knew better than this great historian how to make the most of such a situation. Indeed it would be hard to overestimate the degree to which Bancroft's historical vision dominated the nineteenth-century American mind. In the reminiscences of Henry C. Whitney, *Life on the Circuit with Lincoln,* one sometimes wonders whether Whitney was remembering his former colleague or Bancroft's eulogy.[71]

One must be very careful with Bancroft. The phrase "intuitions of the people" could be construed as the proximate state of majority public opinion at a given time. Read in this way Bancroft could make a good deal of sense. Bancroft continued to adulate Lincoln, who "never thought to electrify the community by taking an advanced position with a banner of opinion, but rather studied to move forward compactly, exposing no detachment in front or rear." Indeed, "the course of his Administration might have been explained as the calculating policy of a shrewd and watchful politician, had there not been seen behind it a fixedness of principle which from the first determined his purpose and grew more intense with every year, consuming his life by its energy."[72]

As Bancroft delivered this oration, Republicans and Democrats in Congress applauded by turns, depending on whether the historian stated the opinions of the radicals or the Johnson Democrats.[73] And Lincoln himself might have recognized something in Bancroft's portrait. Lincoln was careful not to get too far ahead of the politically possible, and Bancroft captured this aspect admirably. But Lincoln's "fixedness of purpose" did not originate with the people. More often, Lincoln saw himself as struggling to get the people to understand matters as he thought they really were. "Although President Jackson had said, 'Never for a moment believe that the great body of the citizens . . . can deliberately intend to do wrong,' Lincoln was dubious," one historian noted. He "was no democrat as the word was understood in his century."[74] While prudence dictated a careful and "halting" course—even by Bancroft's standards—Lincoln found it necessary to guide public opinion, and not, as Bancroft had it, to let himself be guided by it. And Bancroft missed just how much Lincoln did indeed try to "electrify the community." In the 1850s Lincoln sought to rouse the North against the encroachments of the slave power, and most of his speeches were intended both to help shape public perceptions and to rouse public will. It was this heroic task, after all, that elevated Lincoln's speeches and gave them their lasting appeal.

With his eulogy, Bancroft forwarded the cause of his Democratic Party at the expense of Lincoln's Whig heritage. "Bancroft and his fellow Brahmins contributed to forming the popular image of Lincoln that was to prevail for many years," according to Richard N. Current, an image in which "the wartime president had little to do, as an agent in his own right, with the events of the Civil War," at least "until the end, when he was planning exactly the Reconstruction policy that his successor tried to carry out." But, as Current notes, "Bancroft was quite unaware of the complexities of Lincoln's personality, his real concern for the rights of the freedmen, his conduct of the war in the role of commander-in-chief, or the way he made himself a statesman by behaving like a politician." Bancroft was preoccupied with political purposes of his own, and the Johnson administration could find support for its views on Reconstruction in his presentation of Lincoln. The point of Bancroft's eulogy was that Lincoln would not have pushed for a moral reconstruction of the South, that his postwar policies would have looked a lot like Johnson's. When one considers Bancroft's impatience with Lincoln's slow moves toward emancipation, this seems shamelessly hypocritical. In the matter of Reconstruction, no amount of temporizing was too much.[75]

Bancroft did more than obscure Lincoln's wartime leadership. Bancroft built upon the log-cabin theme that Lincoln's handlers had used to effect at the Chicago Convention in 1860. It was a theme that obscured Lincoln's ambitious quest for respectability and extraordinary achievement, and one that continues to distort our understanding of Lincoln today. Thus even before he was in the grave, Lincoln's self-conscious efforts to rise to intellectual respectability and then to the loftier heights of literary fame began to lose place in the American memory to a more Democratic "man of the people." Lincoln had rejected this sentimental, Democratic belief in the people when he asserted the need for active moral leadership, which is to say, when he joined the Whig Party. Since J. G. Randall in 1940 described both Republicans and Democrats as "a blundering generation" bringing about a "needless" war, Lincoln has been seen as a "liberal statesman" similar to Woodrow Wilson, which has, stunningly, reincarnated Lincoln as a Democrat.[76] Along with the Reconstruction period, liberal consensus historians of the twentieth century found their Lincoln in Bancroft's eulogy, meaning that Lincoln's religious rhetoric would be given a peculiar and incidental place in our histories. David Donald stands in a long line of historians from Bancroft on who found in Lincoln a man who stood aloof from reform movements, "an essentially passive" personality.[77] This misses Lincoln almost entirely. Lincoln was closer to a workaholic and a Romantic embodiment of Max Weber's Protestant ethic. As Bancroft read it, Lincoln "disclaimed all praise" for the Emancipation Proclamation, giving the credit to God, and this of course was literally true. "God alone can claim it," said Lincoln.[78] But rather than a serious theological reasoner contemplating the nature of history and his limited but special role in it, Bancroft's Lincoln was a country bumpkin who, to his credit, knew his place, and who expressed his humility in a homely religious language: "He was of a religious turn of mind, without superstition; and the unbroken faith of the mass was like his own."[79] By treating it as evidence of a "passive personality," Bancroft and the liberal historians sanitized, marginalized, and later psychologized Lincoln's attempt to bring a theological and moral perspective to American political life. Even some of our more sympathetic interpreters of Lincoln's leadership have dismissed Lincoln's religious rhetoric in the same sentimental way.

PART THREE

Lincoln's Personal Piety and

Public Performance

Chapter Six

FROM PREDESTINARIAN BAPTIST
TO ROMANTIC INTELLECTUAL

• Lincoln's religious biographers and Lincoln's acquaintances generally agree that he grew up in a predestinarian Baptist household and subsequently went through a skeptical phase. Many also add that through the difficulties of life (the death of two sons and the war in particular) he was brought to a new appreciation of the consoling wisdom of his inherited faith. As Herndon paraphrased Mary Lincoln's account: "Mr. Lincoln had no faith and no hope, in the usual acceptance of those words. He never joined a church; but still, as I believe, he was a religious man by nature. He first seemed to think about the subject when our Willie died, and then more than ever about the time he went to Gettysburg; but it was a kind of poetry in his nature; and he was never a technical Christian."[1] Lincoln's personal experience mirrored many in his generation who felt compelled to reject utilitarianism and to embrace some more or less recognizable form of Christianity. In part Lincoln gave voice to his generation's experiences, both with triumphant material progress and with death and loss, because he personally experienced progress and loss so sharply.

A second trait helped make Lincoln a successful spokesman for America in the mid-nineteenth century: like Edgar Allan Poe, Lincoln was a master of irony. Poe, for instance, described the deepest spiritual difficulty of his generation, the loss of the inherited faith in a life hereafter, in a comic poem about an annoying bird (a poem, incidentally, that Lincoln loved).[2] "The Raven" was not entirely comic. The bird—in Poe's "Sonnet To Science" a vulture—never took his beak from out the poet's Victorian heart. The consciousness of the finality of death inherent in the materialistic worldview of modern science never seems to have left the heart of Lincoln. Probably in part because he was not entirely sure himself, Lincoln rarely let his readers rest in the comfort of knowing exactly where he stood on religious matters.

Lincoln's love of poetry and his gift for language also helped make him an apt prophet for his generation. While many Victorians experienced religious longings, few expressed them more poetically than did Lincoln. In a world of understandable material causation, the traditional miracles—once seen as evidence for the moral truths of Christianity—now became (for many intellectuals at least) incredible. Thus Theodore Parker was led to reverse the old priority and to assert that it was not those miracles but rather the permanent poetic truths of Christianity that all along had been most important.[3] Through poetry, Parker made room at the table of Christianity for the doubting Thomases of a post-Enlightenment, Victorian world. Hardly alone in his generation, Lincoln found a place at the table set by Parker and Poe.[4]

Lincoln may have embodied his generation's experience, but he was also a unique individual. Had he not lived, we may well have had a similar set of state papers—Seward's perhaps; and we may even have had the famous letter to the Widow Bixby consoling her for the loss of five (actually two) dead sons—John Hay may well have written it. But we would not have had Lincoln's Second Inaugural and the Gettysburg Address.[5] There would have been no man so determined to bring certain Christian notions to bear on the great events of the period. Lincoln was part of a Romantic generation that gave new life to religious ideas by rejecting empiricism and materialism and by relying either on a more idealistic epistemology or on poetry. And Lincoln's religious language must be seen in this light. But as a Romantic intellectual Lincoln came to a particular understanding of Christianity, one that reflected aspects of his particular religious past. Lincoln penned his own particular rhapsody on the American Romantic air.

OF PROVIDENCE AND SUPERSTITION

"I always was superstitious," Lincoln wrote to his friend, Joshua Speed, in 1842, "and as part of my superstition, I believe God made me one of the instruments of bringing your Fanny and you together, which union, I have no doubt He had fore-ordained. Whatever he designs, he will do for *me* yet. 'Stand *still* and see the salvation of the Lord' is my text just now."[6] Hinting at his own roots in predestinarian Baptist Churches, Lincoln here quoted Exodus 14:13 or 2 Chronicles 20:17.[7] He described himself as "superstitious," a bit of self-directed irony that leads in two directions. The first shows Lincoln was not a literal believer in the strictest sense. Literal believers do not typically describe their faith in such disparaging terms. The irony here befit a man who came up from rural southern poverty and who, in a scientific age and in a community of aspiration, struggled to attain the respect of the most respectable. Lincoln was aware, as indeed any reasonably literate person in antebellum America had to be, that recent scientific discoveries did not sit squarely with traditional biblical accounts of, for instance, the age of the earth.[8] He was aware of Speed's skepticism in particular. Yet, ironically, Lincoln did not abuse Scripture in this passage, and since it was a private communication he was not concerned with keeping up appearances. The joke was not upon believing Christians, but rather on Lincoln himself. He made fun of himself for taking consolation in a biblical attitude that he and Speed both knew he did not quite literally believe in the usual manner but that he nevertheless could not quite help believing. Though lighthearted, it was a real confession.

More ironic still, Lincoln became more self-assured in his religious pronouncements over time, which points to the second implication of his remark about superstition. For instance, he knew in 1849 that the world was "ten-thousand years old," much older than the standard 4,500 years of literalist biblical interpretation.[9] But in the lectures on discoveries and inventions of 1858–1859 he was willing to acknowledge and work within the biblical time line.[10] By the time of his Second Inaugural his religious language was bold and self-confident. Even more striking were his attempts to ascertain the will of God when he struggled with the question of emancipation. Both the Second Inaugural and his thoughts on emancipation bespoke the kind of trust in Providence that Lincoln had referred to as "superstition" in his 1842 letter to Speed. Lincoln regained something of his former naive faith, a second naïveté, almost in spite of himself.[11]

There are some misunderstandings that linger in presentations of Lincoln's religious nature. According to Ward Hill Lamon, Lincoln recounted an elaborate dream shortly before his assassination in which he saw himself lying in state in the East Room.[12] While none of this familiar story can be substantiated beyond Lamon's dubious secondhand account from long after the fact, it has nevertheless been given credence in very reputable biographies.[13] The providential aspect of Lincoln's faith has been distorted and sentimentalized as a morbid fascination with the impending assassination foretold him, supposedly, in his dreams. This is unfortunate not so much because it portrays Lincoln as a man who could see in Providence an almost personal message from God— indeed he did sometimes describe events in that way—but because it characterizes the president as declining in his powers and looking forward to his own death. Americans are accustomed to the story line of the Civil War in which Lincoln is martyred at the moment of triumph, and the Lamon story makes Lincoln's assassination seem dramatically necessary and inevitable. It is itself a great example of the way Victorians could fictionalize their own experience and an interesting comment on the way memory imitates art. Like a figure in a Dickens or Stowe novel, Lincoln became a man haunted by ghosts, a man who, not unlike Uncle Tom, finally accepted his destined role of a Christian martyr.

At the time of his death though, the still relatively young Lincoln was at the height of his powers. As Mark Neely noted, "John Hay, the only person close to Lincoln in the Presidential years who kept a diary, consistently reported the President in good spirits and in complete control of events. As for his superstition it was not a controlling force by then either. No careful lawyer who dreams of his own death fails, as Lincoln failed, to write a will."[14] Mary Lincoln also reported that her husband was in particularly buoyant spirits as the end of the war approached.[15] The Second Inaugural should be read not as the last, parting words of a dying prophet but as the statement of a vigorous executive who had every intention of living. The Lamon story minimized and continues to minimize the importance of Lincoln's religious language. His providential worldview, an integral part of his strength, becomes a part of a world-weary president's weakness and vacillation.

On the other hand, Lincoln gave some credence to the prophetic power of dreams. He seems to have gained confidence from one dream in particular about "floating toward an unknown shore." To him it seemed to foretell good tidings because it occurred before major Union victories.[16] It may have been no more than a playful admission, like an athlete's lucky socks or an adult's fear of the basement, but the same cannot be said of a more important instance of his reliance on a providential outlook. At perhaps the most crucial moment in his career Lincoln sought an almost immediate revelation of God's will.[17] According to the diary of Salmon P. Chase, the able secretary of the Treasury and Lincoln's persistent rival, the president announced his decision to issue the preliminary Emancipation Proclamation with these words:

> The action of the army against the rebels has not been quite what I should have best liked. But they have been driven out of Maryland, and Pennsylvania is no longer in danger of invasion. When the rebel army was at Frederick, I determined, as soon as it should be driven out of Maryland, to issue a proclamation of emancipation such as I thought most likely to be useful. I said nothing to anyone; but I made the promise to myself and (hesitating a little) to my Maker. The rebel army is now driven out, and I am going to fulfill that promise.[13]

Gideon Welles, the secretary of the navy, who paraphrased Lincoln's remarks, substantiated Chase's account.

> In the course of the discussion that followed, he said that he had made a vow, a covenant, that if God gave us the victory in the approaching battle, he would consider it an indication of divine will and that it was his duty to move forward in the cause of emancipation. It might be thought strange that he had in this way submitted the disposal of matters when the way was not clear to his mind what he should do. God had decided this question in favor of the slaves. He was satisfied it was right, was confirmed and strengthened in his action by the vow and the results. His mind was fixed, his decision made, but he wished his paper announcing his course as correct in terms as it could be made without any change in his determination.

Neither account can be dismissed lightly because Welles's diary in particular is considered by historians to be "one of the best sources of inside information on the Lincoln administration" and because, while neither should be accepted as the exact words of Lincoln, on the essential points the two independent contemporary accounts agree. Much has been made of this episode, and William Wolf did well to begin his study of Lincoln's religion with it. Lincoln here made a kind of bargain with God, and it came close to reducing "man's relationship to God to a transactional level. ('I'll free the slaves if You, God, will give us victory.')" For Wolf, such a "primitive superstition" had "no place in a reasoned faith," and only Lincoln's lack of self-righteousness rescued him from the merely primitive. Nevertheless, Wolf observed, Lincoln's "view of reality had an element of the primitive in it represented by the vow and also by his interest in dreams as foretelling the future."[18]

Lincoln however did not use a trial of God's purposes as a substitute for prudential reasoning and sound judgment.[19] On the contrary, Lincoln's providential interpretation of events was *part of* his rational analysis of his situation. In both the Chase and Welles accounts, Lincoln cited reasons for and against issuing the Emancipation Proclamation. Even outside of any theological bargain or covenant, the Union victory at Antietam strengthened the president's hand in issuing the proclamation. It was not as if he had said to himself that if some completely unrelated event came to pass—say for instance a bright, clear day—he would then proceed with emancipation. For Lincoln, these were *not* "the days of miracles," and he did not expect a direct revelation. "I must study the plain physical facts of the case," he said, "ascertain what is possible and learn what appears to be wise and right."[20]

Again, historians should not sentimentalize Lincoln's confession before his cabinet. It was not the testimony of a man unable to cope with the burdens of office surrendering his own will entirely to the will of God. While Lincoln's faith in Providence may have helped him shoulder what for him was undoubtedly a heavy burden of responsibility, he was not seeking to shirk the load. Nor was he abandoning instrumental reason in favor of magical intervention. Rather Lincoln here assumed, or had faith in, an ultimately moral universe. Like any war effort, the Civil War necessitated a kind of brutal logic in the calculation of human life, and Lincoln was not shy in using such prudential reasoning. Nevertheless his calculus never lapsed into amorality, as it would for Oliver Wendell Holmes, Jr., and this is attributable in part to Lincoln's reliance on Providence and providential reasoning. Faith in Providence demanded a careful analysis of the situation to determine the will of God. But that same faith also allowed one to put an end to such searching and to come down with confidence on one side or the other: the evidence that presented itself, however incomplete, was providentially guided. After striving to comprehend the situation as completely as possible, one had in the end to trust in the right, as God gave one to see it. Thus faith in Providence was not a primitive belief at all—whatever primitive might mean. It was rather a sophisticated set of theological assumptions. It did not replace instrumental reasoning; it supplemented that reasoning with a larger moral and theological perspective. With faith that the universe was ultimately moral—an assumption for which Lincoln well knew there was no shortage of contrary evidence—Lincoln felt supremely confident that he could justify emancipation as the right response to his particular circumstances.

Ironically, Richard Hofstadter's famous remark that the Emancipation Proclamation "had all the moral grandeur of a bill of lading" was not entirely off the mark.[21] Lincoln studied his circumstances very carefully, and he even asked for suggestions from his cabinet. The resulting legal craftsmanship perplexed radical abolitionists at the time and continues to bother some students today. As he proceeded circumspectly, however, Lincoln operated within the symbol system of Romanticized, Reformed thought, a system he helped fashion for the purpose. "Sincerely believ[ing it] to be an act of justice, warranted by the Constitution, upon military necessity," Lincoln remained confident that emancipation accorded not only with the Constitution but also with the highest powers of the universe as best he could discern them.[22] Whether or not he used the word "covenant," as Welles said, Lincoln here seems to have been in an optimistic mood about his ability to discern the will of God. He was *strengthened* in his reasoning by having made a trial of it. Working as he did within a predestinarian and providential description of the world, he replicated in a certain measure one of several classic ethical responses to that worldview, the covenantal response.[23]

In this Lincoln's words echoed such seventeenth-century covenantal documents as, for instance, "A Model of Christian Charity," in which "if the Lord shall please to hear us, and bring us in peace to the place we desire, then hath he ratified this Covenant and sealed our Commission and will expect a strict performance of the articles contained in it."[24] Lincoln everywhere assumed an ultimately inscrutable divinity, and covenantal theory had its origins with the Bible and with the medieval nominalists who rejected the rationalism and natural law of Aquinas because it compromised the absolute sovereignty of God. Refusing to hold God within the bounds of human reason, nominalists chose instead to rely for guidance in human affairs on the Bible as the sovereign word of God.[25] Through history and through the history of God's covenants with his people, God chose of his own accord to reveal himself, and thus his will became only somewhat knowable. In the Second Inaugural two years later, Lincoln would find a different, more radical, yet similarly classical response to the ethical problems presented by assuming a just but ultimately inscrutable God. But here in 1862–1863 he asked from the country (and received) an absolute commitment to a moral crusade, a crusade for a vision of American liberty in which, in the long run, slavery had no place. He was emboldened to do so by his confidence in discerning the will of God. The war and emancipation came late in Lincoln's religious development, but the point here is both to correct the misunderstanding that Lincoln thought he could foretell the future through dreams and, at the same time, to acknowledge that he strove to see the world in providential terms. He sought to discern the will of God in that Providence (as well as from Scripture and reason), and he sought to order his conduct according to that discernment.

A still further misunderstanding that continues to plague our portrayals of Lincoln's religion lies in the notion that he somehow read the Bible naturally or naively, in the absence of any interference from formal church teachings. Writing in 1959, William Wolf saw in Lincoln "a biblical Christian." "The Bible quite apart from the competing churches was his source of inspiration."[26] Presenting Lincoln's religion that way prevented his capture by any particular denomination, probably reflecting the needs of the consensus period, when the ideal American was seen as a mainstream Protestant, Catholic, or Jew. Since Lincoln himself did not officially join any denomination, there was no need to dwell either on his predestinarian Baptist heritage or on the predestinarian and Presbyterian views of his pastors. One could simply assert that Lincoln's own religious vision sprang somehow immediately from the Bible.

As any anthology of creeds and confessions will amply attest, however, the Bible does not read itself, and the doctrine of predestination is largely the achievement of postbiblical writers (though indeed those writers found justification for their thought in Scripture).[27] Lincoln's profound reading of the Bible should not be seen as a personal trait. It reflected, rather, a theologically astute political culture and a Reformed theological heritage. "Raised a predestinarian Baptist," conceded Wolf, "Lincoln never became a Baptist, but he never ceased to be a predestinarian." "Although the Bible would be his primary inspiration for this insight," that is, predestination, Wolf conceded that Lincoln "may have been helped somewhat in its articulation by the Calvinistic doctrine of predestination as expounded by two distinguished Old-School Presbyterian pastors under whom he would sit in Springfield and in Washington."[28] While Lincoln was not orthodox in the sense that he subscribed to a particular statement of faith as it was then accepted by any denomination, he nevertheless spoke as a man fully immersed in the world of Reformed Christianity in the middle of the nineteenth century.

In addition, Wolf's nondenominational interpretation relied on some dubious sources. According to her son in 1916, Aminda Rogers Rankin dictated in 1889 a conversation she allegedly remembered having with Lincoln in 1846. Wolf cites the quote,

> I doubt the possibility, or propriety, of settling the religion of Jesus Christ in the models of man-made creeds and dogmas. It was a spirit in the life that He laid stress on and taught, if I read aright. I know I see it to be so with me.
>
> The fundamental truths reported in the four gospels as from the lips of Jesus Christ, and that I first heard from the lips of my mother, are settled and fixed moral precepts with me. I have concluded to dismiss from my mind the debatable wrangles that once perplexed me with distractions that stirred up, but never absolutely settled anything. I have ceased to follow such discussions or be interested in them.
>
> I cannot without mental reservations assent to long and complicated creeds and catechisms. If the church would ask simply for assent to the Savior's statement of the substance of the law: "Thou shalt love the Lord thy God with all thy heart, and with all thy soul, and with all thy mind, and thy neighbour as thyself,"—that church would I gladly unite with.[29]

Though there is "more than average doubt" about the authenticity of this quotation, it continues to affect our perception of Lincoln.[30] The first two paragraphs in particular are doubtful. While the last paragraph may be more reliable, it almost exactly duplicates a description of Lincoln's religion published in 1865. Henry C. Deming, a Connecticut politician and an officer during the Civil War, reported after the war that Lincoln said these words to *him.* Though it was reported after the fact and can be taken as no more than a paraphrase, Deming's account may be accurate in part or in whole.[31] When Rankin talked to her son, she may well have confused that earlier account with her own recollections. But, even if Deming's account is true to Lincoln's words in the essentials, that does not change the fact that Lincoln was adept at using the whole host of theological words and word systems, and that he did so with apparent relish. Assuming Lincoln did endorse greater tolerance of theological diversity and a correspondingly open church, it does not follow that he was uninterested in the particulars of theological controversy. The doctrine of predestination and the emphasis on providential reasoning to which it sometimes led did not follow simply from the New Testament commandment to love God with all thy heart, soul, and mind and thy neighbor as thyself. It reflected a specific denominational past.

But the source of the Rankin quotation is doubtful, and it implies an anti-intellectualism alien to the lawyer and politician. Lincoln was not the frontier innocent of simple biblical faith he has been portrayed to be. At several points in his career, including in the Second Inaugural, he took careful and even carefully original positions in the "debatable wrangles" of theology. The Lincoln of the Illinois bar and of the great debates loved fine distinctions and rigorous controversy—he even made an adult study of Euclid. Wolf followed Benjamin Thomas in asserting that Lincoln "must have" been disturbed by the denominational feuding on the frontier.[32] Eager to ensure that Lincoln was not captured by conventional religiosity, early biographers needed a nondenominational Lincoln. Similarly, the twentieth-century need for a Judeo-Christian Lincoln led later scholars to dismiss as incidental one of the abiding sources of his thought, predestinarian Baptist and Presbyterian doctrine, even though William Herndon observed that Lincoln's "early Baptist training made him a fatalist to the day of his death."[33] The consistency with which predestinarian themes and providential considerations recur in Lincoln's writings is one of their most definitive characteristics and cannot be seen merely as a "natural" expression of frontier religiosity. (The frontier was in fact dominated by a Methodism that did not stress providential reasoning to the same degree.) In his own Romanticized way, Lincoln sided with his parents and grandparents in the denominational controversies of the antebellum period, momentarily revitalizing ideas that had previously found their most potent expression in the great Reformed confessions of Westminster, Savoy, and Philadelphia.

Another source of misunderstanding surrounding Lincoln's use of predestinarian thought might be termed the psychological reading. David Donald's recent biography discounts the religious and intellectual character of Lincoln's thought by treating it as evidence of his "passive personality." Donald's Lincoln was reluctant "to take the initiative and make bold plans; he preferred to respond to the actions of others." This may seem on its face to be a rather bizarre reading; a man whose political ambition supposedly knew no rest, who helped organize two political parties in Illinois and who guided one of them to a national majority, who was involved in more than 5,000 cases large and small before both federal and state courts, who found time to dabble in short stories, poems, and lectures, and who still managed to memorize Shakespeare and large portions of the Bible, Lincoln must have worked compulsively. And Donald himself admitted that, "like thousands of Calvinists who believed in predestination, he worked indefatigably for a better world—for himself, for his family, and for his nation."[34]

But the more serious point of interpretation Donald was making was not the psychological one that Lincoln was "essentially passive." Rather, Donald meant to assert that Lincoln was not controlling, doctrinaire, or authoritarian in his approach to political ethics, and his interpretation of Lincoln's political philosophy and religious views were much influenced, he wrote, by John Rawls. Donald did not provide a psychological analysis of Lincoln's character so much as an interpretation of Lincoln's lifework as an expression of philosophical liberalism. Lincoln's "passivity," Donald continued, "made for a pragmatic approach to problems, a recognition that if one solution was fated not to work another could be tried. 'My policy is to have no policy' became a kind of motto for Lincoln—a motto that infuriated the sober, doctrinaire people around him who were inclined to think that the President had no principles either." Make no mistake; Donald here implied that religious people were both sober and doctrinaire.[35]

Donald admired in Lincoln the "*Negative Capability* . . . of being in uncertainties, Mysteries, doubts, without any irritable reaching after fact and reason."[36] And there is certainly something to the idea that the assumption of radical depravity led Lincoln to suspend judgment and be more flexible. The emphasis on providential reasoning was originally made necessary by the rejection of the excessive reliance on natural reason of Aristotle and Aquinas, because such emphasis on independent human reason abrogated the sovereignty of God. Thus providential thought tended to be historically, rather than philosophically, minded. Answering abstract questions of legal philosophy was not an end in itself for Lincoln, nor did he attempt to deduce logical solutions to the problems he faced from abstract statements of political philosophy. Rather he tried to ascertain from his historical situation "*where* we are and *whither* we are tending, [that] we could then better judge *what* to do, and *how* to do it."[37] Nothing in Lincoln suggests that he intended to use the secular power to enforce rational natural law. In the eyes of his antislavery critics his ethics were situational in the extreme. Yet even when his providential, or circumstantial, ethical outlook gave his superior analytical powers a workout, he nevertheless remained extremely anxious about consistency and principle. With all its legal precision and its lack of "moral grandeur," the Emancipation Proclamation is as good an example as any.

Lincoln held off on declaring emancipation until he could establish its necessity as a legitimate war measure under the constitutional war powers of the president. Late in the war he was willing to put logic aside in fostering the return of the seceded states so-called to "their practical relation with the

Union," without settling the "merely pernicious abstraction" of just what their status had been while they were out of it.[38] But that was an exception; and he certainly never renounced "any irritable reaching after fact and reason." More often he strained his powers to convince the public to see the moral problems he faced in the same subtle shades of light and shadow in which he saw them. It is therefore a mistake to read into Lincoln a form of liberalism and pragmatism that avoided pronouncing moral judgments and that authorized coercion only for the sake of expanding freedom. As Boritt discovered in Lincoln's economic thought, Lincoln's moralism could not be reduced to the desire to increase freedom, economic or otherwise. While Lincoln was acquainted with liberal political theory, he knew it largely as the theory of his opponents.

By sentimentalizing Lincoln's religious words, the liberal interpretation of Lincoln overlooks the role older Reformed theological debates about polity and salvation played in Lincoln's formulation of the problems confronting the country. It is perfectly appropriate, indeed essential, to put Lincoln's political writings into the context of Clay, Calhoun, and Webster as well as of Jefferson, Madison, and Hamilton. But there was more to the antebellum American mind than the liberal Enlightenment heritage. Lincoln was well schooled in the older yet ongoing tradition of theological disputation. While it gave rise to the liberal theories of John Locke, this line of development maintained a far stronger substantive theological perspective than did either Locke or his American successors in the pantheon of liberal thought. With the statements of Westminster, Savoy, and Philadelphia, respectively, Presbyterians, Congregationalists, and Baptists formed the three largest branches of Reformed orthodoxy in America. The Baptist Philadelphia Confession modified the London Confession, which modified the Congregationalist Savoy Declaration, which itself modified the great Westminster Confession of 1647. Because Lincoln based so much of his understanding of American political life on an analogy with the life of the churches he knew, the historical disputes over church polity and the role of civil magistrates must also be considered essential background for understanding Lincoln's words. In addition to the Constitution and the Declaration of Independence, the cadences and phrases of this religious heritage also resound in Lincoln's mature writing. Lincoln's Reformed heritage led to his emphasis on predestination and Providence and encouraged the creedal definition of American nationality that was evident in all of his nationalist utterances.

EARLY REFORMED ENVIRONMENT

Lincoln grew up in a Baptist household, and the Lincoln family history parallels in many ways the history of Protestantism in America. At this point, intellectual history and the social history of the Lincoln family merge. In England the Lincoln family belonged to a parish that rejected the "Popish practices" under Charles I, and in America the Lincolns began as Congregationalists. Samuel Lincoln (1622–?) arrived in Salem with the Great Migration in 1637 and settled in Hingham.[39] Samuel's son, Mordecai (1657–1727), was a prominent ironworker. Similar to the Independents of England, Congregationalists in America were the party of Cromwell. With the Savoy Declaration of 1658, English Congregationalists accepted the rigorous Reformed theology of Westminster, adapting the articles on church polity and the role of the civil magistracy as fit the Congregational model. American Congregationalists adopted these Savoy measures at Boston in 1680 and again at Saybrook in 1708. From the Congregationalist point of view, in the act of establishing a state church the Presbyterians at Westminster granted undue power to the civil magistrate to maintain that church, including the power to convoke synods. Congregationalists put stronger stress on the idea that God's visible church could be kept pure of the unconverted. Thus they insisted on evidence of the work of the Spirit for full church membership and limited the power of the magistrate in church matters to punishing blasphemy and the like.[40]

Around 1744, during what is known as the First Great Awakening, some Congregationalist Churches sided with the New Lights. According to the New Lights, some of the established Congregationalists churches, the so-called "standing order," had fallen away from the insistence on a truly converted ministry and membership. In response, New Lights reemphasized the necessary work of the Holy Spirit, both in conversion and in the true call to ministry. They founded "pious Congregational" or "Separate" churches, and some of these New Light Churches took what seemed the logical step of rejecting infant baptism in favor of baptizing only the converted into God's visible church.[41] Thus the mother church of most American Baptists was the Congregational Church, which itself shared most of the Westminster Confession with the Presbyterians.

So-called Regular Baptists, also known as Calvinistic or Particular Baptists (from their belief in particular as opposed to general atonement), were Calvinists in doctrine and Independents in church polity; and they accepted formal written creeds, not as binding tests of faith, but as declarations of faith prevailing at the time in the denomination. In addition to the statement agreed to by the members of an individual church, they accepted the Philadelphia Confession of 1742, which was an adaptation of the London Confession of 1689. At Philadelphia, the American Baptists strengthened London's "closed communion" rule, which restricted communion to those baptized as adults, by adding a treatise on discipline and an article enjoining the laying on of hands prior to baptism. Another new article not only allowed the practice of singing in worship but commended it as a divine ordinance.[42]

Though Congregationalists in polity, Baptists rejected the New England Congregationalist "theocracy," preferring for theological reasons a radical free-church model. They rejected any notion of a Christian state in favor of a more radically Augustinian two kingdoms teaching, and on this point they out-Calvined Calvin. The heavenly and the earthly kingdoms were separate and distinct. "Christians would freely associate themselves with Christ's church and live as pilgrims in a hostile world. Baptists did not deny the legitimacy of the worldly structures, but saw them as a part of God's creative, not His salvic, action."[43] In other words, the state was necessary in a fallen world, but to see in it any hope for mankind's salvation was blasphemy. On this point they were in some ways closer to Luther than to Calvin. Though they would have rejected Luther's reliance on secular power to establish the church, they agreed with him that ultimately the world would not be transformed by human striving. This relatively radical two kingdoms tradition echoed repeatedly in the thoughts and writings of Abraham Lincoln.

Lincoln's family left New England for the frontier, and there, after a brief Quaker interlude, they associated themselves with the Baptists of Virginia and Kentucky. Mordecai Lincoln, Jr. (1686–1736), moved to Monmouth County, New Jersey, and then to Berks County, Pennsylvania. His son and Lincoln's great-grandfather, John Lincoln (1716–1788), married a Quaker and moved to Rockingham County, Virginia, which was as far back as Lincoln himself traced his paternity. Lincoln was vaguely aware that there were Quakers in his paternal family line.[44] Because of the Indian hostilities, it was difficult for John Lincoln to maintain a Quaker's pacifism on the Virginia and Kentucky frontier, and he appears to have switched from the Quaker to the Baptist denomination. In the aftermath of the American Revolution the British incited the Indians to resist American westward expansion, provoking widespread bloodshed, particularly in Kentucky in the 1780s.[45] John's son and President Lincoln's grandfather, Captain Abraham Lincoln (1744–1786), moved from Virginia to Kentucky in 1782 where he was killed by Indians a few years afterward.[46] "The story of his death by the Indians," Lincoln later wrote, "and of Uncle Mordecai, then fourteen years old, killing one of the Indians, is the legend more strongly than all others imprinted upon my mind and memory."[47] As the story came down to the future president, his grandfather was killed, "not in battle, but by stealth, when he was laboring to open a farm in the forest."[48] In the existing record, Lincoln never mentioned his grandfather without relating this story.[49] Captain Lincoln was buried in the Long Run Baptist Church Cemetery of Jefferson County, Kentucky. Though an Episcopalian, his wife was buried in the First Regular Baptist Church's Mill Creek Cemetery in Hardin County, Kentucky. Lincoln's respect for the Quaker faith as well as his rejection of the Quaker's radical individualism and pacifism had its roots in this family history. That legacy became apparent in the terms with which Lincoln reacted to the radical antislavery movement's similarly radical ethical stance. Unlike other prominent Republicans, Lincoln never dallied with either ethical perfectionism or pacifism.

While in Kentucky, Lincoln's father Thomas was a Separate Baptist, rejecting all formal creeds and statements of faith except those in the Bible. Baptists in particular were known for their insistence on freedom of conscience, and Separates took this to the extreme.[50] Rather than a distaste for theological disputation, the insistence on absolute freedom of conscience in matters of faith reflected something close to its opposite; theological argument re-

mained a mainstay of Baptist piety. (Similarly, Abraham Lincoln's unwillingness formally to join a particular church in no way implied an impatience
with theological reasoning.) Instead of bringing "peace to the church," however, the Separate experiment of relying solely on individual conscience and
the Bible soon proved inadequate. Not unlike the Quakers on this point, the
Separates did not stress a learned ministry and had no official creed. They
were very successful in revivals and forming new churches, but various here-
sies crept in among them, especially Arminianism, or the reliance on the individual's works for salvation rather than God's free grace and the work of the
Holy Spirit. In Virginia the Separates reunited with the Regular Baptists as
early as 1787 on the basis of adherence to the Philadelphia Confession (with
explanations).[51] In Kentucky, the Separate experiment lasted a little longer.
Eventually the more Calvinistic Kentucky Separates with whom the Lincoln's
migrated to Indiana in 1816 cast off their Arminian (later, Free Will) Baptist
brethren and joined with the Regular Baptists to form the United Baptists.[52]
Lincoln's determination to maintain some purity of doctrine and to see the
American state as requiring a creedal statement like the Declaration of Independence reflected this failed experience with noncreedal churches. Other
Republicans were willing to dally with Douglas in the Lecompton struggle or
to compromise on slavery extension in the secession winter because they believed that they would come out ahead. Lincoln by contrast was willing to
concede on practical issues but unwilling to compromise on the substance of
antislavery commitment that he held to be more important. While practical
arrangements remained secondary and, to the annoyance of ethical perfec-
tionists, negotiable, the creed, or central idea, was primary—and of even
more importance than the reality of human bondage.

Though a Separate, Lincoln's father supervised the building of the Pigeon
Creek (Regular) Baptist Church in 1821. When the Kentucky Separates made
peace with the Regulars in 1823, he joined the Pigeon Creek church "by letter" from the Little Mount Separate Baptist Church back in Kentucky, his
wife joining "by experience" in the same year. Thereafter it seems he was a
regular member. His daughter and Abraham Lincoln's sister, Sarah, was married in the church and died in childbirth shortly thereafter. The articles of
faith adopted by the Little Pigeon Baptist Church were carefully crafted (if
carelessly spelled), and they repeated the essentials of Reformed doctrine.
"We believe in one god the Father the word & the holley gost who haith created all things that are created by the word of his power for his pleasure,"
stated the first article. The second article declared that in the Bible could be
found everything necessary to man's salvation, rule of faith, and practice.
The third asserted the fall of man; the fourth, the doctrines of election, calling, regeneration, and sanctification; the fifth, the perseverance of the saints;
the sixth, the final judgment; the seventh, that good works were the fruits of
grace that followed after justification; the eighth, that believer's baptism and
the Lord's Supper were ordinances (typical Baptist fare); the tenth, that the
Lord's Supper should be administered at least twice a year; and the eleventh,

that ministers ought to be called and sent of God, come properly recommended, and receive proper recompense.

The ninth article of the Little Pigeon statement instituted the command of foot washing, a ritual common to Baptists of Appalachia. Some Kentucky Baptists took it up as early as 1788 from the thirteenth chapter of John, and it symbolized the need for renewed baptism.[53] Christ insisted on washing the feet of his disciples, saying "anyone who has bathed only needs to have his feet washed to be altogether clean. And you are already clean—though not all of you." Regardless of rank or station, each of the saints, or church members, would wash the feet of another, acknowledging both their need for cleansing, and the requirement of humility. The practice is still common among Primitive Baptists, who in radically Augustinian fashion reject the notion that original sin can be overcome in this world.[54]

At age fourteen, Abraham Lincoln was sexton of the church. The position required his attendance whenever the church was open, and he was known to have mimicked the sermons he heard there.[55] His stepmother, Sarah Bush Lincoln, later told Herndon that "Abe read the bible some, though not as much as said . . . [he] had no particular religion—didnt think of that question at that time, if he ever did." Nevertheless Lincoln was not entirely deaf to the theology surrounding him. "He would hear a sermons preached," she continued, "come home—take the children out—get on a stump or log and almost repeat it word for word."[56] While such imitation may have been no form of flattery, sincere or otherwise, nevertheless Lincoln clearly learned his Reformed orthodoxy well enough to be self-conscious in his use of it.[57] If one loosely equates Calvinism with predestinarianism in the usual manner, Alfred Kazin was correct to say that "something of the Calvinism so natural to the hardships of the frontier clung to the churchless and fatalistic Lincoln." But for most of his life Lincoln was not churchless, and it should go without saying that there was nothing natural to the frontier about either Calvinism or fatalism. Like Wolf, Kazin saw the Baptist beliefs of Lincoln's youth as "primitive." But Kentucky Baptists did not follow some form of "nature religion" or "superstitious" theology.[58] Their religion was rather a finely articulated result of centuries of religious development. Wolf was closer to the truth when he noted that "frontier religion was the vehicle of culture for this Hoosier youth."[59] Lincoln was well catechized. The revivalist methods of Separate Baptists in Virginia resulted in significant black membership, and Lincoln may even have imbibed some of his early antislavery convictions from the preachers at Pigeon Creek.[60] His father's deep antislavery convictions may also have been related to early experiences with biracial Kentucky Separate Baptists.

Other sources of religious education for Lincoln included the Lincoln family copy of Starke Dupuy's *Hymns and Spiritual Songs*, a hymnbook (without musical notation) full of the kind of rhymed quadrameter Lincoln later wrote himself.[61] The first entry in the *Collected Works of Abraham Lincoln* (and therefore the oldest thing in Lincoln's hand) includes a quotation of the opening of an Isaac Watts Hymn, "Time what an empty vapor tis," with a marginal notation about the meter.[62] Among the hymnbook's songs still popular today were "Amazing Grace" and "Come Thou Fount of Every Blessing."

But Lincoln's scant formal education outside of church also included heavy doses of Reformed theology, often in the form of stories celebrating the wisdom of Providence amid apparent woes, with paeans to the joys of Christianity and life eternal. "Every occurrence in the universe is *Providential:* because it is the consequence of those laws which Divine Wisdom has established as most productive of the general good," according to *The Kentucky Preceptor.* "But to select individual facts, as more directed by the hand of Providence than others, because we think we see a particular good purpose answered by them, is an infallible inlet to error and superstition." Other passages dripped with a kind of early Romanticism that may have had an effect on Lincoln: "Eternal fountain of feeling! It is here I *trace thee, and this is thy divinity which stirs within me;* not that in some sad and sickening moment, 'my soul shrinks back upon herself, and startles at destruction'— mere pomp of words! but that I feel some generous joys and generous cares beyond myself—all comes from thee, *great,* great sensorium of the world!" The expectation of the conversion experience was everywhere taken for granted, and Paul's conversion was urged as an argument for the truth of Christianity: "the example of St. Paul may assure us of the mercy of God towards mistaken consciences, and ought to inspire us with the most enlarged charity and good will towards those, whose erroneous principles mislead their conduct." In Lincoln's early environment there was simply no escaping the overwhelming cultural force of Reformed Christianity.[63]

As a former Separate and active member of the church, Lincoln's father was aware of the Old School and antimission impulses that arose in the 1820s and 1830s. One of the Kentucky preachers who became active in the Little Pigeon association of Indiana later withdrew to join the antimission Baptists.[74] Like their Separate Baptist predecessors, antimission Baptists rejected the educated ministry, insisting that God alone through free grace and the Holy Spirit could work the conversion of the sinner. William Warren Sweet wrote that "the anti-mission Baptists were ultra-Calvinistic in doctrine, were opposed to academic or theological education for the ministry, and were hostile to all societies for the promotion of the spiritual and social welfare of mankind. They thought that God in His own time and His own way would bring His elect to repentance and redemption. Any effort on the part of man to assist God in his redemptive work was therefore not only presumptuous, but wicked."[65] They rejected revivalistic means of grace and conversion such as missionary activity and even Sunday schools. "Stand still and see the salvation of the Lord," would have been a favorite text, because any active attempt to promote conversion necessarily implied an unwillingness to wait on God's sovereign pleasure. They were extremely hostile to any notion of a Christian state and thus tended to be Democrats rather than Whigs. Lincoln's father was an antislavery Whig, which at least on the issue of slavery would have put him in sympathy with the missionary societies and probably precluded any antimission involvement on the part of the Lincoln family. Nevertheless, the antimission impulse of Kentucky constituted an important minority within Reformed Christianity in the antebellum period, and it pointed to an ambivalence in the American Protestant mind regarding the relationship between politics and the state, one that runs through the writings of Lincoln.[66]

Unlike his sister, Lincoln did not join the church his father built. He would screen his religious experience through the ironic filter of post-Enlightenment, Romantic thought. Nevertheless a pervasive tension ran through all his writings, between the attempt to make Christian ideals relevant to the state through positive moral action and the fear that so doing amounted to a renunciation of reliance on God and the idolatrous worship of the worldly. During the war he would most closely link the fate of the northern view of American civilization with Christian ideals, but in the end he is best noted for his attempts to temper the arrogance of postmillennialist evangelical thought. On the one hand, the nation, like a church, was based on an articulated common creed, a set of narratives, and a set of sacred texts. Lincoln, indeed, spoke of national purpose in tones usually heard in church. On the other hand, the nation was not the Church.

YOUNG MAN LINCOLN

Between the time he left his family in 1831 and his literal and metaphorical arrival as an adult around the time of his marriage, Lincoln found room to explore a variety of intellectual possibilities, and in this period he does indeed seem to have been unchurched.[67] He did not, however, lose his interest in theological matters, a point that deserves stress. If it is true that after an encounter with convincing skepticism one can never quite go back to an earlier and perhaps more naive faith, then it is equally true that, having once incorporated the complexities of a religious worldview, one rarely shakes off its influences completely; one rarely loses interest in the questions of ultimate meaning raised by religion. And what was remarkable about the Romantic period was the degree to which people were conscious of their unique historical and spiritual situation. Lincoln's New Salem and early Springfield period was marked by intellectual exploration.

Paine's *Age of Reason,* Gibbon's *Decline and Fall of the Roman Empire,* Volney's *Ruins of Civilization,* and Voltaire are generally cited as works that Lincoln encountered in his twenties, along with Shakespeare and Burns.[68] With the possible exception of Shakespeare, each of these writers challenged Christianity in some way, and each enjoyed a somewhat naughty reputation. Paine of course openly attacked the teachings of Christianity as immoral and looked to human reason for something akin to salvation. Gibbon's entire historical vision blamed Christianity for the decline of Roman virtue. Volney saw in religion an unnatural and life-negating asceticism and predicted the union of all religions to be based on the more reasonable Epicureanism typical of late-eighteenth-century France.[69] For all his depth, even Burns questioned the justice of double predestination in a manner reminiscent of Voltaire, which doubtless added to the appeal for Lincoln of "Holy Willie's Prayer" and other poems of Burns.[70] Not only did Burns speak to Lincoln's emerging skepticism, but like Lincoln, the Scottish poet revolted against a specifically Calvinist religious past. After a religious early education, Lincoln began to absorb the Enlightenment.

Based on exhaustive editorial work on sources originally gathered by William Herndon, Douglas L. Wilson has recently endorsed the story that Lincoln wrote a book on "infidelity" during the New Salem years.[71] As the picturesque story goes, the scandalous book was snatched from the author and dashed into the fire to save his already portentous career. But in a campaign document of 1846 Lincoln seems to have denied the book's existence: "That I am not a member of any Christian Church, is true; but I have never denied the truth of the Scriptures; and I have never spoken with intentional disrespect of religion in general, or of any denomination of Christians in particular."[72] In any case, Lincoln and his intellectual companions argued their way through what was a wrenching shift in American culture away from an inherited Calvinism, through the skepticism of the Enlightenment, and to the sometimes uneasy zeal of the Romantic. In argument among themselves they took various positions that would have been viewed as scandalous to many others, and from the sources it is unclear whether Lincoln tended at that time to argue something like Painite infidelity or some form of universalism. (All of the sources, it must be said, are secondhand and sometimes thirdhand accounts from long after the events in question. And the matter is further complicated by a lack of clarity in the use of the word "infidelity.")[73]

Some of those who recollected having discussions about religion with Abraham Lincoln during the 1830s and 1840s characterized his position as a form of universalism, that is, he expressed discontent with the doctrine of double predestination by which some are destined before birth to damnation.[74] According to Mentor Graham, Lincoln based his argument on a close reading of 1 Corinthians 15:22, "for as in Adam all die, even so in Christ shall all be made alive." At other times the sources had Lincoln denying the authenticity of the Scriptures in the fashion of Paine. Though one might dispute Wilson's assertion that the evidence for this is "very strong," it may be true that Lincoln wrote a more radically Painite and "infidel" book.[75] Given the conflicting sources, it is probably best to adopt a skeptical attitude toward the precise nature of Lincoln's arguments during this period, since he may well have argued some form of Painism or universalism or, at various times, both. Indeed he may well have adopted in argument some other positions that are now completely forgotten. What does seem certain is that Lincoln abandoned any straightforward or literal version of his inherited belief. Equally certain and equally important, he never lost interest in theological disputation.

Existing Lincoln writings from before his move to Springfield in 1837 come to some seventy-seven pages, most of which consist of surveying business, legal documents, and legislative enactments or amendments.[76] The first notice of religion that survives in Lincoln's adult writings came in 1832, soon after he struck out on his own. In "To the People of Sangamo County" Lincoln suggested that education was important because it could enable every man both to read history (and thereby learn to appreciate the value of free institutions) and to read the Scriptures and other moral works.[77] The next surviving Lincoln writing concerning religion was a satire that Lincoln probably wrote in 1834. The piece was a send-up of Peter Cartwright, the famous Methodist circuit rider who would run against Lincoln in the 1846 congressional election. Writing under the name of his friend Sam Hill, Lincoln called Cartwright "a most abandoned hypocrite (I will not say in religion—for of this I pretend to know nothing—but) in politics."[78] Lincoln was deputy postmaster under Hill, and Hill's son was one of those who later claimed that Lincoln wrote a book on infidelity. The first accusations of Lincoln's infidelity arose in 1846, and if Peter Cartwright was behind them he may have been trying to even the score.[79]

The next reference to religion came in a private letter from 1837. Lincoln confessed he was lonely in his new residence at Springfield. "I have been spoken to by but one woman since I've been here, and should not have been by her, if she could have avoided it. I've never been to church yet, nor probably shall not be soon. I stay away because I am conscious I should not know how to behave myself." Too much of this correspondence is missing to know exactly what was at issue or whether Lincoln's statements were in some way ironic. Lincoln appears to have associated churchgoing with the society of women, though that may be reading too much into the passage. Lincoln's self-consciousness about class and respectability was genuine, and his humility appears real. Perhaps he was trying to find a tactful way to get rid of the addressee, Mary Owens, by calling attention to his failings. Without knowing more about his relationship with Owens; without knowing, for instance, whether she generally encouraged Lincoln to go to church; or whether Lincoln here invented an excuse for not going; it is difficult to make much of the confession.[80]

Not until 1838 does an important document pertaining to religion appear in the relatively scant record.[81] The Lyceum Address of January 1838 marked the beginning of a transition in Lincoln's life from backwoods New Salem legislator to member of the Springfield elite. The subject was "the perpetuation of our political institutions," and the lecture called for a kind of political religion. As recent disturbances with antiabolition mobs had attested, the memories of shared sacrifice during the American Revolution no longer provided adequate social cement, and in most un-Jacksonian fashion Lincoln therefore advocated "reverence for the constitution and laws." Here he picked up on the theme he first touched on in his 1832 announcement for the state assembly. Like the church of his father he had left, the nation had both a creed and sacred texts, and these, rather than any underlying social contract, lent it moral and legal identity. In effect his 1832 campaign document had called for a national catechism, and Lincoln repeated the call in 1838. "In history," said Lincoln, "we hope [the scenes of the revolution] will be read of, and recounted, so long as the bible shall be read;—but even granting that they will, their influence *cannot be* what it heretofore has been." Thus, in addition to these histories, political reason required a "reverence for the Constitution and the laws."[82]

Lincoln was putting forward a rather conservative solution. "Let every American, every lover of liberty, every well wisher to his posterity, swear by the blood of the Revolution, never to violate in the least particular, the laws of the country; and never to tolerate their violation by others."[83] But he was troubled by the conservative implications of his theory. Lincoln's reverence for the laws was never absolute. If there were bad laws, they should be borne only until repealed. Because he believed the laws were legitimate in spite of the fact that they protected the institution of slavery, Lincoln was not an abolitionist. Nevertheless, he remained open to a standard of right and wrong that was higher even than the Union. Since he believed slavery to be wrong, he was sympathetic to the antislavery message in a way that Bancroft or Van Buren or Douglas could not be, at least not in public. It is time once and for all to dispense with the notion that Lincoln's devotion to the Union was akin to "religious mysticism."[84] The idea originated with an apologist for the South and, indeed, can only be maintained at the expense of Lincoln's antislavery commitment. For Lincoln, America was emphatically *not* an "absolute good." As Major L. Wilson summed it up, "if Van Buren can be seen as a priest of political religion, the position Lincoln defined made room for a prophet."[85]

This puts us in a better position to understand the last sentences of Lincoln's Lyceum Address.

> Let those materials be moulded into *general intelligence, sound morality* and, in particular, *a reverence for the constitution and laws;* and, last; that we improved to the last; that we remained free to the last; that we revered his name to the last; that, during his long sleep, we permitted no hostile foot to pass over or desecrate his resting place; shall be that which to learn the last trump shall awaken our Washington.
>
> Upon these let the fabric of freedom rest, as the rock of its basis; and as truly as has been said of the only greater institution, *"the gates of hell shall not prevail against it."*[86]

The "last trump" was a figure of speech more than a literal reality, but for Bancroft and the Democrats history in its essentials had already come to an end; the last trump had already sounded. The overt Christian eschatology, or theory of the end of time, of Lincoln's Lyceum Address has seldom been remarked upon, but Lincoln deliberately began the lecture by placing the American people "under date of the nineteenth century of the Christian era." He overtly framed American history within the larger and more fundamental compass of Christian eschatology, and he explicitly rejected any interpretation of America as a divine fulfillment. Throughout the address he presented history as an open-ended affair from which he drew an inescapable moral: to "improve to the last." Where Bancroft saw an inevitable and progressive dialectic between the parties of reform and those of conservatism, Lincoln in this speech was quite deliberately more orthodox and even Augustinian. In the 1850s Lincoln would see in the slavery issue "the eternal struggle between these two principles—right and wrong—throughout the world. They are the two principles that have stood face to face from the beginning of time; and will ever continue to struggle."[87]

Lincoln's last sentence has received comparatively little attention, but given the elaborate theological self-conception articulated by the Democrats it was nothing short of stunning. Perry Miller began his great history of American thought with "the Augustinian Strain of Piety."[88] From there he—and Sacvan Bercovitch after him—charted the steady declension of that Augustinian piety into the worship of the American way of life itself.[89] "Gradually in America the nation emerged as the primary agent of God's meaningful activity in history. Hence Americans bestowed on it a catholicity of destiny similar to that which theology attributes to the universal church."[90] Though Whigs tended to use it as a summons to further moral striving, the founding "upon a rock," already a cliché, implicitly equated the church with the republic: virtually all of the great American intellectuals of the antebellum period followed Bancroft and equated America with the church universal in some fashion or other.[91] And postmillennialism was so prevalent in American churches of the period that "in 1859 the nondenominational *American Theological Review,* characterized these views as 'the commonly received doctrine.'"[92]

In a brief phrase that could not have been calculated to catch votes or to appease local religious sentiment, Lincoln revealed a theological thoughtfulness that surpassed Emerson, Thoreau, Hawthorne, and even the early Melville. Almost in the same breath that he called for a reverence for the law as a "political religion," he was troubled enough by the implications of his metaphor to note that America was not the church universal, let alone the church triumphant. And the remark was not an isolated incident in Lincoln's literary life; Lincoln quietly attempted to temper the chiliasm of his Romantic cohort—hence, for instance, his revision of "chosen country" from Jefferson's First Inaugural to "almost chosen people" at Trenton in 1861 (if the *New York Tribune* can be trusted) and hence, finally, his lectures on discoveries and inventions.[93] All our actions, including those regarding slavery, remained under the judgment of history—and of God.

In the Lyceum Address, Lincoln established the analogy between the United States and the Protestant churches that would characterize his writings on the nature of the Union (later, the "nation") throughout his career. Like the church, the state was bound by a kind of reverence. And, like the church, the American nation could "live through all time."[94] Lincoln came perilously close to worshipping American institutions, and he knew it.

While he knew that this amounted to putting the created before the creator, nevertheless he channeled some if not all of his religious energies into his thinking about American law and politics. Lincoln clearly had religious feelings for his country. He more than admired the great statesmen of the American founding; he revered them, and he aspired to be one of them. But Lincoln was also careful enough to note that the church was a "higher institution" than the American state. Thus, in a manner uncharacteristic for the age in which he lived, he struggled to articulate a form of Romantic nationalism that avoided deification of the state. Over time the prophetic possibilities for social criticism in this analogy between church and state would become more dominant. Lincoln would use the national creed to critique the national practice.

Perry Miller found that, in the Lyceum Address, Lincoln was poised ambiguously between Common Sense philosophy and the insurgent Romanticism of the 1830s and 1840s. Lincoln warned against men of "loftiest genius," a Caesar or a Napoleon, and offered as an antidote "Reason, cold, calculating, unimpassioned reason." Yet Miller found in Lincoln's argument "no abstract hostility to the sublime" or even, "in any modern sense, opposition to the romantic." Indeed, Lincoln was sure that, "by an eloquence which romantics could hardly equal," he was "opposing the cold circumspection of legal rationality to the fantastic exercises of romantic genius."[95] But Romanticism had an even greater effect on the young Lincoln than Miller imagined. At an early stage, Lincoln was clearly conscious of Romantic developments. Lincoln might have initially sided with the Enlightenment establishment, but so had Emerson. And Miller oddly missed the fact that, in addition to cold, calculating, unimpassioned reason, here Lincoln already called for a "political religion" that was more than the mere exercise of instrumental reason. Finally, Lincoln was in a process of development that a decade later resulted in his paean to the sublimity of Niagara Falls. Miller drew a distinction without a difference; if Lincoln eventually surpassed the Romantics in style, it was because he would become one of them.

In addition to uncovering the early skepticism of the young Lincoln and his circle, Douglas Wilson has also provided a great service in emphasizing Lincoln's subsequent Byronic phase. Wilson summed up Lincoln's New Salem early adulthood: though not an atheist, he "was so strongly critical of orthodox Christian beliefs that he sometimes looked like one of his more conventional friends, rejecting the divinity of Christ, the infallibility of the Scriptures, and an afterlife," Wilson noted of Lincoln's early adulthood. He was "something of a deist in the tradition of Jefferson, Voltaire, and Paine. Whereas these three were all decidedly upbeat about the prospects of a less superstitious and more rational world, however, Lincoln's outlook remained fatalistic. Here Wilson began to address the important differences between Lincoln and the Enlightenment figures he mentioned. It is safe to say Lincoln grappled more deeply with the consequences of a material cosmos than did Jefferson, Voltaire, or Paine. Wilson continued: "where others could appeal to a religious faith for hope and comfort in the contemplation of death, Lincoln's fatalistic deism, with no expectation of an afterlife, seems to have left him with a palpable sense of dread and staring into the abyss."[96] A year later he wrote that, "if ever I feel the soul within me elevate and expand to those dimensions not wholly unworthy of its Almighty Architect, it is when I contemplate the cause of my country, deserted by all the world beside, and I standing up boldly and alone and hurling defiance at her victorious oppressors. Here without contemplating consequences, before High Heaven, and in the face of the world, I swear eternal fidelity to the just cause, as I deem it, of the land of my life, my liberty and my love."[97] The phrase "Almighty Architect" may have been an echo of Paine and the Enlightenment, but the passage as a whole was Romantic.

Lincoln became enamored with the poetry of Lord Byron in the 1830s. Along with two of his closest personal friends, Joshua Speed and Henry C. Whitney, Lincoln dwelt lovingly upon *Childe Harold's Pilgrimage*, which was, among other things, a long *sic transit gloria mundi*, a meditation on the transience of existence. Wilson successfully tied Lincoln's famed melancholy to Byron's famed *Weltschmertz*. Science, said Poe, had "dragged Diana from her car," and Byron did Poe one better in the poem "Darkness," depicting a "dream, which was not all a dream," in which the bright sun was extinguished. A kind of Hobbesian war of all against all ensued in which even the animals joined, and the people were forced to grapple with the inevitability of their impending doom. Here, in a poem Lincoln also loved, was an early figure for the death of God and for the consequent confrontation with the empty universe that came along with it. Like many in his Romantic cohort, Lincoln appears to have had great difficulty with the implications of the scientific worldview for religion, not only with the loss of simple trust in the reality of a life hereafter but especially also with the implication that human striving ultimately had no meaning. He experienced deep depression brought on in part by the realization of the finality of death. Like the great poets, he found consolation in the ambition for lasting fame. He determined to live in such a way as to be remembered, and both literary and political ambition therefore became necessary parts of his character. Lincoln's legendary ambition and the Byronic tone of some of his early perorations, his other literary efforts, and even the lectures on discoveries and inventions all stem in part from this source. Thus, while it would leave marks, the blithe and superficial skepticism of Voltaire, Paine, Gibbon, and Jefferson did not in the end obscure the religious attitude, the Christian posture, the piety of Abraham Lincoln.[98]

Indeed, Lincoln may well have found a rationale for the classic notions of predestination and Providence in what he called "the doctrine of necessity— that is, that the human mind is impelled to action, or held in rest by some power, over which the mind itself has no control."[99] Even throughout Lincoln's skeptical early adulthood, that doctrine remained, along with all the moral and theological attitudes that such a position inevitably entailed.[100] There can be profound differences between equally deterministic descriptions of the world, and properly speaking Lincoln's thought was neither fatalistic nor mechanistic but providential. While the Fates are not necessarily benevolent, they are relatively friendly compared with the vast cosmic indifference of scientific determinism: with the Fates one was entitled to be angry. And the hidden yet ultimately benevolent God of biblical monotheism represents another possibility altogether. Thus regardless of the depth of his skepticism, Lincoln never accepted the humanism and free will of the Enlightenment. For one thing, Lincoln's version of necessity was theological rather than mechanistic.[101] The point of the doctrine of necessity for Lincoln was not the abstract philosophical one that, after all, everything has a cause and every cause an antecedent cause and so on, and thus free will is illusory. If Lincoln personalized his God only very rarely—take for instance his promise to God to issue the Emancipation Proclamation after a victory—he nonetheless always assumed that the universe was morally guided. It might be difficult to fathom, and the specific mechanism of divine guidance might be unclear, but from the perspective of an inscrutable God human history had meaning. "I am almost ready to say this is probably true," Lincoln would later suggest, "that God wills this contest [the Civil War] and wills that it shall not end yet. By his mere quiet power, on the minds of the now contestants, He could have either *saved* or *destroyed* the Union without a human contest."[102]

Typically tentative, Lincoln expressed himself with a double conditional: "almost," "probably." Nevertheless his doctrine of necessity required a personal response: he needed to adopt an attitude of humility toward life and death that adequately took into account the degree to which human beings are not entirely in control of events. So while Lincoln backed up the doctrines of predestination and Providence with what may have seemed a more up to date and intellectually respectable doctrine of necessity, his piety remained remarkably constant.[103] For instance, while he unconsciously assumed his own superiority over the men around him (and this would disturb the vanity of men like Salmon Chase), he was known for his magnanimity and for his profound humility. He could be ambitious without being vain. Further, he was able to remain calm in the midst of extremely difficult circumstances because he took consolation from knowing that, ultimately, events were not in his hands.

How exactly a doctrine of necessity squared with ethical responsibility was another question altogether, but it was one that the freethinking determinist no less than the Old School Presbyterian had to face, and the question preoccupied others of the time as well—one has only to think of Melville's endless musings about chance, free will, and necessity. And in the Second Inaugural Lincoln would face the issue squarely. Despite his bouts of skepticism and his consequent Romantic reformulation, he cast his lot in some degree with Reformed Doctrine and in particular with the Old School emphasis on predestination.[104] The decision put Lincoln in conflict with Methodism and with the emergent "New School" that made Arminian concessions to the Enlightenment belief that mankind was indeed free to shape its destiny if only it resolved to do so. During his 1846 congressional campaign against the Methodist circuit rider, Peter Cartwright, Lincoln noted of his doctrine of necessity that he had "always understood this same opinion to be held by several of the Christian denominations."[105] Contrary to the notion that Lincoln remained aloof from theological debates, he here somewhat ironically took an essentially Reformed stand against his Methodist opponent. Perhaps he assumed that no matter what he said he would not receive the Methodist vote. Thus from his childhood Baptist roots to the New Salem years and to his presidency, there would be important changes in the way Lincoln understood the world. Nevertheless, with Lincoln the sense remained constant that he was not the superman Ahab; he was not entirely free to shape his destiny. In the end it was his underlying piety that allowed Lincoln to reconstruct a usable form of Christianity.

The importance of poetry for Lincoln's development can hardly be overstated. In addition to generating a critique of the scientific and utilitarian worldview on the grounds of humankind's highest spiritual aspirations, Byron, Poe, and the Romantic poets provided renewed access to the religious tradition. The fragment at Niagara reveals that, through the medium of poetry, Lincoln was able to put himself into a symbolic and poetic relationship with the world, which even led him to experiment with poems of his own. The Romantic poets expressed Lincoln's own disillusionment with Enlightenment materialism and utilitarianism. He did not have to feel ashamed or bashful about the fact that he found a material world vapid. An intellectually viable piety was provided for him. It would have been scandalous to literalists who busied themselves about the task of reconciling Enlightenment thought with the biblical narrative in thousands of pages of tedious argument, but Lincoln could hold his head up in church, confident that with a few bold strokes of a poet's pen his thoughts on religion could cut to the heart of human experience and be rendered consonant with the deepest thinkers of his age.[106] All of Lincoln's biographers have remarked on his passion for the Romantic poets, but the path usually goes nowhere in their narratives. Only a superb intellectual confidence could produce a work like the Gettysburg Address. Indeed, a superb intellectual confidence is apparent through most of Lincoln's career. Lincoln could gain intellectual confidence from his mastery of storytelling, of the law, of Euclid, of constitutional disputation, and of politics. But Lincoln also found much of that confidence in an ironic but sincere poetic reappropriation of his ancestral faith.

Chapter Seven

POETRY AND RELIGIOUS ORTHODOXY
IN THE SECOND INAUGURAL

• Lincoln was particularly depressed in early 1841, a time when it seems he rediscovered the Bible. Perhaps the death of Ann Rutledge called up memories of the deaths in early life of his mother and sister, or perhaps his early career frustrations, the dissolution of his legal partnership, and his new Springfield environment left him alienated and unsure of himself; perhaps his troubled engagement to Mary Todd contributed to his sense of gloom. In any case, his friends thought him near suicide.[1] Michael Burlingame described his situation:

> To recuperate from the emotional earthquake that had shaken him so badly, Lincoln took a vacation in the summer of 1841, spending four weeks at Joshua Speed's family home in Kentucky. There he benefited, as Herndon put it, from the "congenial associations at the Speed farm, the freedom from unpleasant reminders, the company of his staunch friend, and above all the motherly care and delicate attention of Mrs. Speed." According to Speed, his mother solicitously looked after Lincoln, and one day, when she observed him "very melancholy," she "with a woman[']s instinct being much pained at his deep depression" presented him with a Bible, "advising him to read it, [and] to adopt its precepts."[2]

Lincoln made reference to the gift a few months after returning to Springfield: "Tell your mother that I have not got her 'present' (the Oxford Bible) with me; but that I intend to read it regularly when I return home. I doubt not that it is really, as she says, the best cure for the 'Blues' could one but take it according to the truth."[3]

By his own account, Lincoln gave up arguing for his doctrine of necessity about this time, but in poetic Christian form he would return to it for the rest of his life.[4] In the letter to Mary Speed, Lincoln quoted and explained a providential passage from a French proverb. The occasion was his return trip from the South and his reaction to a group of slaves "strung together like so many fish upon a trot-line." They had been sold down the river and yet, Lincoln noted, they nevertheless laughed and joked more than anyone else on the steamboat. "How true it is," wrote Lincoln, "that 'God tempers the wind to the shorn lamb,' or in other words, that He renders the worst of human conditions tolerable, while He permits the best, to be nothing better than tolerable."

The letter thus presents the reader not only with Lincoln's early distaste for the institution of slavery but also with the paradox of Lincoln's approach to the Bible and religion. At the same moment he expressed doubts about the literal veracity of the Bible, he was capable of using religious poetry expertly. Typical of Lincoln was the choice of passages; the view of God was providential. In poetic fashion Lincoln applied a providential interpretation to the concrete world in front of him, in this case to the apparent paradox that the enslaved devoted more time than the nominally free did to the arts of music and humor—arts that, as he described in the lectures on discoveries and inventions, he held above all others. Not coincidentally, people like Thoreau and Melville shared similar observations about the aridity of American life at about the same time.[5] Lincoln's poetic reappropriation of orthodox Protestant Christianity in his first years in Springfield may well have solved a difficult political problem—he certainly was not going to win elections by pointing out the logical deficits of the biblical narrative—but it clearly served more personal needs. There was something more than discretion or political expediency in his use of biblical and religious poetry.[6] The letter to the Speeds, close friends in Kentucky, could not have been calculated to win favor of any relevance in Springfield. From this point on in Lincoln's life the biblical language for which he is known became more pronounced as he left the "infidel" talk of his youth behind him and embarked on an almost private literary career, frequently drawing on his deep understanding of Christian thought and poetry.

If, as eyewitnesses later attested, Lincoln continued during his early Springfield years to make fun of the paradoxes inherent in a Christian worldview, little of it comes through in his correspondence with his friend Joshua Speed or his family.[7] In fact Lincoln appears to have taken the lead in bringing his friend to a greater appreciation of religion. Speed feared for the life of his recent bride, and Lincoln eagerly pressed upon his friend the value of her religion.

> I hope and believe, that your present anxiety and distress about *her* health and *her* life, must and will forever banish those horrid doubts, which I know you sometimes felt, as to the truth of your affection for her. If they can be once and forever removed, (and I almost feel a presentiment that the Almighty has sent your present affliction expressly for that object) surely, nothing can come in their stead, to fill their immeasurable measure of misery. The death scenes of those we love, are surely painful enough; but these we are prepared to, and expect to see. They happen to all, and all know they must happen. Painful as they are, they are not an unlooked-for-sorrow. Should she, as you fear, be destined to an early grave, it is indeed, a great consolation to know that she is so well prepared to meet it. Her religion, which you once disliked so much, I will venture you now prize most highly.

The impression given by this correspondence is one of a man sincerely convinced of the consolation of religion at a time when death was an all too familiar visitor.[8] This in no way proves that Lincoln himself had come to a literal belief in a life hereafter; in other moods, he continued to have good fun at the expense of religion. In the letter to Speed cited at the beginning of chapter 6, Lincoln made fun of his "superstition" as well as of himself. But the passage rules out the notion that he was secretly dismissive of religion. If the exact nature of his belief or unbelief remained ambiguous, by 1842 his respect for religion was obviously sincere. And it was something more than respect at a distance. In an effort to find coherence and meaning in events, Lincoln constantly struggled with the language of Providence.

MORE ORTHODOX THAN THOU

In the existing record these early developments in Lincoln's religious outlook found their fullest expression in the "Address to the Washington Temperance Society of Springfield, Illinois."[9] "One of the most important speeches expressing Lincoln's political philosophy," it presented, according to Herman Belz, "a searching critique of the attitude and methods of the reformers of his day."[10] For Belz the speech was most remarkable because in it Lincoln challenged the self-righteous approach taken by many advocates of the temperance movement that so radically changed the drinking habits of Americans during this period.[11] "A drop of honey catches more flies than a gallon of gall," said Lincoln, and with that he praised the Washingtonians for their more effective approach to the problem of alcoholism.[12] In the Washingtonian scheme, recovering alcoholics joined together to take a pledge of abstinence, and rather than using denunciation or legislative prohibition they relied on persuasion to convince the habitual drinker to stop for his own good. Virtually abstinent himself, Lincoln had never been active in the temperance movement.[13] The address provided him not only with an opportunity to speak outside of the courtroom or the legislature but with an opportunity to clarify his reasoning on the reform movements of the period.

The address has traditionally been used to separate Lincoln from those reform movements.[14] Lincoln, or so the reasoning went, displayed none of the misguided self-righteousness of more avowed abolitionists like Salmon P. Chase, for instance. Lincoln did warn, it is true, against the dangers that self-righteousness presented to the very cause its advocates claimed to promote. The Temperance Address paralleled Lincoln's early protest against an antiabolition resolution in the Illinois legislature of 1837. Lincoln there joined another representative in stating "that the institution of slavery is founded on both injustice and bad policy; but that the promulgation of abolition doctrines tends rather to increase than to abate its evils."[15]

But in both cases the antiself-righteousness interpretation, while important, threatens to obscure the more obvious point that in gratuitous fashion Lincoln publicly allied himself with two of the pet causes of the revivalists. If Lincoln separated himself from the more radical reformers of the antebellum period, he consistently expressed solidarity with their goals. What is more, he here addressed the evangelicals *on their own terms*. Two weeks earlier he had been selected to eulogize a member of the Temperance Society, a task he performed expertly. In the eulogy, published in the *Sangamo Journal*,

Lincoln already displayed full command of a form he would bring to perfection at Gettysburg. More important here, he used the language of disinterested benevolence so fundamental to the antebellum reform movements.[16] Seen in this light, the Temperance Address was the first great installment of Lincoln's Romantic and Christian political thought.

The address began with an unrestrained millennial vision, and at first reading one is almost tempted to think Lincoln had to be kidding.

> The cause (temperance) itself seems suddenly transformed from a cold abstract theory, to a living, breathing, active, and powerful chieftain, going forth "conquering and to conquer." The citadels of his great adversary are daily being stormed and dismantled; his temples and his altars, where the rites of his idolatrous worship have long been performed, and where human sacrifices have long been wont to be made, are daily desecrated and deserted. The trump of the conqueror's fame is sounding from hill to hill, from sea to sea, and from land to land, and calling millions to his standard at a blast.[17]

To anyone familiar either with the *Whig Review* and the *Democratic Review* or with postmillennial Protestant polemics, however, this kind of purple prose should be all too familiar.[18] Taking almost blasphemous liberties with Christian symbolism in this manner was typical of the literary style of the antebellum period.

Probably reflecting the desire of scholars to show Lincoln off at his best, this is not the kind of quotation preferred by Lincoln's historians. If mentioned at all, this overblown oratory has generally been dismissed as a kind of youthful overreaching that reflected more a nod to social convention than fidelity to the original genius Lincoln was later to become. But if this was one of Lincoln's most important speeches, some attempt must be made to explain the passages that have not aged so well. In the address Lincoln treated temperance as a cause perhaps more important even than the cause of republican institutions—high praise coming from Lincoln. And he would call up the slavery issue as well by comparing intemperance to the moral death of slavery.[19] As in the Lyceum Address, Lincoln here used the millennial language of the last trump, and for the moment at least he seems to have allowed himself to be swept up in the optimism of the time. Like the writers of the *Whig Review*, Lincoln here used language that bridged the Romantic with more traditional Christian symbol systems. In particular, the juxtaposition of "cold abstract theory" with "a living, breathing, active, and powerful chieftain" was reminiscent of the antiutilitarian writings of the *Whig Review*.

Lincoln continued:

> But when one, who has long been known as a victim of intemperance, bursts the fetters that have bound him, and appears before his neighbors "clothed, and in his right mind," a redeemed specimen of long lost humanity, and stands up with tears of joy trembling in eyes, to tell of the miseries *once* endured, *now* to be endured no more forever; of his once naked and starving children now

clad and fed comfortably; of a wife long weighed down with woe, weeping, and a broken heart, now restored to health, happiness, and renewed affection; and how easily it all is done, once it is resolved to be done; however simple is language, there is a logic, and an eloquence in it, that few, with human feelings, can resist. They cannot say that *he* desires a union of church and state, for he is not a church member; they can not say *he* is vain of hearing himself speak, for his whole demeanor shows, he would gladly avoid speaking at all; they cannot say *he* speaks for pay for he receives none, and asks for none. Nor can his sincerity in any way be doubted; or his sympathy for those he would persuade to imitate his example, be denied.[20]

The fact that Lincoln advocated relatively moderate means of achieving humanitarian goals like antislavery and temperance should not be allowed to obscure his deep affinity with the humanitarian reform movements of the antebellum period. Writings like this make it easier to fit Lincoln into the world of Harriet Beecher Stowe. He took enough pride in the speech to send it to Speed and his wife begging them to read it; and in spite of its evangelical tone he did not find it necessary to apologize to his skeptical friend.[21]

In the speech he used the language of the conversion experience, though not the austere language of conversion associated with the Puritans or with Jonathan Edwards, a form of piety maintained in this period by such fringe groups as the Primitive Baptists and antimission Baptists. Rather he reflected the heyday of nineteenth-century evangelicalism when the prevailing assumption held that one *could* simply choose this day whom one would serve.[22] Thus in place of an absolute sense of dependence on the Almighty, an overt optimism about the capacity of human beings to choose good (Pelagianism) momentarily slipped in here, an attitude more typical of Methodism, revivalist Congregationalism, and New School Presbyterianism than of radical Calvinism or of the mature Lincoln: one had merely to resolve to be temperate and it was done.

This was not Lincoln at his most psychologically astute, and it becomes clear later in the speech that he did not quite mean to endorse free will the way it appears here. But Lincoln did make common cause with humanitarian reformers. He went so far as to suggest that, in the temperance revolution, "we shall find a stronger bondage broken; a viler slavery, manumitted; a greater tyrant deposed" than the political revolution of 1776 in which "the world [had] found a solution of that long mooted problem, as to the capability of man to govern himself," the "germ" of which "has vegetated, and still is to grow and expand into the universal liberty of mankind."[23] (Notice the Romantic historical theory with its organic rather than mechanical metaphor.) And he took the evangelical's part against a Democratic Party objection that held that the northern reform movements sought an illicit combination of church and state. Though he objected to some of their methods, he repeatedly went out of his way to assert that their moral concerns were legitimate. As a Whig and as a Republican he would go further to insist that the reforms were legitimate *political* concerns as well.

Much in this speech was reminiscent of Theodore Dwight Weld and the humanitarianism of the "antislavery impulse."[24] Weld was concerned especially with the rational immortal soul, degraded and imbruted by slavery. That idea was implicit in the link that Lincoln made between temperance and antislavery. Intemperance, said Lincoln, left its victims "prostrate in the chains of moral death." He looked for a "happy day, when, all appetites controlled, all passions subdued, all matters subjected, *mind*, all conquering *mind*, shall live and move the monarch of the world." Thus, when Lincoln looked for a "Reign of Reason," he was not at odds with the revival, nor was he endorsing the deism of Thomas Paine.[25]

At this point in his career, Lincoln gave a relatively standard evangelical defense of "moral suasion."

> On this point, the Washingtonians greatly excel the temperance advocates of former times. Those whom they desire to convince and persuade, are their old friends and companions. They know they are not demons, nor even the worst of men. *They* are practical philanthropists; and *they* glow with a generous and brotherly zeal, that mere theorizers are incapable of feeling. Benevolence and charity possess *their* hearts entirely; and out of the abundance of their hearts, their tongues give utterance. "Love through all their actions runs, and all their words are mild." In this spirit they speak and act, and in the same, they are heard and regarded. And when such is the temper of the advocate, and such of the audience, no good cause can be unsuccessful.

This from the man who accepted war rather than let the nation perish. The Temperance Address *was* youthful, and it *was* conventional. If, as Belz suggested, the Temperance Address was "one of the most important speeches expressing Lincoln's political philosophy," however, it was not because it presented "a searching critique of the attitude and methods of the reformers of his day." On the contrary, it was perfectly in line with the irenic, optimistic spirit of those humanitarian reform movements—and, one should add, naively so. Sentiments like these led others to pacifism. It was perfectly in line with Theodore Dwight Weld and the antislavery impulse, and it was perfectly in line with the revivals. To be sure, there were some minor Lincolnian deviations, moments when his darker understanding of the human condition showed through.[26] And Lincoln distanced himself from the *radical* wing of reform, including especially radical abolitionism. But taken as a whole, the Temperance Address was among Lincoln's most optimistic productions. Far from rejecting the spirit of reform in this speech, Lincoln embraced it.

There were some rather original ideas, however. By drawing on his solid understanding of the Christian thought Lincoln inaugurated the important rhetorical tactic of outorthodoxing the orthodox. Many scholars have been tempted to claim that Lincoln's God was one that left little room or need for a savior. Words like "Providence" and "Almighty" occur in his writings far more frequently than do references to the Second Person. Nevertheless Lincoln's cautioning against self-righteousness presupposed the Atonement.

"But," say some, "we are no drunkards; and we shall not acknowledge ourselves such by joining a Reformed drunkard's society, whatever our influence might be." Surely no Christian will adhere to this objection. If they believe, as they profess, that Omnipotence condescended to take on himself the form of sinful man, and, as such, to die an ignominious death for their sakes, surely they will not refuse submission to the infinitely lesser condescension, for the temporal, and perhaps eternal salvation, of a large, erring, and unfortunate class of their own fellow creatures. Nor is the condescension very great.

In my judgment, such of us as have never fallen victims, have been spared more from the absence of appetite, then from any mental or moral superiority over those who have.[27]

The last remark implied that perhaps there was more to becoming temperate than merely choosing to be so, which contradicted Lincoln's opening remarks that resolving to be temperate was enough. Lincoln here returned to his habitual belief that one was not entirely or even primarily in control of one's own choices. One therefore needed to adopt a posture of humility, forgiveness, and thankfulness. (And this suggests a necessary corrective to any exaggerated use of Lincoln as the prototypical self-made man.)

Perhaps more important here, Lincoln made explicit use of the Second Person in the Temperance Address. The speech—in fact a sermon—was an exhortation to imitate Christ. By appealing to Christ's example Lincoln's aim was to thwart self-righteousness. However much they might surpass Lincoln in literal professions of faith, any would-be orthodox Christians could act in a more Christian spirit of forgiveness and humility were they to adopt the program of the Washingtonians. Loosely construed, this was Lincoln's version of the Pharisee and the publican, and Lincoln left no one guessing as to who belonged in the temple: he sided with the recovering alcoholics. Though Lincoln here denounced denunciation, the speech was not a critique of humanitarian reform. Rather, it was a profoundly Christian counter to any self-congratulatory pharisaism that might have crept in among the faithful.

Lincoln quite literally returned to his early church education to make the point:

By the Washingtonians, this system of consigning the habitual drunkard to hopeless ruin, is repudiated. *They* adopt a more enlarged philanthropy. *They* go for present as well as future good. *They* labor for all *now* living, as well as all *hereafter* to live. *They* teach hope to all—*despair* to none. As applying to *their* cause, *they* deny the doctrine of unpardonable sin. As in Christianity it is taught, so in this *they* teach, that

"While the lamp holds out to burn,
The vilest sinner may return."

And, what is matter of the most profound gratulation, they, by experiment upon experiment, and example upon example, prove the maxim to be no less true in the one case than in the other. On every hand we behold those, who but yesterday, were the chief of sinners, now the chief apostles of the cause.[28]

The quotation was from Isaac Watts's *Hymns and Spiritual Songs,* a body of hymnody that Lincoln encountered in his youth.[29] Lincoln found a use for his early Kentucky Baptist training after all. The last paragraph also deserves noting because it replicates in the essentials the passages from Lincoln's early schoolbooks, which, as noted earlier, held out the conversion of Paul as a model. Thus "even the vilest of sinners" had the possibility of becoming an apostle Paul.

Lincoln here used Scripture to confront evangelicals with an even more radically orthodox Christian message. Lincoln deliberately countered his use of the more Methodist language of moral suasion and free will with the core, orthodox Protestant belief that, of his own sovereign will, God chose whom to redeem. Redemption was not based on human choices or ethical merit. The tactic of outorthodoxing the orthodox and the use of Christian thought and imagery would characterize Lincoln's speeches and writings for the rest of his life. While he may or may not have become more concerned with religion and religious issues after the loss of his sons and during the war, few if any of his later speeches were more deeply Christian than this early one. Lincoln found his basic rhetorical strategy and persona early. By the early 1840s he had moved beyond the skepticism that separated him from his Baptist boyhood. Though not quite a converted evangelical Christian, Lincoln was nevertheless on his way to becoming a Romantic Christian intellectual.

One confusing passage of the Temperance Address deserves clarification:

> If, then, what I have been saying be true, is it wonderful, that *some* should think and act *now,* as *all* thought and acted *twenty years ago?* The universal *sense* of mankind, on any subject, is an argument, or at least an *influence* not easily overcome. The success of the argument in favor of the existence of an over-ruling Providence, mainly depends upon that sense; and men ought not, in justice, to be denounced for yielding to it, in any case, or for giving it up slowly, *especially,* where they are backed by interest, fixed habits, or burning appetites.[30]

It is difficult to imagine that this analogy between changing public opinion on the temperance issue and, of all things, the belief in Providence was an effective argument. Even those paying careful attention probably missed the point: since the universal sense of mankind was the chief argument in favor of the belief in Providence, it ought also to be respected in the matter of alcohol abuse. If evangelicals relied on the Common Sense philosophy to establish moral and theological truths such as the existence of God, they ought not to be too self-righteous if heavy drinkers acquired their attitudes about drinking from that same universal opinion. Here Lincoln may have been taunting New School evangelicals with the unexpected consequences of their own doctrine, but he may also have been somewhat confused; the argument is oddly self-contradictory.

Again, Lincoln's personal intellectual development paralleled the intellectual history of the West. Whereas elsewhere in the address Lincoln already used more Romantic idioms, in his transition from skepticism to Romanticism he seems here to have dallied momentarily with the Common Sense school.[31] The Temperance Address not only endorsed the ethical tactic of moral suasion common to evangelicals, it also made peculiar use of their epistemological theories and faculty psychology, showing that, whatever one wants to say about Lincoln and religion, he made a personal study of the religious philosophy available in his day. Essential background for this passage was the emerging Old School–New School split in the Presbyterian Church. "In answer to the skepticism of Hume, [the Common Sense philosophy taught that all men] could reliably recognize truth when they saw it. Not only could they be sure of the existence of the material world, but also of certain self-evident truths," from logic and mathematics to the existence of God and principles of morality.[32] Reform-minded New Schoolers relied on the Common Sense philosophy to justify their optimistic approach toward revivals as well as toward temperance, antislavery, and their unusually literal-minded readings of Scripture.[33] In the Temperance Address, Lincoln explicitly grappled with the Common Sense philosophy that dominated the religious colleges of antebellum America.

But Lincoln also seemed to undermine the evangelical mainstays—moral suasion, the Common Sense philosophy, and freedom of the will—even as he cited them. Where evangelical New Schoolers asserted that man was a free agent, Lincoln made contradictory appeals to the orthodox Calvinist thought he learned as a youth. And by acknowledging variability in the "universal sense of mankind" Lincoln undermined the Common Sense argument for the "existence of an over-ruling Providence." If, as changing attitudes toward alcohol attested, the universal sense of mankind or "universal public opinion" varied with time and place, how then could it be used to justify the belief in anything, let alone in the existence of God? Lincoln was on the verge of discovering the Achilles' heel of Common Sense thought: in fact there *was* no common moral sense, no self-evident truth. Just five months later he would write the letter to Speed in which he referred to his own belief in Providence as "superstition," something no convinced Common Sense religious thinker would ever say. Like the *Whig Review,* Lincoln left room for the idea of "human nature, which is God's decree, and never can be reversed."[34] But this was reserved for negative pronouncements about human weakness, selfishness, and inability—for Original Sin. Rapid changes in the way people organized their lives gave rise to slang terms like "Old Fogy" and made it apparent that moral categories had a history. The reality of shifting mores in a world of historical change made the existence of any positive, innate ideas impossible to maintain.

Eventually Romanticism allowed Lincoln to articulate his radically providential Calvinism more clearly. The Fragment on Niagara Falls shows that Lincoln eventually abandoned the language of Common Sense philosophy altogether. Common Sense New School Presbyterians explicitly rejected any religion that found "'pleasure in the contemplation of the starry heavens; of hills, and streams, and lakes, of the landscape and of the ocean; and [was] willing in these things to admire and praise the existence and perfections of the Creator.' Such a religion, said [Albert] Barnes, may be of some artistic value. But it was [no] different from ancient paganism and could not be preached."[35] And in the Second Inaugural Lincoln would leave behind any hint of New School evangelical faith in human agency. The Romantics insisted that all perception required a prior act of intuition—that was Poe's point. All perception was also interpretation. Through poetry and religion, knowledge of God came before experience, and Lincoln perceived the world through the poetic interpretive framework of a God of history. He strained to see the hand of Providence in the events of his life. Through this poetic struggle with the interpretive language of Providence and predestination he would find meaning in the Civil War.

ROMANTIC CHRISTIANITY IN POLITICS

One of the first political issues to arise for Lincoln after his articulation of Romantic Christian political theory came with the defeat of Henry Clay and the election of Polk in 1844. Strikingly, Lincoln did not just assume the theological stance widely held by opponents of slavery; he actually took up the theological debate on his own. While he might have surrendered theology to the more radically, and indeed self-righteously, abolitionist wing of the antislavery movement, he instead justified his particular brand of moderate antislavery by reemphasizing the doctrine of original sin and denying the postmillennialist possibility of worldly perfection. He heartily accepted the theological terms of the debate, but he insisted that in his moderate position he was actually more orthodox than the orthodox or, more precisely, more orthodox than the pietists.

Lincoln believed that the defection of antislavery Whigs to the Liberty Party had cost Henry Clay and the Whigs the state of New York in 1844.[36] According to Lincoln, the Whigs were as opposed to the extension of slavery as the Liberty Party—even more so. The "Whig abolitionists" of New York's "burned over," or revivalist, northern districts were morally responsible for the disastrous election of Polk and the consequent Mexican Cession. In rejecting the perfectionism of James G. Birney's 1844 Liberty Party, Lincoln appealed directly to the Gospel of Matthew.

> What was their process of reasoning, I can only judge from what a single one of them told me. It was this: "We are not to do *evil* that *good* may come." This general, proposition is doubtless correct; but did it apply? If by your votes you could have prevented the *extension*, &c. of slavery, would it not have been *good* and not *evil* so to have used your votes, even though it involved the casting of them for a slaveholder? By the *fruit* the tree is to be known. An *evil* tree can not bring forth *good* fruit. If the fruit of electing Mr. Clay would have been to prevent the extension of slavery, could the act of electing have been *evil*. . . . I hold it to be a paramount duty of us in the free states, due to the Union of the states, and perhaps to liberty itself (paradox though it may seem) to let the slavery of

the other states alone; while, on the other hand, I hold it to be equally clear, that we should never knowingly lend ourselves directly or indirectly, to prevent that slavery from dying a natural death—to find new places for it to live in, when it can no longer exist in the old. Of course I am not now considering what would be our duty, in cases of insurrection among the slaves.[37]

In hindsight the last line has an ominous ring. Here Lincoln hinted that, while the North should not knowingly prevent the "natural" death of slavery, the Constitution did indeed require the North to aid the South in suppressing a slave rebellion. And in the case of John Brown's attempted insurrection, Lincoln would attempt to allay southern fears of northern complicity by dismissing him as a lawless "enthusiast."[38] Lincoln never faltered in his respect for positive law. From an orthodox point of view, Brown was a radical pietist who did not adequately understand that the complexities of the human condition required allegiance both to the revealed will of God and to the positive law of the created order.

But Lincoln here made a more important point concerning Christian ethics. After dispensing with the idea that one could become righteous before God through sacramental acts or even ethical behavior, after claiming that only through faith in Christ could one be saved, the apostle Paul nevertheless sought to lay a foundation for some kind of ethical discrimination. The freedom of a Christian was not the freedom to do evil. This idea became central in the Protestant Reformation, and Lincoln here challenged the legitimacy of the Liberty Party on very familiar orthodox grounds. Any spiritual descendent of Martin Luther had to know that action taken merely for the sake of appearing righteous was unholy, especially when it had adverse effects, when it did not bring forth "good fruits." Lincoln had delivered essentially the same sermon in the Temperance Address, but here one can get a better sense for the power of his rhetorical strategy. In apologizing for his own more cautious approach he challenged the evangelical antislavery party on its own religious grounds.

In 1848, political antislavery activists nominated the archenemy of Whiggery and abolitionism, Martin Van Buren, because they could not support the slaveholder Zachary Taylor. Predictably Lincoln objected. He feared that the Free-Soil Party would again split the antislavery vote and help elect the Democratic candidate, Lewis Cass of Michigan. Not unlike Polk, Cass was a Democrat of the Young America style, who along with Stephen Douglas originated the doctrine of popular sovereignty as a solution to the problem of slavery in the territories. Lincoln "felt certain" that if Cass were elected "the plans of farther extension of slavery would meet no check." In a somewhat imperfect report of a Massachusetts speech in 1848, Lincoln again took what amounted to an orthodox line against theological perfectionism.

In declaring that they would "do their duty and leave the consequences to God," [the Liberty Party men] merely gave an excuse for taking a course that they were not able to maintain by a fair and full argument. To make this declaration did not show what their duty was. If it did we should have no use for judgment, we might as well be made without intellect, and when divine or human law does not clearly point out what *is* our duty, we have no means of finding out what it is by using our most intelligent judgment of the consequences. If there were divine law, or human law for voting for Martin Van Buren, or if a fair examination of the consequences and first reasoning would show that voting for him would bring about the ends they pretended to wish—then he [Lincoln] would give up the argument. But since there was no fixed law on the subject, and since the whole probable result of their action would be an assistance in electing Gen. Cass, he must say that they were behind the Whigs in their advocacy of the freedom of the soil.[39]

Theologically Lincoln stood between those who pressed a pietistic line that emphasized individual righteousness even at the expense of instrumental reasoning—a line of thought that found its most logical expression in William Lloyd Garrison or Henry David Thoreau—and those genteel thinkers like Edward Everett who as inheritors of eighteenth-century rationalism were too skeptical of enthusiastic moral claims to challenge the existing social order, even when that order included slavery.[40] Lincoln was orthodox here in the sense that he took a complex position that acknowledged both "divine and human law." During the war he explained himself: "I have done, and shall do, the best I could and can, in my own conscience, under my oath to the law."[41] As a lawyer, Lincoln had defended a slaveholder seeking the return of his slaves. Lincoln's sense of his duties and responsibilities to his calling as a lawyer and then as president accorded with his Romantic reappropriation of classical Calvinism.

Simply put, Lincoln was not called to rewrite the Constitution—at least not yet. When that time came he would lend support to what became the Thirteenth Amendment, but in the meantime he could justify acting as the lawyer for a slaveholding plaintiff in an action for recovery of slaves. Lincoln lived with paradoxes and contradictions, but by 1848 he had achieved a serene confidence in his powers of analysis, and until late in the war for him the paradoxes often only seemed. With carefully constructed explanations rooted in orthodox Calvinism, he constantly balanced commitments to higher and positive law. Here again the Emancipation Proclamation comes to mind. Allegiance to the Constitution required a technically limited and carefully circumspect proclamation; nevertheless he firmly believed emancipation to be an act of justice transcendentally defined. While he agreed that both simple caution and the Constitution required that slavery be allowed to continue where it already existed, he also insisted that it be treated as a wrong. Far from passive, Lincoln was very sure of himself. He carefully laid the groundwork in public opinion for the Emancipation Proclamation, and his stance accorded with his definition of leadership and statesmanship.

Lincoln's forceful leadership on the issue of slavery has been described in terms of Aristotelian prudential thought, but it is difficult to justify his refusing to compromise in 1860–1861 and going to war on prudential grounds.[42] Nothing in Aristotle led to antislavery conviction, and, more important, nothing in the tradition of prudence would lead Lincoln and the Republican Party finally to draw a line at the extension of slavery in the territories, saying "this far and no further." Most important of all, Lincoln and his generation did not use classical language in the manner of the Enlightenment. Rather they used a Protestant and Augustinian language, one that helped them muster the nerve finally to oppose the slave power by force. Though carefully guarded and restrained by a kind of prudential view imbedded in doctrines like the Trinity and "calling," a quest for righteousness, a desire to be no further implicated in what they saw as a monstrous crime, led Lincoln and the Republicans to call what they hoped against hope was a southern bluff and, then, to fight a terrible war.

In a sense Lincoln participated in denominational politics. His position on the slavery issue accorded with those taken by the Old School Presbyterians against their more evangelical New School rivals. But, again, it was not because Lincoln made a profession of faith to the Old School. Rather, Old School Calvinism accorded better with his sense of human dependence on a superintending Providence than did the humanism of other theological options available to him. In its repudiation of church tradition, The New School was too extreme in its support of otherwise admirable causes. Lincoln and Old School Calvinists probably would have agreed in supporting gradual emancipation and colonization, conscientiously refusing a more radical position.[43]

Lincoln could discuss theological questions with the clergymen in his acquaintance. His wife Mary made a profession of faith to the Reverend James Smith of the First Presbyterian Church of Springfield after the death of their son Eddie in 1850. Whether the Lincolns were attracted to the Old School Presbyterian preacher because his more orthodox Augustinian doctrines better accorded with Lincoln's own views or because Mary chose Smith after he had helped her grieve over the death of her second son, there is a certain harmony between some of the positions Lincoln took and the tenets of Old School Presbyterianism. As an adult Lincoln seems to have had an aversion to triumphal Methodism, preferring a learned, antirevivalist, Old School Presbyterian clergy. Smith and Lincoln shared an interest both in temperance and colonization, and colonization was the cause of more cautious antislavery activists who would not go so far as to countenance violations of law in the service of emancipation.[44] Like Lincoln, the Old School did not join the more Arminian New Schoolers in condemning the Fugitive Slave Act.[45] They were less optimistic about the human condition, less optimistic that the Heavenly Kingdom could be made real on earth, and therefore more willing to accept moral compromise when necessary to preserve legal restraints on sinful humanity. Nevertheless they were not entirely hostile to the missionary endeavors of the period.

James Smith was the author of a book, *The Christian's Defence,* which Lincoln read, and thus Lincoln found an interlocutor in the minister of First

Presbyterian, where he and Mary attended.[46] *The Christian's Defence* was an exhaustive attempt to defend the truth of a fairly literal-minded biblical Christianity against the attacks of various "atheistical" thinkers including Tom Paine and David Hume. Smith had hardly produced an original work of theology, and he seems to have been oblivious to the new Romantic sensibility and the possibilities it held for placing piety on a different footing than the literalism typical of the eighteenth-century Common Sense school.[47] Thus William J. Wolf probably overestimated the impact on Lincoln of Smith's literalistic defense of Scripture. With his young Whig colleagues, Lincoln moved away from empiricism even in this post-Humean Common Sense form—and indeed away from the Enlightenment preoccupation with natural science in general—to a preoccupation with poetry, theology, and history. Nevertheless Lincoln probably took an interest in Smith's epistemological ruminations, which were typical of a period in which epistemology had become all-important. And Smith was a qualified expositor of the classical Christian heritage. While Lincoln could not follow Smith's literalism step for step, which helps explain why he did not give evidence of conversion and join the church, his speeches may nevertheless owe some of their theological surefootedness to Smith's orthodox demonstrations.

Much has been made of the fact that Lincoln did not join the church. But by twentieth-century standards he may well have qualified as a member of the First Presbyterian Church in Springfield and later of the New York Avenue Presbyterian Church in Washington, D.C. In mid-nineteenth-century America membership in a Reformed denomination was generally contingent upon producing evidence of conversion. One was accepted into church membership either "by testimony" of conversion or "by letter" from a previous church. Thus the fact that Lincoln did not become a full member of any particular church must be seen in its historical context. He participated at the Presbyterian churches where his wife was a full member; he attended, he paid rent for a pew, and his son Tad was baptized in 1855.[48]

While much of what he wrote about Providence, for instance, would have gained ready assent, especially from an Old School Presbyterian of the time, the point is not to claim that Lincoln was a Presbyterian or that Lincoln learned everything he knew about theology from James Smith. But a fair understanding of Lincoln's religious rhetoric must take into account his childhood in a predestinarian Baptist world and his later gravitation toward a similarly orthodox Calvinist church. There simply is no such thing as a naive reading of Scripture, and Lincoln would doubtless have read the Bible much differently had he grown up Methodist or Roman Catholic. As a Romantic intellectual, Lincoln laid down his piety on a somewhat unorthodox epistemological foundation, one that allowed him to work out his own particular poetic synthesis. But in other ways he remained true to a particular Reformed Christian heritage as he understood it. As is apparent in the *Whig Review* and elsewhere, Lincoln in some ways sought to be rather *more* orthodox than his fellow Christians, of whom many laid claim to full church membership. Without claiming to speak for a particular church or for God, he confronted professing Christians with the disparity between their professions and their practice. From the somewhat comfortable position of the nominal outsider he could assume a prophetic tone without exposing himself to charges of hypocrisy he might have faced had he committed himself more formally to a particular creed.

Even the points at which he seems most at variance with particular Reformed doctrines—say for instance his leanings in the direction of universalism, the doctrine that, as opposed to merely an "elect" group, mankind is destined for salvation universally—Lincoln spoke always in the language of Calvinism. Universalism was a kind of minority belief that appeared in the debates of the period, one that in some ways was more consonant with the optimistic, transcendental democracy of Bancroft's sort than with a strictly Calvinist position of Old School Presbyterianism. According to Mentor Graham, Lincoln argued for a form of universalism while in New Salem (1831–1837), and Isaac Cogdal and William Herndon reported a similar set of conversations with Lincoln in the late 1850s. But the secondhand accounts of Lincoln's religion in the 1850s merit a note of caution. According to William Barton, Lincoln's universalism remained essentially Calvinist in its underlying rationale and therefore should not be confused with the Universalist denomination. Lincoln incorporated "wide departures from conventional orthodoxy" into his religious thinking, but his foundation was always "the old-time predestinarianism which he heard in his youth and never outgrew." And he was conscious that he built his religious system on that Calvinist foundation. He did not, for the most part, adopt the pose of a naive reader of Scripture. Rather he took self-conscious positions regarding various theological options available to him. Once again the "rail-splitter" Lincoln has obscured the self-conscious intellectual. His self-conscious theological positioning—and the self-conscious theology of those around him—lends the popular debates of the period their particular flavor and clearly distinguishes them from anything the Enlightenment or the twentieth century produced. While Lincoln did not join a particular denomination, he knew his creeds and was a master of the confessional game.[49]

Again, Lincoln did not make his intellectual discoveries entirely on his own. William Herndon had one of the largest libraries in the state, which may help explain Lincoln's attachment to his junior partner. Though Douglas Wilson has done much to rehabilitate Herndon he has yet to receive his full due. Lincoln rose to prominence at the bar and in politics in shoulder-to-shoulder, day-to-day fellowship with a genuinely curious and genuinely intellectual legal partner. Herndon eagerly kept abreast of intellectual developments in the East; corresponded with William Lloyd Garrison, Wendell Phillips, and Joshua Giddings; and maintained a correspondence with Theodore Parker that lasted until Parker's death.[50] After Lincoln's death, Herndon performed a remarkable and original feat of scholarship in carefully generating testimony from the still-living witnesses to Lincoln's early life. And perhaps no one was in a position to spend more time in conversation with the adult Lincoln than Herndon.

Lincoln had tremendous intellectual ambitions, and yet he was not a great reader of books. Thus he would have both enjoyed and benefited from the banter of a bibliophile like Herndon. Along with Herndon, Jesse Fell, and Isaac Cogdal, Lincoln's other friends from the circuit and bar provided intellectual companionship. When they began practicing law, the profession itself was rooted in the world of moral and theological reflection. Along with Fell, Herndon and Lincoln read and discussed the works of William Ellery Channing and Theodore Parker. And Fell reported that, if "called upon to designate an author whose views most nearly represented Mr. Lincoln's on [the subject of religion, he] would say that author was Theodore Parker." Herndon was a transcendentalist, and Lincoln's less giddy, more cautious approach, both to epistemological questions and to the question of slavery, blinded Herndon somewhat to Lincoln's genuinely Romantic tendencies. As his Niagara Falls remarks showed, Lincoln enjoyed pulling the wool over Herndon's eyes in precisely that regard. But Herndon was not entirely blind to Lincoln's Romantic sensibility, and he was eager to associate Lincoln with Parker. In spite of Lincoln's "infidelity," his lack of belief that "the Bible is the divine special revelation of God," Herndon said that Lincoln was "a *thoroughly religious man*—a man of exalted notions of right—justice—duty, etc."[51]

As Fell described it, Lincoln, while unorthodox, was firm in his belief in a "superintending and overruling Providence that guides and controls the operations of the world, but maintained that law and order, and not their violation or suspension, are the appointed means by which this Providence is exercised."[52] If true, this constituted a serious disagreement between Lincoln and the Reverend James Smith. Smith defended a more traditional approach to the question by maintaining against Hume that the witness of supernatural miracles was as valid as any other kind of secondhand empirical knowledge upon which people perforce rely.[53] Lincoln never joined Smith in arguing that Providence worked by miraculously setting the usual laws of nature in abeyance from time to time. But there was more to Lincoln's view of Providence than Fell's teleological restatement of natural law. For Lincoln the human mind "was impelled to action, or held in rest by some power, over which the mind itself has no control."[54] For Lincoln, God worked his will by acting directly on the minds of historical actors, and that belief allowed Lincoln to express his sense of the presence of God in terms far more immediate than those of Fell (or, for that matter, those of Fell's fellow Unitarian, George Bancroft, for whom "the people" could intuit the will of God but the individual could not).[55]

Mary Lincoln, too, was a genuine intellectual. She attended Ward's Academy in Lexington, Kentucky, and spent four years at "the select finishing school of Madame Victorie Mentelle."[56] She was a reader of French and German, a rare accomplishment in antebellum Springfield—especially for a woman—and the works in French and German checked out for the Lincoln White House from the Library of Congress were in all probability borrowed for her.[57] Her husband attended the theater as well as the opera with her, and thus despite her faults, Mary Lincoln probably deserves some credit for sharing with him a wider world of literature and thereby enriching his intellectual life.

. . .

The effect of Lincoln's theological and religious influences on his political thought was broad and persistent. His quarrel with Douglas in the middle and late 1850s had an important theological dimension, and he carried his basic religious outlook with him to Washington. Lincoln used the Bible to illustrate his remarks more often in the 1850s than has been fully recognized. He was not shy about using his superior understanding of Christianity and the Bible against Douglas, often with comic effect for those who knew their Scripture.[58] And as usual there was a serious import to Lincoln's remarks. In the Protestant churches it was not the institution of the church but the Bible, the symbols, the creeds, and the standards that required ultimate loyalty. For Lincoln, reverence for the Declaration of Independence, for the Constitution, for the laws, and for the Revolution gave moral focus to political action in much the same way the Bible and the Philadelphia Confession functioned for Baptists or the Bible and the Westminster Confession functioned for Presbyterians. As Allen Guelzo put it, "the Declaration came to assume the role of a substitute scripture, and the Fathers the role of political patriarchs in creating what Lincoln called in 1838 a 'civil religion.'"[59] The analogy between a Protestant church and the national state formed the basis of Lincoln's Romantic nationalism.

For Lincoln, at least since 1852, Jefferson's Declaration was Scripture, and John C. Calhoun was a "heretic."[60] Lincoln was serious when, for instance, he called Douglas to repentance.[61] Where Douglas insisted that such theological ideas as "sin" should be confined to personal private morality, Lincoln joined Theodore Weld in applying the concept to public political behavior. The emphasis was not on the liberal value of consent but rather on the more substantive moral program of equality. Lincoln insisted that there were higher transcendent standards to which the nation had dedicated itself and which gave meaning to American history. The nation's ideals were rooted in the biblical injunction to love thy neighbor as thyself and to earn one's bread by the sweat of one's own brow—ideals that he and his generation simply read into the Declaration of Independence. Such beliefs explain Lincoln's insistence on stigmatizing the institution of slavery both as immoral and as contrary to the principles on which American institutions were founded.[62] Far more than any particular policy toward slavery in the states or territories, it was Lincoln's stigmatizing of the southern way of life that offended the South.

It is easy to forget that Republicans took seriously the idea that slavery might become national in the decade leading to the Civil War. Yet southern politicians and editors were saying essentially the same thing from the opposite perspective. By 1860, they were demanding the nationalization of chattel slavery as a matter of moral as well as constitutional property rights, which must be born in mind when thinking about postbellum, liberal states' rights apologetics for the Confederacy.[63] States' rights were everywhere honored and valued, North and South, before, during, and after the war. Yet for too long liberal states' rights apologetics have obscured what was really at stake for both sides in 1860. By that time the South insisted on a national policy toward the institution of slavery at least as vociferously as the North demanded that slavery be placed on the path to "ultimate extinction." Both North and South were in the grips of a Romantic quest for righteousness, and the efforts of both precluded any liberal accommodation of the sectional difficulty.

Lincoln addressed that split in his "House Divided" position of 1858, which he carried into the election of 1860. Lincoln explained it in the peroration of another speech that helped to make his career, the Cooper Institute Address in February 1860. The speech made Lincoln a viable candidate in the Northeast and solidified his role as chief Republican spokesman.

> Nor can we justifiably withhold [full national recognition, i.e., legal nationalization of slavery], on any ground save our conviction that slavery is wrong. If slavery is right, all words, acts, laws, and constitutions against it, are themselves wrong, and should be silenced, and swept away. If it is right, we cannot justly object to its nationality—its universality; if it is wrong, they cannot justly insist upon its extension—its enlargement. All they ask, we could readily grant, if we thought slavery right; all we ask, they could as readily grant, if they thought it wrong. Their thinking it right, and our thinking it wrong, is the precise fact upon which depends the whole controversy. Thinking it right, as they do, they are not to blame for desiring its full recognition, as being right; but, thinking it wrong, as we do, can we yield to them? Can we cast our votes with their view, and against our own? In view of our moral, social, and political responsibilities, can we do this?
>
> Wrong as we think slavery is, we can yet afford to let it alone where it is, because that much is due to the necessity arising from its actual presence in the nation; but can we, while our votes will prevent it, allow it to spread into the National Territories, and to overrun us here in these Free States? If our sense of duty forbids this, then let us stand by our duty, fearlessly and effectively. Let us be diverted by none of those sophistical contrivances wherewith we are so industriously plied and belabored—contrivances such as groping for some middle ground between the right and the wrong, vain as the search for a man who should be neither a living man nor a dead man—such as a policy of "don't care" on a question about which all true men do care—such as Union appeals beseeching true Union men to yield to Disunionists, reversing the divine rule, and calling, not the sinners, but the righteous to repentance—such as invocations to Washington, imploring men to unsay what Washington said, and undo what Washington did.
>
> Neither let us be slandered from our duty by false accusations against us, nor frightened from it by menaces of destruction to the Government nor of dungeons to ourselves. LET US HAVE FAITH THAT RIGHT MAKES MIGHT, AND IN THAT FAITH, LET US, TO THE END, DARE TO DO OUR DUTY AS WE UNDERSTAND IT.[64]

This was Lincoln at perhaps his most self-righteous. Even here he did not vilify the South, but the desire to emphasize Lincoln's tolerance should not obscure his central point: the Republicans were the "righteous" while the disunionists were the "sinners." Lincoln interpreted in religious terms the southern demands that the North refrain from denouncing the wrong of slavery—and this was not an anomalous, personal characteristic of Lincoln's. Rather, the logic of the situation on both sides demanded moral clarity. The questions really were, Who is righteous, and who should repent? There could be no liberal, consensual solution to what had become a conflict of fundamental moral beliefs.

But this led Lincoln almost ineluctably to a dangerous heresy. When he pushed to "reinaugurate the good old 'central ideas' of the Republic," Lincoln came close to joining his evangelical allies in equating the cause of his Republican Party with the will of God "We *can* do it," he said. "The human heart *is* with us—God is with us. We shall again be able not to declare that, 'all states as States, are equal,' nor yet that 'all citizens as citizens are equal,' but to renew the broader, better declaration, including both these and much more, that 'all *men* are created equal.'"[65] In mustering the North's will to oppose slavery's expansion, to resist secession, and finally to abolish slavery and finish a war that turned out to be far more painful than anyone had anticipated, Lincoln virtually equated American civilization with the coming Kingdom.

A PURLOINED LETTER

Early in the war and continuing through the Gettysburg Address, Lincoln leaned decidedly toward an optimistic description of American national purpose and destiny. His view was apparent in the peroration to the Wisconsin State Fair Speech as well as in the First Inaugural and his handling of the Emancipation Proclamation. To muster national purpose, he relied on the rhetoric of America's special place in the history of the salvation of mankind. The Gettysburg Address is perhaps the best example of this, and as such it is the greatest expression of nineteenth-century Romantic nationalism. The works of Tennyson and Kipling pale in comparison.

Opening with "Four score and seven" forced Lincoln's listeners and readers to do some quick math and to settle on the Declaration of Independence rather than the Constitution as the key to the origins of American nationality. On Lincoln's reading this made substantive equality rather than the social contract or consent of the governed the foundation of American government, and Lincoln thus reasserted his contention that American nationality was at core antislavery. But simply by calling to mind the language of the King James Bible, the peculiar dating was calculated to put American history into the biblical narrative. Lincoln's New Testament emphasis was apparent as well in his treatment of the battlefield casualties in terms of sacrificial death. "Greater love hath no man than this, that a man lay down his life for his friends," and whether or not Lincoln had John 15:13 in mind he returned to the theme of his Temperance Address and the imitation of Christ.

The soldiers gave their lives that the nation might live. Thus the American nation became the special object of Christlike sacrifice.

Beginning in 1776 with a "continent" and then a "nation," moving to the "now" with a "battlefield" and a "portion of that field," Lincoln had systematically narrowed the range and focus of his remarks to the here and now, closing the first section of the address with the dismissive remark that "it is altogether fitting and proper that we should do this." There was something mundane, even hackneyed, about a funeral oration. (This was precisely parallel to the antithesis Lincoln set up in the first part of the Niagara Falls meditation discussed earlier.) Also typical of Lincoln was the call to further striving. His listeners were to continue with the ghastly war effort in order to ensure that the nation have a "new birth of freedom," and that government of, by, and for the people "shall not perish from the earth." This accorded with the aims of the war, which had always been to preserve the Union and which, since January, included the emancipation of the slaves as well. Lincoln here also returned to an idea he articulated at the Wisconsin State Fair in 1859. The idea was that through intense human striving it was possible to hope that the "onward and upward" course of American civilization might never pass away. A kind of immortality could be achieved through rededication to the national project.[66]

To the emphasis on moral striving Lincoln had made in 1859, at Gettysburg he added the religious element of sacrificial death and resurrection. In the second section of his speech Lincoln exploded the narrow context of the first section into the realm of timeless transcendental meaning: "But, in a larger sense. . . ." And the transcendental meaning Lincoln had in mind was that the blood sacrifice on the battlefield required a response of devotion. Whereas in the Lyceum Address he recommended reverence for the laws as an intellectual matter, here at Gettysburg he mustered the emotive power actually to generate that feeling. It was a triumph of Romantic literature. Lincoln displayed precisely the quality that the *Whig Review* had ascribed to "Genius." The rebirth of the nation became the object of genuine religious awe.

The Gettysburg Address marked the apex in the development of Lincoln's Romantic nationalism. With the triple victories of 1863—Vicksburg, Gettysburg, and Chattanooga—Lincoln was at his most self-confident. While still in Indiana Lincoln likely had read William Grimshaw's *History of the United States: From Their First Settlement as Colonies, to the Cession of Florida, in Eighteen Hundred and Twenty-one*, a one-volume history that went through fifteen large editions.[67] Albert Beveridge quoted the last paragraph from it in his Lincoln biography, emphasizing the similarity between Grimshaw's antislavery vision of the meaning of Jefferson and American civilization on the one hand and Lincoln's own later pronouncements on the other. Grimshaw wrote:

> Let us not only declare by words, but demonstrate by our actions, that "all men are created equal; that they are endowed by their creator, with the same inalienable rights: that among these are life, liberty and the pursuit of happiness." Let

us venerate the instruction of that great and amiable man to whom, chiefly, under Providence, the United States are indebted for their liberties; the world for a common hero: "That there exists an indissoluble union between virtue and happiness, between duty and advantage."[68]

The parallel between this passage and the Cooper Institute peroration, while striking, reflects a certain conventionality in both works. But Grimshaw accorded better than Bancroft with Lincoln's brand of nationalism. Grimshaw was Whiggish in support of internal improvements, a national bank, and public support of inventions through patent laws. In addition to looking for an eventual end to slavery, he was sympathetic to the Native Americans as well. (Grimshaw was also more interested in historical particularity than was Bancroft.) Whether Lincoln in any way had Grimshaw in mind, the historical vision he articulated at Gettysburg reflected the tendency common in the period to see equality as the meaning of American civilization and to see American history as progressive. But especially the providential understanding of the meaning of America comes through in passages like Grimshaw's. Thus Lincoln did not invent anything at Gettysburg. Nor did he somehow trick his audience into accepting a new vision of American history and identity.[69] Rather, at Gettysburg Lincoln demonstrated what literary genius and a lot of hard work could do with otherwise trite and conventional stuff.

Ironically, what was actually original to Lincoln developed through the crisis of confidence bordering on despair that followed upon the unexpected military setbacks in the summer of 1864 and that brought with it the prospect of losing his reelection battle.[70] As late as May 30, 1864, Lincoln expressed his certainty that the North fought on the side of God and Christianity. In one short, relatively unknown passage, Lincoln managed to squeeze in what for him were the guiding scriptural passages of his administration:

In response to the preamble and resolutions of the American Baptist Home Mission Society, which you did me the honor to present, I can only thank you for thus adding to the effective and almost unanimous support which the Christian communities are so zealously giving to the country, and to liberty. Indeed it is difficult to conceive how it could be otherwise with any one professing christianity or even having ordinary perceptions of right and wrong. To read in the Bible, as the word of God himself, that "In the sweat of *thy* face shalt thou eat bread," and to preach therefrom that, "In the sweat of *other mans* faces shalt thou eat bread," to my mind can scarcely be reconciled with honest sincerity. When brought to my final reckoning, may I have to answer for robbing no man of his goods; yet more tolerable even this, than for robbing one of himself, and all that was his. When a year or two ago, those professedly holy men of the South, met in the semblance of prayer and devotion, and, in the name of Him who said "As ye would all men should do unto you, do ye even so unto them" appealed to the christian world to aid them in doing to a whole race of men, as they would have not man do unto themselves, to

> my thinking, they contemned and insulted God and His church, far more than
> did Satan when he tempted the Saviour with the Kingdoms of the earth. The
> devils attempt was no more false, and far less hypocritical. But let me forbear,
> remembering it is also written "Judge not, lest ye be judged."[71]

Much of this would appear in his Second Inaugural, particularly the passage from Genesis about eating one's bread from the sweat of one's face and the Gospel passage about not judging. Though the letter ends with Lincoln's refusal to judge, the conciliatory gesture was far too little and came far too late to have much effect. Lincoln may have known that he *should* not judge, but he in fact *did*. And the self-righteousness is obvious enough. Thus the passage has remained in relative obscurity while the much more interesting Second Inaugural has assumed the rank of literary classic and theological wonder.

The passage was written at a time when the war was still progressing relatively well, and it was thus quite openly self-righteous. Grant's relentless grind had already resulted in the battles of the Wilderness and Spotsylvania Courthouse, and in the West William T. Sherman had assumed command; but Cold Harbor and the seemingly endless siege of Petersburg were yet to come. As the summer wore on, the promised victories of spring never came, and in the meantime Lincoln had his reelection prospects to consider. Grant lost nearly 100,000 men in six weeks of fighting. By mid-August Lincoln's advisors were telling him that his reelection was "an impossibility," and on August 23 he wrote a "Memorandum Concerning His Probable Failure of Re-election," in which he expressed his desire to cooperate with the new president-elect before the inauguration.[72]

Sherman's victory at Atlanta finally came in September, and two days later Lincoln wrote to the Quaker Eliza P. Gurney. Lincoln had met with Gurney in October 1862, at a time when despite the narrow victory at Antietam and the preliminary Emancipation Proclamation the war was not going well. Lincoln's Niagara Falls meditation also coincided with a period of setback for him. In difficult times Lincoln turned to Romantic poetry and to religion. In the fall of 1862 he worried about Democratic advances in the congressional elections.[73] Now nearly two years later Lincoln sent a reply to Gurney that touched on themes that would recur in the Second Inaugural:

> The purposes of the Almighty are perfect, and must prevail, though we erring
> mortals may fail to accurately perceive them in advance. We hoped for a happy
> termination of this terrible war long before this; but God knows best, and has
> ruled otherwise. We shall yet acknowledge His wisdom and our own error
> therein. Meanwhile we must work earnestly in the best light He gives us, trust-
> ing that so working still conduces to the great ends He ordains. Surely He in-
> tends some great good to follow this mighty convulsion, which no mortal
> could make, and no mortal could stay.[74]

Lincoln went on to offer consolation to the Society of Friends for their particular difficulty in opposing both slavery and the war that would abolish it, emphasizing that each person had to work by the light of his or her own conscience.

In the darkest nights of the war Lincoln had considered the dreadful possibility that the North might actually lose. Generally speaking most northerners considered that possibility only to recoil from such a worldview-shattering prospect. For evangelicals as well as for a quasi-secular intellectual like Bancroft, such a possibility entailed the destruction of all that had given meaning to their lives. Bancroft momentarily pondered the futility of his great historical project: what would be the point in explaining the origins of a republic that no longer existed? Not only would it have proven to be just another ephemeral human institution, but also the United States could hardly have represented even a foretaste of the telos of all history. Bancroft, however, soon took solace in the inevitability of the North's victory. The Civil War was just another struggle to rid America of vestigial aristocratic elements, and it in no way really threatened the American project. Self-doubt was for the faint of heart, and what was needed was a more persistent faith that the God of history was on our side. Thus the war only reinforced Bancroft's earlier opinions.[75]

Lincoln refused Bancroft's easy consolation and, in fact, drew the opposite conclusion. For the president, perhaps more than for anyone else, the possibility of a Confederate victory had been real. As much as for Bancroft, such a possibility had shattering consequences. But unlike Bancroft Lincoln continued to take the possibility of defeat seriously, even after the threat had passed. Everything he had worked for in his life and almost everything he had believed in found meaning only in the context of the American democratic project. But if that project and if that nation were only one among many—as indeed his radically Augustinian Calvinism had contended—and if in God's good time that nation might perish from the earth after all, then for Lincoln America could not represent God's Kingdom on earth or the telos of world history. Even to flirt with such rhetoric as Lincoln had at Gettysburg was blasphemy. The meaning of America in Lincoln's imagination had to be revised, reevaluated, and scaled back: this was the task of the Second Inaugural Address.

Lincoln was reminded by the awful events of the summer of 1864 that the results of the war had not been in his or anyone else's hands. He returned to his doctrine of necessity.

> Neither party expected for the war, the magnitude, or the duration, which it has already attained. Neither anticipated that the *cause* of the conflict might cease with, or even before, the conflict itself should cease. Each looked for an easier triumph, and a result less fundamental and astounding. Both read the same Bible, and pray to the same God; and each invokes His aid against the other. It may seem strange that any men should dare to ask a just God's

assistance in wringing their bread from the sweat of other men's faces; but let us judge not that we be not judged. The prayers of both could not be answered; that of neither has been answered fully. The Almighty has His own purposes."[76]

Not even Lincoln could resist one last jab at the South for its dedication to slavery. But here the self-righteousness was muted as it had not been a year previously. Lincoln returned to the providential thinking that was so characteristic in early life but that since he assumed the responsibilities of office had been apparent only in a few moments of self-doubt such as the emancipation decision and the military deadlock of the fall of 1862 and winter of 1863.

For David Donald and others, Lincoln ducked some of the responsibility for the war in passages like this one, which shifted "some of the responsibility for all the suffering."[77] Though there may be something to Donald's supposition, Lincoln did not give up his belief in the justness of his cause. He did not here apologize for prosecuting the war with the likes of Grant, Sherman, and Sheridan. The point of the speech was not to "let go and let God." Lincoln prosecuted the war with an incredible confidence in his own ability to sort out moral tangles. And it was Lincoln who urged his generals into bloody battle, risking the threat of dictatorship, or so he sarcastically put it, if only they might bring back victories.[78] Lincoln demanded of himself and of others that they continue to strive "with firmness in the right, as God [gave them] to see the right." Thus, if the providential interpretation had a comforting effect for Lincoln personally, it was on some deeper, unconscious level. Within his providential and deterministic outlook Lincoln refused to relax the moral demands he made on himself and on the nation.

Rather than comfort himself by shifting responsibility to God, Lincoln said that in this speech he had indicted *himself* most of all. To Thurlow Weed he wrote: "Men are not flattered by being shown that there has been a difference of purpose between the Almighty and them. To deny it, however, in this case, is to deny that there is a God governing the world. It is a truth which I thought needed to be told; and as whatever of humiliation there is in it, falls most directly on myself, thought others might afford for me to tell it."[79]

What humiliation? If Lincoln still clung to the belief that by his best lights his cause was just, and if the Almighty alone could claim the consequences, then he should have been beyond reproach. But in the Second Inaugural he returned to another idea that he first articulated in the Temperance Address. This time he accused himself of too narrowly equating his purposes with those of God, and this clue to the meaning of the Second Inaugural has largely been overlooked. The question that begs to be asked is just when and how did Lincoln equate his own purposes with those of God?

Any system of determinism that denies the free will of human beings runs into a problem of whether people, individually or collectively, can be held morally responsible for their actions. In the Second Inaugural, Lincoln—reflecting on a predetermined providential world—simply asserted such responsibility. In spite of the fact that we are impelled to act as we do by forces that are beyond our control and that are ultimately in the hands of

God, we nevertheless remain responsible. Again Lincoln quoted Matthew and applied the lesson:

> "Woe unto the world because of offences! for it must needs be that offences come; but woe to that man by whom the offence cometh!" If we shall suppose that American Slavery is one of those offences which, in the Providence of God, must needs come, but which, having continued through His appointed time, He now wills to remove, and that He gives to both North and South, this terrible war, as the woe due to those by whom the offence came, shall we discern therein any departure from those divine attributes which the believers in a Living God always ascribe to Him: Fondly do we hope—fervently do we pray—that this mighty scourge of war may speedily pass away. Yet, if God wills that it continue, until all the wealth piled by the bond-man's two hundred and fifty years of unrequited toil shall be sunk, and until every drop of blood drawn with the lash, shall be paid by another drawn with the sword, as was said three thousand years ago, so still it must be said: "the judgments of the Lord, are true and righteous altogether."

In the passage that immediately precedes the quotation from Matthew, Jesus warned the Pharisees against harming the children: "But whoso shall offend one of these little ones which believe in me, it were better for him that a millstone were hanged about his neck, and that he were drowned in the depth of the sea." Not only was Lincoln guilty in the manner of the Pharisees of equating his own purposes with those of God, but perhaps also he recalled to mind the fact that as a lawyer he had tried an action on the part of a slaveowner for the recovery of his slaves. Or perhaps he had in mind his more recent and, by his own logic, legally necessary reluctance to emancipate. Whereas a year earlier he congratulated himself on his lack of complicity in slavery, by this interpretation his own actions placed him among those by whom the offense came. Perhaps again he had in mind the fact that he had misjudged the union sentiments of the South and deprecated the warnings that southern threats of secession and war were serious. The passage from Matthew immediately following the quotation said that "wherefore if thy hand or thy foot offend thee, cut them off, and cast them from thee." Before a God of such exacting justice, Lincoln had no choice but to throw himself on God's mercy.

In Edgar Allan Poe's "A Purloined Letter," the missing note is hidden in front of the investigator, Monsieur G——, the prefect of the Parisian police. The letter has been turned inside out and resealed. Failing to consider the intellect of his opponent, the prefect fails also to see the letter hidden in front of him. But by duly considering the nature of the brilliant villain, the even more brilliant C. Aguste Dupin expects just such a brilliant ruse; only he is able to see the letter for what it is. Thus Romantics like Poe stressed that truly to perceive required a prior intuition, a prior conceptual leap. The problem Lincoln set for himself was to discern the will of God in Providence. And, by his own account, he had earlier failed in this task because he had failed duly to consider the nature of God.

The raw materials of the Second Inaugural should have been apparent to Lincoln for some time. Lincoln had always struggled with the interpretative framework of Providence to find meaning in experience, and the arrogance of the American self-conception had always bothered him. The protracted years of war; the wounded, the dying, and the dead; the problem of slavery in a war ostensibly to preserve a Union that protected slavery—it had all been in front of him all along. And yet, like the purloined letter, he had not quite seen it. The experience of devastating stalemate in the summer of 1864 led Lincoln to the belief that his cause would fail, which in turn led him to reconsider the implications of his providential worldview. At last he was able to grasp the letter all along purloined in that experience. The world would go on even without a triumphant American nation, and thus the cause of the Union was not necessarily the cause of God. Moral striving by one's best lights remained an inescapable duty, but no one, not even America, could escape complicity in the sins of the world. Lincoln returned to the piety of his boyhood and to the radically Augustinian notion that original sin could not be overcome in this world. Neither the North, nor America, nor Abraham Lincoln could be counted fully among the righteous. Even if the war were to continue until it destroyed American civilization entirely, "the judgments of the Lord, are true and righteous altogether."

According to George M. Marsden, people of all denominations in the North saw in the preservation of the nation, in earthly progress through reform and struggle, the approach of the second coming of Christ. Americans' "acquaintance with apocalyptic imagery was reflected and reinforced in the words of the most famous war hymn, 'His truth is marching on.'" From pulpits across America, the spiritual reign of Christ was taught to be drawing near, and "the approach of the advent was urged as a reason to hasten earthly progress."[80] That millennialism had justified both the humanitarian reform movements, of which antislavery was first and foremost, and the fervent belief in American democracy, to which the Gettysburg Address had ministered.

Lincoln now denied all of this. It is therefore a mistake to read the Second Inaugural exclusively, or even primarily, as a plea for compassion toward the South. Almost 1,500 years earlier Augustine had faced a similar dashing of all earthly, political hope with the sack of Rome in 410. The prospect of Union defeat in the Civil War put Lincoln into something similar to Augustine's situation. Like Rome or Nineveh or Tyre, America could not represent the City of God. Thus the Second Inaugural was not a call to a triumphant North to be magnanimous in victory. Those who fought on the right hand of God in a millennial struggle could afford to be condescending. Rather, it was a call to humility. The meaning of the war for Lincoln was that no man, no nation, could claim a right to triumph. America was no longer the culmination of world history: merely one nation among many that, while endeavoring to remain firm in the right, remained no closer to the Kingdom of God than any other. All alike remained under the judgment of God.

NOTES

INTRODUCTION

1. Isaac Newton Arnold, *The History of Abraham Lincoln, and the Overthrow of Slavery* (Chicago: Clarke, 1866); David B. Chesebrough, *"No Sorrow like Our Sorrow": Northern Protestant Ministers and the Assassination of Lincoln* (Kent, Ohio: Kent State University Press, 1994); J. G. Holland, *Life of Abraham Lincoln* (Springfield, Mass.: G. Bill, 1866); Harold Holzer, "'Columbia's Noblest Sons': Washington and Lincoln in Popular Prints," *Journal of the Abraham Lincoln Association* 15, no. 1 (1994): 40; Harold Holzer, *Lincoln Seen and Heard* (Lawrence: University Press of Kansas, 2000), 31; Harold Holzer and Mark E. Neely, *Mine Eyes Have Seen the Glory: The Civil War in Art* (New York: Orion Books, 1993); Mark E. Neely, Jr., *The Fate of Liberty: Abraham Lincoln and Civil Liberties* (New York: Oxford University Press, 1991), "The Irrelevance of Mercy."

2. For a brief general bibliography on the subject of Lincoln and religion, see Allen C. Guelzo, *Abraham Lincoln: Redeemer President* (Grand Rapids, Mich.: William B. Eerdmans, 1999), 465–72; Mark A. Noll, "'Both . . . Pray to the Same God': The Singularity of Lincoln's Faith in the Era of the Civil War," *Journal of the Abraham Lincoln Association* 18, no. 1 (1997): 1n. On Herndon and Lincoln's religion, Noll cites David Herbert Donald, *Lincoln's Herndon* (New York: Alfred A. Knopf, 1948), 212–16, 236–38, 256–57, 271–82. On Lincoln's humor, see P. M. Zall, ed., *Abe Lincoln Laughing: Humorous Anecdotes from Original Sources by and about Abraham Lincoln* (Berkeley: University of California Press, 1982), 7–8. On the supposed book, see Guelzo, *Abraham Lincoln,* 21; and John Hill to Herndon, in Douglas L. Wilson and Rodney O. Davis, eds., *Herndon's Informants: Letters, Interviews, and Statements about Abraham Lincoln* (Urbana: University of Illinois Press, 1998), 61–62.

3. Edmund Wilson, *Patriotic Gore: Studies in the Literature of the American Civil War* (New York: Oxford University Press, 1962), 106.

4. G. George Fox, *Abraham Lincoln's Religion: Sources of the Great Emancipator's Religious Inspiration* (New York: Exposition Press, 1959), 21.

5. Robert W. Johannsen, *Stephen A. Douglas* (New York: Oxford University Press, 1973), 640–41.

6. As one reviewer wryly pointed out, "that such concepts as Original Sin, the Atonement, and the Resurrection might actually have serious and enduring meanings for people simply escapes the attention of some historians" (Robert McColley, "Review Essay: *The Inner World of Abraham Lincoln,* by Michael Burlingame and *Abraham Lincoln: From Skeptic to Prophet,* by Wayne C. Temple," *Journal of the Abraham Lincoln Association* 17, no. 2 [1996]: 60).

7. Theodore Parker, "Discourse of the Transient and Permanent in Christianity," in Perry Miller, ed., *The Transcendentalists: An Anthology* (Cambridge, Mass.: Harvard University Press, 1950).

8. Benjamin P. Thomas, *Portrait for Posterity: Lincoln and His Biographers* (New Brunswick, N.J.: Rutgers University Press, 1947), 89.

9. Quoted in ibid., 83, 79–80.

10. William H. Herndon and Jesse W. Weik, *Herndon's Life of Lincoln*, ed. Paul M. Angle (1942; rpt., New York: Da Capo Press, 1983), 466.

11. In the third debate with Stephen Douglas at Jonesboro, Lincoln did quote a passage from Thompson Campbell that used the term "human rights," but he did so in response to an interrogatory and in no way did he endorse the views of the quotation. See Roy P. Basler, ed., *The Collected Works of Abraham Lincoln*, 8 vols. (New Brunswick, N.J.: Rutgers University Press, 1953–1955), 3:123; Don E. Fehrenbacher, ed., *Speeches and Writings*, by Abraham Lincoln, 2 vols. (New York: Literary Classics of the United States, 1989), 1:611 (published as vols. 45–46 of the Library of America series). The phrase also occurs in a perhaps imperfect press paraphrase of Lincoln's remarks to Senator John Conness, *Cincinnati Gazette*, Nov. 17, 1863 (Basler, ed., *Collected Works*, 7:13). Finally, the phrase occurs in "To the workingmen of Manchester," Jan. 19, 1863 (Basler, ed., *Collected Works*, 6:64; Fehrenbacher, ed., *Speeches and Writings*, 2:432), but the message looks to be the work of Seward or Hay.

12. Daniel Kilham Dodge, *Abraham Lincoln: The Evolution of His Literary Style*, introduced by James Hurt (1900; rpt., Urbana: University of Illinois Press, 2000), 31; Guelzo, *Abraham Lincoln*, 106–10.

13. The chief monuments in this field of the literature include the chapter "The Instrument of God" in Richard Nelson Current, *The Lincoln Nobody Knows* (New York: Hill and Wang, 1958). See also Edmund Wilson's famous endorsement of Alexander H. Stephens's observation "that Lincoln's love of the Union was a species of religious mysticism," in David Herbert Donald, *Lincoln* (New York: Simon & Schuster, 1995), 337; Wilson, *Patriotic Gore*; and Wayne C. Temple, *Abraham Lincoln: From Skeptic to Prophet* (Mahomet, Ill.: Mayhaven, 1995). See also McColley, "Review Essay," 54. Throughout this passage, I make free use of McColley's essay.

14. Writing in 1920, William E. Barton did not have access to Basler's authoritative *Collected Works of Abraham Lincoln*. Nevertheless he was perhaps for that reason exceptionally careful with secondhand accounts in his book *The Soul of Abraham Lincoln* (New York: George H. Doran, 1920). In 1959, Fox in *Abraham Lincoln's Religion* explicitly refused to limit himself to Basler's selections; and Wolf, who engaged in no such anti-Basler polemic, nevertheless credited many secondhand accounts of Lincoln's words that were recalled only long after the events in question. See William J. Wolf, *Lincoln's Religion*, published in 1959 as *The Almost Chosen People* (Philadelphia: Pilgrim Press, 1970), 8. (Compare Wolf's endorsement of Basler with his use of secondhand quotations throughout his book.) See also Harlan Hoyt Horner, *The Growth of Lincoln's Faith* (New York: Abingdon Press, 1939); Elton Trueblood, *Abraham Lincoln: Theologian of American Anguish* (New York: Harper & Row, 1973). Fortunately, we now have *The Recollected Words of Abraham Lincoln*, compiled and edited by Don E. and Virginia Fehrenbacher (Stanford, Calif.: Stanford University Press, 1996). By evaluating and grading the mountain of material attributed to Lincoln but not included in Basler's *Collected Works* and, more important, by providing a brief rationale for the grade of authenticity given, this book made the otherwise daunting task of evaluating sources much simpler. In addition, we now have a reliable guide to the other recollections of Abraham Lincoln that Herndon so diligently gathered after the war from Lincoln's former neighbors and friends (Wilson and Davis, eds., *Herndon's Informants*). To some extent we can get around Herndon by using the material directly for ourselves. The same is now true for much other reminiscence material gathered by Lincoln's early biographers in Michael Burlingame, ed., *At Lincoln's side: John Hay's Civil War Correspondence and Selected Writ-

ings (Carbondale: Southern Illinois University Press, 2000); Michael Burlingame, ed., *Lincoln's Journalist: John Hay's Anonymous Writings for the Press, 1860–1864* (Carbondale: Southern Illinois University Press, 1998); Michael Burlingame, ed., *An Oral History of Abraham Lincoln: John G. Nicolay's Interviews and Essays* (Carbondale: Southern Illinois University Press, 1996); Michael Burlingame and John R. T. Ettlinger, eds., *Inside Lincoln's White House: The Complete Civil War Diary of John Hay* (Carbondale: Southern Illinois University Press, 1997); William Osborn Stoddard and Michael Burlingame, *Inside the White House in War Times: Memoirs and Reports of Lincoln's Secretary* (Lincoln: University of Nebraska Press, 2000). Though each of the books in the tradition of religious biography remains useful, one must take the time to compare the citations with the *Collected Works*, with the *Recollected Words*, and with *Herndon's Informants*, carefully excluding any dubious quotations and the conclusions drawn from them.

15. William Barton, for example, assembled from diverse writings and contexts a "Creed of Abraham Lincoln in his own words" (*Soul of Abraham Lincoln*, 291–300). This "Creed" is reprinted in Wolf, *Lincoln's Religion*, 195–96.

16. David Hein and Glen E. Thurow did not concentrate on Lincoln's private belief in this way, but for their part they analyzed Lincoln as a systematic thinker whose meaning was to be found in relation to the world of systematic political science and theology. This can be a useful exercise, especially for the political scientist and the theologian, but the historian's task is different. See also Joseph R. Fornieri, "Biblical Republicanism: Abraham Lincoln's Civil Theology" (Ph.D. diss., Catholic University of America, 1996), 14–15; David Hein, "Lincoln's Faith: Commentary on 'Abraham Lincoln and American Political Religion,'" in Gabor S. Boritt and Norman O. Forness, eds., *The Historian's Lincoln: Pseudohistory, Psychohistory, and History* (Urbana: University of Illinois Press, 1988); David Hein, "Lincoln's Theology and Political Ethics," in Kenneth W. Thompson, ed., *Essays on Lincoln's Faith and Politics* (Lanham, Md.: University Press of America, 1983); Glen E. Thurow, "Abraham Lincoln and American Political Religion," in Boritt and Forness, eds., *Historian's Lincoln*.

17. Hein, "Lincoln's Theology and Political Ethics."

18. Daniel Feller, *The Jacksonian Promise: America, 1815–1840* (Baltimore: Johns Hopkins University Press, 1995); Guelzo, *Abraham Lincoln;* Charles Grier Sellers, *The Market Revolution: Jacksonian America, 1815–1846* (New York: Oxford University Press, 1991); Harry L. Watson and Eric Foner, *Liberty and Power: The Politics of Jacksonian America* (New York: Hill and Wang, 1990).

19. Christopher Lasch, Gary Wills, and John Patrick Diggins have published widely read books that challenge the secular Enlightenment image of American nationality. While Wills puts the Gettysburg Address into the Romantic context of the rural cemetery movement to splendid effect, only Diggins joins the older school of religious interpretation represented by Perry Miller and Sacvan Bercovitch. Diggins lays important groundwork when he contrasts Lincoln with Machiavelli to refute Pocock's republican interpretation, but a more closely contextual approach is needed. John P. Diggins, *The Lost Soul of American Politics: Virtue, Self-Interest, and the Foundations of Liberalism* (New York: Basic Books, 1984); Christopher Lasch, *The True and Only Heaven: Progress and Its Critics* (New York: W. W. Norton, 1991); Garry Wills, *Under God: Religion and American Politics* (New York: Simon and Schuster, 1990). For a rejoinder to Diggins, see Brian F. Danoff, "Lincoln, Machiavelli, and American Political Thought," *Presidential Studies Quarterly* 30, no. 2 (2000): 290–311. On Lincoln and technology, see Robert V. Bruce, *Lincoln and the Tools of War* (Indianapolis: Bobbs-Merrill, 1956).

20. Eric Foner, "The Causes of the American Civil War," in Eric Foner, ed., *Politics and Ideology in the Age of the Civil War* (London: Oxford University Press, 1974), 19.

The article also appeared in Robert P. Swierenga ed., *Beyond the Civil War Synthesis: Political Essays of the Civil War Era* (Westport, Conn.: Greenwood Press, 1975), 3–15; as well as in *Civil War History* 20 (1974): 201. Cited in Richard Carwardine, "Lincoln, Evangelical Religion, and American Political Culture in the Era of the Civil War," *Journal of the Abraham Lincoln Association* 18, no. 1 (1997): 50.

21. "Address to the Washington Temperance Society of Springfield," Feb. 22, 1842, Basler, ed., *Collected Works*, 1:271–79; Fehrenbacher, ed., *Speeches and Writings*, 1:81–90. Compare with Ian R. Tyrrell, *Sobering Up: From Temperance to Prohibition in Antebellum America, 1800–1860* (Westport, Conn.: Greenwood Press, 1979).

22. For the new political historians, see William E. Gienapp, *The Origins of the Republican Party, 1852–1856* (New York: Oxford University Press, 1987); Michael F. Holt, *The Rise and Fall of the American Whig Party: Jacksonian Politics and the Onset of the Civil War* (New York: Oxford University Press, 1999); James L. Huston, *The Panic of 1857 and the Coming of the Civil War* (Baton Rouge: Louisiana State University Press, 1987); Mark W. Summers, *The Plundering Generation: Corruption and the Crisis of the Union, 1849–1861* (New York: Oxford University Press, 1987).

23. On "free labor" appeals, see Gienapp, *Origins of the Republican Party*, 356–57. For Republicans' replacing the Whigs, see Gienapp, *Origins of the Republican Party*, 13–35. At the outset of the passage, Geinapp asserted that the Whig Party's problems "stemmed less from the slavery question than from the rise of ethnocultural issues" but the analysis that then follows seems to support precisely the opposite conclusion. See also 86–87 as well as Richard L. McCormick, "The Republican Party's Tortuous Path to 'Victorious Defeat,'" *Reviews in American History* 16 (1988): 398. For the House Divided speech, see Basler, ed., *Collected Works*, 2:461–69; Fehrenbacher, ed., *Speeches and Writings*, 1:426–34.

24. William E. Gienapp, "Nativism and the Creation of a Republican Majority in the North before the Civil War," *Journal of American History* 72 (1985): 354.

25. Clifford Geertz, "Ideology as a Cultural System," in David E. Apter, ed., *Ideology and Discontent* (New York: Free Press, 1964), 63–64, quotation on 63; Francis X. Sutton, *The American Business Creed* (Cambridge, Mass.: Harvard University Press, 1956), 4. On language and experience, see Robert E. Shalhope, "Thomas Jefferson's Republicanism and Antebellum Southern Thought," *Journal of Southern History* 42, no. 4 (1976): 533–35. Shalhope cites Erik H. Erikson, *Young Man Luther: A Study in Psychoanalysis and History* (New York: W. W. Norton, 1958), 22.

26. On issues of interpretation, see Gienapp, "Nativism and the Creation of a Republican Majority," 356; Holt, *Rise and Fall of the American Whig Party*, 28–32. At points Holt relied on the *American Review: A Whig Journal of Politics, Literature, Art, and Science* (New York: Wiley and Putnam, 1845–1852, hereafter cited as the *Whig Review*) to help establish the intellectual character of the American Whigs (212, 234, 247, 349). I go into the *Whig Review* in greater detail and less apologetically. For a critique of Holt on this point, see Eric Foner, review of *The Political Crisis of the 1850s*, by Michael F. Holt, *American Historical Review* 84, no. 2 (1979); Major L. Wilson, review of *The Political Crisis of the 1850s*, by Michael F. Holt, *Journal of Southern History* 44, no. 4 (1978): 635–36. Holt himself stressed the roles both of political leadership and of ideas in exacerbating the tensions leading up to the Civil War. Still he oddly continues to eschew elite discourse. See Joel H. Silbey, "'Doomed to Misfortune—If not Dissolution.'" *Virginia Quarterly Review* 76, no. 2 (2000): 351–57; Holt, *Rise and Fall of the American Whig Party*, 349.

27. On the role of evangelical activism, see Richard J. Carwardine, *Evangelicals and Politics in Antebellum America* (New Haven, Conn.: Yale University Press, 1993); William Brock, *Parties and Political Conscience: American Dilemmas, 1840–1850* (Millwood, N.Y.: KTO Press, 1979); Noll, "'Both . . . Pray to the Same God.'"

28. On evangelical support for the Republican Party, see Carwardine, "Lincoln, Evangelical Religion, and American Political Culture," 50. For a lively debate on the use of Marxist, or sort-of Marxist, categories in the analysis of the American antislavery movement, see Thomas Bender, ed., *The Antislavery Debate: Capitalism and Abolitionism as a Problem in Historical Interpretation* (Berkeley: University of California Press, 1992); Daniel Walker Howe, "The Evangelical Movement and Political Culture in the North during the Second Party System," *Journal of American History* 77 (1991): 1216–39.

29. Quote from Howe, "Evangelical Movement," 1220–22. See also Thomas L. Haskell, "Capitalism and the Origins of the Humanitarian Sensibility," *American Historical Review* 90 (1985): 339–61, 547–66; Daniel Walker Howe, "The Market Revolution and the Shaping of Identity in Whig-Jacksonian America," in Melvyn Stokes and Stephen Conway, ed., *The Market Revolution in America: Social, Political, and Religious Expressions, 1800–1880* (Charlottesville: University Press of Virginia, 1996); Gregory H. Singleton, "Protestant Voluntary Organizations and the Shaping of Victorian America," in Daniel Walker Howe, ed., *Victorian America* ([Philadelphia]: University of Pennsylvania Press, 1976), 55–56.

30. On critiques of market capitalism, see Paul Goodman, *Of One Blood: Abolitionism and the Origins of Racial Equality* (Berkeley: University of California Press, 1998); John Stauffer, "Beyond Social Control: The Example of Gerrit Smith," *American Transcendental Quarterly* 11, no. 3 (1997): 234–60.

31. For Lincoln's use of the utilitarian phrase, see "Speech to Germans at Cincinnati, Ohio," Feb. 12, 1861, in Basler, ed., *Collected Works*, 4:202. For the economics of slavery, see "On Sectionalism," ca. July 1856, in Basler, ed., *Collected Works*, 2:352; Fehrenbacher, ed., *Speeches and Writings*, 1:372.

32. Robert P. Swierenga, "Ethnoreligious Political Behavior in the Mid-Nineteenth Century: Voting, Values, Cultures," in Mark A. Noll, ed., *Religion and American Politics: From the Colonial Period to the 1980s* (New York: Oxford University Press, 1990), 148.

33. Noll, "'Both . . . Pray to the Same God,'" 24–25.

34. Ibid., 1.

35. That is, Transcendentalists like Emerson and Thoreau, a few odd evangelical Romantics like Edwards A. Park and Horace Bushnell, and the Mercersburg theology of Philip Schaff and John Nevin. For the pervasiveness of the Scottish Common Sense School and the minimal impact of Romanticism, see Daniel Walker Howe, *Making the American Self: Jonathan Edwards to Abraham Lincoln* (Cambridge, Mass.: Harvard University Press, 1997), 190 and passim; George M. Marsden, "Everyone One's Own Interpreter? The Bible, Science, and Authority in Mid-Nineteenth-Century America," in Nathan O. Hatch and Mark A. Noll, eds., *The Bible in America: Essays in Cultural History* (New York: Oxford University Press, 1982), 82 and passim.

36. Garry Wills, *Lincoln at Gettysburg: The Words that Remade America* (New York: Simon & Schuster, 1992), 77–78, 104–5.

37. Brock, *Parties and Political Conscience*, 139.

CHAPTER 1

1. George B. Forgie, whose *Patricide in the House Divided* otherwise has the most extensive discussion of Lincoln's relationship to Young America, only once briefly refers to this lecture (*Patricide in the House Divided: A Psychological Interpretation of Lincoln and His Age* [New York: W. W. Norton, 1979], 254). In his effort to press a psychological interpretation, Forgie probably overestimates Lincoln's filiopiety and undoubtedly overstates his conservatism. Olivier Fraysse put the First Lecture on Discoveries and Inventions to good use in his *Lincoln, Land, and Labor, 1809–60*, trans. Sylvia Neely (Urbana:

University of Illinois Press, 1994), 33–34. See also William E. Barton, *The Life of Abraham Lincoln*, 2 vols. (Indianapolis: Bobbs-Merrill, 1925), 1:405, 408; Douglas L. Wilson, "Lincoln's Declaration," in *Lincoln before Washington: New Perspectives on the Illinois Years* (Urbana: University of Illinois Press, 1997), 177.

2. Harry V. Jaffa and Robert W. Johannsen, eds., *In the Name of the People: Speeches and Writings of Lincoln and Douglas in the Ohio Campaign of 1859* (Columbus: Ohio State University Press, 1959), vii–x.

3. Thomas F. Schwartz, "The Springfield Lyceums and Lincoln's 1838 Speech," *Illinois Historical Journal* 83, no. 1 (1990); Donald M. Scott, "The Popular Lecture and the Creation of a Public in Mid-Nineteenth-Century America," *Journal of American History* 66 (1980): 791–809.

4. Stephen B. Oates, *With Malice toward None: The Life of Abraham Lincoln* (New York: Harper & Row, 1976), 98; Gabor S. Boritt, *Lincoln and the Economics of the American Dream* (Urbana: University of Illinois Press, 1994), 189.

5. Here I follow Oates, *With Malice toward None*, 160–61, on Lincoln's law practice at this time and p. 60 and p. 75 on his already recognized speechwriting abilities.

6. Wayne C. Temple, "Lincoln as a Lecturer on 'Discoveries, Inventions, and Improvements,'" *Jacksonville Journal Courier*, May 23, 1982; Wayne C. Temple, "Lincoln the Lecturer, Parts I–II," *Lincoln Herald* 101 (1999): 94–110, 146–63.

7. See Basler, ed., *Collected Works*, 2:437–42, 3:356–63; Fehrenbacher, ed., *Speeches and Writings*, 2:3–11.

8. Fehrenbacher and Fehrenbacher, eds., *Recollected Words of Abraham Lincoln*, 490.

9. Basler, ed., *Collected Works*, 3:359; Fehrenbacher, ed., *Speeches and Writings*, 2:6.

10. See Temple, "Lincoln as a Lecturer"; Temple, "Lincoln the Lecturer," 102, 161–62.

11. "To William Morris," Mar. 28, 1859, Basler, ed., *Collected Works*, 3:374.

12. Ibid., 356.

13. Fehrenbacher and Fehrenbacher, eds., *Recollected Words of Abraham Lincoln*, 340; Temple, "Lincoln the Lecturer," 153–54.

14. Fehrenbacher and Fehrenbacher, eds., *Recollected Words of Abraham Lincoln*, 78, 241–42; see also 270–71.

15. Brock, *Parties and Political Conscience*, ix–xvi, 35.

16. For example, the publisher's title to the address Lincoln delivered at the Cooper Institute reads "The Address of the Hon. Abraham Lincoln, in Vindication of the Policy of the Framers of the Constitution and the Principles of the Republican Party . . ." (Basler, ed., *Collected Works*, 3:522).

17. Allen C. Guelzo, "Abraham Lincoln and the Doctrine of Necessity," *Journal of the Abraham Lincoln Association* 18, no. 1 (1997): 76.

18. Basler, ed., *Collected Works*, 3:356; Fehrenbacher, ed., *Speeches and Writings*, 2:3. Edward Ladd Widmer also quotes these sentences but does not discuss Lincoln at length in "Young America: Democratic Cultural Nationalism in Ante-bellum New York" (Ph.D. diss., Harvard University, 1993).

19. See Johannsen, *Stephen A. Douglas*, chap. 15.

20. Edward J. Kempf, *Abraham Lincoln's Philosophy of Common Sense: An Analytical Biography of a Great Mind* ([New York]: New York Academy of Sciences, 1965), xxi and 190. See also, for instance, Johannsen, *Stephen A. Douglas*, 371.

21. See Merle Curti, "Young America," in *Probing Our Past* (New York: Harper, 1955); David B. Danbom, "The Young America Movement," *Journal of the Illinois State Historical Society* 67, no. 3 (1974); Johannsen, *Stephen A. Douglas*, chap. 15; Donald S. Spencer, *Louis Kossuth and Young America: A Study of Sectionalism and Foreign Policy, 1848–1852* (Columbia: University of Missouri Press, 1977); John Stafford, *The Literary Criticism of "Young America":*

A Study in the Relationship of Politics and Literature, 1837–1850 (Berkeley: University of California Press, 1952); Edward L. Widmer, *Young America: The Flowering of Democracy in New York City* (New York: Oxford University Press, 1999); Widmer, "Young America."

22. Danbom, "Young America Movement," 299–300.

23. Joel Porte, ed., *Essays and Lectures,* by Ralph Waldo Emerson (New York: Literary Classics of the United States, 1983), 1353 (published as vol. 15 of the Library of America series). The honors for coining the term "Young America" have also been accorded to Edwin De Leon in a South Carolina College commencement address of 1845. See Curti, "Young America," 219–20; Perry Miller, *The Raven and the Whale* (New York: Harcourt Brace, 1956); Stafford, *Literary Criticism of "Young America."*

24. Porte, ed., *Essays and Lectures,* 213.

25. Charles Reagan Wilson, *Baptized in Blood: The Religion of the Lost Cause, 1865–1920* (Athens: University of Georgia Press, 1980).

26. R. W. B. Lewis, *The American Adam: Tragedy and Tradition in the Nineteenth Century* (Chicago: University of Chicago Press, 1955).

27. Albert K. Weinberg, *Manifest Destiny: A Study of Nationalist Expansionism in American History* (1935; rpt., Chicago: Quadrangle Books, 1963).

28. Siert F. Riepma, "'Young America': A Study in American Nationalism before the Civil War" (Ph.D. diss., Western Reserve University, 1939); Spencer, *Louis Kossuth and Young America;* quotation from Dale Roger Prentiss, "Economic Progress and Social Dissent in Michigan and Mississippi, 1837–1860" (Ph.D. diss., Stanford University, 1990), 149.

29. Marvin Meyers, *The Jacksonian Persuasion* (New York: Vintage, 1960); Widmer, "Young America," 12.

30. Howe, "Market Revolution," 268; Sellers, *Market Revolution.* Howe cites Lawrence Frederick Kohl, *The Politics of Individualism: Parties and the American Character in the Jacksonian Era* (New York: Oxford University Press, 1989); Louise L. Stevenson, *Scholarly Means to Evangelical Ends: The New Haven Scholars and the Transformation of Higher Learning in America, 1830–1890,* New Studies in American Intellectual and Cultural History (Baltimore: Johns Hopkins University Press, 1986).

31. Thomas R. Hietala, *Manifest Design: Anxious Aggrandizement in Late Jacksonian America* (Ithaca, N.Y.: Cornell University Press, 1985), 55–94.

32. Johannsen, *Stephen A. Douglas,* 344.

33. Widmer, "Young America," 54; Hietala, *Manifest Design,* 10.

34. Porte, ed., *Essays and Lectures,* 227, 213.

35. Johannsen, *Stephen A. Douglas,* 344–45; Hietala, *Manifest Design,* 11, 97–122.

36. Basler, ed., *Collected Works,* 3:357; Fehrenbacher, ed., *Speeches and Writings,* 2:3–4.

37. Johannsen, *Stephen A. Douglas,* 661, 84.

38. See especially the "Address to the Washington Temperance Society of Springfield," Basler, ed., *Collected Works,* 1:271; Fehrenbacher, ed., *Speeches and Writings,* 1:81.

39. Lilian Handlin, *George Bancroft, the Intellectual as Democrat* (New York: Harper & Row, 1984), 255.

40. Carwardine, *Evangelicals and Politics,* 66, 95, 270.

41. Basler, ed., *Collected Works,* 3:360; Fehrenbacher, ed., *Speeches and Writings,* 2:6–7. This passage points to the fact that some form of the two lectures was originally delivered as one. The material of the First Lecture begins with a long discussion of biblical inventions (Basler, ed., *Collected Works,* 2:437–42), which is likely where Lincoln first related the story about Adam and Eve that he had "passed unnoticed before."

42. "On the connotation of needle and thread in America at that time, see chap. 10 of *Huckleberry Finn.* Linking inventions with sexual curiosity makes Lincoln a forerunner of Freud" (Frayssé, *Lincoln, Land, and Labor,* 40).

43. Basler, ed., *Collected Works*, 2:437.

44. "To Lyman Trumbull," Dec. 11, 1858, ibid., 3:345; Fehrenbacher, ed., *Speeches and Writings*, 1:832.

45. Stephen A. Douglas, "'See the Conquering Hero Comes': Principles of Stephen A. Douglas Illustrated in His Speeches," 1860, Joseph Regenstein Library, University of Chicago.

46. "To Lyman Trumbull," Dec. 11, 1858, Basler, ed., *Collected Works*, 3:345; Fehrenbacher, ed., *Speeches and Writings*, 1:832.

47. "To Lyman Trumbull," Feb. 3, 1859, Basler, ed., *Collected Works*, 3:355–56; Fehrenbacher, ed., *Speeches and Writings*, 2:2.

48. This contrasts somewhat with Danbom, "Young America Movement," 303. For Danbom, after 1856 Young America "lived on only in the haunting rhetoric of political opponents."

49. Stephen A. Douglas, "Speech of Senator S. A. Douglas at the Meeting in Odd-Fellows' Hall, New Orleans, on Monday Evening, December 6, 1858," 1859, Joseph Regenstein Library, University of Chicago, 9–10. For Pierre Soulé, see Spencer, *Louis Kossuth and Young America*, 37, 105.

50. Basler, ed., *Collected Works*, 2:4.

51. Ibid., 1:433; Fehrenbacher, ed., *Speeches and Writings*, 1:162.

52. "Autobiography Written for John L. Scripps," ca. June 1860, Basler, ed., *Collected Works*, 4:66; Fehrenbacher, ed., *Speeches and Writings*, 1:166.

53. Basler, ed., *Collected Works*, 1:438; Fehrenbacher, ed., *Speeches and Writings*, 1:166–67.

54. Basler, ed., *Collected Works*, 1:431; Fehrenbacher, ed., *Speeches and Writings*, 1:161.

55. Mark E. Neely, *The Last Best Hope of Earth: Abraham Lincoln and the Promise of America* (Cambridge, Mass.: Harvard University Press, 1993), 26.

56. Boritt, *Lincoln and the Economics of the American Dream*, 29, 138.

57. See for instance Phillip S. Paludan, "Lincoln's Prewar Constitutional Vision," *Journal of the Abraham Lincoln Association* 15, no. 2 (1994): 17 and passim; David Zarefsky, "'Public Sentiment is Everything': Lincoln's View of Political Persuasion," *Journal of the Abraham Lincoln Association* 15, no. 2 (1994): 23–40. Paludan cites "Speech at Columbus, Ohio," Sept. 16, 1859, Basler, ed., *Collected Works*, 3:400–403; Fehrenbacher, ed., *Speeches and Writings*, 31–33.

58. Mark E. Neely, Jr., "Lincoln and the Mexican War: An Argument by Analogy," *Civil War History: A Journal of the Middle Period* 24, no. 1 (1978): 15.

59. "Speech at Tremont, Illinois," May 2, 1840, Basler, ed., *Collected Works*, 1:209–10 (for an additional letter, "To John T. Stuart," Mar. 1, 1840, see 206); Paul Simon, *Lincoln's Preparation for Greatness: The Illinois Legislative Years* (Urbana: University of Illinois Press, 1971), 130, 136–37, 214.

60. "Speech on the Sub-Treasury," Dec. 26, 1840, Basler, ed., *Collected Works*, 1:177; Fehrenbacher, ed., *Speeches and Writings*, 1:63. On Lincoln's use of invective, see Robert Bray, "'The Power to Hurt': Lincoln's Early Use of Satire and Invective," *Journal of the Abraham Lincoln Association* 16, no. 1 (1995): 55 and passim.

61. Gienapp, *Origins of the Republican Party*, 67 and passim; Michael F. Holt, "The Politics of Impatience: The Origins of Know Nothingism," *Journal of American History* 60 (1973): 314.

62. Gienapp, *Origins of the Republican Party*, 181–86, 260–63.

63. Johannsen, *Stephen A. Douglas*, 498–99.

64. Meyers, *Jacksonian Persuasion*, 19.

65. As the *Whig Review* put it, "Is the people, though singly but erring mortals, at once invested with infallibility, like a pope, as soon as it assembles and puts on the tiara of sovereignty? It is a slavish doctrin to think so" ("The Progress and Disorganization," July 1845, 96).

66. Gabor S. Boritt, "A Question of Political Suicide: Lincoln's Opposition to the Mexican War," *Journal of the Illinois State Historical Society* 67, no. 1 (1974): 87, 92; "To William H. Herndon," Feb. 1, 1848, Basler, ed., *Collected Works*, 1:446–48; Fehrenbacher, ed., *Speeches and Writings*, 1:172–73.

67. Holt, *Rise and Fall of the American Whig Party*, 176, 219, 233, 245, 249–55.

68. Carwardine, *Evangelicals and Politics*, 235–40.

69. *Congressional Globe*, 33d Cong., 1854, 23, pt. 1: 617.

70. Ibid., 618.

71. Ibid., 617–19.

72. Ibid., 619.

73. Robert W. Johannsen, ed., *The Letters of Stephen A. Douglas* (Urbana: University of Illinois Press, 1961), 302.

74. *Congressional Globe*, 33d Cong., 1854, 23, pt. 1: 620.

75. Carwardine, *Evangelicals and Politics*, 95–96.

76. *Congressional Globe*, 33d Cong., 1854, 23, pt. 1: 621.

77. Meyers, *Jacksonian Persuasion*, 20.

78. Gilbert H. Barnes, *The Antislavery Impulse, 1830–1844* (Gloucester, Mass.: P. Smith, 1933), 180.

79. *Congressional Globe*, 33d Cong., 1854, 23, pt. 1: 621.

80. Ibid. On Douglas's fears of theocracy, see Carwardine, *Evangelicals and Politics*, 184–85.

81. *Congressional Globe*, 33d Cong., 1854, 23, pt. 1: 622.

82. "Reply to Chicago Emancipation Memorial, Washington, D.C.," Sept. 13, 1862, Basler, ed., *Collected Works*, 5:419–25; Fehrenbacher, ed., *Speeches and Writings*, 2:361–67.

83. Johannsen, ed., *Letters of Stephen A. Douglas*, 311. On Douglas and theocracy, see, for instance, David Zarefsky, *Lincoln, Douglas, and Slavery: In the Crucible of Public Debate* (Chicago: University of Chicago Press, 1990).

84. *Congressional Globe*, 33d Cong., 1854, 23, pt. 1: 623.

85. Ibid.

86. Edward Purcell, *The Crisis of Democratic Theory: Scientific Naturalism and the Problem of Value* (Lexington: University Press of Kentucky, 1973), 269. Here, as elsewhere, I use the term "liberal" in the classical sense of Locke or Jefferson or Lord Acton rather than in the New Deal sense of Franklin Roosevelt or Lyndon Johnson.

87. Weinberg, *Manifest Destiny*, 128.

88. Johannsen, ed., *Letters of Stephen A. Douglas*, 348.

89. In the entire discussion of Kossuth and the impact of his visit, I follow Spencer, *Louis Kossuth and Young America*.

90. Ibid., 100, 106, 116. Spencer quotes Douglas from *Proceedings at the Banquet of the Jackson Democratic Association, Washington, Eighth of January, 1852* (Washington, D.C., 1852), 10–11.

91. Spencer, *Louis Kossuth and Young America*, 44.

92. Widmer, "Young America," 56n.

93. Spencer, *Louis Kossuth and Young America*, 118.

94. Johannsen, *Stephen A. Douglas*, 369, 373; Spencer, *Louis Kossuth and Young America*, 120.

95. Stephen A. Douglas, "Speech of Mr. Douglas, of Illinois, on the Monroe Doctrine, delivered in the U.S. Senate, Feb. 14, 1853," Joseph Regenstein Library, University of Chicago, 7.

96. Johannsen, ed., *Letters of Stephen A. Douglas*, 237.

97. Stephen A. Douglas, "To George Nicholas Sanders," in ibid., 480.

98. The clauses of the Clayton-Bulwer Treaty Douglas cited on this point were, first, "The boundary line established by this article shall be religiously respected by each of the two Republics [Mexico and the U.S.], and no change shall ever be made therein except by the express and free consent of both nations lawfully given by the general government of each, in conformity with its own constitution" and, second, "That while the United States disclaim any designs upon the Island of Cuba inconsistent with the laws of nations and with their duties to Spain. . . ." (Douglas, "Speech of Mr. Douglas, of Illinois, on the Monroe Doctrine," 7).

99. *Congressional Globe*, 33d Cong., 1854, 23, pt. 1: 618.

100. David A. Nichols, *Lincoln and the Indians: Civil War Policy and Politics* (Columbia: University of Missouri Press, 1978).

101. Lewis, *American Adam*.

102. "The Fate of Mexico," *United States Magazine and Democratic Review* 41 (May 1858) (hereafter cited as *Democratic Review*). Italics in original.

103. Quoted in Johannsen, *Stephen A. Douglas*, 570.

104. See Boritt and Forness, eds., *Historian's Lincoln*, 175–204; LaWanda Cox, *Lincoln and Black Freedom: A Study in Presidential Leadership* (Columbia: University of South Carolina Press, 1981); Benjamin Quarles, *Lincoln and the Negro* (New York: Oxford University Press, 1962); Simon, *Lincoln's Preparation for Greatness*, 121–37. For a brief review of the literature on this subject, see Donald, *Lincoln*, 633, note from p. 221.

105. Gienapp, "Nativism and the Creation of a Republican Majority," 533.

106. Boritt, *Lincoln and the Economics of the American Dream*, 223.

107. "Message to Congress in Special Session," July 4, 1861, Basler, ed., *Collected Works*, 4:426. Fehrenbacher, ed., *Speeches and Writings*, 2:250.

108. See especially Thomas Wentworth Higginson, *Army Life in a Black Regiment*, ed. Howard N. Meyer (1869; rpt., New York: W. W. Norton, 1984).

109. "Speech on the Dred Scott Decision," June 26, 1857, Basler, ed., *Collected Works*, 2:409; Fehrenbacher, ed., *Speeches and Writings*, 1:402–3.

110. "Fate of Mexico," *Democratic Review*, 342.

111. "Address at Cooper Institute," Basler, ed., *Collected Works*, 3:548; Fehrenbacher, ed., *Speeches and Writings*, 2:128.

112. Johannsen, *Stephen A. Douglas*, 506.

113. Quoted in ibid., 399.

114. Ibid.

115. Basler, ed., *Collected Works*, 3:357–58; Fehrenbacher, ed., *Speeches and Writings*, 2:4.

116. Thomas Arnold, *Introductory Lectures on Modern History, Delivered in Lent Term, MDCCCXLII. With the Inaugural Lecture Delivered in December, MDCCCXLI*, 4th ed. (London: B. Fellows, 1849), 32.

117. Walter H. Conser, Jr., *Church and Confession: Conservative Theologians in Germany, England, and America, 1815–1866* ([Macon, Ga.]: Mercer University Press, 1984), 133–34.

118. Basler, ed., *Collected Works*, 3:360; Fehrenbacher, ed., *Speeches and Writings*, 2:7.

119. Louis Hartz, *The Liberal Tradition in America: An Interpretation of American Political Thought since the Revolution* (New York: Harcourt Brace Jovanovich, 1955).

120. Basler, ed., *Collected Works*, 3:363; Fehrenbacher, ed., *Speeches and Writings*, 10.

121. Oates, *With Malice toward None*, 178.

122. Boritt, *Lincoln and the Economics of the American Dream*, 74. Writes Boritt, "Thinking in terms of a permanent economic revolution was second nature to Whigs of Lincoln's generation but not to those of Webster's, though they, too, were fond of speaking of great transformations" (ibid., 167).

123. Ibid., 8.

124. Basler, ed., *Collected Works*, 3:472; Fehrenbacher, ed., *Speeches and Writings*, 2:91.

125. Basler, ed., *Collected Works*, 3:362–63; Fehrenbacher, ed., *Speeches and Writings*, 2:10.

126. Basler, ed., *Collected Works*, 3:362; Fehrenbacher, ed., *Speeches and Writings*, 2:9.

127. Gienapp, "Nativism and the Creation of a Republican Majority," 533.

128. Frances P. Cobbe, ed., *The Collected Works of Theodore Parker: Minister of the Twenty-eighth Congregational Society at Boston. . .*, vol. 6 (London: Trübner, 1864), 240–86.

129. Basler, ed., *Collected Works*, 3:363; Fehrenbacher, ed., *Speeches and Writings*, 2:10.

130. Sacvan Bercovitch, *The American Jeremiad* (Madison: University of Wisconsin Press, 1978), 113; Conrad Cherry, ed., *God's New Israel: Religious Interpretations of American Destiny* (Englewood Cliffs, N.J.: Prentice-Hall, 1971), 116–17; Handlin, *George Bancroft*, 129.

131. Basler, ed., *Collected Works*, 3:357–58; Fehrenbacher, ed., *Speeches and Writings*, 2:4.

132. Basler, ed., *Collected Works*, 3:358; Fehrenbacher, ed., *Speeches and Writings*, 2:5.

133. See the *Whig Review*.

134. Basler, ed., *Collected Works*, 3:356–57; Fehrenbacher, ed., *Speeches and Writings*, 2:3.

135. Bruce, *Lincoln and the Tools of War*; Temple, "Lincoln as a Lecturer," 3–4.

136. Basler, ed., *Collected Works*, 3:359; Fehrenbacher, ed., *Speeches and Writings*, 2:6.

137. Temple, "Lincoln as a Lecturer," 12; Temple, "Lincoln the Lecturer," 161.

138. Temple, "Lincoln as a Lecturer," 6; Temple, "Lincoln the Lecturer," 154.

139. Basler, ed., *Collected Works*, 3:481–82; Fehrenbacher, ed., *Speeches and Writings*, 2:101.

140. Basler, ed., *Collected Works*, 3:481; Fehrenbacher, ed., *Speeches and Writings*, 2:100.

141. According to George M. Marsden, "by far the most prevalent apocalyptic view among American Protestants in the Civil War era is known technically as 'postmillennialism.' It teaches that Christ will not come again until *after* a millennium of prolonged progress on earth and special spiritual blessings. In the writings of the day this view was often designated 'Spiritualist': because its advocates believed that the promised Kingdom of Christ would be manifested in the reign of the Holy Spirit over the hearts of his people. The millennial kingdom, which was expected to last for an indeterminate time (some said a literal thousand years), was not to be an entirely new age. Rather, it would be an extension of the spiritual kingdom that Christ had introduced at the time of his first advent, when he had established his Church as the agency through which the Holy Spirit would be made manifest. The Millennium would be marked by a great revival of Christianity and the conversion of all the nations of the world, so that the numbers of the saved would far exceed those of the lost. It was also expected to bring radical social-reforms, including the cessation of wars, the end of enslavements and oppressions, triumph over all forms of vice, and a great extension of learning and the arts. After this would be the Second Coming and Judgment by Christ, the creation of 'a New Heavens and a New Earth,' and the everlasting reign of Christ over his people" (George M. Marsden, *The Evangelical Mind and the New School Presbyterian Experience: A Case Study*

of Thought and Theology in Nineteenth-Century America, Yale Publications in American Studies, vol. 20 [New Haven, Conn.: Yale University Press, 1970], 185).

142. "Address to the Wisconsin State Agricultural Society," Sept. 30, 1859, Basler, ed., *Collected Works,* 3:481; Fehrenbacher, ed., *Speeches and Writings,* 2:100.

143. Danbom, "Young America Movement," 297.

144. Ibid., 305.

145. Fraysse, *Lincoln, Land, and Labor;* Daniel Walker Howe, "Why Abraham Lincoln Was a Whig," *Journal of the Abraham Lincoln Association* 16, no. 1 (1995).

146. Danbom, "Young America Movement," 306.

147. J. David Greenstone, *The Lincoln Persuasion: Remaking American Liberalism,* Princeton Studies in American Politics (Princeton, N.J.: Princeton University Press, 1993).

148. Barnes, *Antislavery Impulse,* 79.

149. Lewis, *American Adam,* 7.

150. Lasch, *True and Only Heaven,* 16.

CHAPTER 2

1. Lester J. Cappon, ed., *The Adams-Jefferson Letters: The Complete Correspondence between Thomas Jefferson and Abigail and John Adams* (Chapel Hill: University of North Carolina Press, 1959), 569–70.

2. Ibid., 571.

3. Thomas Jefferson, "To John Holmes," Monticello, Apr. 22, 1820, Adrienne Koch and William Peden, eds., *The Life and Selected Writings of Thomas Jefferson* (New York: Modern Library, 1944).

4. Brock, *Parties and Political Conscience,* 68–69.

5. Merle Curti, "Mr. Locke, America's Philosopher, 1783–1861," in *Probing Our Past,* 85–86.

6. Merle Curti clearly articulated this idea in an essay revealingly titled "Mr. Locke, America's Philosopher, 1783–1861." While, as quoted above, Curti did explicate the Romantic, anti-Lockean reaction in American thought, his pragmatist assumptions led him to dismiss Romanticism as only "bringing about an increasing qualification and enrichment of the basic Lockean philosophy" (ibid., 98).

7. George Bancroft, *Oration Delivered on the Fourth of July, 1826* (Northampton, Mass.: T. Watson Shepard, 1826), 23.

8. No less than their Soviet adversaries, Cold War "consensus" historians remained under the sway of one of Hegel's brilliant students. Much of the following discussion of Bancroft's romanticism follows David W. Noble, *Historians against History: The Frontier Thesis and the National Covenant in American Historical Writing since 1830* (Minneapolis: University of Minnesota Press, 1965), chaps. 1–2.

9. Walter H. Conser summarized the traditional view of Romanticism when he defined it as a "break from rationalism and a critique of the Enlightenment. Protesting against the narrowness of rationalist categories and their understanding of human nature, denying the adequacy of the Enlightenment's eudaemonistic ethics, and challenging the easy equation of morality and outward behavior, romanticism contested the rationalist assumptions on several fronts. . . . Romantics claimed that life was an ineffable mystery." (*Church and Confession,* 28–29). I agree fully with this traditional assessment. I only want to add that what explains this impulse was the desire to live once again as though life had some higher significance. Thus I see Romanticism as, at root, a religious urge. See also M. H. Abrams, *Natural Supernaturalism: Tradition and Revolution in Romantic Literature* (New York: W. W. Norton, 1971), 11–13, 29, and passim; Anne C. Rose, *Victorian America and the*

Civil War (Cambridge: Cambridge University Press, 1992); René Wellek, "The Concept of Romanticism," in *Concepts of Criticism*, ed. Stephen G. Nichols (New Haven, Conn.: Yale University Press, 1963). Anne C. Rose has recently stated the case slightly differently. In *Victorian America and the Civil War*, Rose argued "that at the heart of American Victorian culture was romanticism, the impulse to search in secular pursuits for answers to questions once settled by traditional religion." If there is any significant difference at all between my treatment and hers, it is that, whereas Rose saw Victorianism as essentially secularizing in spirit, I see it as a neoreligious reaction to the secularism of the Enlightenment. But since we both argue that Victorianism and Romanticism were religious responses to a religious crisis, these are clearly two sides of the same coin. M. H. Abrams also saw Romanticism as part of the process of secularization, but it was not "the deletion and replacement of religious ideas but rather the assimilation and reinterpretation of religious ideas, as constitutive elements in a world view founded on secular premises." The only quibble I would raise with this "secularization-hypothesis" of Abrams and Rose is that it makes sense only in retrospect. Romantics themselves did not know that Darwin would ultimately undermine their attempts to replace materialism with a higher sensibility; rather, they sincerely hoped to save the world from materialism. Thus it seems more in keeping with the spirit of the Romantics themselves to treat Romanticism as an attempt to stem the tide of secularism and materialism than to make it part of the secularization process itself.

10. *Illinois State Journal*, Feb. 14, 1859, Feb. 21, 1859.

11. For Lincoln's poems and his story, see Basler, ed., *Collected Works*, 1:336–79, 384–89, 392; Fehrenbacher, ed., *Speeches and Writings*, 1:120–22, 130–39, 141–43, 145–49.

12. "To Andrew Johnston," Apr. 18, 1846, Basler, ed., *Collected Works*, 1:378; Fehrenbacher, ed., *Speeches and Writings*, 1:137.

13. *Illinois State Journal*, Feb. 14, 1859, Feb. 21, 1859.

14. Basler, ed., *Collected Works*, 2:437–42.

15. Ibid., 438.

16. Donald, *Lincoln*, 164.

17. Phillip S. Paludan, *A Covenant with Death: The Constitution, Law, and Equality in the Civil War Era* (Urbana: University of Illinois Press, 1975), 68.

18. Frank Freidel, *Francis Lieber: Nineteenth-Century Liberal* (Baton Rouge: Louisiana State University Press, 1947), 63–81.

19. Basler, ed., *Collected Works*, 2:437.

20. Allan Nevins, *The Emergence of Lincoln*, vol. 1, *Douglas, Buchanan, and Party Chaos, 1857–1859* (New York: Charles Scribner's Sons, 1950), 391. See also Boritt, *Lincoln and the Economics of the American Dream*, 189.

21. Basler, ed., *Collected Works*, 2:442.

22. Ibid., 3:358–59; Fehrenbacher, ed., *Speeches and Writings*, 2:5.

23. Basler, ed., *Collected Works*, 2:440.

24. Fraysse, *Lincoln, Land, and Labor*, 33.

25. Ibid., 34.

26. Basler, ed., *Collected Works*, 2:10–11. Fehrenbacher, ed., *Speeches and Writings*, 1:222–24.

27. Basler, ed., *Collected Works*, 2:437–42.

28. Elizabeth R. McKinsey, *Niagara Falls: Icon of the American Sublime*, Cambridge Studies in American Literature and Culture (Cambridge: Cambridge University Press, 1985), 97.

29. Ibid., 52, 86–108.

30. James A. Secord, ed., *Vestiges of the Natural History of Creation and Other Evolutionary Writings* (Chicago: University of Chicago Press, 1994), ix–xlv and passim.

Vestiges was the subject of not one but two lengthy and sharply critical reviews in the *Whig Review:* "The Author of the Vestiges of the Natural History of Creation," February 1846; "A Sequel to 'Vestiges of the Natural History of Creation,'" April 1846. See also Guelzo, *Abraham Lincoln,* 108.

31. Barton, *Soul of Abraham Lincoln,* 166–71, 255, 265; Herndon and Weik, *Herndon's Life of Lincoln,* ed. Angle, 354; Secord, ed., *Vestiges,* ix–x, xxvi.

32. James Smith, *The Christian's Defence,* 2 vols. (Cincinnati: J. A. James, 1843), vol. 2.

33. Donald, *Lincoln,* 132.

34. Quoted from John J. Duff, *A. Lincoln, Prairie Lawyer* (New York: Rinehart, 1960), 102. See also Dodge, *Abraham Lincoln,* 31.

35. While David Donald rejected Herndon's extreme gloss that "Lincoln did not appreciate nature" (*Lincoln's Herndon,* 128), he chose to accept Herndon's testimony of some thirty years after the fact rather than take seriously the words of a draft document in Lincoln's hand. His reluctance to read Lincoln as a self-conscious, reflective (let alone Romantic or religious) intellectual is typical of an entire generation of scholars and reflects the intellectual needs of the "consensus period," when American history was supposed to be about agreement, not argument; about Jefferson, not Jonathan Edwards; about practical problem solving, not philosophy or literature.

On Herndon as a historian, see Douglas L. Wilson's series of courageous essays in which he has convincingly revised the excessive tendency of scholars to discount Herndon's testimony. See especially "Herndon's Legacy," in *Lincoln before Washington,* 25–26 and passim; "William H. Herndon and the 'Necessary Truth,'" in *Lincoln before Washington.* Nevertheless, on the subject of Lincoln's intellectual tendencies, Herndon was a poor judge. And he had a positive program that involved minimizing Lincoln's religious tendencies so as not to give credence to the view that Lincoln was in any way a conventional sectarian.

36. Donald, *Lincoln,* 165. Lincoln cited from "Eulogy on Henry Clay," July 6, 1852, Basler, ed., *Collected Works,* 2:126; Fehrenbacher, ed., *Speeches and Writings,* 1:264.

37. Wills, *Lincoln at Gettysburg.*

38. Conrad Cherry, *Nature and the Religious Imagination from Edwards to Bushnell* (Philadelphia: Fortress Press, 1980), 9.

39. Basler, ed., *Collected Works,* 1:178–79; Fehrenbacher, ed., *Speeches and Writings,* 1:64–65.

40. Wilson, *Baptized in Blood.*

41. The entire document lacks the usual clarity of Lincoln. In addition, both the words "sublime Christian Heroism" and the words "Human Rights" were uncharacteristic. No autograph draft exists, and Seward seems to have handled the matter, though doubtless with Lincoln's approval (Basler, ed., *Collected Works,* 6:63–65; Fehrenbacher, ed., *Speeches and Writings,* 2:431–33).

42. "Speech at Independence Hall," Feb. 22, 1861, Basler, ed., *Collected Works,* 4:240–1; Fehrenbacher, ed., *Speeches and Writings,* 2:213–14.

43. "To William H. Seward," June 28, 1862, Basler, ed., *Collected Works,* 5:291–92; Fehrenbacher, ed., *Speeches and Writings,* 2:335.

44. Henry F. May, *The Enlightenment in America* (New York: Oxford University Press, 1976), 97.

45. Lydia Maria Child, *Anti-Slavery Catechism* (Newburyport, Mass.: C. Whipple, 1839), 69, quoted from John L. Thomas, ed., *Slavery Attacked: The Abolitionist Crusade* (Englewood Cliffs, N.J.: Prentice-Hall, 1965), 69. See Greenstone, *Lincoln Persuasion,* 245.

46. James M. McPherson, *For Cause and Comrades: Why Men Fought in the Civil War* (New York: Oxford University Press, 1997).

47. Greenstone, *Lincoln Persuasion,* 108.

48. Jefferson quotations cited in ibid., 85, 102, drawn from Koch and Peden, eds., *Life and Selected Writings of Thomas Jefferson,* 397–402.

49. "Fragment on the Struggle Against Slavery," ca. July 1858, Basler, ed., *Collected Works,* 2:482; Fehrenbacher, ed., *Speeches and Writings,* 1:437–38.

50. Barnes, *Antislavery Impulse.*

51. Nevins, *Emergence of Lincoln,* vol. 1, *Douglas, Buchanan, and Party Chaos,* 410–11.

52. Gienapp, "Nativism and the Creation of a Republican Majority," 554; Brooks D. Simpson, "Two More Roads to Sumter," *Reviews in American History* 17 (1989): 229.

53. "To the People of Sangamo County," Mar. 9, 1832, Basler, ed., *Collected Works,* 1:8; Fehrenbacher, ed., *Speeches and Writings,* 1:4.

54. Cappon, ed., *Adams-Jefferson Letters,* 434.

55. "Second Lecture on Discoveries and Inventions," Basler, ed., *Collected Works,* 3:358; Fehrenbacher, ed., *Speeches and Writings,* 2:4.

56. Noble, *Historians against History,* 16.

57. Henry C. Whitney, *Life on the Circuit with Lincoln* (Boston: Estes & Lauriat, 1892), 214.

58. This is of course a bit facile. One could just as easily give credit to, for example, Edward Everett's Cambridge oration of August 1824. See Edward Everett, *Orations and Speeches on Various Occasions,* 2d ed., vol. 1 (Boston: Charles C. Little and James Brown, 1850), 9–44. This section was prepared before Andrew Burstein published *America's Jubilee: How in 1826 a Generation Remembered Fifty Years of Independence* (New York: Alfred A. Knopf, 2001). See also Burstein's *On Sentimental Democracy: The Evolution of America's Self-Image* (New York: Hill and Wang, 1999).

59. Merrill D. Peterson, *The Jefferson Image in the American Mind* (New York: Oxford University Press, 1960), 3; Burstein, *America's Jubilee,* 268.

60. Cherry, *Nature and the Religious Imagination,* 138.

61. Bancroft, *Oration delivered on the Fourth of July, 1826,* 3.

62. Ibid., 4.

63. Bercovitch, *American Jeremiad,* 138.

64. May, *Enlightenment in America,* 9–10.

65. George Bancroft, *Literary and Historical Miscellanies* (New York: Harper and Brothers, 1855), 505.

66. Noble, *Historians against History,* 27–28; May, *Enlightenment in America,* 361–62.

67. Bancroft, *Literary and Historical Miscellanies,* 409.

68. Bancroft, *Oration delivered on the Fourth of July, 1826,* 20.

69. Handlin, *George Bancroft,* 3–26.

70. Bercovitch, *American Jeremiad.*

71. Bancroft, *Literary and Historical Miscellanies,* 424–25.

72. Robert H. Canary, *George Bancroft,* ed. Sylvia E. Bowman (New York: Twayne, 1974), 25.

73. Basler, ed., *Collected Works,* 1:159–79; Fehrenbacher, ed., *Speeches and Writings,* 1:44–65.

74. Handlin, *George Bancroft,* 180–81.

75. Ibid., 182.

76. Bancroft, *Oration Delivered on the Fourth of July, 1826,* 23.

77. Ibid., 25.

78. Ibid., 7.

79. George Bancroft, *History of the United States, from the Discovery of the American Continent,* vol. 3 (Boston: Little, Brown, 1840), 396.

80. George Bancroft, *History of the United States, from the Discovery of the American Continent,* vol. 4 (Boston: Little, Brown, 1852), 157–58.

81. Bancroft, *Literary and Historical Miscellanies,* 440.

82. Bercovitch, *American Jeremiad,* 117–18.

83. Noble, *Historians against History.*

84. Bancroft, *Literary and Historical Miscellanies,* 504.

85. On Jefferson's beliefs, see Cappon, ed., *Adams-Jefferson Letters,* 591–94. On Adams, see ibid., 372–75.

86. Bercovitch, *American Jeremiad,* 140 and passim.

87. Bancroft, *History,* 3:398.

88. Ibid., 398–99.

89. Bancroft, *Literary and Historical Miscellanies,* 446.

90. Bercovitch, *American Jeremiad,* 107.

91. Bancroft, *History,* 4:10; Bancroft, *Literary and Historical Miscellanies,* 491–92.

92. Bancroft, *Literary and Historical Miscellanies,* 470–71.

93. Herman Melville, *Battle-Pieces and Aspects of the War,* ed. Lee Rust Brown (New York: Da Capo Press, 1995), 63.

94. Sheldon M. Novick, ed., *The Collected Works of Justice Holmes: Complete Public Writings and Selected Judicial Opinions of Oliver Wendell Holmes,* Holmes Devise Memorial Edition, vol. 3 (Chicago: University of Chicago Press, 1995), 137.

95. Bercovitch, *American Jeremiad,* 144.

96. *Southern State Rights, Free Trade and Anti-Abolition Tract No. 1* (Charleston: Walker & Burke, 1844), 32.

97. Meyers, *Jacksonian Persuasion.*

98. *Southern State Rights,* 24.

99. Ibid., 25.

100. "Thomas Jefferson to James Madison," Sept. 6, 1789, Koch and Peden, eds., *Life and Selected Writings of Thomas Jefferson,* 491, quoted in Greenstone, *Lincoln Persuasion,* 78.

101. Canary, *George Bancroft,* 30, 36–40.

102. Ibid., 31.

103. Ibid., 37.

104. *Southern State Rights,* 28.

105. Ibid., 27.

106. Handlin, *George Bancroft,* 192.

107. Canary, *George Bancroft,* 31.

108. Handlin, *George Bancroft,* 216, 232.

109. Frederick Merk, *Manifest Destiny and Mission in American History: A Reinterpretation* (New York: Vintage, 1963), 156, 194–95.

110. See Boritt, *Lincoln and the Economics of the American Dream,* 137–42. Mark E. Neely makes important qualifications to Boritt's claim that Lincoln actively opposed expansion ("Lincoln and the Mexican War," 13–17).

111. Holt, *Rise and Fall of the American Whig Party,* 176, 219, 233, 245, 249–55.

112. Neely, "Lincoln and the Mexican War," 14.

113. Boritt, *Lincoln and the Economics of the American Dream,* 139–40.

114. Quoted in Neely, "Lincoln and the Mexican War," 13.

115. Boritt, *Lincoln and the Economics of the American Dream,* 139–40.

116. Ibid., 259.

117. Carwardine, *Evangelicals and Politics,* 46. On the negative assessment of Lincoln, see Wilson, *Patriotic Gore,* 75.

118. Whitney, *Life on the Circuit with Lincoln,* 214.

119. "Second Lecture on Discoveries and Inventions," Basler, ed., *Collected Works*, 3:363; Fehrenbacher, ed., *Speeches and Writings*, 2:10.

120. "To Joshua F. Speed," Aug. 24, 1855, Basler, ed., *Collected Works*, 2:323; Fehrenbacher, ed., *Speeches and Writings*, 1:363.

121. Bancroft, *Literary and Historical Miscellanies*, 514–17.

122. Bancroft, *History*, 4:11.

123. Bancroft, *Oration delivered on the Fourth of July, 1826*, 26; Basler, ed., *Collected Works*, 5:537; Fehrenbacher, ed., *Speeches and Writings*, 537.

124. Handlin, *George Bancroft*, 148.

125. "Address to the Washington Temperance Society," Feb. 22, 1842, Basler, ed., *Collected Works*, 1:275; Fehrenbacher, ed., *Speeches and Writings*, 1:85–86.

CHAPTER 3

1. Brock, *Parties and Political Conscience*, ix; Holt, *Rise and Fall of the American Whig Party*, 10–11.

2. Daniel Walker Howe, *The Political Culture of the American Whigs* (Chicago: University of Chicago Press, 1979), 77.

3. Brock, *Parties and Political Conscience*, 189.

4. Carwardine, *Evangelicals and Politics*, 65. Thomas Ritchie quote unknown.

5. On Whig fears of demagoguery, see Thomas Brown, *Politics and Statesmanship: Essays on the American Whig Party* (New York: Columbia University Press, 1985), 9.

6. Holt, *Rise and Fall of the American Whig Party*, 49, 17. See also 28–32.

7. Ibid., 64.

8. Ibid., 10, 41, 66–69.

9. Ibid., 14, 30.

10. Carwardine, *Evangelicals and Politics*, 253, 278.

11. Ibid., 45.

12. See Frank Luther Mott, *A History of American Magazines, 1741–1850* (Cambridge, Mass.: Harvard University Press, 1938), 750–54.

13. Adrienne Koch and William Peden, eds., *The Selected Writings of John and John Quincy Adams* (New York: Alfred A. Knopf, 1946), 288–89.

14. "Has the State a Religion?" *Whig Review*, March 1846, 284.

15. "Speech at Independence Hall," Feb. 22, 1861, Basler, ed., *Collected Works*, 4:240–41; Fehrenbacher, ed., *Speeches and Writings*, 2:213–14; Greenstone, *Lincoln Persuasion*, 236.

16. "Progress and Disorganization," *Whig Review*, 99, second quotation on 90.

17. Abrams, *Natural Supernaturalism*, 11.

18. "Progress and Disorganization," *Whig Review*, 91.

19. Mott, *History of American Magazines*, 752.

20. "Progress and Disorganization," *Whig Review*, 91–92, 94.

21. Ibid., 93.

22. Charles Sumner, "War System of the Commonwealth of Nations [1849]," in *Annals of America*, vol. 7, *1841–1849: Manifest Destiny*, ed. William Benton (Chicago: Encyclopaedia Britannica, 1976), 550.

23. "Speech to Indians," Mar. 23, 1863, Basler, ed., *Collected Works*, 6:152; Fehrenbacher, ed., *Speeches and Writings*, 2:441–42.

24. Brown, *Politics and Statesmanship*, 12.

25. "Progress and Disorganization," *Whig Review*, 93.

26. Ibid., 98.

27. David F. Ericson, *The Shaping of American Liberalism: The Debates over Ratification, Nullification, and Slavery* (Chicago: University of Chicago Press, 1993), 137.

28. "Our Country," *Whig Review*, March 1845, 277.

29. "Progress and Disorganization," *Whig Review*, 95.

30. Ibid., 97.

31. Gienapp, *Origins of the Republican Party*, 364–65.

32. "Progress and Disorganization," *Whig Review*, 95.

33. Meyers, *Jacksonian Persuasion*, 13.

34. Perry Miller, *The New England Mind: The Seventeenth Century* (1939; rpt., New York: Beacon, 1961), 199.

35. David J. Harkness, *Lincoln and Byron, Lovers of Liberty* (Harrogate, Tennessee: Department of Lincolniana of Lincoln Memorial University, 1941); David J. Harkness and R. Gerald McMurtry, *Lincoln's Favorite Poets* (Knoxville: University of Tennessee Press, 1959), 37–53; Douglas L. Wilson, "Abraham Lincoln and the 'Spirit of Mortal,'" in *Lincoln before Washington*, 33; Douglas L. Wilson, *Honor's Voice: The Transformation of Abraham Lincoln* (New York: Alfred A. Knopf, 1998), 59, 190–93, 197–98, 205, 252, 256, 262, 275, 292–94, 310–11, 320, 349–51, 366. See also Wilson and Davis, eds., *Herndon's Informants*, 789.

36. Perry Miller, *Nature's Nation* (Cambridge, Mass.: Belknap Press of Harvard University Press, 1967), 199.

37. For Barnard, see Mott, *History of American Magazines*, 752. For Colton, see Donald Frank Andrews, "The American Whig Review, 1845–1852: Its History and Literary Contents" (Ph.D. diss., University of Tennessee, 1977), 21.

38. "Our Position—Introductory," *Whig Review*, January 1845, 1–2.

39. "The Position of the Parties," *Whig Review*, January 1845, 9.

40. "Introductory," *Whig Review*, 2.

41. Ibid., 3.

42. "Our Country," *Whig Review*, 275.

43. Cobbe, ed., *Collected Works of Theodore Parker*, 6:240.

44. For a historiographical discussion of Whig thought, see Brown, *Politics and Statesmanship*, 2–3.

45. See, for instance, "Has the State a Religion?" *Whig Review*, 284.

46. William J. Novak, *The People's Welfare: Law and Regulation in Nineteenth-Century America*, Studies in Legal History (Chapel Hill: University of North Carolina Press, 1996).

47. "Position of the Parties," *Whig Review*, 9.

48. Carwardine, "Lincoln, Evangelical Religion, and American Political Culture," 32.

49. "Introductory," *Whig Review*, 2.

50. "To Joshua F. Speed," Aug. 24, 1855, Basler, ed., *Collected Works*, 2:323; Fehrenbacher, ed., *Speeches and Writings*, 1:363.

51. "Theodore Frelinghuysen," *Whig Review*, January 1845, 100.

52. "Our Country," *Whig Review*, 276.

53. The piece is attributed to Bellows in David Brion Davis, ed., *Antebellum American Culture: An Interpretive Anthology* (Lexington, Mass.: D. C. Heath, 1979), 111.

54. "Influence of the Trading Spirit upon the Social and Moral Life of America [1845 in the *Whig Review*]," in *Annals of America*, vol. 7, *1841–1849: Manifest Destiny*, ed. Benton, 267.

55. Ibid., 268.

56. "European Views of American Democracy.—De Tocqueville," *Democratic Review* 1, no. 1 (1837): 91–107; "European Views of American Democracy. No. II. M. De Tocqueville," *Democratic Review* 2, no. 8 (1838): 337–57.

57. "Influence of the Trading Spirit," *Whig Review*, 269.

58. Ibid., 266–67.

59. John M. Murrin, "Religion and Politics in America from the First Settlements to the Civil War," in Noll, ed., *Religion and American Politics*, 28. As we will see, Lincoln's doctrine of necessity can be seen as a return to a more truly Calvinist orthodoxy.

60. See for instance Seward to Thurlow Weed, quoted in Brock, *Parties and Political Conscience*, 306.

61. Basler, ed., *Collected Works*, 2:409–10; Fehrenbacher, ed., *Speeches and Writings*, 1:403.

62. "Influence of the Trading Spirit," *Whig Review*, 269.

63. Ibid., 270–71.

64. See Cherry, *Nature and the Religious Imagination*, 9–10 and passim.

65. Hugh Chisholm, ed., *The Encyclopaedia Britannica: A Dictionary of Arts, Sciences, Literature, and General Information*, 29 vols. (New York: Encyclopaedia Britannica, 1911), 20:628–29.

66. "Influence of the Trading Spirit," *Whig Review*, 271–72.

67. Cherry, *Nature and the Religious Imagination*; Greenstone, *Lincoln Persuasion*; Perry Miller, *Errand into the Wilderness* (Cambridge, Mass.: Belknap Press of Harvard University Press, 1956), 184–203.

68. "Thoughts on Reading," *Whig Review*, May 1845, 492, second quotation on 485.

69. "Poe's Tales," *Whig Review*, September 1845, 306–9.

70. "Thoughts on Reading," *Whig Review*, 489–93.

71. Ibid., 489.

72. Ibid., 494.

73. "The Bhagvat Geeta and the Doctrine of Immortality," *Whig Review*, September 1845, 267–68.

74. "Thoughts on Reading," *Whig Review*, 489.

75. Cherry, *Nature and the Religious Imagination*.

76. "Thoughts on Reading," *Whig Review*, 492.

77. Ibid., 490.

78. "Metaphysics of Bear Hunting: An Adventure in the San Saba Hills," *Whig Review*, July 1845, 172. "Metaphysics of Bear Hunting" was probably written by Charles Wilkins Webber (Andrews, "American Whig Review," 112).

79. Carwardine, *Evangelicals and Politics*, 10.

80. Miller, *Errand into the Wilderness*, 200.

81. "The Study of Plato," *Whig Review*, August 1845, 168.

82. Ibid.

83. Ibid.

84. "Fragment on the Pro-Slavery Theology," [1858?], Basler, ed., *Collected Works*, 3:204–5; Fehrenbacher, ed., *Speeches and Writings*, 1:685–86.

85. I am thinking here of, for example, Archibald Macliesh and "The Irresponsibles."

86. "Introductory," *Whig Review*, 2.

CHAPTER 4

1. Howe, *Political Culture of the American Whigs*, 79, second quotation on 71.

2. Morton J. Horwitz, *The Transformation of America Law, 1780–1860*, Studies in Legal History (Cambridge, Mass.: Harvard University Press, 1977); James Willard Hurst, *Law and the Conditions of Freedom: In the Nineteenth-Century United States* (Madison: University of Wisconsin Press, 1956). Perry Miller dwelt more on religion and Romanticism in law. See Perry Miller, *The Life of the Mind in America: From the Revolution to the Civil War* (New York: Harcourt, Brace & World, 1965), bk. 2.

3. Duff, *A. Lincoln*, 128.

4. In other senses of course the law in this period could be called "liberal"—especially in the negatively defined, Hartzian sense: the law was neither socialist nor did it favor the landed property rights of an aristocracy.

5. Arthur Bestor, "The American Civil War as a Constitutional Crisis," *American Historical Review* 69, no. 2 (1964): 327–52.

6. Basler, ed., *Collected Works*, 4:263–64; Fehrenbacher, ed., *Speeches and Writings*, 2:216–17.

7. George Bowyer, *Commentaries on Universal Public Law* (London: V & R. Stevens and G. S. Norton, 1854), 15.

8. Ibid., 204, 206.

9. Brock, *Parties and Political Conscience*, 171.

10. The book is in the Lincoln collection of the special collections of the Joseph Regenstein Library at the University of Chicago.

11. Basler, ed., *Collected Works*, 4:264; Fehrenbacher, ed., *Speeches and Writings*, 2:217.

12. Harry V. Jaffa, *Crisis of the House Divided: An Interpretation of the Issues in the Lincoln-Douglas Debates* (Garden City, N.Y.: Doubleday, 1959).

13. George Fitzhugh, author of *Cannibals All* and *Sociology for the South*.

14. Jaffa, *Crisis of the House Divided*, v.

15. "Has the State a Religion?" *Whig Review*, 273.

16. Ibid., 274–75, 288, 289.

17. Ibid., 278–79. On the well-regulated society, see Novak, *People's Welfare*.

18. "Has the State a Religion?" *Whig Review*, 280–81.

19. Ibid., 282.

20. Ibid., 284.

21. Basler, ed., *Collected Works*, 3:550–51; Fehrenbacher, ed., *Speeches and Writings*, 2:416–17.

22. For a portrait of the southern side, I rely on Brock, *Parties and Political Conscience*.

23. Albert A. Woldman, for instance, apologized for the Matson case in this way in *Lawyer Lincoln* (1936; rpt., New York: Carrol & Graf, 1994), 60–71.

29. While none of this discussion of Lincoln's slavery-related cases is new or original to me, I insert it here because these revealing episodes remain relatively unknown; and thus no treatment of Lincoln's legal practice, however cursory, can responsibly pass them in silence.

24. *Bailey* v. *Cromwell* et al., 4 Ill. 232 (1841). See Dan W. Bannister, *Lincoln and the Illinois Supreme Court*, ed. Barbara Hughett (Springfield, Ill.: Dan W. Bannister, 1994), 133.

25. Duff, *A. Lincoln*, 130–49.

26. Oates, *With Malice toward None*, 101.

27. Duff, *A. Lincoln*, 86–87.

28. Anton-Hermann Chroust, "Abraham Lincoln Argues a Pro-Slavery Case," *American Journal of Legal History* 5 (1961): 305.

29. Miller, *Life of the Mind in America*, 205.

30. Donald, *Lincoln*, 103–4.

31. Benjamin P. Thomas, *Abraham Lincoln: A Biography* (New York: Alfred A. Knopf, 1952), 112.

32. On the Republican Party as "revival-style," see Carwardine, *Evangelicals and Politics*, 263, 297.

33. Brock, *Parties and Political Conscience*, 300–301.

34. Ibid., 300, 304.

35. Quoted in ibid., 296.

36. For a treatment of Seward's higher-law position, see ibid., 300–316.

37. Quoted in Bestor, "American Civil War as a Constitutional Crisis," 344.

38. William H. Seward, "California, Union, and Freedom," in *Congressional Globe*, 31st Cong., 1st sess., 1850, appendix, 268.

39. Ibid., 268–69.

40. Ibid., 261–62.

41. Ibid., 268–69.

42. Ibid., 262, 268.

43. Brock, *Parties and Political Conscience*, 230–31.

44. Carwardine, *Evangelicals and Politics*, 14–17.

45. Seward, "California, Union, and Freedom," 265.

46. Ibid.

47. See for instance Gal. 5:13–6:15.

48. Henry David Thoreau, "Civil Disobedience [1849]," in *Annals of America*, vol. 7, *1841–1849: Manifest Destiny*, ed. Benton, 545.

49. See Morna D. Hooker, *The Gospel according to St. Mark*, Black's New Testament Commentaries (Peabody, Mass.: Hendrickson, 1991), 278–81.

50. Thoreau, "Civil Disobedience," 544.

51. Seward, "California, Union, and Freedom," 268.

52. See Brock, *Parties and Political Conscience*, 388, 300–317.

53. "Speech to the Scott Club," Aug. 26, 1852, Basler, ed., *Collected Works*, 2:156; Fehrenbacher, ed., *Speeches and Writings*, 1:295–96.

54. Brock, *Parties and Political Conscience*, 300.

55. Basler, ed., *Collected Works*, 4:482–83, 6:155–57, 496–97, 8:55–56; Fehrenbacher, ed., *Speeches and Writings*, 2:264–65, 520–21, 637–38; Temple, *Abraham Lincoln*, 164–65, 225–26.

56. Brock, *Parties and Political Conscience*, 142.

57. Boritt, *Lincoln and the Economics of the American Dream*, 71, 240.

58. Howe, *Political Culture of the American Whigs*, 302. This presupposition permeates the narratives of consensus historians like Arthur Schlesinger, Jr., and Daniel Boorstin. Though they used it in part as a whipping boy, such historians as Richard Hofstadter, Perry Miller, Louis Hartz, and Sacvan Bercovitch (the darker side of the consensus, one might say) shared this basic picture of American history. Neoprogressive historians like Eric Foner were even more economically minded, and iconoclastic tendencies notwithstanding there seems to be little impulse among current historians to challenge their forebears on this. In line with a subtly teleological "modernization theory," but counter to much of his evidence, Daniel Walker Howe was likewise led to see the Republican party as a move "away from paternalism toward a more impersonal, secular society."

59. Boritt, *Lincoln and the Economics of the American Dream*, 11.

60. Howe, *Political Culture of the American Whigs*, 9; Hietala, *Manifest Design*, 96–97.

61. Bancroft, *Literary and Historical Miscellanies*, 515–16.

62. Boritt, *Lincoln and the Economics of the American Dream*. In emphasizing the economic aspects of Lincoln's thought, Boritt built in part on the work of Eric Foner, who emphasized the economic vision of the Republican party in the 1850s and placed "at the center of the Republican ideology . . . the notion of 'free labor.'" Like Boritt, Foner acknowledged an important moral element in the antislavery crusade of the Republican party in the 1850s; and he noted that Republican leaders "did develop a policy which recognized the essential humanity of the Negro." Because of the undeniably racist views so prevalent in northern society and because of the consequent lack of sympathy for the crusade of the abolitionists and the plight of the slaves themselves, however, Foner

emphasized the ways Republicans also appealed to the self-interest of voters with a free-soil ideology; and Boritt's "dream" corresponded closely with Foner's "ideology." Foner also stressed the way Republicans cast slavery as the enemy of values like the dignity of labor, the Protestant ethic, social mobility, and economic independence. More than the "convenient rationalization of material interests," moral opposition to slavery, a belief in the cultural superiority of northern society, and an economic interest in the free-soil territory as an area of opportunity for northern labor all combined to form a coherent free-soil ideology (Eric Foner, *Free Soil, Free Labor, Free Men: The Ideology of the Republican Party before the Civil War* [New York: Oxford University Press, 1970], 9, 261, 265, 13–16).

63. Richard Hofstadter, *The American Political Tradition and the Men Who Made It* (1948; rpt., New York: Vintage, 1974), 118.

64. Boritt, *Lincoln and the Economics of the American Dream*, viii–ix, 11, 30, 43, 78, 117, 278. Significantly, Boritt did not include among the elements of Lincoln's dream the ideal of economic independence that Foner had attributed to his fellow Republicans (*Lincoln and the Economics of the American Dream*, 185–88).

65. Joseph Dorfman, *The Economic Mind in American Civilization*, 5 vols. (New York: Viking, 1946–1959), 2:967 and passim.

66. Basler, ed., *Collected Works*, 7:512; Boritt, *Lincoln and the Economics of the American Dream*, 278; Fehrenbacher, ed., *Speeches and Writings*, 2:624.

67. Boritt, *Lincoln and the Economics of the American Dream*, ix.

68. Basler, ed., *Collected Works*, 3:356–63; Fehrenbacher, ed., *Speeches and Writings*, 2:3–11.

69. Boritt, *Lincoln and the Economics of the American Dream*, 113. Boritt here cites Edmund Wilson, *To the Finland Station: A Study in the Writing and Acting of History* (Garden City, N.Y.: Doubleday, 1953), 298.

70. Boritt, *Lincoln and the Economics of the American Dream*, 113, 142.

71. Ibid., 58, 103, 113, 193.

72. Ibid., 20–23, 64, 67, 77, quotation on 22; Meyers, *Jacksonian Persuasion*, 13.

73. As I hope to show in a future writing, this is clear in the rhetoric both of Stephen Douglas and of the *Democratic Review*.

74. Howe, *Political Culture of the American Whigs*, 289. Howe nevertheless continued to see in "Jacksonians" like Douglas a "pre-modern" animus (300).

75. Michael F. Holt, *Political Parties and American Political Development from the Age of Jackson to the Age of Lincoln* (Baton Rouge: Louisiana State University Press, 1992), 316–17.

76. Boritt, *Lincoln and the Economics of the American Dream*, 234.

77. Douglas, "Speech of Senator S. A. Douglas at the Meeting in Odd-Fellows' Hall, New Orleans," 9–10.

78. Greenstone, *Lincoln Persuasion*, 232. See also "On Sectionalism," ca. July 1856, Basler, ed., *Collected Works*, 2:351–52; Fehrenbacher, ed., *Speeches and Writings*, 1:372.

79. "Speech at Chicago," Mar. 1, 1859, Basler, ed., *Collected Works*, 3:366–67; Fehrenbacher, ed., *Speeches and Writings*, 2:13–14.

80. Boritt, *Lincoln and the Economics of the American Dream*, 256. See also 162, 175.

81. For the debate on the nature of American slavery, see Robert William Fogel and Stanley L. Engerman, *Time on the Cross: The Economics of American Negro Slavery*, 2 vols. (Boston: Little, Brown, 1974); Eugene D. Genovese, *The World the Slaveholders Made: Two Essays in Interpretation* (New York: Pantheon, 1969); Kenneth M. Stampp, *The Peculiar Institution: Slavery in the Ante-bellum South* (New York: Alfred A. Knopf, 1956). See also Lawrence B. Goodheart, Richard D. Brown, and Stephen G. Rabe, eds., *Slavery in American Society*, 3d ed., Problems in American Civilization (Lexington, Mass.: D. C. Heath, 1993); Guelzo, *Abraham Lincoln*, 134–38, 459.

82. "Fragment on Sectionalism," ca. July 23, 1856; "To W. H. Wells," Jan. 8, 1859; "Speech at Hartford," Mar. 5, 1860, Basler, ed., *Collected Works*, 2:351, 3:349, 4:2–13, 16; Boritt, *Lincoln and the Economics of the American Dream*, 163; Fehrenbacher, ed., *Speeches and Writings*, 1:372, 2:1.

83. See for instance Lincoln's remark on "the invention of negroes, or, of the present mode of using them, in 1434," in the "Second Lecture on Discoveries and Inventions," Basler, ed., *Collected Works*, 3:362; Fehrenbacher, ed., *Speeches and Writings*, 2:9. But the position is everywhere apparent in his treatment of the peculiar institution throughout the 1850s. Attitudes toward blacks had changed for the worse, largely owing to the rise of king cotton.

84. Boritt, *Lincoln and the Economics of the American Dream*, 160–62.

85. Ibid., 155–56, 163–64.

86. "Annual Message to Congress," Dec. 3, 1861, Basler, ed., *Collected Works*, 5:52; Fehrenbacher, ed., *Speeches and Writings*, 2:296. For a critique, see Phillip S. Paludan, "Commentary on 'Lincoln and the Economics of the American Dream,'" in Boritt and Forness, eds., *Historian's Lincoln*, 116–23.

87. Boritt, *Lincoln and the Economics of the American Dream*, 185–89.

88. Basler, ed., *Collected Works*, 3:472; Fehrenbacher, ed., *Speeches and Writings*, 2:91.

89. "Annual Message to Congress," Dec. 3, 1861, Basler, ed., *Collected Works*, 5:52–53; Fehrenbacher, ed., *Speeches and Writings*, 2:296–97.

90. Dorfman, *Economic Mind in American Civilization*, 2:699.

91. Howe, *Political Culture of the American Whigs*, 101.

92. Francis Wayland, *The Elements of Intellectual Philosophy* (Boston: Phillips, Sampson, 1854); Francis Wayland, *The Elements of Moral Science* (New York: Cooke, 1835); Francis Wayland, *The Elements of Political Economy* (Boston: Gould, Kendall, and Lincoln, 1837).

93. Porte, ed., *Essays and Lectures*, 260, 375.

94. Boritt, *Lincoln and the Economics of the American Dream*, 117–18.

95. Joyce Appleby, *Capitalism and a New Social Order: The Republican Vision of the 1790s* (New York: New York University Press, 1984), 4. Scholars have dated this shift variously; for some, liberalism was implicit from the first colonial beginnings (Hartz, *Liberal Tradition in America*, 3); others dated it with Jefferson's Declaration, the Constitution of 1789, or Jefferson's election in 1800 (Appleby, *Capitalism and a New Social Order*, 3); the ascendancy of Jackson in the 1830s (Lance Banning, "Jeffersonian Ideology Revisited: Liberal and Classical Ideas in the New American Republic," *William and Mary Quarterly*, 3d ser., 43 [1986]: 3–34); or even as late as the rise of the Republican Party in the 1850s (Howe, *Political Culture of the American Whigs*, 280, 299). Much rides on the debate, because where one places this shift usually determines who gets the blame or praise for "modernity." Boritt placed the shift with Henry Clay in the 1820s, but the process was ongoing. At stake in this debate is how exactly one should define "liberal" and "republican."

96. Diggins, *Lost Soul of American Politics*, 3–17.

97. Boritt, *Lincoln and the Economics of the American Dream*.

98. Brown, *Politics and Statesmanship*, 5.

99. Howe, *Political Culture of the American Whigs*, 155.

100. "To Anson G. Henry," Nov. 19, 1858, Basler, ed., *Collected Works*, 3:339; Fehrenbacher, ed., *Speeches and Writings*, 1:831.

101. Donald, *Lincoln*, 542, 544.

102. "Speech at Cincinnati," Sept. 17, 1859, quoted in Dorfman, *Economic Mind in American Civilization*, 2:907; Fehrenbacher, ed., *Speeches and Writings*, 2:84.

103. Boritt, *Lincoln and the Economics of the American Dream.*

104. Basler, ed., *Collected Works,* 3:475; Fehrenbacher, ed., *Speeches and Writings,* 2:94.

105. Basler, ed., *Collected Works,* 3:479–80; Fehrenbacher, ed., *Speeches and Writings,* 2:98–99.

106. Bender, ed., *Antislavery Debate,* 19.

107. "Notes on the Practice of Law," [1850?], Basler, ed., *Collected Works,* 2:81; Fehrenbacher, ed., *Speeches and Writings,* 1:245.

108. "Second Inaugural Address," Mar. 4, 1865, Basler, ed., *Collected Works,* 1:411–12, 8:333; Fehrenbacher, ed., *Speeches and Writings,* 2:687; Wayland cited in Boritt, *Lincoln and the Economics of the American Dream,* 123, 333n.9 (drawn from Wayland, *Elements of Political Economy,* 107, 111, 167).

109. Howe, *Political Culture of the American Whigs,* 297.

110. Ibid.

111. Paludan, "Commentary on 'Lincoln and the Economics of the American Dream,'" 121.

112. "Address to the Wisconsin State Fair," Sept. 30, 1859, Basler, ed., *Collected Works,* 3:477–82; Fehrenbacher, ed., *Speeches and Writings,* 2:96–101.

113. Paludan, "Commentary on 'Lincoln and the Economics of the American Dream,'" 120.

114. Charles Hubert Coleman, *Abraham Lincoln and Coles County, Illinois* (New Brunswick, N.J.: Scarecrow Press, 1955). As Paludan noted, but for the war Ulysses Grant would have remained floundering on the frontier just like Lincoln's less successful relations.

115. Boritt, *Lincoln and the Economics of the American Dream,* 180–81.

116. Thomas F. Schwartz, "Lincoln Never Said That," *For the People: A Newsletter of the Abraham Lincoln Association* 1, no. 1 (1999): 4.

117. Boritt, *Lincoln and the Economics of the American Dream,* 128. See also Hofstadter, *American Political Tradition,* 135–36.

118. Foner, "Causes of the American Civil War," 33.

119. Boritt, *Lincoln and the Economics of the American Dream,* 179–80, 218.

120. Bancroft, *Literary and Historical Miscellanies,* 512–13.

121. Greenstone, *Lincoln Persuasion,* 252; Holt, *Rise and Fall of the American Whig Party,* 117.

122. Miller, *Nature's Nation,* 120.

CHAPTER 5

1. Greenstone, *Lincoln Persuasion,* 197, 203, 227; J. David Greenstone, "The Transient and the Permanent in American Politics: Standards, Interests, and the Concept of 'Public,'" in J. David Greenstone, ed., *Public Values and Private Power in American Politics* (Chicago: University of Chicago Press, 1982).

2. Basler, ed., *Collected Works,* 2:255; Fehrenbacher, ed., *Speeches and Writings,* 1:315.

3. For an analysis of the "self-interest-oriented" liberalism of Stephen Douglas and his tradition, I am indebted to Greenstone, *Lincoln Persuasion;* Greenstone, "Transient and the Permanent in American Politics."

4. Basler, ed., *Collected Works,* 2:276; Fehrenbacher, ed., *Speeches and Writings,* 1:339.

5. Basler, ed., *Collected Works,* 2:275–76; Fehrenbacher, ed., *Speeches and Writings,* 1:339.

6. Herbert Storing, "Slavery and the Moral Foundations of the American Repub-

lic," in Robert H. Horwitz, ed., *The Moral Foundations of the American Republic*, 2d ed. (Charlottesville: University Press of Virginia, 1979), 325–26.

7. Dorothy Ross, *The Origins of American Social Science* (Cambridge: Cambridge University Press, 1991).

8. John Lauritz Larson, "Liberty by Design: Freedom, Planning, and John Quincy Adams's American System," in Mary O. Furner and Barry Supple, eds., *The State and Economic Knowledge: The American and British Experiences* (Cambridge: Cambridge University Press), 88–90.

9. Ibid., 92.

10. Holt, *Political Parties and American Political Development*, 40–45.

11. "The Moral of the Crisis," *Democratic Review*, October–December 1837, 119.

12. Here I reverse Allen Guelzo's argument (*Abraham Lincoln*, 252).

13. Basler, ed., *Collected Works*, 2:220–21; Fehrenbacher, ed., *Speeches and Writings*, 1:301–2. This belief in the positive role of government was accepted as orthodox in the Whig-dominated legal theory of the period. See, for instance, the words of one book from the Lincoln-Herndon law office library: "Law is not intended merely to restrain man from injustice and war, but to direct human society to the common welfare; and its origin and use are to be found in the very nature of man impressed upon him by his Creator" (Bowyer, *Commentaries on Universal Public Law*, 29).

14. Compare, for instance, a former Democrat like Chase with a former Whig like Seward, both Republicans. See Brock, *Parties and Political Conscience*, 307.

15. Greenstone, *Lincoln Persuasion*, 220.

16. "Speech at Kalamazoo," Aug. 27, 1856, Basler, ed., *Collected Works*, 2:363–64; Fehrenbacher, ed., *Speeches and Writings*, 1:379.

17. Foner, *Free Soil, Free Labor, Free Men*.

18. "Speech on the Dred Scott Decision," June 26, 1857, Basler, ed., *Collected Works*, 2:409; Fehrenbacher, ed., *Speeches and Writings*, 1:402.

19. Greenstone, *Lincoln Persuasion*, 251.

20. Mark E. Neely, Jr., "The Civil War and the Two-Party System," in James M. McPherson, ed., *"We Cannot Escape History": Lincoln and the Last Best Hope of Earth* (Urbana: University of Illinois Press, 1995), 100.

21. Greenstone, *Lincoln Persuasion*, 220, 236.

22. Basler, ed., *Collected Works*, 2:276; Fehrenbacher, ed., *Speeches and Writings*, 1:340.

23. Diggins, *Lost Soul of American Politics*, 298–303; John P. Frank, *Lincoln as a Lawyer* (Urbana: University of Illinois Press, 1961), 113–15; Howe, *Political Culture of the American Whigs*, 290; Jaffa, *Crisis of the House Divided*, 318; Phillip S. Paludan, *The Presidency of Abraham Lincoln*, American Presidency Series, vol. 29 (Lawrence: University Press of Kansas, 1994), 221; Cushing Strout, *Making American Tradition: Visions and Revisions from Ben Franklin to Alice Walker* (New Brunswick, N.J.: Rutgers University Press, 1990), 149–50; Trueblood, *Abraham Lincoln*, 69–70; Garry Wills, *Inventing America: Jefferson's Declaration of Independence* (Garden City, N.Y.: Doubleday, 1978), xxii–xxiv; Wills, *Lincoln at Gettysburg*, 38, 90–120; Wilson, "Lincoln's Declaration," 172; Wolf, *Lincoln's Religion*, 95–96. Allen C. Guelzo has gone the furthest to date in driving home the point—made more quietly by other historians of Lincoln—that Lincoln was not as Jeffersonian as a cursory reading of some of his speeches might imply (*Abraham Lincoln*, 5–14, 193–96). In an attempt to present a contrary view, Drew R. McCoy cites James G. Randall (*Lincoln, the Liberal Statesman* [New York: Dodd, Mead, 1947], 179) in his "Lincoln and the Founding Fathers: A Reconsideration," *Journal of the Abraham Lincoln Association* 16, no. 1 (1995): 1–13. In his last paragraph, McCoy unwittingly undermines his thesis when he

acknowledges that Madison would almost surely have had nothing to do with Lincoln's policy of "containment" of slavery. Indeed, one might say that Lincoln put the ideal of equality ahead of his belief in union, though it is better to say that for Lincoln the two were inseparable and that a nation with a permanent institution of slavery was not worth preserving. McCoy is right to point out that the founders sometimes *sounded* antislavery the way Lincoln did. Lincoln's interpretation of the founding nevertheless remains open to serious challenge (Zarefsky, "'Public Sentiment is Everything,'" 36–37). I do not believe that Lincoln was aware that he had recast the Enlightenment of the founders in a more activist, Romantic mold. The role of Samuel Chase, who saw the founding as antislavery in precisely the same way Lincoln did, is examined in John Niven, "Lincoln and Chase, a Reappraisal," *Journal of the Abraham Lincoln Association* 12 (1991): 3–5.

24. Quoted in Diggins, *Lost Soul of American Politics*, 300, from "Speech on the Dred Scott Decision," June 26, 1857, Basler, ed., *Collected Works*, 2:405; Fehrenbacher, ed., *Speeches and Writings*, 1:398.

25. "Portion of Speech at Republican Banquet in Chicago," Dec. 10, 1856, Basler, ed., *Collected Works*, 2:385; Fehrenbacher, ed., *Speeches and Writings*, 1:385–86.

26. "Lincoln's reply to Douglas, First Debate at Ottawa," Aug. 21, 1858, Basler, ed., *Collected Works*, 3:30; Fehrenbacher, ed., *Speeches and Writings*, 1:527; Robert W. Johannsen, ed., *The Lincoln-Douglas Debates of 1858* (New York: Oxford University Press, 1965), 67.

27. "To Joshua F. Speed," Aug. 24, 1855, Basler, ed., *Collected Works*, 2:325; Fehrenbacher, ed., *Speeches and Writings*, 1:363.

28. Basler, ed., *Collected Works*, 2:270; Fehrenbacher, ed., *Speeches and Writings*, 1:333.

29. "To James T. Hale," Jan. 11, 1861, Basler, ed., *Collected Works*, 4:172; Fehrenbacher, ed., *Speeches and Writings*, 2:197.

30. "To Thurlow Weed, Dec. 17, 1860, Basler, ed., *Collected Works*, 4:154; Fehrenbacher, ed., *Speeches and Writings*, 2:192.

31. "Speech at Columbus," Sept. 16, 1859, and "Speech at New Haven," Mar. 6, 1860, Basler, ed., *Collected Works*, 3:423–25; Fehrenbacher, ed., *Speeches and Writings*, 2:56–58, 138.

32. Frank J. Williams, "Abraham Lincoln—Our Ever-Present Contemporary," in McPherson, ed., *"We Cannot Escape History,"* 142.

33. Citations here could be multiplied indefinitely. See for instance "Speech on the Sub-Treasury," Dec. 26, 1839; "Notes for Speeches," ca. Sept. 1859; "Speech at Columbus," Sept. 16, 1859; or "Speech at Cincinnati," Sept. 17, 1859; Basler, ed., *Collected Works*, 1:177, 3:397–99, 403–5, 412–17, 440, 449–51; Fehrenbacher, ed., *Speeches and Writings*, 1:63, 2:27–29, 33, 36, 44–50, 61, 71–74.

34. Greenstone, *Lincoln Persuasion*, 108.

35. "Speech on the Dred Scott Decision," June 26, 1857, Basler, ed., *Collected Works*, 2:399, 402; Fehrenbacher, ed., *Speeches and Writings*, 1:390, 394.

36. "Lincoln's Reply to Douglas, First Debate at Ottawa," Aug. 21, 1858, Basler, ed., *Collected Works*, 3:27; Fehrenbacher, ed., *Speeches and Writings*, 1:524–25; Johannsen, ed., *Lincoln-Douglas Debates*, 64–65.

37. "The Spirit of Liberty," *Whig Review*, December 1845, 618–19.

38. Robert W. Johannsen, "Stephen A. Douglas, 'Harper's Magazine,' and Popular Sovereignty," *Mississippi Valley Historical Review* 45, no. 1 (1958): 613.

39. Richard Nelson Current, "Bancroft's Lincoln," in *Speaking of Abraham Lincoln: The Man and His Meaning for Our Times* (Urbana: University of Illinois Press, 1983), 173.

40. Handlin, *George Bancroft*, 262–63.

41. M. A. De Wolfe Howe, ed., *The Life and Letters of George Bancroft*, 2 vols. (New York: Charles Scribner's Sons, 1908), 2:129–31; Johannsen, *Stephen A. Douglas*, 584.

42. Johannsen, *Stephen A. Douglas*, 599.

43. George Bancroft, "To Stephen A. Douglas," 1858, Joseph Regenstein Library, University of Chicago, 1.

44. Handlin, *George Bancroft*, 255–67.

45. Two later volumes ending with the Constitution of 1789 reflected the Civil War experience and Bancroft's desire to settle questions about the nature of the Constitution that arose in the aftermath of secession. See George Bancroft, *History of the United States, from the Discovery of the American Continent*, vol. 9 (Boston: Little, Brown, 1866); George Bancroft, *History of the United States, from the Discovery of the American Continent*, vol. 10 (Boston: Little, Brown, 1874); Handlin, *George Bancroft*, 285–86, 324–26.

46. Handlin, *George Bancroft*, 263.

47. Ibid., 264.

48. Bancroft, "To Stephen A. Douglas," 1.

49. Merrill D. Peterson, *Lincoln in American Memory* (New York, Oxford: Oxford University Press, 1994), 36–37.

50. Howe, ed., *Life and Letters of George Bancroft*, 2:132–33.

51. Ibid., 134.

52. Johannsen, *Stephen A. Douglas*, 852.

53. Howe, ed., *Life and Letters of George Bancroft*, 2:148, second quotation on 2:137.

54. Ibid., 138–39, 141–42.

55. Noted in Lincoln's reply; see "To George Bancroft," Nov. 18, 1861, Basler, ed., *Collected Works*, 5:26; Howe, ed., *Life and Letters of George Bancroft*, 2:143.

56. Howe, ed., *Life and Letters of George Bancroft*, 2:153–54.

57. George Bancroft, "Oration, pronounced in Union Square, April 25, 1865 at the Funeral Obsequies of Abraham Lincoln in the City of New York," *Pulpit and Rostrum: Sermons, Orations, Popular Lectures, Etc.* 34–35 (June 1865): 8; Howe, ed., *Life and Letters of George Bancroft*, 2:158.

58. Howe, ed., *Life and Letters of George Bancroft*, 2:154–55; Current, "Bancroft's Lincoln," 177.

59. Quoted in Current, "Bancroft's Lincoln," 177. See Howe, ed., *Life and Letters of George Bancroft*, 2:155–56.

60. Quoted in Current, "Bancroft's Lincoln," 178.

61. "To George Bancroft," Feb. 29, 1864, Basler, ed., *Collected Works*, 7:22, 212. Current related the same tale in almost exactly the same order. I repeat it here, with apologies, because it is particularly telling encounter. Current did not, however, see Lincoln as necessarily ironic here ("Bancroft's Lincoln," 177).

62. George Bancroft, "Speech of Mr. Bancroft at the New York Union Meeting, April 20, 1863," in *The League for Union: Speeches of the Hon. George Bancroft and James Milliken, Esq.* (Philadelphia: William S. and Alfred Martien, 1863), 15–16.

63. Bancroft, "Oration, pronounced in Union Square, April 25, 1865," 7–8.

64. Ibid., 10.

65. George Bancroft, *Abraham Lincoln, a Tribute: An Address Delivered February 12, 1866 before a Joint Session in the House Chamber at the Memorial for Abraham Lincoln* (New York: A. Wessels, 1908), 19.

66. George Bancroft, "The Place of Abraham Lincoln in History," *Atlantic Monthly* 15, no. 92 (1865): 763.

67. George Bancroft, *Literary and Historical Miscellanies*, 444–80; Current, "Bancroft's Lincoln," 174–75, 182.

68. Bancroft, *Abraham Lincoln, a Tribute*, 25.

69. Ibid., 52–53, 68.

70. Ibid., 66–67.

71. Compare, for instance, Bancroft's tribute with this passage: "He possessed, in a higher degree than that of any other statesman known to fame, the power and faculty of clear and comprehensive statement; in this respect he was so clear and lucid, that it was easy to follow his arguments; his language was composed of plain Anglo-Saxon words and almost always absolutely without adornment; his arguments, though logical and profound, were conveyed to the mind by such easy approaches, that the ordinary understanding could readily grasp and comprehend them" (Whitney, *Life on the Circuit with Lincoln*, 62).

72. Bancroft, *Abraham Lincoln, a Tribute*, 68–69.

73. Handlin, *George Bancroft*, 284–85; Howe, ed., *Life and Letters of George Bancroft*, 2:159.

74. Phillip S. Paludan, "Emancipating the Republic: Lincoln and the Means and Ends of Antislavery," in McPherson, ed., *"We Cannot Escape History,"* 51.

75. Current, "Bancroft's Lincoln," 185, second quotation on 184; Handlin, *George Bancroft*, 284.

76. Allen C. Guelzo, "Review Essay: *The Inner World of Abraham Lincoln*, by Michael Burlingame and *Abraham Lincoln: From Skeptic to Prophet*, by Wayne C. Temple," *Journal of the Abraham Lincoln Association* 17, no. 2 (1996): 42.

77. Donald, *Lincoln*, 14.

78. Current, "Bancroft's Lincoln," 179; "To Albert G. Hodges," Apr. 4, 1864, Basler, ed., *Collected Works*, 7:282; Fehrenbacher, ed., *Speeches and Writings*, 2:586.

79. Bancroft, "Place of Abraham Lincoln in History," 763.

CHAPTER 6

1. Herndon and Weik, *Herndon's Life of Lincoln*, ed. Angle, 359–60, 412–15. See also Barton, *Soul of Abraham Lincoln*, 229–30. This is Herndon's reconstruction, from his notes, of what Mary Lincoln related to him in September 1866. For the notes, see Wilson and Davis, eds., *Herndon's Informants*, 358, 360.

2. Wilson, "Abraham Lincoln and the 'Spirit of Mortal,'" 137.

3. Miller, *Nature's Nation*, 134–49; Parker, "Discourse of the Transient and Permanent in Christianity."

4. For Lincoln's relationship with Parker and Channing, see Barton, *Soul of Abraham Lincoln*, 172–80.

5. Of course this assumes Hay would have reached the White House without Lincoln, an entirely fanciful assumption on my part. More seriously, on the authenticity of the Bixby letter, see Michael Burlingame, "New Light on the Bixby Letter," *Journal of the Abraham Lincoln Association* 16, no. 1 (1995).

6. "To Joshua F. Speed," Jan 4., 1842, Basler, ed., *Collected Works*, 1:289; Fehrenbacher, ed., *Speeches and Writings*, 1:95.

7. Fehrenbacher, ed., *Speeches and Writings*, 1:860n.

8. Witness, for instance, the publication data for Robert Chambers's *Vestiges of the Natural History of Creation*, which Lincoln read. The book ran to eleven editions between and 1844 and 1860, selling about one-half million copies (Secord, ed., *Vestiges*, xxvi–xxvii, chap. 2, n. 30).

9. "Fragment on Niagara Falls," [late September 1848?], Basler, ed., *Collected Works*, 2:10–11; Fehrenbacher, ed., *Speeches and Writings*, 1:222–24.

10. Basler, ed., *Collected Works*, 2:437–42.

11. Mark I. Wallace, *The Second Naiveté: Barth, Ricoeur, and the New Yale Theology,* Studies in American Biblical Hermeneutics, vol. 6 (Macon, Ga.: Mercer University Press, 1995).

12. Fehrenbacher and Fehrenbacher, eds., *Recollected Words of Abraham Lincoln,* 292–93.

13. For a critique of this tradition, see ibid., 535n.294. The Fehrenbachers cite Jim Bishop, *The Day Lincoln Was Shot* (New York: Harper, 1955), 54–56; Oates, *With Malice toward None,* 425–26; Carl Sandburg, *Abraham Lincoln: The War Years,* 4 vols. (New York: Harcourt, Brace & World, 1939), 4:243–45; Wolf, *Lincoln's Religion,* 28–29.

14. Mark E. Neely, Jr., *The Abraham Lincoln Encyclopedia* (New York: McGraw-Hill, 1982), 248.

15. Wilson and Davis, eds., *Herndon's Informants,* 357–59.

16. Fehrenbacher and Fehrenbacher, eds., *Recollected Words of Abraham Lincoln,* 398, 486–87.

17. Compare Guelzo, *Abraham Lincoln,* 342.

18. Fehrenbacher and Fehrenbacher, eds., *Recollected Words of Abraham Lincoln,* 96, 474; Wolf, *Lincoln's Religion,* 28.

19. Ibid., 30, 148.

20. "Reply to Chicago Emancipation Memorial," Sept. 13, 1862, Basler, ed., *Collected Works,* 5:420; Fehrenbacher, ed., *Speeches and Writings,* 2:361.

21. Hofstadter, *American Political Tradition,* 169.

22. "Final Emancipation Proclamation," Jan. 1, 1863, Basler, ed., *Collected Works,* 6:30; Fehrenbacher, ed., *Speeches and Writings,* 2:425.

23. For a covenantal interpretation of this episode, see Wolf, *Lincoln's Religion,* 148–53.

24. Robert C. Winthrop, ed., *Life and Letters of John Winthrop, Governor of the Massachusetts-Bay Company at Their Emigration to New England,* 2d ed., 2 vols. (Boston: Little, Brown, 1869), 2:18–20.

25. Robert Mackintosh, in *Encyclopaedia Britannica,* ed. Chisholm, 11th ed. (New York: Encyclopaedia Britannica, 1911), s.v. "Theology."

26. Wolf, *Lincoln's Religion,* 193, second quotation on 42.

27. See for instance "Predestination" in William Cathcart, ed., *The Baptist Encyclopaedia: A Dictionary of the Doctrines, Ordinances, Usages, Confessions of Faith, Sufferings, Labors, and Successes, and of the General History of the Baptist Denomination in All Lands* (Philadelphia: L. H. Everts, 1881), 934–37.

28. Wolf, *Lincoln's Religion,* 48, 78.

29. Fehrenbacher and Fehrenbacher, eds., *Recollected Words of Abraham Lincoln,* 373–74; Wolf, *Lincoln's Religion,* 51.

30. Fehrenbacher and Fehrenbacher, eds., *Recollected Words of Abraham Lincoln,* liii.

31. See ibid., 137; Wolf, *Lincoln's Religion,* 74–75.

32. Wolf, *Lincoln's Religion,* 41–42.

33. Herndon and Weik, *Herndon's Life of Lincoln,* ed. Angle, 56, quoted in Wolf, *Lincoln's Religion,* 11.

34. Donald, *Lincoln,* 47, 514. I also discuss this at the end of chap. 5.

35. Ibid., 17.

36. Ibid., 15.

37. "'House Divided' Speech," June 16, 1858, Basler, ed., *Collected Works,* 2:461; Fehrenbacher, ed., *Speeches and Writings,* 2:426.

38. "Speech on Reconstruction," Apr. 11, 1865, Basler, ed., *Collected Works,* 8:403; Fehrenbacher, ed., *Speeches and Writings,* 2:699.

39. Temple, *Abraham Lincoln,* 5. I rely on Temple for this account of Lincoln's paternal family line.

40. Philip Schaff, ed., *The Creeds of Christendom, with a History and Critical Notes,* 4th ed., vol. 3, *Bibliotheca Symbolica Ecclesiae Universalis* (1877; rpt., New York: Harper & Brothers, 1919), 718–20, 723.

41. Cathcart, ed., *Baptist Encyclopaedia,* 1041.

42. Philip Schaff, ed., *The Creeds of Christendom, with a History and Critical Notes,* 6th ed., vol. 1, *Bibliotheca Symbolica Ecclesiae Universalis* (1877; rpt., New York: Harper & Brothers, 1931), 845, 852–53, 855; Schaff, ed., *Creeds of Christendom,* 3:738–41; Cathcart, ed., *Baptist Encyclopaedia,* 266.

43. J. Gordon Melton, ed., *The Encyclopedia of American Religions,* 2 vols. (Wilmington, N.C.: McGrath, 1978), 1:366.

44. "Autobiography Written for Campaign," ca. June 1860; "To Solomon Lincoln," Mar. 6, 1848; "To David Lincoln," Apr. 2, 1848, Basler, ed., *Collected Works,* 1:456, 462, 4:60–61; Fehrenbacher, ed., *Speeches and Writings,* 1:160; Temple, *Abraham Lincoln,* 5.

45. George Brown Tindall and David E. Shi, *America: A Narrative History,* 4th ed., 2 vols. (New York: W. W. Norton, 1996), 1:320.

46. Louis Austin Warren, *Lincoln's Parentage and Childhood: A History of the Kentucky Lincolns Supported by Documentary Evidence* (New York: Century, 1926), 3–9.

47. "To Jesse Lincoln," Apr. 1, 1854, Basler, ed., *Collected Works,* 2:217; Fehrenbacher, ed., *Speeches and Writings,* 1:300.

48. "To Jesse W. Fell, Enclosing Autobiography," Dec. 20, 1859, Basler, ed., *Collected Works,* 3:511; Fehrenbacher, ed., *Speeches and Writings,* 2:107.

49. Basler, ed., *Collected Works,* 4:37, 117.

50. William G. McLoughlin, *Soul Liberty: The Baptists' Struggle in New England, 1630–1833* (Hanover, N.H.: University Press of New England for Brown University Press, 1991).

51. J. H. Spencer, *A History of Kentucky Baptists,* 2 vols. (Cincinnati: Printed for the author, 1886), 1:482; Warren, *Lincoln's Parentage and Childhood,* 234.

52. Warren, *Lincoln's Parentage and Childhood,* 233–34.

53. William Warren Sweet, ed., *Religion on the American Frontier: A Collection of Source Material,* vol. 1, *The Baptists, 1783–1830* (New York: Henry Holt, 1931), 429–30.

54. James L. Peacock and Ruel W. Tyson, *Pilgrims of Paradox: Calvinism and Experience among the Primitive Baptists of the Blue Ridge,* Smithsonian Series in Ethnographic Inquiry (Washington, D.C.: Smithsonian Institution Press, 1989), 3 and passim.

55. Louis A. Warren, *Lincoln's Youth: Indiana Years, Seven to Twenty-one, 1816–1830* (Indianapolis: Indiana Historical Society, 1959), 121–22.

56. Wilson and Davis, eds., *Herndon's Informants,* 107.

57. Thomas, *Portrait For Posterity,* 47–48.

58. Alfred Kazin, *God and the American Writer* (New York: Alfred A. Knopf, 1997), 123–24, 135.

59. Wolf, *Lincoln's Religion,* 28, 39.

60. Sweet, ed., *Religion on the American Frontier,* 78; Michael Burlingame, "'I Used to Be a Slave': The Origins of Lincoln's Hatred of Slavery," in *The Inner World of Abraham Lincoln* (Urbana: University of Illinois Press, 1994), 21; Warren, *Lincoln's Youth,* 117.

61. Warren, *Lincoln's Youth,* 115–16.

62. Basler, ed., *Collected Works,* 1:1. For a discussion, see Wilson, "Abraham Lincoln and the 'Spirit of Mortal,'" 140.

63. "A Teacher," ed., *The Kentucky Preceptor, Containing a Number of Useful Lessons for Reading and Speaking*, 3d ed. (Lexington, Ky: Maccoun, Tilford, 1812), 63, 79, 89, 117. On Lincoln's use of this book, see Wilson and Davis, eds., *Herndon's Informants*, 126.

64. Warren, *Lincoln's Youth*, 119–20.

65. Sweet, ed., *Religion on the American Frontier*, 67.

66. Carwardine, *Evangelicals and Politics*, 14–18.

67. Wilson, *Honor's Voice*, 210.

68. Albert J. Beveridge, *Abraham Lincoln, 1809–1858*, 2 vols. (Boston and New York: Houghton Mifflin, 1928), 1:138–39; Donald, *Lincoln*, 48–49; Wilson and Davis, eds., *Herndon's Informants*, 21, 24, 31, 80, 90, 141, 172, 179, 210, 374, 420, 499, 513, 519, 577; Rufus Rockwell Wilson, *What Lincoln Read* (Washington, D.C.: Pioneer, 1932), 42.

69. Wilson, *Honor's Voice*, 78–80.

70. Ibid., 72–76; Wilson and Davis, eds., *Herndon's Informants*, 251, 577.

71. Douglas Wilson's turn of phrase here is worth noting: "There is little reason to doubt that Lincoln may have written an essay on what the Bible says about eternal damnation [i.e. one on universal atonement], but the evidence that he wrote another, more provocative one that Samuel Hill wanted destroyed is independent and very strong" (*Honor's Voice*, 81).

72. "Handbill Replying to Charges of Infidelity," July 31, 1846, Basler, ed., *Collected Works*, 1:383; Fehrenbacher, ed., *Speeches and Writings*, 1:139.

73. Barton, *Soul of Abraham Lincoln*, 175, 239–40.

74. For the universalist side of the argument, see ibid., 138–39, 240. Despite Douglas Wilson's laudable work with Herndon's sources, on the whole I still find Barton more convincing. Without dismissing the material collected by Herndon that Wilson relies on, Barton's account generally squares better with the Lincoln of the *Collected Works*. At the same time, Barton's treatment of Herndon's sources remains perfectly plausible.

75. Wilson, *Honor's Voice*, 81–85. Wilson seems particularly eager to cast Lincoln's thought in the mold of Thomas Paine, even though there is evidence, at least as credible, that Lincoln also argued for some form of universalism during this period—and long afterward. Wilson himself cited some of this evidence for universalism on (Wilson, *Honor's Voice*, 80). While the evidence is far from unimpeachable on either side, Wilson based his analysis on the resemblance of some of *the descriptions* of Lincoln's arguments with those of Thomas Paine's *Age of Reason*. Of course other descriptions do not resemble Paine quite so much. And the witnesses whose accounts do match Paine may after all have been remembering Paine, whose book they could still read, rather than Lincoln, whose "book," if there was one, had been dashed into the flames. After firmly establishing that Lincoln at least flirted with various forms of "infidelity," Wilson pushed beyond his evidence in asserting the precise nature of Lincoln's beliefs to be Painite. He has advanced an interpretation of Lincoln's religious rhetoric as essentially disingenuous and manipulative, and his case appears stronger if one accepts the Painite interpretation of his early "infidelity" rather than the universalist one. Universalism was unorthodox and scandalous at the time, which would explain Lincoln's reticence in religious matters without making his soaring religious rhetoric entirely disingenuous. "The clarity of Paine's prose," he wrote, "and the incisive lucidity of his rationalism made his writings popular with thoughtful readers of the day, particularly those inclined toward freethinking" (77). But the day—if by "the day" Wilson meant after the mid-1830s—was one in which Paine's works did not enjoy the popularity they had during the American Revolution. Nevertheless Wilson pressed an Enlightenment interpretation: "In embracing Burns, Paine, and Volney, Lincoln was casting his lot with the

rationalism of the Enlightenment and the skeptical spirit of the eighteenth century. As he was to indicate in many ways in the years ahead, he thought of himself as committed to the cause of reason" (85). Reason, though, had taken on a whole new set of connotations in the nineteenth century, which is precisely what is at issue. From the perspective of our investigation, however, it makes little difference. Even if Lincoln were disingenuous, the *significance* of his religious language would remain unaffected. What he said is more important than what he may or may not have "believed"—whatever exactly one means by that. More important, had he seen religion as merely a means to catching votes, he would have sounded much more conventional than he did. The Second Inaugural, for example, was not calculated to make the evangelicals happy. In spite of his skepticism, Lincoln was drawn to a religious description of the human condition for far deeper reasons than mere ambition, mere utility, or even mere morality; and this placed him not in the Enlightenment of Paine but solidly in the Romantic camp.

76. Basler, ed., *Collected Works*, 1:1–77.

77. "To the People of Sangamo County," Mar. 9, 1832, ibid., 8; Fehrenbacher, ed., *Speeches and Writings*, 1:4. This passage was treated more thoroughly in chap. 2.

78. Douglas L. Wilson, "Abraham Lincoln versus Peter Cartwright," in *Lincoln Before Washington*, 63.

79. "Handbill Replying to Charges of Infidelity," July 31, 1846, Basler, ed., *Collected Works*, 1:382; Fehrenbacher, ed., *Speeches and Writings*, 1:139–40; Guelzo, *Abraham Lincoln*, 51; Wilson, "Abraham Lincoln versus Peter Cartwright," 55.

80. "To Mary S. Owens," May 7, 1837, Basler, ed., *Collected Works*, 1:78–79; Fehrenbacher, ed., *Speeches and Writings*, 1:18–19.

81. For a brief review of the literature on this lecture, see Neely, *Fate of Liberty*, 265. See also Donald, *Lincoln*, 611. Mark Neely lays at the feet of Edmund Wilson most of the blame for the modern myth that Lincoln foresaw his own rise to power and the Emancipation Proclamation in this lecture (Mark Neely, "Lincoln's Lyceum Speech and the Origins of a Modern Myth," *Lincoln Lore*, no. 1776–1777 [1987]: 1–4). Neely shows that, whatever other strengths they have, several important Lincoln books are nevertheless deeply flawed by their acceptance of this interpretation: including Dwight G. Anderson, *Abraham Lincoln: The Quest for Immortality* (New York: Alfred A. Knopf, 1982); Forgie, *Patricide in the House Divided*; Jaffa, *Crisis of the House Divided*; Wilson, *Patriotic Gore*. For a "classical republican" interpretation of the Lyceum Address, see Major L. Wilson, "Lincoln on the Perpetuation of Republican Institutions: Whig and Republican Strategies," *Journal of the Abraham Lincoln Association* 16, no. 1 (1995): 19 and passim.

82. See Basler, ed., *Collected Works*, 1:108–15; Fehrenbacher, ed., *Speeches and Writings*, 1:28–36.

83. Basler, ed., *Collected Works*, 1:112; Fehrenbacher, ed., *Speeches and Writings*, 1:32.

84. Wilson, *Patriotic Gore*, 99.

85. Major L. Wilson, "Lincoln and Van Buren in the Steps of the Fathers: Another Look at the Lyceum Address," *Civil War History* 29, no. 3 (1983): 209.

86. Basler, ed., *Collected Works*, 1:115. Fehrenbacher, ed., *Speeches and Writings*, 1:36.

87. "Lincoln's Reply to Douglas, Seventh Debate at Alton," Oct. 15, 1858, Basler, ed., *Collected Works*, 3:315; Fehrenbacher, ed., *Speeches and Writings*, 1:810–11; Johannsen, ed., *Lincoln-Douglas Debates*, 319.

88. Miller, *New England Mind*, 3.

89. Bercovitch, *American Jeremiad*.

90. John Edwin Smylie, "National Ethos and the Church," *Theology Today*, October 1963, cited in Cherry, ed., *God's New Israel*, 13.

91. Bercovitch, *American Jeremiad*, 146.

92. Marsden, *Evangelical Mind*, 186.

93. Cherry, ed., *God's New Israel*, 107; "Address to the New Jersey Senate," Feb. 21, 1861, Basler, ed., *Collected Works*, 4:236; Fehrenbacher, ed., *Speeches and Writings*, 2:209.

94. "Address to the Young Men's Lyceum," Jan. 27, 1838, Basler, ed., *Collected Works*, 1:109; Fehrenbacher, ed., *Speeches and Writings*, 1:29.

95. Miller, *Life of the Mind in America*.

96. Wilson, *Honor's Voice*, 187, 189.

97. "Speech on the Sub-Treasury," Dec. 26, 1839, Basler, ed., *Collected Works*, 1:178–79; Fehrenbacher, ed., *Speeches and Writings*, 1:65.

98. Wilson, *Honor's Voice*, 189–91, 309.

99. "Handbill Replying to Charges of Infidelity," July 31, 1846, Basler, ed., *Collected Works*, 1:382; Fehrenbacher, ed., *Speeches and Writings*, 1:139.

100. See Guelzo, "Abraham Lincoln and the Doctrine of Necessity." My discussion parallels Guelzo's to a large extent. Guelzo does explore the possibility of a utilitarian origin of Lincoln's doctrine of necessity, though one mediated through his experience as a practicing lawyer. Given Lincoln's devotion to the common law (75) and given the range of evidence of an antiutilitarian interpretation, Guelzo's reading seems tenuous. Still, it is possible that Lincoln adopted elements of the utilitarian worldview even while he generally rejected its moral superficiality and thus gravitated toward its Romantic antipode. Romanticism was a reaction to as much as a rejection of utilitarianism.

101. Compare Guelzo, *Abraham Lincoln*, 116–21. Guelzo interprets Lincoln in the light of J. S. Mill's and Jeremy Bentham's scientific determinism. Lincoln may or may not have found this attractive in his early years, but he always gave his discussions of determinism theological and moral dimensions alien to the great utilitarians.

102. "Meditation on the Divine Will," ca. early September 1862, Basler, ed., *Collected Works*, 5:403–4; Fehrenbacher, ed., *Speeches and Writings*, 2:359.

103. This essentially follows Barton: "It is quite possible that Abraham Lincoln never became a Christian of the type who could have expressed his faith in terms of the Bateman interview; it is equally possible that even in those callow years when he was reading Tom Paine and Volney and writing sub-sophomoric effusions on things he knew little about, the germ of religious faith was actually present even in his doubt" (*Soul of Abraham Lincoln*, 155).

104. Guelzo, *Abraham Lincoln*, 154–55.

105. "Handbill Replying to Charges of Infidelity," July 31, 1846, Basler, ed., *Collected Works*, 1:382; Fehrenbacher, ed., *Speeches and Writings*, 1:139; Guelzo, "Abraham Lincoln and the Doctrine of Necessity," 65.

106. Smith, *Christian's Defence*, vol. 2.

CHAPTER 7

1. Michael Burlingame, "Lincoln's Depressions: 'Melancholy Dript from Him as He Walked,'" in *Inner World of Abraham Lincoln*, 96–101; Wilson, *Honor's Voice*, 309.

2. Burlingame, "Lincoln's Depressions," 101–2.

3. "To Mary Speed," Sept. 27, 1841, Basler, ed., *Collected Works*, 1:261; Fehrenbacher, ed., *Speeches and Writings*, 1:75.

4. "Handbill Replying to Charges of Infidelity," July 31, 1846, Basler, ed., *Collected Works*, 1:382; Fehrenbacher, ed., *Speeches and Writings*, 1:139.

5. See for instance Robert F. Sayre, ed., *Henry David Thoreau: A Week on the Concord*

and Merrimack Rivers: Walden; or, Life in the Woods: The Maine Woods: Cape Cod, Library of America, vol. 28 (New York: Literary Classics of the United States, 1985), 326–28.

6. See Wilson, *Honor's Voice,* 309–12. Wilson suggests that Lincoln learned to neutralize the possible negative political effects of his infidelity by studying the Christian apologists and presenting himself as an earnest candidate for conversion. The obvious question would be, Why would he present himself in this way to his closest friend, Joshua Speed, who was, if anything, more skeptical than Lincoln was? (see 311, 368n.54.) Or why learn so much and so well? The obvious relish with which Lincoln used Christian poetry and the Bible both in public and in private communications suggests a more genuine relationship with the tradition, though perhaps one not quite reaching literal belief. He did not merely learn a few standard apologetic turns of phrase; he ranged far, wide, and deep into the Christian tradition, and he expressed his findings masterfully. If it was merely a charade of self-presentation, it was a remarkable charade indeed.

7. Wilson, *Honor's Voice,* 186–87.

8. "To Joshua F. Speed," Feb. 3, 1842, Basler, ed., *Collected Works,* 1:267–68, 270, 289; Fehrenbacher, ed., *Speeches and Writings,* 1:78–79, 80, 95.

9. My treatment of this speech differs considerably from the most extensive recent treatment: Lucas E. Morel, "Lincoln among the Reformers: Tempering the Temperance Movement," *Journal of the Abraham Lincoln Association* 20, no. 1 (1999): 1–34.

10. Herman Belz, "Review Essay: Salmon P. Chase and the Politics of Racial Reform," *Journal of the Abraham Lincoln Association* 17, no. 2 (1996): 22.

11. Tyrrell, *Sobering Up.*

12. "Address to the Washington Temperance Society," Feb. 22, 1842, Basler, ed., *Collected Works,* 1:273; Fehrenbacher, ed., *Speeches and Writings,* 1:83.

13. Neely, *Abraham Lincoln Encyclopedia,* 306.

14. Donald, *Lincoln,* 82–83.

15. "Protest in the Illinois Legislature on Slavery," Mar. 3, 1837, Basler, ed., *Collected Works,* 1:75; Fehrenbacher, ed., *Speeches and Writings,* 1:18.

16. "Eulogy on Benjamin Ferguson," Feb. 8, 1842, Basler, ed., *Collected Works,* 1:268–69.

17. Ibid., 271; Fehrenbacher, ed., *Speeches and Writings,* 1:81.

18. Marsden, *Evangelical Mind,* 185–86.

19. Basler, ed., *Collected Works,* 1:278–79; Fehrenbacher, ed., *Speeches and Writings,* 1:89–90.

20. Basler, ed., *Collected Works,* 1:272; Fehrenbacher, ed., *Speeches and Writings,* 1:81–82.

21. "To Joshua F. Speed," Mar. 27, 1842, July 4, 1842, Basler, ed., *Collected Works,* 1:282–83, 290; Fehrenbacher, ed., *Speeches and Writings,* 1:93, 96.

22. Marsden, *Evangelical Mind,* 81.

23. Basler, ed., *Collected Works,* 1:278–79; Fehrenbacher, ed., *Speeches and Writings,* 1:89.

24. Barnes, *Antislavery Impulse.*

25. Basler, ed., *Collected Works,* 1:278–79; Fehrenbacher, ed., *Speeches and Writings,* 1:89–90.

26. See for instance the passage quoted earlier from Basler, ed., *Collected Works,* 1:275–76; Fehrenbacher, ed., *Speeches and Writings,* 1:85–86.

27. Basler, ed., *Collected Works,* 1:277–78; Fehrenbacher, ed., *Speeches and Writings,* 1:88.

28. Basler, ed., *Collected Works,* 1:276; Fehrenbacher, ed., *Speeches and Writings,* 1:86.

29. Warren, *Lincoln's Youth*, 118.

30. Basler, ed., *Collected Works*, 1:275; Fehrenbacher, ed., *Speeches and Writings*, 1:85.

31. On Scottish Enlightenment Common Sense and faculty psychology in Lincoln's Lyceum and Temperance Address, see Howe, *Making the American Self*, 141–45.

32. Marsden, *Evangelical Mind*, 48.

33. Marsden, "Everyone One's Own Interpreter?"

34. Basler, ed., *Collected Works*, 1:273; Fehrenbacher, ed., *Speeches and Writings*, 1:83.

35. Marsden, *Evangelical Mind*, 111.

36. "To Williamson Durley," Oct. 3, 1845, Basler, ed., *Collected Works*, 1:347–48; Fehrenbacher, ed., *Speeches and Writings*, 1:111; Eric Foner and John A. Garraty, eds., *The Reader's Companion to American History* (Boston: Houghton Mifflin, 1991), 336.

37. "To Williamson Durley," Oct. 3, 1845, Basler, ed., *Collected Works*, 1:347–48; Fehrenbacher, ed., *Speeches and Writings*, 1:111–12.

38. "Address at Cooper Institute," Feb. 27, 1860, Basler, ed., *Collected Works*, 3:541; Fehrenbacher, ed., *Speeches and Writings*, 2:125.

39. Basler, ed., *Collected Works*, 2:3–4.

40. Greenstone, *Lincoln Persuasion*, 265–82. In some ways I have replicated Greenstone's argument here.

41. "To Eliza P. Gurney," Sept. 4, 1864, Basler, ed., *Collected Works*, 7:535; Fehrenbacher, ed., *Speeches and Writings*, 2:627.

42. Jaffa, *Crisis of the House Divided*.

43. Marsden, *Evangelical Mind*, 99–101.

44. Temple, *Abraham Lincoln*, 57.

45. Carwardine, *Evangelicals and Politics*, 180–83.

46. Wolf, *Lincoln's Religion*, 67, 80, 82–86.

47. Smith, *Christian's Defence*, 2:362–64; Wolf, *Lincoln's Religion*, 83.

48. Temple, *Abraham Lincoln*, 43–57, 60.

49. Ibid., 89; Wilson, *Honor's Voice*, 80; Barton, *Soul of Abraham Lincoln*, 238, 240.

50. Herndon and Weik, *Herndon's Life of Lincoln*, ed. Angle, xvii, xxi, xxxvii.

51. Ibid., xlv, 329, 351–52, 359.

52. Ibid., 358.

53. Smith, *Christian's Defence*, 2:362–64.

54. "Handbill Replying to Charges of Infidelity," July 31, 1846, Basler, ed., *Collected Works*, 1:382; Fehrenbacher, ed., *Speeches and Writings*, 1:139.

55. For instance, "Speech at Chicago," July 10, 1858, Basler, ed., *Collected Works*, 2:458; Fehrenbacher, ed., *Speeches and Writings*, 1:454. On Fell's Unitarianism, see Neely, *Abraham Lincoln Encyclopedia*, 108.

56. Neely, *Abraham Lincoln Encyclopedia*, 181.

57. Ibid., 180; Wilson, *What Lincoln Read*, 67–68, 93–95. The books borrowed include, in French, the works of Hugo and Balzac and, in German, those of Goethe, Shiller, Richter, and Schlegel. Mary was probably responsible for the borrowing of Hawthorne, Dickens, and Emerson as well.

58. See for instance "Speech at Springfield," July 17, 1858, Basler, ed., *Collected Works*, 2:510–11; Fehrenbacher, ed., *Speeches and Writings*, 1:466–67.

59. Guelzo, *Abraham Lincoln*, 196.

60. "Eulogy on Henry Clay," July 6, 1852, Basler, ed., *Collected Works*, 2:130–31; Fehrenbacher, ed., *Speeches and Writings*, 1:269.

61. See "Speech at Springfield," July 17, 1858, Basler, ed., *Collected Works*, 2:510–11; Fehrenbacher, ed., *Speeches and Writings*, 1:466–67.

62. Greenstone, *Lincoln Persuasion*, 19.

63. The editor of Lincoln's "Address at Cooper Institute," Feb. 27, 1860, added footnotes to the printed edition of 1860, which appear also in Basler's *Collected Works*. These footnotes quote the relevant southern politicians and writers (Basler, ed., *Collected Works*, 3:548n.37).

64. Ibid., 549–50; Fehrenbacher, ed., *Speeches and Writings*, 2:129–30.

65. Marsden, *Evangelical Mind*, 182–98; "Portion of Speech at Republican Banquet," Dec. 10, 1856, Basler, ed., *Collected Works*, 2:385; Fehrenbacher, ed., *Speeches and Writings*, 1:386.

66. Basler, ed., *Collected Works*, 3:482; Fehrenbacher, ed., *Speeches and Writings*, 2:101.

67. The evidence for Lincoln's reading Grimshaw rests on one witness long after the fact. See Wilson and Davis, eds., *Herndon's Informants*, 109n.

68. Beveridge, *Abraham Lincoln*, 1:74. The quotation is from William Grimshaw, *History of the United States: From Their First Settlement as Colonies, to the Cession of Florida, in Eighteen Hundred and Twenty-one* (Philadelphia: Grigg & Elliott, 1824), 301.

69. Wills, *Lincoln at Gettysburg*.

70. Even in his eventual denial that victory necessarily represented the favorable judgment of God, Lincoln was not entirely alone. Though Lincoln would have had difficulty with his biblical literalism, the Old School stalwart Charles Hodge of Princeton came to much the same conclusion about the inscrutability of Providence (Guelzo, *Abraham Lincoln*, 414).

71. "To George B. Ide, James R. Doolittle, and A. Hubbell," May 30, 1864, Basler, ed., *Collected Works*, 7:368; Fehrenbacher, ed., *Speeches and Writings*, 2:596–97.

72. "Memorandum Concerning His Probable Failure of Re-election," Aug. 23, 1864, Basler, ed., *Collected Works*, 7:514; Fehrenbacher, ed., *Speeches and Writings*, 2:624.

73. Basler reproduces Lincoln's part of the interview with Mrs. Gurney giving it the date of Oct. 26, 1862 (*Collected Works*, 5:478). According to that source, Lincoln expressed views very similar to those he expressed in 1864 to Mrs. Gurney and in the Second Inaugural. "If after endeavoring to do my best in the light which he affords me, I find my efforts fail, I must believe that for some purpose unknown to me, He wills it otherwise. . . ." The source is in an unknown hand, the date is in yet another hand, and Fehrenbacher omits it from the selected works entirely. If true to Lincoln in the fall of 1862, however, it would not necessarily refute the basic contention that Lincoln returned to a greater emphasis on the will of God late in the war. In fact the troubles in the summer of 1864 may have called to mind those of the fall of 1862.

74. "To Eliza P. Gurney," Sept. 4, 1864, *Collected Works*, 7:535; Fehrenbacher, ed., *Speeches and Writings*, 2:627.

75. See chap. 5.

76. Basler, ed., *Collected Works*, 8:332–33; Fehrenbacher, ed., *Speeches and Writings*, 2:686–87.

77. Donald, *Lincoln*, 515. See also Boritt, *Lincoln and the Economics of the American Dream*, 256.

78. "To Joseph Hooker," Jan. 26, 1863, Basler, ed., *Collected Works*, 6:78–79; Fehrenbacher, ed., *Speeches and Writings*, 2:433–34.

79. "To Thurlow Weed," Mar. 15, 1865, Basler, ed., *Collected Works*, 8:356; Fehrenbacher, ed., *Speeches and Writings*, 2:689.

80. Marsden, *Evangelical Mind*, 184.

BIBLIOGRAPHY

Abrams, M. H. *Natural Supernaturalism: Tradition and Revolution in Romantic Literature.* New York: W. W. Norton, 1971.

Anderson, Dwight G. *Abraham Lincoln: The Quest for Immortality.* New York: Alfred A. Knopf, 1982.

Andrews, Donald Frank. "The American Whig Review, 1845–1852: Its History and Literary Contents." Ph.D. diss., University of Tennessee, 1977.

Appleby, Joyce. *Capitalism and a New Social Order: The Republican Vision of the 1790s.* New York: New York University Press, 1984.

Arnold, Isaac Newton. *The History of Abraham Lincoln, and the Overthrow of Slavery.* Chicago: Clarke, 1866.

Arnold, Thomas. *Introductory Lectures on Modern History, Delivered in Lent Term, MDCC-CXLII. With the Inaugural Lecture Delivered in December, MDCCCXLI.* 4th ed. London: B. Fellows, 1849.

Bancroft, George. *Abraham Lincoln, a Tribute: An Address Delivered February 12, 1866 before a Joint Session in the House Chamber at the Memorial for Abraham Lincoln.* New York: A. Wessels, 1908.

———. *History of the United States, from the Discovery of the American Continent.* Vol. 3. Boston: Little, Brown, 1852.

———. *History of the United States, from the Discovery of the American Continent.* Vol. 4. Boston: Little, Brown, 1840.

———. *History of the United States, from the Discovery of the American Continent.* Vol. 9. Boston: Little, Brown, 1866.

———. *History of the United States, from the Discovery of the American Continent.* Vol. 10. Boston: Little, Brown, 1874.

———. *Literary and Historical Miscellanies.* New York: Harper and Brothers, 1855.

———. *Oration Delivered on the Fourth of July, 1826.* Northampton, Mass.: T. Watson Shepard, 1826.

———. "Oration, Pronounced in Union Square, April 25, 1865 at the Funeral Obsequies of Abraham Lincoln in the City of New York." *Pulpit and Rostrum: Sermons, Orations, Popular Lectures, Etc.* 34–35 (June 1865): 3–13.

———. "The Place of Abraham Lincoln in History." *Atlantic Monthly* 15, no. 92 (1865): 757–64.

———. "Speech of Mr. Bancroft at the New York Union Meeting, April 20, 1863." In *The League for Union: Speeches of the Hon. George Bancroft and James Milliken, Esq.* Philadelphia: William S. and Alfred Martien, 1863.

———. "To Stephen A. Douglas." 7. 1858. Joseph Regenstein Library, University of Chicago.

———. "To Stephen A. Douglas." 16. 1858. Joseph Regenstein Library, University of Chicago.

———. "To Stephen A. Douglas." 24. 1858. Joseph Regenstein Library, University of Chicago.

Banning, Lance. "Jeffersonian Ideology Revisited: Liberal and Classical Ideas in the New American Republic." *William and Mary Quarterly,* 3d ser., 43 (1986): 3–34.

Bannister, Dan W. *Lincoln and the Illinois Supreme Court.* Edited by Barbara Hughett. Springfield, Ill.: Dan W. Bannister, 1994.

Barnes, Gilbert H. *The Antislavery Impulse, 1830–1844.* Gloucester, Mass.: P. Smith, 1933.

Barton, William E. *The Soul of Abraham Lincoln.* New York: George H. Doran, 1920.

Basler, Roy P., ed. *The Collected Works of Abraham Lincoln.* 8 vols. New Brunswick, N.J.: Rutgers University Press, 1953–1955.

Belz, Herman. "Review Essay: Salmon P. Chase and the Politics of Racial Reform." *Journal of the Abraham Lincoln Association* 17, no. 2 (1996): 22–40.

Bender, Thomas, ed. *The Antislavery Debate: Capitalism and Abolitionism as a Problem in Historical Interpretation.* Berkeley: University of California Press, 1992.

Bercovitch, Sacvan. *The American Jeremiad.* Madison: University of Wisconsin Press, 1978.

Bestor, Arthur. "The American Civil War as a Constitutional Crisis." *American Historical Review* 69, no. 2 (1964): 327–52.

Beveridge, Albert J. *Abraham Lincoln, 1809–1858.* 2 vols. Boston and New York: Houghton Mifflin, 1928.

Bishop, Jim. *The Day Lincoln Was Shot.* New York: Harper & Brothers, 1955.

Boritt, Gabor S. *Lincoln and the Economics of the American Dream.* Urbana: University of Illinois Press, 1994.

———. "A Question of Political Suicide: Lincoln's Opposition to the Mexican War." *Journal of the Illinois State Historical Society* 67, no. 1 (1974): 79–100.

Boritt, Gabor S., and Norman O. Forness, eds. *The Historian's Lincoln: Pseudohistory, Psychohistory, and History.* Urbana: University of Illinois Press, 1988.

Bowyer, George. *Commentaries on Universal Public Law.* London: V. & R. Stevens and G. S. Norton, 1854.

Brock, William. *Parties and Political Conscience: American Dilemmas, 1840–1850.* Millwood, N.Y.: KTO Press, 1979.

Brown, Thomas. *Politics and Statesmanship: Essays on the American Whig Party.* New York: Columbia University Press, 1985.

Bruce, Robert V. *Lincoln and the Tools of War.* Indianapolis: Bobbs-Merrill, 1956.

Burlingame, Michael. "'I Used to Be a Slave': The Origins of Lincoln's Hatred of Slavery." In *The Inner World of Abraham Lincoln,* 20–56. Urbana: University of Illinois Press, 1994.

———. "Lincoln's Depressions: "Melancholy Dript from Him as He Walked"." In *The Inner World of Abraham Lincoln,* 92–122. Urbana: University of Illinois Press, 1994.

———. "New Light on the Bixby Letter." *Journal of the Abraham Lincoln Association* 16, no. 1 (1995): 59–71.

———, ed. *At Lincoln's Side: John Hay's Civil War Correspondence and Selected Writings.* Carbondale: Southern Illinois University Press, 2000.

———, ed. *Lincoln's Journalist: John Hay's Anonymous Writings for the Press, 1860–1864.* Carbondale: Southern Illinois University Press, 1998.

———, ed. *An Oral History of Abraham Lincoln: John G. Nicolay's Interviews and Essays.* Carbondale: Southern Illinois University Press, 1996.

Burlingame, Michael, and John R. T. Ettlinger, eds. *Inside Lincoln's White House: The Complete Civil War Diary of John Hay.* Carbondale: Southern Illinois University Press, 1997.

Burstein, Andrew. *America's Jubilee: How in 1826 a Generation Remembered Fifty Years of Independence.* New York: Alfred A. Knopf, 2001.

———. *On Sentimental Democracy: The Evolution of America's Self-Image.* New York: Hill and Wang, 1999.

Canary, Robert H. *George Bancroft.* Edited by Sylvia E. Bowman. New York: Twayne, 1974.

Cappon, Lester J., ed. *The Adams-Jefferson Letters: The Complete Correspondence between Thomas Jefferson and Abigail and John Adams.* Chapel Hill: University of North Carolina Press, 1959.

Carwardine, Richard. *Evangelicals and Politics in Antebellum America.* New Haven, Conn.: Yale University Press, 1993.

———. "Lincoln, Evangelical Religion, and American Political Culture in the Era of the Civil War." *Journal of the Abraham Lincoln Association* 18, no. 1 (1997): 27–56.

Cathcart, William, ed. *The Baptist Encyclopaedia: A Dictionary of the Doctrines, Ordinances, Usages, Confessions of Faith, Sufferings, Labors, and Successes, and of the General History of the Baptist Denomination in All Lands.* Philadelphia: L. H. Everts, 1881.

Cherry, Conrad. *Nature and the Religious Imagination from Edwards to Bushnell.* Philadelphia: Fortress Press, 1980.

———, ed. *God's New Israel: Religious Interpretations of American Destiny.* Englewood Cliffs, N.J.: Prentice-Hall, 1971.

Chesebrough, David B. *"No Sorrow like Our Sorrow": Northern Protestant Ministers and the Assassination of Lincoln.* Kent, Ohio: Kent State University Press, 1994.

Child, Lydia Maria. *Anti-Slavery Catechism.* Newburyport, Mass: C. Whipple, 1839.

Chisholm, Hugh, ed. *The Encyclopaedia Britannica: A Dictionary of Arts, Sciences, Literature, and General Information.* 29 vols. New York: Encyclopaedia Britannica, 1911.

Chroust, Anton-Hermann. "Abraham Lincoln Argues a Pro-Slavery Case." *American Journal of Legal History* 5 (1961): 299–308.

Cobbe, Frances P., ed. *The Collected Works of Theodore Parker: Minister of the Twenty-eighth Congregational Society at Boston. . .* Vol. 6. London: Trübner, 1864.

Coleman, Charles Hubert. *Abraham Lincoln and Coles County, Illinois.* New Brunswick, N.J.: Scarecrow Press, 1955.

Congressional Globe. 46 vols. Washington, D.C., 1834–1873.

Conser, Walter H., Jr. *Church and Confession: Conservative Theologians in Germany, England, and America, 1815–1866.* [Macon, Ga.]: Mercer University Press, 1984.

Current, Richard Nelson. "Bancroft's Lincoln." In *Speaking of Abraham Lincoln: The Man and His Meaning for Our Times,* 172–86. Urbana: University of Illinois Press, 1983.

———. *The Lincoln Nobody Knows.* New York: Hill and Wang, 1958.

Curti, Merle. "Mr. Locke, America's Philosopher, 1783–1861." In *Probing Our Past,* 69–118. New York: Harper, 1955.

———. "Young America." In *Probing Our Past,* 219–45. New York: Harper, 1955.

Danbom, David B. "The Young America Movement," *Journal of the Illinois State Historical Society* 67, no. 3 (1974): 294–306.

Danoff, Brian F. "Lincoln, Machiavelli, and American Political Thought." *Presidential Studies Quarterly* 30, no. 2 (2000): 290–311.

Davis, David Brion, ed. *Antebellum American Culture: An Interpretive Anthology.* Lexington, Mass.: D.C. Heath, 1979.

Democratic Review. "European Views of American Democracy.—De Tocqueville." *United States Magazine and Democratic Review* 1, no. 1 (1837): 91–107.

———. "European Views of American Democracy. No. II. M. De Tocqueville." *United States Magazine and Democratic Review* 2, no. 8 (1838): 337–57.

———. "The Fate of Mexico," *United States Magazine and Democratic Review* 41 (May 1858): 337–46.

———. "The Moral of the Crisis." *United States Magazine and Democratic Review* 1 (October–December 1837): 108–22.

Diggins, John P. *The Lost Soul of American Politics: Virtue, Self-Interest, and the Foundations of Liberalism.* New York: Basic Books, 1984.

Dodge, Daniel Kilham, *Abraham Lincoln: The Evolution of His Literary Style.* Introduced by James Hurt. 1900. Reprint, Urbana: University of Illinois Press, 2000.

Donald, David Herbert. *Lincoln.* New York: Simon & Schuster, 1995.

———. *Lincoln's Herndon.* New York: Alfred A. Knopf, 1948.

Dorfman, Joseph. *The Economic Mind in American Civilization.* 5 vols. New York: Viking, 1946–1959.

Douglas, Stephen A. "'See the Conquering Hero Comes': Principles of Stephen A. Douglas Illustrated in His Speeches." 1860. Joseph Regenstein Library, University of Chicago.

———. "Speech of Senator S. A. Douglas at the Meeting in Odd-Fellows' Hall, New Orleans, on Monday Evening, December 6, 1858." 1859. Joseph Regenstein Library, University of Chicago.

Duff, John J. *A. Lincoln, Prairie Lawyer.* New York: Rinehart, 1960.

Ericson, David F. *The Shaping of American Liberalism: The Debates over Ratification, Nullification, and Slavery.* Chicago: University of Chicago Press, 1993.

Erikson, Erik H. *Young Man Luther: A Study in Psychoanalysis and History.* New York: W. W. Norton, 1958.

Everett, Edward. *Orations and Speeches on Various Occasions.* 2d ed. Vol. 1. Boston: Charles C. Little and James Brown, 1850.

Fehrenbacher, Don E., ed. *Speeches and Writings,* by Abraham Lincoln. Vols. 45–46, Library of America. New York: Literary Classics of the United States, 1989.

Fehrenbacher, Don E., and Virginia Fehrenbacher, eds. *Recollected Words of Abraham Lincoln.* Stanford, Calif.: Stanford University Press, 1996.

Feller, Daniel. *The Jacksonian Promise: America, 1815–1840.* Baltimore: Johns Hopkins University Press, 1995.

Fogel, Robert William, and Stanley L. Engerman. *Time on the Cross: The Economics of American Negro Slavery.* 2 vols. Boston: Little, Brown, 1974.

Foner, Eric. "The Causes of the American Civil War." In *Politics and Ideology in the Age of the Civil War,* edited by Eric Foner, 15–33. London: Oxford University Press, 1974.

———. *Free Soil, Free Labor, Free Men: The Ideology of the Republican Party before the Civil War.* New York: Oxford University Press, 1970.

———. Review of *The Political Crisis of the 1850s,* by Michael F. Holt. *American Historical Review* 84, no. 2 (1979): 555–56.

Foner, Eric, and John A. Garraty, eds. *The Reader's Companion to American History.* Boston: Houghton Mifflin, 1991.

Forgie, George B. *Patricide in the House Divided: A Psychological Interpretation of Lincoln and His Age.* New York: W. W. Norton, 1979.

Fornieri, Joseph R. "Biblical Republicanism: Abraham Lincoln's Civil Theology." Ph.D. diss., Catholic University of America, 1996.

Fox, G. George. *Abraham Lincoln's Religion: Sources of the Great Emancipator's Religious Inspiration.* New York: Exposition Press, 1959.

Frank, John P. *Lincoln as a Lawyer.* Urbana: University of Illinois Press, 1961.

Fraysse, Olivier. *Lincoln, Land, and Labor, 1809–60.* Translated by Sylvia Neely. Urbana: University of Illinois Press, 1994.

Freidel, Frank. *Francis Lieber: Nineteenth-Century Liberal.* Baton Rouge: Louisiana State University Press, 1947.

Geertz, Clifford. "Ideology as a Cultural System." In *Ideology and Discontent*, edited by David E. Apter, 47–76. New York: Free Press, 1964.

Genovese, Eugene D. *The World the Slaveholders Made: Two Essays in Interpretation*. New York: Pantheon, 1969.

Gienapp, William E. "Nativism and the Creation of a Republican Majority in the North before the Civil War." *Journal of American History* 72 (1985): 529–59.

———. *The Origins of the Republican Party, 1852–1856*. New York: Oxford University Press, 1987.

Goodheart, Lawrence B., Richard D. Brown, and Stephen G. Rabe, eds. *Slavery in American Society*. 3d ed. Problems in American Civilization. Lexington, Mass.: D. C. Heath, 1993.

Goodman, Paul. *Of One Blood: Abolitionism and the Origins of Racial Equality*. Berkeley: University of California Press, 1998.

Greenstone, J. David. *The Lincoln Persuasion: Remaking American Liberalism*. Princeton Studies in American Politics. Princeton, N.J.: Princeton University Press, 1993.

———. "The Transient and the Permanent in American Politics: Standards, Interests, and the Concept of 'Public.'" In *Public Values and Private Power in American Politics*, edited by J. David Greenstone, 286. Chicago: University of Chicago Press, 1982.

Grimshaw, William. *History of the United States: From Their First Settlement as Colonies, to the Cession of Florida, in Eighteen Hundred and Twenty-one*. Philadelphia: Grigg & Elliott, 1824.

Guelzo, Allen C. "Abraham Lincoln and the Doctrine of Necessity." *Journal of the Abraham Lincoln Association* 18, no. 1 (1997): 57–81.

———. *Abraham Lincoln: Redeemer President*. Grand Rapids, Mich.: William B. Eerdmans, 1999.

———. "Review Essay: *The Inner World of Abraham Lincoln*, by Michael Burlingame and *Abraham Lincoln: From Skeptic to Prophet*, by Wayne C. Temple." *Journal of the Abraham Lincoln Association* 17, no. 2 (1996): 41–51.

Handlin, Lilian. *George Bancroft, the Intellectual as Democrat*. New York: Harper & Row, 1984.

Harkness, David J. *Lincoln and Byron, Lovers of Liberty*. Harrogate, Tenn.: Department of Lincolniana of Lincoln Memorial University, 1941.

Harkness, David J., and R. Gerald McMurtry. *Lincoln's Favorite Poets*. Knoxville: University of Tennessee Press, 1959.

Hartz, Louis. *The Liberal Tradition in America: An Interpretation of American Political Thought since the Revolution*. New York: Harcourt Brace Jovanovich, 1955.

Haskell, Thomas L. "Capitalism and the Origins of the Humanitarian Sensibility," *American Historical Review* 90 (1985): 339–61, 547–66.

Hein, David. "Lincoln's Faith: Commentary on 'Abraham Lincoln and American Political Religion.'" In *The Historian's Lincoln: Pseudohistory, Psychohistory, and History*, edited by Gabor S. Boritt, 144–48. Urbana: University of Illinois Press, 1988.

———. "Lincoln's Theology and Political Ethics." In *Essays on Lincoln's Faith and Politics*, edited by Kenneth W. Thompson, 103–79. Lanham, Md.: University Press of America, 1983.

Herndon, William H., and Jesse W. Weik. *Herndon's Life of Lincoln*. Edited by Paul M. Angle. 1942. Reprint, New York: Da Capo Press, 1983.

Hietala, Thomas R. *Manifest Design: Anxious Aggrandizement in Late Jacksonian America*. Ithaca, N.Y.: Cornell University Press, 1985.

Higginson, Thomas Wentworth. *Army Life in a Black Regiment*. Edited by Howard N. Meyer. 1869. Reprint, New York: W. W. Norton, 1984

Hofstadter, Richard. *The American Political Tradition and the Men Who Made It.* 1948. Reprint, New York: Vintage, 1948.

Holland, J. G. *Life of Abraham Lincoln.* Springfield, Mass.: G. Bill, 1866.

Holt, Michael F. *Political Parties and American Political Development from the Age of Jackson to the Age of Lincoln.* Baton Rouge: Louisiana State University Press, 1992.

———. "The Politics of Impatience: The Origins of Know Nothingism." *Journal of American History* 60 (1973): 309–31.

———. *The Rise and Fall of the American Whig Party: Jacksonian Politics and the Onset of the Civil War.* New York: Oxford University Press, 1999.

Holzer, Harold. "'Columbia's Noblest Sons': Washington and Lincoln in Popular Prints." *Journal of the Abraham Lincoln Association* 15, no. 1 (1994): 23–69.

———. *Lincoln Seen and Heard.* Lawrence: University Press of Kansas, 2000.

Holzer, Harold, and Mark E. Neely. *Mine Eyes Have Seen the Glory: The Civil War in Art.* New York: Orion Books, 1993.

Hooker, Morna D. *The Gospel according to St. Mark.* Black's New Testament Commentaries. Peabody, Mass.: Hendrickson, 1991.

Horner, Harlan Hoyt. *The Growth of Lincoln's Faith.* New York: Abingdon Press, 1939.

Horwitz, Morton J. *The Transformation of America Law, 1780–1860.* Studies in Legal History. Cambridge, Mass.: Harvard University Press, 1977.

Howe, Daniel Walker. "The Evangelical Movement and Political Culture in the North during the Second Party System." *Journal of American History* 77 (1991): 1216–39.

———. *Making the American Self: Jonathan Edwards to Abraham Lincoln.* Cambridge, Mass.: Harvard University Press, 1997.

———. "The Market Revolution and the Shaping of Identity in Whig-Jacksonian America." In *The Market Revolution in America: Social, Political, and Religious Expressions, 1800–1880,* edited by Melvyn Stokes and Stephen Conway, 259–81. Charlottesville: University Press of Virginia, 1996.

———. *The Political Culture of the American Whigs.* Chicago: University of Chicago Press, 1979.

———. "Why Abraham Lincoln Was a Whig," *Journal of the Abraham Lincoln Association* 16, no. 1 (1995).

Howe, M. A. De Wolfe, ed. *The Life and Letters of George Bancroft.* 2 vols. New York: Charles Scribner's Sons, 1908.

Hurst, James Willard. *Law and the Conditions of Freedom: In the Nineteenth-Century United States.* Madison: University of Wisconsin Press, 1956.

Huston, James L. *The Panic of 1857 and the Coming of the Civil War.* Baton Rouge: Louisiana State University Press, 1987.

Illinois State Journal, Feb. 14–21, 1859.

Jaffa, Harry V. *Crisis of the House Divided: An Interpretation of the Issues in the Lincoln-Douglas Debates.* Garden City, N.Y.: Doubleday, 1959.

Jaffa, Harry V. and Robert W. Johannsen, eds. *In the Name of the People: Speeches and Writings of Lincoln and Douglas in the Ohio Campaign of 1859.* Columbus: Ohio State University Press, 1959.

Johannsen, Robert W. *Stephen A. Douglas.* New York: Oxford University Press, 1973.

———. "Stephen A. Douglas, 'Harper's Magazine,' and Popular Sovereignty." *Mississippi Valley Historical Review* 45, no. 1 (1958): 606–31.

———, ed. *The Lincoln-Douglas Debates of 1858.* New York: Oxford University Press, 1965.

Kazin, Alfred. *God and the American Writer.* New York: Alfred A. Knopf, 1997.

Kempf, Edward J. *Abraham Lincoln's Philosophy of Common Sense: An Analytical Biography of a Great Mind*. [New York]: New York Academy of Sciences, 1965.

Koch, Adrienne, and William Peden, eds. *The Life and Selected Writings of Thomas Jefferson*. New York: Modern Library, 1944.

———, eds. *The Selected Writings of John and John Quincy Adams*. New York: Alfred A. Knopf, 1946.

Larson, John Lauritz. "Liberty by Design: Freedom, Planning, and John Quincy Adams's American System." In *The State and Economic Knowledge: The American and British Experiences*, edited by Mary O. Furner and Barry Supple. Cambridge: Cambridge University Press.

Lasch, Christopher. *The True and Only Heaven: Progress and Its Critics*. New York: W. W. Norton, 1991.

Lewis, R. W. B. *The American Adam: Tragedy and Tradition in the Nineteenth Century*. Chicago: University of Chicago Press, 1955.

McColley, Robert. "Review Essay: *The Inner World of Abraham Lincoln*, by Michael Burlingame and *Abraham Lincoln: From Skeptic to Prophet*, by Wayne C. Temple." *Journal of the Abraham Lincoln Association* 17, no. 2 (1996): 52–60.

McCormick, Richard L. "The Republican Party's Tortuous Path to 'Victorious Defeat.'" *Reviews in American History* 16 (1988): 396–402.

McCoy, Drew R. "Lincoln and the Founding Fathers: A Reconsideration." *Journal of the Abraham Lincoln Association* 16, no. 1 (1995): 1–13.

McKinsey, Elizabeth R. *Niagara Falls: Icon of the American Sublime*. Cambridge Studies in American Literature and Culture. Cambridge: Cambridge University Press, 1985.

Mackintosh, Robert. "Theology." In *Encyclopaedia Britannica*, edited by Hugh Chisholm, vol. 26, 772–85. New York: Encyclopaedia Britannica, 1911.

McLoughlin, William G. *Soul Liberty: The Baptists' Struggle in New England, 1630–1833*. Hanover, N.H.: University Press of New England for Brown University Press, 1991.

McPherson, James M. *For Cause and Comrades: Why Men Fought in the Civil War*. New York: Oxford University Press, 1997.

Marsden, George M. *The Evangelical Mind and the New School Presbyterian Experience: A Case Study of Thought and Theology in Nineteenth-Century America*. Yale Publications in American Studies, vol. 20. New Haven, Conn.: Yale University Press, 1970.

———. "Everyone One's Own Interpreter? The Bible, Science, and Authority in Mid-Nineteenth-Century America." In *The Bible in America: Essays in Cultural History*, edited by Nathan O. Hatch and Mark A. Noll, 79–100. New York: Oxford University Press, 1982.

May, Henry F. *The Enlightenment in America*. New York: Oxford University Press, 1976.

Melton, J. Gordon, ed. *The Encyclopedia of American Religions*. 2 vols. Wilmington, North Carolina: McGrath, 1978.

Melville, Herman. *Battle-Pieces and Aspects of the War*. Edited by Lee Rust Brown. New York: Da Capo Press, 1995.

Merk, Frederick. *Manifest Destiny and Mission in American History: A Reinterpretation*. New York: Vintage, 1963.

Meyers, Marvin. *The Jacksonian Persuasion*. New York: Vintage, 1960.

Miller, Perry. *Errand into the Wilderness*. Cambridge, Mass.: Belknap Press of Harvard University Press, 1956.

———. *The Life of the Mind in America: From the Revolution to the Civil War*. New York: Harcourt, Brace & World, 1965.

———. *Nature's Nation*. Cambridge, Mass.: Belknap Press of Harvard University Press, 1967.

———. *The New England Mind: The Seventeenth Century.* 1939. Reprint, New York: Beacon, 1961.

———. *The Raven and the Whale.* New York: Harcourt Brace, 1956.

Morel, Lucas E. "Lincoln among the Reformers: Tempering the Temperance Movement." *Journal of the Abraham Lincoln Association* 20, no. 1 (1999): 1–34.

Mott, Frank Luther. *A History of American Magazines, 1741–1850.* Cambridge, Mass.: Harvard University Press, 1938.

Murrin, John M. "Religion and Politics in America from the First Settlements to the Civil War." In *Religion and American Politics from the Colonial Period to the 1980s,* edited by Mark A. Noll, 19–43. New York: Oxford University Press, 1990.

Neely, Mark E., Jr. *The Abraham Lincoln Encyclopedia.* New York: McGraw-Hill, 1982.

———. "The Civil War and the Two-Party System." In *"We Cannot Escape History": Lincoln and the Last Best Hope of Earth,* edited by James M. McPherson, 86–104. Urbana: University of Illinois Press, 1995.

———. *The Fate of Liberty: Abraham Lincoln and Civil Liberties.* New York: Oxford University Press, 1991.

———. *The Last Best Hope of Earth: Abraham Lincoln and the Promise of America.* Cambridge, Mass.: Harvard University Press, 1993

———. "Lincoln and the Mexican War: An Argument by Analogy." *Civil War History: A Journal of the Middle Period* 24, no. 1 (1978): 5–24.

———. "Lincoln's Lyceum Speech and the Origins of a Modern Myth." *Lincoln Lore,* no. 1776–1777 (1987): 1–4.

Nevins, Allan. *The Emergence of Lincoln.* Vol. 1, *Douglas, Buchanan, and Party Chaos, 1857–1859.* New York: Charles Scribner's Sons, 1950.

Nichols, David A. *Lincoln and the Indians: Civil War Policy and Politics.* Columbia: University of Missouri Press, 1978.

Niven, John. "Lincoln and Chase, a Reappraisal." *Journal of the Abraham Lincoln Association* 12 (1991): 1–15.

Noble, David W. *Historians against History: The Frontier Thesis and the National Covenant in American Historical Writing since 1830.* Minneapolis: University of Minnesota Press, 1965.

Noll, Mark A. "'Both . . . Pray to the Same God': The Singularity of Lincoln's Faith in the Era of the Civil War." *Journal of the Abraham Lincoln Association* 18, no. 1 (1997): 1–26.

Novak, William J. *The People's Welfare: Law and Regulation in Nineteenth-Century America.* Studies in Legal History. Chapel Hill: University of North Carolina Press, 1996.

Novick, Sheldon M., ed. *The Collected Works of Justice Holmes: Complete Public Writings and Selected Judicial Opinions of Oliver Wendell Holmes.* Holmes Devise Memorial Edition. Vol. 3. Chicago: University of Chicago Press, 1995.

Oates, Stephen B. *With Malice toward None: The Life of Abraham Lincoln.* New York: Harper & Row, 1976.

Paludan, Phillip S. "Commentary on 'Lincoln and the Economics of the American Dream.'" In *The Historian's Lincoln: Pseudohistory, Psychohistory, and History,* edited by Gabor S. Boritt and Norman O. Forness, 116–23. Urbana: University of Illinois Press, 1988.

———. *A Covenant with Death: The Constitution, Law, and Equality in the Civil War Era.* Urbana: University of Illinois Press, 1975.

———. "Emancipating the Republic: Lincoln and the Means and Ends of Antislavery." In *"We Cannot Escape History": Lincoln and the Last Best Hope of Earth,* edited by James M. McPherson, 45–62. Urbana: University of Illinois Press, 1995.

———. *The Presidency of Abraham Lincoln*. American Presidency Series, vol. 29. Lawrence: University Press of Kansas, 1994.

Parker, Theodore. "Discourse of the Transient and Permanent in Christianity." In *The Transcendentalists: An Anthology*, edited by Perry Miller, 259–83. Cambridge, Mass: Harvard University Press, 1950.

Peacock, James L., and Ruel W. Tyson. *Pilgrims of Paradox: Calvinism and Experience among the Primitive Baptists of the Blue Ridge*. Smithsonian Series in Ethnographic Inquiry. Washington, D.C.: Smithsonian Institution Press, 1989.

Peterson, Merrill D. *The Jefferson Image in the American Mind*. New York: Oxford University Press, 1960.

———. *Lincoln in American Memory*. New York: Oxford University Press, 1994.

Porte, Joel, ed. *Essays and Lectures,* by Ralph Waldo Emerson. Vol. 15, Library of America. New York: Literary Classics of the United States, 1983.

Prentiss, Dale Roger. "Economic Progress and Social Dissent in Michigan and Mississippi, 1837–1860." Ph.D. diss., Stanford University, 1990.

Purcell, Edward. *The Crisis of Democratic Theory: Scientific Naturalism and the Problem of Value*. Lexington: University Press of Kentucky, 1973.

Randall, James G. *Lincoln, the Liberal Statesman*. New York: Dodd, Mead, 1947.

Riepma, Siert F. "'Young America': A Study in American Nationalism before the Civil War." Ph.D. diss., Western Reserve University, 1939.

Rose, Anne C. *Victorian America and the Civil War*. Cambridge: Cambridge University Press, 1992.

Ross, Dorothy. *The Origins of American Social Science*. Cambridge: Cambridge University Press, 1991.

Sandburg, Carl. *Abraham Lincoln: The War Years*. 4 vols. New York: Harcourt, Brace & World, 1939.

Sayre, Robert F., ed. *A Week on the Concord and Merrimack Rivers: Walden; or, Life in the Woods: The Maine Woods: Cape Cod,* by Henry David Thoreau. Vol. 28. Library of America. New York: Literary Classics of the United States, 1985.

Schaff, Philip, ed. *The Creeds of Christendom, with a History and Critical Notes*. 4th ed. Vol. 3, *Bibliotheca Symbolica Ecclesiae Universalis*. 1877. Reprint, New York: Harper & Brothers, 1919.

———. *The Creeds of Christendom with a History and Critical Notes*. 6th ed. Vol. 1, *Bibliotheca Symbolica Ecclesiae Universalis*. 1877. Reprint, New York: Harper & Brothers, 1931.

Schwartz, Thomas F. "Lincoln Never Said That." *For the People: A Newsletter of the Abraham Lincoln Association* 1, no. 1 (1999): 4–6.

———. "The Springfield Lyceums and Lincoln's 1838 Speech." *Illinois Historical Journal* 83, no. 1 (1990): 45–49.

Scott, Donald M. "The Popular Lecture and the Creation of a Public in Mid-Nineteenth-Century America," *Journal of American History* 66 (1980): 791–809.

Secord, James A., ed. *Vestiges of the Natural History of Creation and Other Evolutionary Writings*. Chicago: University of Chicago Press, 1994.

Sellers, Charles Grier. *The Market Revolution: Jacksonian America, 1815–1846*. New York: Oxford University Press, 1991.

Seward, William H. "California, Union, and Freedom." *Congressional Globe,* 31st Cong., 1st sess., 1850, appendix, 260–69.

Shalhope, Robert E. "Thomas Jefferson's Republicanism and Antebellum Southern Thought." *Journal of Southern History* 42, no. 4 (1976): 529–56.

Silbey, Joel H. "'Doomed to Misfortune—If Not Dissolution.'" *Virginia Quarterly Review* 76, no. 2 (2000): 351–57.

Simon, Paul. *Lincoln's Preparation for Greatness: The Illinois Legislative Years.* Urbana: University of Illinois Press, 1971.

Simpson, Brooks D. "Two More Roads to Sumter." *Reviews in American History* 17 (1989): 225–31.

Singleton, Gregory H. "Protestant Voluntary Organizations and the Shaping of Victorian America." In *Victorian America*, edited by Daniel Walker Howe, 47–58: [Philadelphia]: University of Pennsylvania Press, 1976.

Smith, James. *The Christian's Defence.* 2 vols. Cincinnati: J. A. James, 1843.

Smylie, John Edwin. "National Ethos and the Church." *Theology Today*, October 1963, 313–17.

Southern State Rights, Free Trade and Anti-Abolition Tract No. 1. Charleston, S.C.: Walker & Burke, 1844.

Spencer, Donald S. *Louis Kossuth and Young America: A Study of Sectionalism and Foreign Policy, 1848–1852.* Columbia: University of Missouri Press, 1977.

Spencer, J. H. *A History of Kentucky Baptists.* 2 vols. Cincinnati: Printed for the author, 1886.

Stampp, Kenneth M. *The Peculiar Institution: Slavery in the Ante-bellum South.* New York: Alfred A. Knopf, 1956.

Stafford, John. *The Literary Criticism of "Young America": A Study in the Relationship of Politics and Literature, 1837–1850.* Berkeley: University of California Press, 1952.

Stauffer, John. "Beyond Social Control: The Example of Gerrit Smith." *American Transcendental Quarterly* 11, no. 3 (1997): 234–60.

Stoddard, William Osborn, and Michael Burlingame. *Inside the White House in War Times: Memoirs and Reports of Lincoln's Secretary.* Lincoln: University of Nebraska Press, 2000.

Storing, Herbert J. "Slavery and the Moral Foundations of the American Republic." In *The Moral Foundations of the American Republic*, 2d ed., ed. Robert H. Horwitz, 214–33. Charlottesville: University Press of Virginia, 1979.

Strout, Cushing. *Making American Tradition: Visions and Revisions from Ben Franklin to Alice Walker.* New Brunswick, N.J.: Rutgers University Press, 1990.

Summers, Mark W. *The Plundering Generation: Corruption and the Crisis of the Union, 1849–1861.* New York: Oxford University Press, 1987.

Sumner, Charles. "War System of the Commonwealth of Nations [1849]." In *Annals of America.* Vol. 7, *1841–1849: Manifest Destiny*, edited by William Benton, 548–51. Chicago: Encyclopaedia Britannica, 1849.

Sutton, Francis X. *The American Business Creed.* Cambridge, Mass.: Harvard University Press, 1956.

Sweet, William Warren, ed. *Religion on the American Frontier: A Collection of Source Material.* Vol. 1, *The Baptists, 1783–1830.* New York: Henry Holt, 1931.

Swierenga, Robert P. "Ethnoreligious Political Behavior in the Mid-Nineteenth Century: Voting, Values, Cultures." In *Religion and American Politics: From the Colonial Period to the 1980s*, edited by Mark A. Noll, 146–71. New York: Oxford University Press, 1990.

"Teacher, A," ed. *The Kentucky Preceptor, Containing a Number of Useful Lessons for Reading and Speaking.* 3d ed. Lexington, Ky.: Maccoun, Tilford, 1812.

Temple, Wayne C. *Abraham Lincoln: From Skeptic to Prophet.* Mahomet, Ill.: Mayhaven, 1995.

———. "Lincoln as a Lecturer on 'Discoveries, Inventions, and Improvements.'" *Jacksonville Journal Courier*, May 23, 1982.

———. "Lincoln the Lecturer, Parts I–II." *Lincoln Herald* 101 (1999): 94–110, 146–63.

Thomas, Benjamin P. *Abraham Lincoln: A Biography*. New York: Alfred A. Knopf, 1952.

———. *Portrait for Posterity: Lincoln and His Biographers*. New Brunswick, N.J.: Rutgers University Press, 1947.

Thomas, John L., ed. *Slavery Attacked: The Abolitionist Crusade*. Englewood Cliffs, N.J.: Prentice-Hall, 1965.

Thoreau, Henry David. "Civil Disobedience [1849]." In *Annals of America*. Vol. 7, *1841–1849: Manifest Destiny*, edited by William Benton, 540–48. Chicago: Encyclopaedia Britannica, 1976.

Thurow, Glen E. "Abraham Lincoln and American Political Religion." In *The Historian's Lincoln: Pseudohistory, Psychohistory, and History*, edited by Gabor S. Boritt and Norman O. Forness, 125–43. Urbana: University of Illinois Press, 1988.

Tindall, George Brown, and David E. Shi. *America: A Narrative History*. 4th ed. 2 vols. New York: W. W. Norton, 1996.

Trueblood, Elton. *Abraham Lincoln: Theologian of American Anguish*. New York: Harper & Row, 1973.

Tyrrell, Ian R. *Sobering Up: From Temperance to Prohibition in Antebellum America, 1800–1860* Westport, Conn.: Greenwood Press, 1979.

Wallace, Mark I. *The Second Naiveté: Barth, Ricoeur, and the New Yale Theology*. Studies in American Biblical Hermeneutics, vol. 6. Macon, Ga.: Mercer University Press, 1995.

Warren, Louis Austin. *Lincoln's Parentage and Childhood: A History of the Kentucky Lincolns Supported by Documentary Evidence*. New York: Century, 1926.

———. *Lincoln's Youth: Indiana Years, Seven to Twenty-one, 1816–1830*. Indianapolis: Indiana Historical Society, 1959.

Watson, Harry L., and Eric Foner. *Liberty and Power: The Politics of Jacksonian America*. New York: Hill and Wang, 1990.

Wayland, Francis. *The Elements of Intellectual Philosophy*. Boston: Phillips, Sampson, 1854.

———. *The Elements of Moral Science*. New York: Cooke, 1835.

———. *The Elements of Political Economy*. Boston: Gould, Kendall, and Lincoln, 1837.

Weinberg, Albert K. *Manifest Destiny: A Study of Nationalist Expansionism in American History*. 1935. Reprint, Chicago: Quadrangle Books, 1963

Wellek, René. "The Concept of Romanticism." In *Concepts of Criticism*, edited by Stephen G. Nichols, 160–7. New Haven, Conn.: Yale University Press, 1963.

Whig Review. "The Author of the Vestiges of the Natural History of Creation." *American Review: A Whig Journal of Politics, Literature, Art, and Science*, February 1846, 168–79.

———. "The Bhagvat Geeta and the Doctrine of Immortality." *American Review: A Whig Journal of Politics, Literature, Art, and Science*, September 1845, 267–78.

———. "Has the State a Religion?" *American Review: A Whig Journal of Politics, Literature, Art, and Science*, March 1846, 273–89.

———. "Influence of the Trading Spirit Upon the Social and Moral Life of America [1845]." In *Annals of America*. Vol. 7, *1841–1849: Manifest Destiny*, edited by William Benton, 266–72. Chicago: Encyclopaedia Britannica, 1976.

———. "Introductory." *American Review: A Whig Journal of Politics, Literature, Art, and Science*, January 1845, 1–4.

———. "Metaphysics of Bear Hunting: An Adventure in the San Saba Hills." *American Review: A Whig Journal of Politics, Literature, Art, and Science*, July 1845, 171–88.

———. "Our Country." *American Review: A Whig Journal of Politics, Literature, Art, and Science,* March 1845, 275–79.

———. "Our Position—Introductory." *American Review: A Whig Journal of Politics, Literature, Art, and Science,* July 1845, 1–2.

———. "Poe's Tales." *American Review: A Whig Journal of Politics, Literature, Art, and Science,* September 1845, 306–09.

———. "The Position of the Parties." *American Review: A Whig Journal of Politics, Literature, Art, and Science,* January 1845, 5–21.

———. "The Progress and Disorganization." *American Review: A Whig Journal of Politics, Literature, Art, and Science,* July 1845, 90–99.

———. "A Sequel to 'Vestiges of the Natural History of Creation.'" *American Review: A Whig Journal of Politics, Literature, Art, and Science,* April 1846, 383–96.

———. "The Spirit of Liberty." *American Review: A Whig Journal of Politics, Literature, Art, and Science,* December 1845, 614–22.

———. "The Study of Plato." *American Review: A Whig Journal of Politics, Literature, Art, and Science,* August 1845, 163–70.

———. "Theodore Frelinghuysen." *American Review: A Whig Journal of Politics, Literature, Art, and Science,* January 1845, 99–103.

———. "Thoughts on Reading." *American Review: A Whig Journal of Politics, Literature, Art, and Science,* May 1845, 483–96.

Whitney, Henry C. *Life on the Circuit with Lincoln.* Boston: Estes & Lauriat, 1892.

Widmer, Edward Ladd. "Young America: Democratic Cultural Nationalism in Antebellum New York." Ph.D. diss., Harvard University, 1993.

———. *Young America: The Flowering of Democracy in New York City.* New York: Oxford University Press, 1999.

Williams, Frank J. "Abraham Lincoln—Our Ever-Present Contemporary." In *"We Cannot Escape History": Lincoln and the Last Best Hope of Earth,* edited by James M. McPherson, 139–57. Urbana: University of Illinois Press, 1995.

Wills, Garry. *Inventing America: Jefferson's Declaration of Independence.* Garden City, N.Y.: Doubleday, 1978.

———. *Lincoln at Gettysburg: The Words That Remade America.* New York: Simon & Schuster, 1992.

———. *Under God: Religion and American Politics.* New York: Simon & Schuster, 1990.

Wilson, Charles Reagan. *Baptized in Blood: The Religion of the Lost Cause, 1865–1920.* Athens: University of Georgia Press, 1980.

Wilson, Douglas L. "Abraham Lincoln and the 'Spirit of Mortal.'" In *Lincoln before Washington: New Perspectives on the Illinois Years,* 133–48. Urbana: University of Illinois Press, 1997.

———. "Abraham Lincoln versus Peter Cartwright." In *Lincoln before Washington: New Perspectives on the Illinois Years,* 55–73. Urbana: University of Illinois Press, 1997.

———. "Herndon's Legacy." In *Lincoln before Washington: New Perspectives on the Illinois Years,* 21–36. Urbana: University of Illinois Press, 1997.

———. *Honor's Voice: The Transformation of Abraham Lincoln.* New York: Alfred A. Knopf, 1998.

———. "Lincoln's Declaration." In *Lincoln before Washington: New Perspectives on the Illinois Years,* 166–81. Urbana: University of Illinois Press, 1997.

———. "William H. Herndon and the 'Necessary Truth.'" In *Lincoln before Washington: New Perspectives on the Illinois Years,* 37–52. Urbana: University of Illinois Press, 1997.

Wilson, Douglas L., and Rodney O. Davis, eds. *Herndon's Informants: Letters, Interviews, and Statements about Abraham Lincoln.* Urbana: University of Illinois Press, 1998.

Wilson, Edmund. *Patriotic Gore: Studies in the Literature of the American Civil War.* New York: Oxford University Press, 1962.

Wilson, Major L. "Lincoln and Van Buren in the Steps of the Fathers: Another Look at the Lyceum Address." *Civil War History* 29, no. 3 (1983): 197–211.

———. "Lincoln on the Perpetuation of Republican Institutions: Whig and Republican Strategies." *Journal of the Abraham Lincoln Association* 16, no. 1 (1995): 15–38.

———. Review of *The Political Crisis of the 1850s,* by Michael F. Holt. *Journal of Southern History* 44, no. 4 (1978): 635–36.

Wilson, Rufus Rockwell. *What Lincoln Read.* Washington, D.C.: Pioneer, 1932.

Winthrop, Robert C., ed. *Life and Letters of John Winthrop: Governor of the Massachusetts-Bay Company at Their Emigration to New England, 1630.* 2d ed. 2 vols. Boston: Little, Brown, 1869.

Woldman, Albert A. *Lawyer Lincoln.* 1936. Reprint, New York: Carrol & Graf, 1994.

Wolf, William J. *Lincoln's Religion.* Published in 1959 as *The Almost Chosen People.* Philadelphia: Pilgrim Press, 1970.

Zall, P. M., ed. *Abe Lincoln Laughing: Humorous Anecdotes from Original Sources by and about Abraham Lincoln.* Berkeley: University of California Press, 1982.

Zarefsky, David. "'Public Sentiment Is Everything': Lincoln's View of Political Persuasion." *Journal of the Abraham Lincoln Association* 15, no. 2 (1994): 23–40.

INDEX